MAKING HOUSTON MODERN

ROGER FULLINGTON
SERIES IN ARCHITECTURE

THE LIFE AND ARCHITECTURE
OF HOWARD BARNSTONE

MAKING HOUSTON MODERN

EDITED BY BARRIE SCARDINO BRADLEY,
STEPHEN FOX, AND MICHELANGELO SABATINO

UNIVERSITY OF TEXAS PRESS ⌄⌄ AUSTIN

Funding for this project has been provided by former dean Michelangelo Sabatino, Rowe Family College of Architecture Dean Endowed Chair and the John Vinci Distinguished Research Fellow, Illinois Institute of Technology. Publication of this book was also made possible in part by support from Roger Fullington and a challenge grant from the National Endowment for the Humanities.

Copyright © 2020 by the University of Texas Press
All rights reserved
Printed in China
First edition, 2020

Requests for permission to reproduce material from this work should be sent to:
Permissions
University of Texas Press
P.O. Box 7819
Austin, TX 78713-7819
utpress.utexas.edu/rp-form

♾ The paper used in this book meets the minimum requirements of ANSI/NISO Z39.48-1992 (R1997) (Permanence of Paper).

Library of Congress Cataloging-in-Publication Data

Names: Bradley, Barrie Scardino, 1945– editor. | Fox, Stephen, 1950– editor. | Sabatino, Michelangelo, editor.
Title: Making Houston modern : Howard Barnstone's life and architecture / edited by Barrie Scardino Bradley, Stephen Fox, and Michelangelo Sabatino.
Identifiers: LCCN 2019034387
ISBN 978-1-4773-2055-6 (cloth)
Subjects: LCSH: Barnstone, Howard. | Architects—United States—Biography. | Modern movement (Architecture) | Houston (Tex.)—Intellectual life. | Barnstone, Howard—Catalogs.
Classification: LCC NA737.B28 M35 2020 | DDC 720.92 [B]—dc23
LC record available at https://lccn.loc.gov/2019034387

doi:10.7560/320556

CONTENTS

FOREWORD. **CALL ME HOWARD, PLEASE!** VI
CARLOS JIMÉNEZ

PREFACE VIII

INTRODUCTION. **WHY HOWARD BARNSTONE WHY?** 3
STEPHEN FOX AND MICHELANGELO SABATINO

I. HOWARD BARNSTONE'S ARCHITECTURE

CHAPTER 1. **BARNSTONE'S PRACTICE** 39
STEPHEN FOX

CHAPTER 2. **TRANSLATING MIES** Barnstone and Houston Modernism 65
MICHELANGELO SABATINO

CHAPTER 3. **TO BE MODERN IN TEXAS** Lone Star Avant-Garde 97
KATHRYN E. HOLLIDAY

II. HOWARD BARNSTONE'S CLIENTS

CHAPTER 4. **A CONSTRUCTIVE CONNECTION** Barnstone and the Menils 121
BARRIE SCARDINO BRADLEY

CHAPTER 5. **AN ARCHITECTURAL FAMILY PORTRAIT** 175
ROBERT BARNSTONE AND DEBORAH ASCHER BARNSTONE

CHAPTER 6. **BARNSTONE'S JEWISH HOUSTON** 199
JOSHUA J. FURMAN

III. HOWARD BARNSTONE'S LIFE

CHAPTER 7. **A SHORT BIOGRAPHY** 221
BARRIE SCARDINO BRADLEY AND STEPHEN FOX

CHAPTER 8. **BARNSTONE AND THE UNIVERSITY OF HOUSTON** 241
BRUCE C. WEBB

CHAPTER 9. **THE WORST THING THAT CAN HAPPEN** Gertrude and Howard 265
OLIVE HERSHEY

CONCLUSION. **MAGICAL MODERNISM** 290
BARRIE SCARDINO BRADLEY, STEPHEN FOX, AND MICHELANGELO SABATINO

AFTERWORD. **LOOKING TOWARD THE FUTURE** 297
THEODORE H. M. PRUDON

APPENDICES
1. INTERVIEW WITH EUGENE AUBRY 300
2. INTERVIEW WITH ANNE SCHLUMBERGER BROWN 307
3. ARCHITECTURAL AWARDS 310

CATALOGUE RAISONNÉ 312

SELECTED BIBLIOGRAPHY 359

CONTRIBUTORS 364

IMAGE CREDITS 368

INDEX 373

FOREWORD
Call Me Howard, Please!

CARLOS JIMÉNEZ

THE FIRST TIME I met Howard Barnstone was an early spring day in 1985. He showed up at my studio with his associate Rudy Colby. They happened to be in the neighborhood and, on an impulse, stopped by. I later learned it was typical of him to drop by unannounced. With a certain nervousness at meeting the legendary architect, I said something like, "It is a true honor to meet you, Mr. Barnstone," to which he quickly replied, "Call me Howard, please!" His elegant response was made more memorable by his patrician smile, now etched in my memory. After exchanging pleasantries, Howard asked me whether I would do some design consultation for his office. At the time, my studio was in my house, and I was struggling financially with several small projects. The prospect of doing design work for one of Houston's preeminent architects, and getting paid for it, seemed like the most auspicious of blessings. I explained that I needed my autonomy and preferred to work at my studio. He agreed, and we settled on an hourly rate for my design services. Soon after that meeting, I received a book on the architecture of John F. Staub, inscribed by its author with a simple "What a delight to have a new friend." I mention these gestures because although our friendship was to be a short one, it arrived at a critical time in my formation.

To students at the University of Houston, as I had been, Howard Barnstone was a mythic figure. I recall seeing him once or twice when he happened to be at what was then called simply the College of Architecture. I knew of him and admired his work. Depending on whom you asked at the college, he was either revered or reviled. One of the first buildings I visited when I arrived in Houston in 1977 was Barnstone & Aubry's Rothko Chapel, which made a deep impression on me. Although I never had Howard Barnstone as a teacher, I was to learn much from him: how to treat and respect aspiring young architects, how to react to difficult clients, and how to remain an outsider within the discipline of architecture.

During my meetings with Howard, we discussed design matters related to his projects. We traveled to two projects he was doing for Schlumberger, one in Ridgefield, Connecticut, the other in Austin. We worked in situ, fine-tuning or modifying designs that were already in construction. What I vividly remember are the conversations on those trips, always filled with Howard's anecdotal wit and boundless charm, though I began to detect a subtle yet deep-seated sadness. He delighted in posing questions out of the blue, right in the middle of a conversation, as if getting an intuitive answer was what mattered most. In time, it became a game of wits between us, presided over by his erudite, laser-like intelligence.

One of the last times I was with him was while driving back from Austin. A storm was building on the horizon, and thundering gusts were shaking the oblivious prairie. We talked about the magical exchange between music and the images it generates in listeners. I mentioned the music of Gustav Mahler and Manuel de Falla, in particular how their compositions give not only sound but also shape and dimension to, say, a lake, a garden, a storm, or a mountain. Suddenly, Howard interrupted me in his gentle, persuasive way, responding that it would be hard to extract such music from the flat Texas prairie we were crossing. Just as I was about to counter, he added: "Though I bet John Cage or Steve Reich would have a field day doing so." The evocative association of "the flat Texas prairie" with "a field day" of musical images caught my imagination. I completely forgot about the impending storm.

Some of my fondest memories of Howard are of visiting him in his office at 5200 Bayard Lane, near Berthea Street. He always seemed happy there. The house possessed a mix of modesty and grandeur, nurtured by the meandering branches of surrounding live oak trees. Our conversations would wander into subjects other than architecture, some redolent of the whims of history, others with a slight wisp of gossip. It was at these moments that I came to appreciate Howard's mischievous sense of humor and his abundant curiosity about all things. This curiosity was never intrusive or indulgent. It was his way of connecting with the world around him or, as the editors of this book point out, with his search for magical delight in all things, whether it was a conversation, a meal, or a work of architecture. The words "magic" and "charm" conjure up the mysteries of the world as few other ideas can and remind us of our privileged time on earth. Could there be a more beautiful framing for any day than starting with a charming morning and ending with a magical sunset? Through his works, Howard could share with others architecture's power to reveal subtle, invisible miracles, reminding us that architecture can be magical.

PREFACE

MAKING HOUSTON MODERN: *The Life and Architecture of Howard Barnstone* examines the work of a prolific, complex, and controversial twentieth-century Houston architect. Barnstone's wit, sensibility, intelligence, and lively imagination enabled him to attract clients and design buildings that engaged in a complex dialectical relationship with raucous Houston. His fierce independence, subtle and droll humor, and love of surprise imbued his buildings, his pronouncements, and his teaching with unexpected turns of thought and perspective that still seem remarkable. Part of what makes Barnstone such a compelling figure involves how, through his buildings, he worked out the tension between his personal sensibilities and his architectural inclinations.

Recognizing Howard Barnstone's significance in the cultural and social history of Houston, the editors invited other scholars to join with them to produce this book, which seeks not only to explain and underscore Barnstone's work in Houston and Texas but also to place Barnstone in the broader panorama of American architectural culture of the post–Second World War era. Barrie Scardino Bradley made Barnstone's acquaintance after she moved to Houston in 1979, and she delighted in his company for almost a decade. Stephen Fox first worked with Barnstone from 1977 to 1979 on the preparation of Barnstone's book on John Staub's architecture. Michelangelo Sabatino became aware of Barnstone's work after he moved to Houston in 2006 to teach at the Gerald D. Hines College of Architecture and Design at the University of Houston. There Sabatino began to discern the effect that Barnstone had on both the college and the course of postwar modern architecture in Houston. This realization led him to propose this book.

In investigating Barnstone and reviewing his architecture, the essays presented here uncover contradictions that explain why the buildings his firms produced are compelling. To that end, *Making Houston Modern* is divided into three sections: "Howard Barnstone's Architecture," "Howard Barnstone's Clients," and "Howard Barnstone's Life." In the first section, Fox investigates Barnstone's architectural practice from the 1940s through the 1980s, identifying him as an auteur who worked through his collaborators to achieve the architectural results he sought. Sabatino employs the concept of translation to analyze how Bolton & Barnstone transposed Miesian design practices to Houston in the 1950s and how these adaptive strategies played out in Barnstone's subsequent post-Miesian architecture. And Kathryn Holliday places Barnstone alongside his architectural peers in Texas whose writings on architecture differentiated their practices from regional modernism, the mainstream of modern architecture in Texas in the 1950s and 1960s, in order to emphasize distinct local urban identities rather than a statewide consensus.

In "Howard Barnstone's Clients," Bradley documents the personal, institutional, and corporate commissions that Dominique and John de Menil awarded Barnstone, as well as a wide range of commissions from their friends and business associates. Deborah Ascher and Robert Barnstone (Howard Barnstone's nephew)—architects themselves—detail Barnstone's architectural work for himself and for members of his extended family in Texas, Indiana, Maine, and Mexico. Finally, Joshua J. Furman looks at Barnstone's interaction with his Jewish clients and tracks the demographic dispersal of Houston's Jewish communities from the late 1940s through the early 1980s.

In "Howard Barnstone's Life," Bradley and Fox contribute a biographical chapter that chronologically examines the details of his life, identifying influential people and significant episodes. Bruce C. Webb situates Barnstone amid the shifting cultural politics of what is now the Gerald D. Hines College of Architecture and Design at the University of Houston, where Barnstone had a major impact on pedagogy and on his students. Olive Hershey profiles Gertrude Barnstone, Howard Barnstone's wife from 1955 to 1968 and a notable Houstonian in her own right, to illuminate the triumphs and tensions that characterized their domestic life.

Carlos Jiménez, professor of architecture at Rice University School of Architecture and an award-winning, internationally recognized architect, discusses his relationship with Howard Barnstone in the foreword. Theodore Prudon, a recognized authority on the preservation of twentieth-century modernism, provides an afterword. The book's appendices include interviews that put Barnstone's work in a personal perspective: one with the distinguished architect Eugene Aubry,

FAIA, Barnstone's former partner, and one with the architect Anne Schlumberger Brown, a niece of Dominique and John de Menil's and a colleague and client of Howard Barnstone's. An accounting of Barnstone's architectural awards is followed by a catalogue raisonné based on the Howard Barnstone Collection at the Houston Metropolitan Research Center of the Houston Public Library (HMRC, HPL).

As with any such collection of essays, there is some overlapping of information, which we have tried to minimize. *Cite: The Architecture and Design Review of Houston* has since 1982 provided commentary on Houston's built environment, both new and historic, and therefore all the authors have found in its pages information that touched some aspect of their work on Barnstone. In many instances there are additional images of a project in several different chapters. Please see the index, where page numbers referring to an image are italicized.

Many people in addition to the essayists contributed to *Making Houston Modern*. Gertrude Barnstone generously gave of her time in interviews with Olive Hershey, along with her memories and photographs. Judge George Barnstone and Lily Barnstone Wells, the two of Howard's children who live in Houston, helped with preparation of this book by lending photographs and providing personal stories during interviews. Willis Barnstone, his daughter Aliki Barnstone, and Marti Franco also shared stories and material.

Several people were involved at various times in the structuring and writing of *Making Houston Modern*, especially William F. Stern, FAIA (1947–2013), who was an enthusiastic proponent of this project but did not live long enough to contribute an essay. Others who shared information, suggestions, photographs, and memories are Anthony Alofsin, FAIA; Serge Ambrose; Geraldine Aramanda; Ryan Arwood; Eugene Aubry, FAIA; Mr. and Mrs. Thomas Bacon; Joel Warren Barna; Mr. and Mrs. P. G. Bell, Jr.; Rudolph Colby; Margaret Culbertson; Catherine W. Essinger; Frances Tarlton Farenthold; Diane Tanking and Blanton Filak; Mr. and Mrs. John Troy Ford; Viviana Frank, FAIA; Patricia S. and Anthony E. Frederick; Nonya Grenader, FAIA, and Jonathan Grenader; William Guest; Theodore B. Gupton; Doreen Wolfson and Frank Herzog; Paul Hester; Benjamin Hill; Katherine S. Howe; Stephen James; Donna Kacmar, FAIA; John Kaliski; Margie and Burdette Keeland; Susan B. Keeton; Lynn and Tynan Kelly; Mr. and Mrs. I. H. Kempner III; Karl Laurence Kilian; Tam K. Kiehnhoff; Lannis E. Kirkland; Ben Koush; D. Jean Krchnak; Judy Kugle; Lars Lerup; Rafael Longoria;, Ann S. Masel; Joseph Mashburn, FAIA; Nancy Mangum McCaslin; Robin Hunt McCorquodale; Adelaide de Menil; William Middleton; Gerald Moorhead, FAIA; Robert Morris; Patricia Belton Oliver, FAIA; Kathryn O'Rourke;

Jane Blaffer Owen; Peter C. Papademetriou; Monica Penick; Charles A. Perlitz III; James Petty; Robert C. Richter, Jr.; Evelyn Fink Rosenthal; Lisa Rosenthal; Frank Rotnofsky; Jon Schwartz; Lois Farfel Stark; Robert A. M. Stern, FAIA; Simone Swan; Linda Leigh Sylvan; Cynthia Rowan Taylor; Anderson Todd, FAIA; Michael Tracy; Drexel Turner; Frank D. Welch, FAIA; Sarah Whiting; Paul Winkler; and Eric M. Wolf.

At the Houston Metropolitan Research Center, the architectural archivist Samantha Bruer and every member of the Texas Room staff at one time or another were of great help. Special thanks to Laney Chávez, manager of the HMRC, and her predecessors, Kemo Curry and Liz Sargent. At the Woodson Research Center, Rice University, Lee Pecht and his staff assisted several contributors in finding images and information. Special thanks also to the Rice Design Alliance for awarding Stephen Fox and Michelangelo Sabatino a Houston Initiatives Grant in 2011 for a Digitization and Public Access project at the Houston Metropolitan Research Center to digitize some of the drawings in the Howard Barnstone Collection (MSS 178). Ryan Arwood, a University of Houston architecture student, worked diligently to scan the selected drawings. In addition, we appreciate the support of the David Dillon Center for Texas Architecture at the University of Texas at Arlington.

Two anonymous readers provided countless suggestions that improved the manuscript enormously—thank you. Our editor, Robert Devens, his assistant, Sarah McGavick, and Lynne Ferguson, senior manuscript editor, at the University of Texas Press were patient and helpful throughout the publication process. We thank them for supporting the project from the time of our first phone calls. For his life and for his work, it is Howard Barnstone to whom we owe the most gratitude.

MAKING HOUSTON MODERN

INTRODUCTION

WHY HOWARD BARNSTONE WHY?

STEPHEN FOX AND
MICHELANGELO SABATINO

THE TITLE OF THIS INTRODUCTION raises the question any investigation of the work of an architect must answer, implicitly or explicitly: Why does this architect merit recognition?[1] The interrogatory form declares the authors' intention of exploring the subject's contradictions. This publication explores the work and life of Howard Barnstone (1923–1987), a twentieth-century American architect of talent and intellect who produced a body of work that still radiates with intensity and affective power.

Howard Barnstone practiced architecture in Houston from 1948 until his death in 1987, an exceptionally fertile period in twentieth-century architecture. Barnstone belonged to a generation of American architects born between 1916 and 1929 whose diversity intensifies the question why?[2] Within this cohort, Romaldo Giurgola, Charles W. Moore, and Robert Venturi were proponents of the postmodern critique of modern architecture. Charles R. Colbert, Craig Ellwood, Pierre Koenig, Victor Lundy, Anderson Todd, and John Zemanek adhered to rigorous, tectonically based design practices throughout their careers. Ulrich Franzen, John M. Johansen, I. M. Pei, Paul Rudolph, and Evans Woollen moved from designing thinly profiled glass-walled structural cages to thickly contoured concrete or masonry containers. Robert E. Allen, Gunnar Birkerts, Hugh Newell Jacobsen, Gyo Obata, and Frank D. Welch explored the effects of tautness, planarity, and geometric projection in their buildings. Barnstone's buildings from the late 1940s to the mid-1980s track the changes in US architecture visible in the works of these architects. Barnstone valued architectural dexterity. His buildings demonstrated consistency through proportions and details rather than through identification with a set of design principles or methods.

Howard Barnstone, 1962.

Among the well-known Texas architects who practiced during the postwar period, Barnstone stood out for his rejection of both modernist functionalism and Texas regionalism.³ Barnstone delighted in defining himself against the dearly held convictions of others. He found support for this propensity in two figures he especially admired: his major client, the Houston businessman and art collector John de Menil (1905–1973), and John de Menil's other architect, Philip Johnson (1906–2005). John de Menil's defiance of Houston's social conventions and Philip Johnson's skepticism about declarations of faith in architectural movements resonated with Barnstone because both stances seemed to call for individual action rather than acquiescence in group thinking. A comparison with John Saunders Chase (1925–2012) of Houston, the first African American licensed to practice architecture in Texas, is telling. Chase sought the support of African American communities in Houston and other Texas cities and towns in order to build a practice in racially segregated Texas in the mid-1950s.⁴ Barnstone, although he insisted on his Jewish identity, fiercely resisted identification with Houston's Jewish communities, even though many of his clients were Jewish. Barnstone's sense of otherness with respect to any social collective reinforced and legitimized his determination to think through his own reactions and interpretations. Yet he also constantly modified this nonconformist stance in the face of his equally ardent desires to control and to belong. The propulsive force of unacknowledged contradiction drove Barnstone emotionally and gave depth to the serene spaces he configured.

To begin to answer the question why, one might advance obvious justifications. Barnstone was one of the most published Houston architects of the 1950s and 1960s. He was an influential teacher at the University of Houston's College of Architecture, the pioneer author of books on the architecture of Houston and the Texas Gulf Coast, and a spirited and provocative commentator on local issues. Barnstone was charming, charismatic, and witty. He was a captivating conversationalist, ever ready to amuse with sly insights and entertaining stories. But such justifications also have to acknowledge a powerful countercurrent: Barnstone could be self-centered, manipulative, envious, paranoid, spiteful, vindictive, caustic, and abusive. He suffered from bipolar disorder, and was inclined to behaviors associated with narcissism and hyperactivity. Barnstone sought to absorb the people around him into his life, as if it were too big for just one person to fill. The experience of working for or being with Barnstone could be exhilarating because he possessed the ability to make life exciting. But it was also stressful and, ultimately for those he recruited, exhausting and often not sustainable.

Barnstone was not the only pronounced individualist among Texas architects of the mid-twentieth century nor, in all likelihood, the only one beset by emotional disorders. He stood out for his cultivated interests, wit, and refined intelligence. Barnstone's younger brother, the poet and translator Willis Barnstone, wrote about his elder brother's instinct for instruction, specifically on how to adopt upper-class behavior, the Anglo-American subjectivity that mesmerized Howard Barnstone.[5] Barnstone possessed a combination of curiosity, unconventionality, and articulateness that enabled him to engage others in thinking through questions in animated conversations. This ability, as demonstrated also by Vivian Gornick and Phillip Lopate, writers from New York who lived for a time in Houston, is a characteristic of Jewish intellectual life in New York, where Howard and his brother Willis Barnstone grew up in the 1920s and 1930s. Howard Barnstone transposed this social skill to Houston. There, shorn of ethnic or class particularity, it seemed fresh and sparkling. It was one of Barnstone's attributes that he attracted lovers (including the actress, artist, and political activist Gertrude Levy, who became

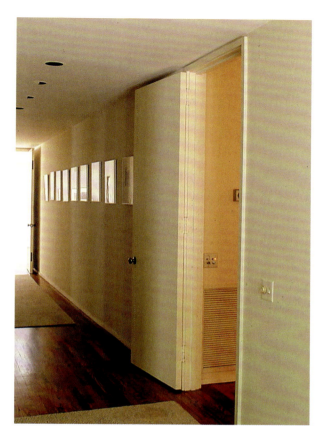

Sue Ledbetter and P. Gervais Bell, Jr., House (1970, Barnstone & Aubry), Houston. Detail showing light switches aligned with doorknobs.

his wife in 1955), clients (especially John de Menil), friends (Jane Blaffer Owen, a patron of Jacques Lipchitz and Philip Johnson and admirer of Paul Tillich), fellow architects (Philip Johnson, Frederick Kiesler, Stanley Tigerman), historians and critics (Peter Blake, Henry-Russell Hitchcock, Esther McCoy, and Colin Rowe), and artists (Forrest Bess, Michael Tracy). Michael Tracy appreciated Barnstone's sensitivity, sensibility, and singularity, qualities that were the more impressive because Barnstone's customary manner of expressing himself was self-effacing and subtle.[6]

Behind this subdued manner, Barnstone exercised a powerful impulse to assert control, a facet of his impulse to instruct. The impression that Barnstone made on others is evident in the extent to which his friends, colleagues, and students wittingly or unwittingly absorbed the traits that identified him as an example of midcentury masculine cool: his verbal mannerisms, his body language, even the kinds of suits he wore. His students Eugene Aubry, William R. Jenkins, and Burdette Keeland, as well as such younger colleagues as Rudolph Colby, modeled their professional and personal identities on Barnstone. Architecturally, the practice of horizontally aligning light-switch plates with door handles testifies to the power of Barnstone's example in Houston. Eugene Aubry, who between 1959 and 1969 was Barnstone's student, employee, and partner, observed that Barnstone inculcated such practices by formulating stories to support what he considered the superiority of doing things his way.[7] These stories almost never promoted such practices as ethically, structurally, or economically preferable, but as the aristocratic way of doing things.

Social class fascinated Barnstone. From at least the time of his matriculation at Yale College in the first half of the 1940s, he was transfixed by American patrician manners. In Houston, he bonded with people whose sense of identity was conditioned by their exposure to and participation in upper-class social life. Barnstone was fascinated by the "discreet charm" (as the Spanish film director Luis Buñuel phrased it) of patrician style, its subtle ceremoniousness and unpretentious sense of assurance, superiority, and propriety.[8] Yet even here, Barnstone refused to surrender. He maintained a critical, even wary, distance, refraining from subjugating himself to a desired identity that he also seemed to feel was alien, even hostile, because he was a modernist, a liberal, and a Jew. Such

INTRODUCTION 7

ambivalence—the ardent pursuit of a desired identity that promised emotional fulfillment, coupled with the rejection of it just as it seemed attainable—haunted Barnstone's career, reinforcing his sense of being a perennial outsider.

Houston, where Barnstone arrived as a Yale architecture graduate and newly licensed architect in 1948, was a city of outsiders and newcomers. Since the 1920s, Houston had expanded in population and territory at what seemed like exponential rates. The US census of 1950 revealed that Houston, which in 1920 had been the third-largest city in Texas (and seventeenth largest in the South), had achieved what once would have seemed impossible: it had surpassed New Orleans to become the largest city in the South.[9] When Barnstone arrived, Houston still thought of itself as a southern city, although as the national news media "discovered" Houston and Texas in the postwar period, they played up its cowboy identity. As the historian Andrew C. Baker argues, this southwestern identity enabled Texans to dissociate their state from the extreme racism that the rise of the civil rights movement provoked in other southern states, while allowing them to hold onto the symbols of white male privilege, a defense of law-and-order policies, and aggressive assertions of individuality.[10] Along with this revisionist identity, Houstonians embraced unimpeded suburban expansion, the construction of freeways, and the proliferation of central air-conditioning as markers of midcentury modernization.[11] Houston thrived during the Second World War as the Defense Plant Corporation, a division of the national government's Reconstruction Finance Corporation, added a layer to the city's oil and natural gas economy by subsidizing construction of a petrochemical refining infrastructure and converting the Houston Ship Channel into an international center of petroleum processing.[12]

Historians of Houston's emergence as a metropolitan center of regional and national consequence have noted the social contradictions that rapid expansion exacerbated.[13] The city's business elite—corporate and independent oilmen, cotton exporters, real estate developers, contractors, bankers, insurance company executives, lawyers, and merchants—tended to be economically progressive but socially conservative. In the 1920s, the lawyer William Clifford Hogg (1875–1930) and his sister, Ima Hogg (1882–1975), invested their oil royalties in efforts to identify Houston culturally as a southern city. Beginning in 1924, they developed what became Houston's most elite residential community, River Oaks, as a model of progressive community-planning standards that Will Hogg hoped the rest of Houston might follow.[14]

Ima Hogg worked with the architects John F. Staub (1892–1981) and Birdsall P. Briscoe (1876–1971), first on several model houses built by the River Oaks Corporation and then on the design of her own house, Bayou Bend (1928), to

Aerial view of downtown Houston, 1952.

formulate a modern but historically saturated southern Creole architectural genre for Houston, which Miss Hogg called Latin Colonial. Ima Hogg was instrumental in founding the Houston Symphony Orchestra (1913) and was a major contributor of art to the Museum of Fine Arts, Houston, built in 1924 with Will Hogg's financial support. After her brother's death, in 1930, she created the Hogg Foundation for Mental Health (1940). (She, her brother, and other family members suffered from depression.) From 1943 to 1948, Ima Hogg served as an elected trustee of the Houston Independent School District, where she sought to ensure a fair distribution of resources in the city's racially segregated public-school system. Ima Hogg devoted the last twenty-five years of her long life to assembling the collection of historic American furniture and art that she presented, along with her house and its gardens, to the Museum of Fine Arts.[15] Miss Hogg was a political liberal.

 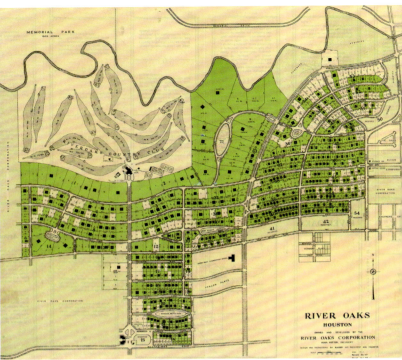

LEFT River Oaks Gate Piers (1926, John F. Staub and Charles W. Oliver), Houston.

RIGHT River Oaks subdivision sales map (1927, H. A. Kipp, civil engineer), Houston.

Nonetheless, River Oaks earned a reputation among upper-middle-income Jewish Houstonians as a neighborhood where they were not welcome.[16]

Riverside Terrace, the elite Houston neighborhood where upper-middle-income Jewish families began to congregate in the mid-1930s, and River Oaks were, by and large, neighborhoods of newcomers. River Oaks and Riverside Terrace, as well as Braeswood, another planned residential neighborhood of the 1920s with elite aspirations, were also where the earliest modern houses in Houston were built, in the mid-1930s. These houses—the L. D. Allen House in Braeswood (Wirtz & Calhoun, 1936),[17] the Ben Proler House in Riverside Terrace (Bailey A. Swenson, 1936), and the Virgil Childress House (Harvin Moore & Hermon Lloyd, 1936) and Robert D. Straus House (John F. Staub, 1936), both in River Oaks— stood out amid their English, Spanish, Italian, French, and Colonial neighbors of the 1920s and 1930s.

In 1937, two Texans who had met while working in Chicago, Fred MacKie (1905–1984) and Karl Kamrath (1911–1988), moved to Houston. By 1940, they had become recognized nationally as Houston's first modern architects. Both partners were inspired by the Usonian modernism of Frank Lloyd Wright.[18] In 1940, Donald Barthelme (1907–1996) also began a modern practice in Houston. In the interwar period, modern residential architecture in elite suburban Houston

(LEFT TO RIGHT) David Courtwright, John F. Staub, and Howard Barnstone at Bayou Bend, River Oaks, Houston, in 1977.

neighborhoods was seen as a marker of stylish progressiveness, not of radical cultural critique.[19]

Following the disruption of the civilian building economy during the Second World War, MacKie & Kamrath and Barthelme resumed their practices in the mid-1940s. But as Kamrath observed in the chapter he contributed to *Houston: Text by Houstonians* (1949), the architecture of postwar Houston was complacent and mediocre.[20] As Philip Johnson quipped to a *Houston Post* reporter in January 1950, "Must we discuss architecture in Houston? It's so dull."[21] Yet no sooner had Kamrath's lament been published than the pendulum began to swing from complacency to modernism.

By 1959, Philip Johnson had designed a flat-roofed glass-walled courtyard-centered house for Dominique and John de Menil (1951)[22] and the new campus of the University of St. Thomas (1958–1959) in Houston.[23] Frank Lloyd Wright had designed the William L. Thaxton, Jr., House, a compact Usonian dwelling in what would become the Memorial suburban village of Bunker Hill, west of River Oaks.[24] Skidmore, Owings & Merrill had designed, with Golemon & Rolfe of Houston, the eighteen-story Medical Towers Building (1956) in the Texas Medical Center.[25] And Ludwig Mies van der Rohe (1886–1969) was the architect of Cullinan Hall (1958), an awesome steel-framed glass-walled addition to the

INTRODUCTION 11

neoclassical Museum of Fine Arts.²⁶ In 1949, the first year that the American Institute of Architects initiated a national design awards program, Donald Barthelme's St. Rose of Lima Catholic Church and School (1948) won an award of merit.²⁷ The next year, the Houston architect Kenneth Franzheim's (1890–1959) most progressive building, Foley's department store (1947) in downtown Houston, won a design award from the AIA as well.²⁸ During Barnstone's first decade of practice in Houston, the field of opportunity lay in the rapidly developing landscapes of suburban Houston. Not until the 1960s would modern architecture began to change the profile of downtown.²⁹

Austin, Bryan, College Station, Corpus Christi, Dallas, El Paso, Fort Worth, Longview, San Antonio, Tyler, and towns in the Lower Río Grande Valley—in short, not only Texas's largest cities but regional ones as well—developed communities of modern architects whose buildings attracted national recognition in the postwar period.³⁰ This process was repeated elsewhere in the South as young architects in Atlanta, Little Rock, Memphis, Miami, New Orleans, Sarasota, and Shreveport produced modern buildings publicized in the national architectural press and recognized with AIA design awards. What set the modern architecture scene in Houston apart from that in other places was the wide variety of modern architecture practiced there. Following MacKie & Kamrath's lead, the architects John S. Chase, Herb Greene (who worked in Houston from 1954 to 1958 for the architect Joseph Krakower), Arthur Moss, and W. Jackson Wisdom and his partner Lenard Gabert designed buildings based on Usonian precepts.³¹

"Contemporary" was the descriptive term used for modern houses based on the ranch-house type. Contemporary architecture rejected historical detail but not, as its proponents saw it, domestic warmth. Contemporary houses and small non-residential buildings were constructed with exterior finishes of ledgestone, thin Roman brick, or redwood (sometimes all three) and low-pitched roofs. Bailey A. Swenson, Wylie W. Vale, and Philip G. Willard and his associate Lucian T. Hood, Jr., pursued the contemporary alternative, sometimes quite flamboyantly. Hood,

L. D. Allen House (1936, Wirtz & Calhoun), 2337 Blue Bonnet, Braeswood, Houston.

OPPOSITE Medical Towers (1956, Golemon & Rolfe with Skidmore, Owings & Merrill), Houston

St. Rose of Lima Catholic Church and School (1948, Donald Barthelme & Associates), Houston.

Swenson, and Willard were especially associated with houses for Jewish clients in Riverside Terrace.[32] Lars Bang, Brooks & Brooks, George Pierce–Abel B. Pierce, Greacen & Brogniez, William N. Floyd, and Milton Foy Martin tended to produce trimly detailed modern buildings that externalized their modular construction.[33] Architectural firms established in the 1930s that took on new design partners in the 1950s—Lloyd, Morgan & Jones and Wilson, Morris, Crain & Anderson—had moved from contemporary ranch-house types during the early and mid-1950s to flat-roofed slab-sided courtyard-centered houses by the end of the decade. This transition reflected the trend that definitively set Houston's postwar modern scene apart from that of other Texan cities: the impact that Ludwig Mies van der Rohe's architectural practices had on Houston, thanks to Philip Johnson and the Menil House. Howard Barnstone and his partner from 1952 to 1961, Preston M. Bolton (1920–2011); Kenneth E. Bentsen (1926–2013); William R. Jenkins (1925–1989); Burdette Keeland (1926–2000); Hugo V. Neuhaus, Jr. (1915–1987), and his partner C. Herbert Cowell (1913–2007); J. Victor Neuhaus III (1926–2018; Hugo Neuhaus's second cousin) and his partner, Harwood Taylor (1927–1988); and Anderson Todd (1921–2018) constituted Houston's Miesian cohort.[34]

Congregation Emanu El Temple (1949, MacKie & Kamrath and Lenard Gabert), Houston.

Whereas architect-designed houses established the character of River Oaks, Riverside Terrace, Braeswood, and other elite Houston neighborhoods in the 1920s, no comparable neighborhoods of architect-designed modern houses in Houston emerged in the 1950s and 1960s. New upper-income neighborhoods were developed during this period in response to Houston's growth in wealth and population, notably the subdivision of Tanglewood in west Houston, to which the Houston Country Club moved in 1957. Also on the west side of Houston was the expansive Memorial sector, a natural pine forest where six suburban villages were incorporated in the 1950s.[35] The subdivision of Meyerland, along Brays Bayou, was set on the flat, treeless plain of southwestern Houston. In each, one-story ranch-type houses, not architect-designed modern houses, dominated the suburban landscape. The small subdivision of Briar Hollow on Buffalo Bayou just west of River Oaks, where two Bolton & Barnstone houses were constructed, and section eight of Meyerland contained concentrations of architect-designed modern houses. Glenbrook Valley on Sims Bayou in southeastern Houston, near William P. Hobby Airport, and Memorial Bend in the Houston portion of Memorial alongside Rummel Creek stand out because of the density of architect-designed modern houses in each, but these were originally marketed to a middle-income

INTRODUCTION 15

clientele.[36] It was among the traditional houses of the 1920s and 1930s in River Oaks, Riverside Terrace, and Braeswood that some of the most conspicuous concentrations of postwar modern domestic architecture were found in Houston. Architect-designed modern houses were integrated into these established landscapes rather than being used to shape new residential landscapes of their own.[37]

The construction of consensus on the virtues of cultural modernity was pursued vigorously in postwar Houston. The establishment of the Alley Theatre in 1947 and the Contemporary Arts Association (CAA) in 1948 originated as protests against the tepid programs of the elite Little Theater of Houston and the Museum of Fine Arts.[38] Gertrude Barnstone (1925–2019) was a star of Little Theater and Alley Theatre productions. The Contemporary Arts Association, with which Barnstone and Bolton were affiliated, counted architecture and design among the arts it promoted. In addition to exhibitions of architecture and design, organized by members of the association and installed in the ingenious one-room Contemporary Arts Museum, designed by MacKie & Kamrath and constructed by association members in 1949, the CAA initiated an annual Modern House Tour in 1952 to showcase architect-designed houses in Houston.[39] The architectural historian Ben Koush described the Modern House Tour as Houston's counterpart to the Case Study program in Los Angeles.[40]

The liberal modernity with which Barnstone was identified occurred in a racially charged atmosphere of intense conflict, in which Gertrude Barnstone became a key player. The landmark US Supreme Court decision in *Smith v. Allwright* (1944), which ruled that racially exclusionary primary elections were unconstitutional, arose from a case filed initially by an African American plaintiff in Houston. So too did the case that resulted in another groundbreaking decision, *Sweatt v. Painter* (1950), which prohibited the University of Texas Law School from excluding African American students because of their race.[41] In reaction to these lawsuits, the state in 1947 acquired Houston College for Negroes, Houston's independent public university for African American students, transformed it into Texas Southern University (TSU), and provided it with graduate professional schools.[42] TSU created an economic base for a stable, expanding African American professional class in Houston and, consequently, a market for more socially exclusive middle-income neighborhoods than the mixed neighborhoods of the historically African American neighborhood of Third Ward, where the university's new campus was located.

Texas Southern University's campus lay on the "color line" separating Third Ward to the north from the white middle-income 1920s-era neighborhood of Washington Terrace to the south. In 1948, a year after TSU became a state

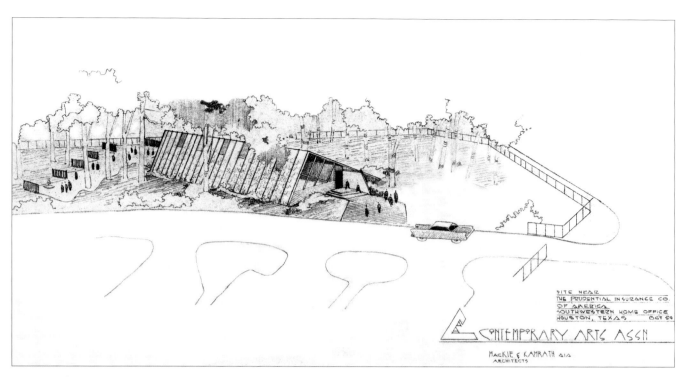

Contemporary Arts Association museum drawing (1949, 1954, MacKie & Kamrath, demolished), Houston.

university, the US Supreme Court ruled in *Shelley v. Kraemer* that deed restrictions mandating racial exclusion were unenforceable. In 1952, Jack Caesar, an African American cattle rancher, bought a house in Riverside Terrace, just south of Washington Terrace. The next year, Caesar's house was dynamited in an act of terror. No one was injured in the blast, but it caused a panic-stricken exodus of white families from the sectors of Riverside Terrace north of Brays Bayou. The historian Barry J. Kaplan notes that white residents constituted 97 percent of the population of this portion of the neighborhood in 1950 (the 3 percent of residents who were African American were servants), 25 percent in 1960, and only 5 percent in 1970. Between 1960 and 1970, the population of the sectors of Riverside Terrace south of Brays Bayou, where two Bolton & Barnstone houses were located, went from 99 percent white in 1960 to 30 percent in 1970.[43] Kaplan points out that although much of Riverside Terrace's Jewish population moved six miles upstream along Brays Bayou to Meyerland, whose first section opened in 1955, a substantial part of Meyerland's population consisted of families that had moved to Houston from elsewhere, an indication of how rapidly Houston's general population continued to be expanded by newcomers.

After students at Texas Southern University led a sit-in in 1960 at the J. Weingarten No. 26 supermarket on Almeda Road (near Riverside Terrace) to

INTRODUCTION 17

Gertrude and Howard Barnstone at the opening of the *Totems Not Taboo* exhibition in Cullinan Hall, Museum of Fine Arts, Houston, 1959.

desegregate its lunch counter, Houston's downtown business elite moved quietly and rapidly to integrate shops, hotels, restaurants, and theaters in the central business district in order to preserve public peace and protect property values.[44] The site of the fiercest ideological conflict in postwar Houston was the board of education of the Houston Independent School District. The historian Don E. Carleton shows how, in Houston, the sense of pervasive crisis was shifted in the mid-1950s from fear of communist subversion of the public schools to fear of racial integration. Carleton analyzes how social stresses created by Houston's rapid expansion exacerbated social tensions and anxiety, which conservative white populist politicians exploited with antigovernment rhetoric and a refusal to accept federal funds for public education in order to evade legal mandates to desegregate the school system.[45] Reactionary populist sentiment was countered by liberal social activism. Appalled by the conduct of the populist majority dominating the board of education, Gertrude Barnstone put her artistic pursuits aside to seek election as a trustee in 1964—and won. As a member of the politically polarized school board, she was a forceful ally of the board's first African American trustee, Hattie Mae Whiting White (elected in 1958), and a second African American trustee, Asberry Butler, Jr., also elected in 1964. The three were critical of the board's efforts to resist court-ordered desegregation, and they repeatedly sought to get the board

Dominique de Menil with Ludwig Mies van der Rohe, seated, at the opening of Cullinan Hall, Museum of Fine Arts, Houston, 1958.

to accept federal funds to improve the quality of public education in Houston.[46]

Gertrude Barnstone's foray into politics brought feature stories in the illustrated national weekly magazines *Look* and the *Saturday Review*. The images in these reports attest to the extent to which the Barnstones had become Houston celebrities by the 1960s. Howard Barnstone was adept at securing publicity for his buildings in nationally circulated architecture journals, efforts that were crucial for gaining recognition in the wider world of American architecture. Barnstone's buildings were also published in the *Houston Post*, the most liberal of Houston's three daily newspapers, and in the *Houston Chronicle*, ensuring that his name was recognized locally. *Texas Architect*, the magazine of the Texas Society of Architects, and the society's statewide design awards program provided additional forums for establishing and maintaining his standing among Texas architects. The effort that Barnstone expended on publicity discloses the extent to which he was compelled to compete for recognition and earn the right to belong. The ambivalence underpinning this compulsion is also disclosed by images.

In the late 1950s, John de Menil commissioned the photographer Eve Arnold to document special events in Houston. Arnold's image of Gertrude and Howard Barnstone standing on one of the runways that Jermayne MacAgy (1914–1964), director of the Contemporary Arts Museum, erected in Cullinan Hall for the second exhibition held in the space, *Totems Not Taboo* (1959), contrasts with their nonappearance at the first exhibition in Cullinan Hall, the dedicatory show in October 1958. Arnold photographed Houston elites old and new in the radiant setting of Cullinan Hall: Ima Hogg and Nina Cullinan, and Mies, seated in one photo next to the young Houston architect Anderson Todd and in another conversing with Dominique de Menil, who kneels beside his chair. Gertrude and Howard Barnstone were not invited to the dedication of Cullinan Hall, although Preston Bolton had been a member of the committee that recommended Mies for the job. Gertrude Barnstone grew up in Houston; she was unfazed by not being invited

INTRODUCTION 19

to parties. Howard Barnstone, though, resented the exclusion; it exacerbated his fear of being an outsider.

Other Texas modern architects—Donald Barthelme and O'Neil Ford of San Antonio, for example—possessed this sense of adversarial singularity, perpetually struggling, as they saw it, to overcome irrationality, prejudice, greed, and compromise.[47] In contrast, the Texas architects Kenneth Bentsen, Preston Bolton, Hugo Neuhaus, Enslie O. Oglesby, and Frank D. Welch gave the impression of being so much at ease in the social milieu to which Barnstone aspired as to be immune to the psychological friction evident in Barnstone's consciousness. This friction surfaced in Barnstone's professional relationships also.

In 1979, Barnstone was commissioned by GreenMark, the residential division of Gerald D. Hines Interests, to design a townhouse complex in First Colony, the planned community that Hines and the Royal Dutch Shell Pension Fund developed on the southwestern outskirts of Houston. After producing a design with which his clients were quite pleased, Barnstone forfeited the commission because he refused to have production work done by another architectural firm, a practice that Hines employed with such architects as Skidmore, Owings & Merrill, I. M. Pei & Partners, and Johnson/Burgee. Philip Johnson added a new chapter to his career as the result of his collaboration with Hines; Johnson conformed to his client's preferred working practices.[48] Barnstone, however, experienced such stress at the prospect of losing control (or perhaps at having to prove himself with a little job before being entrusted with a more important one) that he gave up the opportunity to work with Hines. Barnstone did work successfully with the Schlumberger corporation on two major office complexes in the 1970s and 1980s, one in Ridgefield, Connecticut, and the other in Austin. He was undaunted by scales of operation bigger than a house or by working with architectural teams. It seemed to be his sensitivity to not being acknowledged as "someone," entitled to special consideration and respect, that caused him to jettison the GreenMark project.

Barnstone called attention to himself through the oppositional stances he took. In the Houston zoning battle of 1962, the fourth of five unsuccessful twentieth-century efforts to adopt a zoning ordinance for Houston, Barnstone defied the local liberal consensus to champion nonzoning.[49] During the energy crisis of the mid-1970s, he delighted in driving his big white Oldsmobile convertible (which he nicknamed the "Miami Beach") with the top down and the air-conditioning going full blast in order to "prove" that the energy crisis was merely a hoax to drive up the price of oil. Barnstone loved cars and air-conditioning, as he exclaimed to Esther McCoy when she interviewed him for a report on young US architects published in the Italian journal *Zodiac* in 1963.[50] During a symposium on housing in Houston organized by the Rice Design Alliance in 1977, Barnstone turned on Danny Samuels, a partner in the firm Taft Architects. Samuels had extolled Isabella Court, a 1920s Spanish-style courtyard apartment building in Houston, as a model of low-rise high-density housing. Isabella Court, Barnstone sneered, was nothing but a "stucco slum."[51] At a symposium at the University of Texas at Austin in 1981, Barnstone called Lawrence W. Speck, then a young associate professor of architecture, a "pusher" for advocating regionalism, which Barnstone likened to narcotics.[52] Sitting in the audience, O'Neil Ford, the revered proponent of Texas regionalism, was so incensed that he denounced Barnstone as a "smart-ass." Barnstone responded, with an air of wounded innocence: "Isn't that why you invited me?" Barnstone's disdain disclosed not only his readiness to confront and argue but also his competitiveness. Samuels and Speck belonged to a younger generation of architects and teachers; Barnstone seemed impelled to ridicule them in order to assert his primacy.

The relationship that Barnstone developed with Dominique and John de Menil brings into focus his skill in connecting with the right people. Barnstone said that Hugo Neuhaus initially recommended him to John de Menil to correct several problems the Menils encountered after moving into their Johnson-designed house. Neuhaus, who had been a student at Harvard University's Graduate School of Design at the same time as Johnson in the early 1940s, had a falling-out with Johnson over Neuhaus's administration of the construction of the Menil House and did not want the job.[53] Although Johnson hit it off with John de Menil, he had a tense relationship with Dominique, reflecting the spouses' differences in temperament. John was impulsive, enthusiastic, and commanding; Dominique was rigorous and disciplined. She fixated on resolving details and expected her architects to do likewise. Temperamentally, Barnstone was inclined to the John de Menil–Philip Johnson pole rather than the Dominique de Menil pole. Nevertheless, Barnstone made himself indispensable to the Menils and became part of the entourage of talent they cultivated in Houston after launching themselves as arbiters of artistic modernism, political liberalism, and, eventually, religious ecumenism. John de Menil became Barnstone's social mentor.

Philip Johnson was Barnstone's architectural hero.[54] Johnson's advocacy for architecture as an art and his insistence that architectural design not be subordinated to what he derided as the "crutches" of modern architecture resonated with Barnstone, who persistently defended the autonomy of architecture.[55] Johnson's performance as a cultural arbiter who used his position as director of architecture and design at the Museum of Modern Art, his network of friends and clients, and the buildings he designed to construct an imagined world of elite modernist solidarity appealed to Barnstone—and to John de Menil.[56] That Johnson, like Menil, was nonconformist, outspoken (and well spoken), witty, subversive, and charming endowed him with a charismatic aura that, in Barnstone's estimation, never faded. Johnson's skill at imbuing the rigorous modern architecture of Ludwig Mies van der Rohe with a socially refined identity that legitimized the claims of its inhabitants to cultural authority and leadership made Miesian practices irresistible to Barnstone, as the buildings that Bolton & Barnstone produced during the 1950s make clear.

Johnson mobilized the very instruments that modern architecture had renounced—taste, style, and fashion—to spatially identify a modern, liberal American elite with Miesian architecture in the 1950s. Barnstone shared Johnson's most pronounced architectural disability: he did not draw. He did not share Johnson's aesthetic sensibility, which emerged fitfully in the late 1950s as Johnson moved away from the architectural discipline of Mies. Johnson's camp sensibility, his delight in garish finishes, and his taste for the outré (such as windowless rooms with carpeted walls) did not appeal to Barnstone, who aimed for architectural restraint and spatial exaltation.

Barnstone did share the sensibility of Jermayne MacAgy, whom John de Menil brought to Houston to become the first professional director of the Contemporary Arts Museum in 1955.[57] MacAgy became famous not only for the subjects of the exhibitions she organized but also for the design of her installations, first in MacKie & Kamrath's Contemporary Arts Museum, then in Mies's Cullinan Hall at the Museum of Fine Arts, Houston, and finally at the Gallery of Fine Arts in Jones Hall, Philip Johnson's gallery and auditorium building at the University of St. Thomas (1958).[58] MacAgy exercised her genius for orchestrating spatial relationships between works of art and for staging settings for the display of art in order to create an ecstatic engagement between viewers and art that MacAgy described as "magic."[59]

Another of Barnstone's Menil connections was the museum director James Johnson Sweeney (1900–1986), whom John de Menil brought to Houston in 1961 to become director of the Museum of Fine Arts.[60] It was under the aegis of Sweeney and Menil that Barnstone produced his first book, *The Galveston That Was* (1966).[61] Writing about Victorian Galveston was a kind of therapy for Barnstone, aimed at exploring his own psyche through the "ghostly charm" of the nineteenth-century architecture of the Gulf Coast city, which had experienced great wealth before being almost destroyed by the hurricane of 1900. To frame this theme, Barnstone chose a passage on loss from Edna Ferber's autobiography, *A Kind of Magic*, for the epigraph of *The Galveston That Was*. In Galveston's tragic history, Barnstone

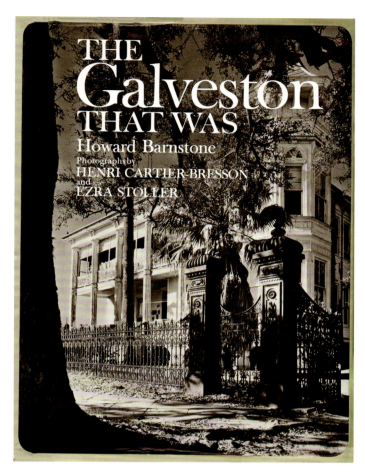

Howard Barnstone, *The Galveston That Was*, cover, first edition (1966).

reflected on melancholy, an ingredient from which he distilled his own magical modernism. Barnstone was assisted in chronicling the decline of Galveston by the photographer Henri Cartier-Bresson, whom John de Menil hired. John de Menil's readiness to persuade (and pay for) an artist of Cartier-Bresson's magnitude to participate in this venture lent Barnstone's book a radiance that extricated it from the confines of parochial regionalism.

The mixture of melancholy, exalted reputation, and opportunism that led to *The Galveston That Was* was heady and intoxicating. Menil resources were capable of evoking social milieus that were glamorous, captivating, and sensational, all effects that, as the anthropologist Pamela G. Smart observes in her book about the Menils, *Sacred Modern*, enabled Dominique and John de Menil to attract a community of support for their projects in Houston in the 1950s and 1960s.[62] The art historian Marcia Brennan, in her book *Curating Consciousness: Mysticism and the Modern Museum*, analyzes the exhibitions that Sweeney organized in Cullinan Hall, which explored dimensions of spirituality through modern art and architecture.[63] Dominique and John de Menil engaged in this exploratory process directly in 1964 when they commissioned the artist Mark Rothko to produce a set of paintings to be installed in a modern chapel in Houston. Although based on an initial design by Johnson, the Rothko Chapel was built to Barnstone & Aubry's plans.[64]

Barnstone was a beneficiary of these extraordinary circumstances, a key contributor to them, but also a victim. In 1968 he suffered a severe episode of manic depression that caused him to be hospitalized and treated with drugs and electroshock therapy. This breakdown occurred in tandem with the dissolution of his marriage to Gertrude Barnstone (they were divorced in 1969) and the termination of his partnership with Aubry. Melancholy suffused Barnstone's life. A similar emotional upheaval claimed Mark Rothko, who killed himself in 1970, three years after completing the paintings for the chapel but before construction of the building. Barnstone cited the title of the last exhibition that Jermayne MacAgy organized at the Contemporary Arts Museum, *The Romantic Agony* (1959), as a way of conceptualizing his suffering. This identification indicated the extent to which language, whether grave or comical, served him as a repository for emotions. Barnstone's love of words and wordplay helped him reassert self-control in order to reconstruct his life and his architectural career in the 1970s. The father of three children, Barnstone lived from the early 1970s until 1987 with male companions. He denied that he was homosexual, and his conduct was consistently in line with prevailing codes of masculinity. As this transition demonstrated, though, the ambivalence characteristic of his conduct, like his determination not to acknowledge contradiction, was existential.

Barnstone's architectural career rebounded in the 1970s. He rebuilt his practice with the help of a succession of talented architectural students from the University of Houston, where he was a tenured professor. Barnstone taught a seminar rather than design studios, as he had done before his breakdown. Anne Schlumberger Brown, who enrolled in the architecture school after Barnstone remodeled two houses for her, remembers Barnstone's class—ostensibly about city planning—with delight. For each class session, he would bring articles he had torn out of the *Houston Post* or the *New York Times*, which became the basis for highly entertaining discussions. If conversation flagged, Barnstone filled in with social gossip, which Anne Brown found especially amusing, since she knew the people he was talking about.[65] Barnstone, Victor Lundy, and the architect and teacher John Zemanek, who had also been edged out as a studio instructor, pursued methods of seminar instruction that were idiosyncratic by the bureaucratic standards of later academic pedagogy.[66] Yet these were the classes that University of Houston architecture students of the 1970s and 1980s remembered.

In the mid-1970s, Barnstone embarked on another book, a survey of the houses of John F. Staub, Houston's foremost country-house architect from the 1920s through the 1950s.[67] In Staub (who was then in his eighties and an enthusiastic participant in the project), Barnstone encountered a subtle architect of place whose houses were contextually responsive and spatially animated even though based on historical models. Barnstone was especially fascinated by Staub's ability to produce architecture that framed Houston's elite as an upper class. In 1977, Barnstone bought a house on Shadowlawn Circle that Staub had designed in 1926. The house had been abandoned by descendants of the family that built it, so Barnstone was able to pick it up for a bargain (he was convinced he had a knack for real estate investments), and rehabilitate it with panache.[68] Barnstone loved to entertain at Shadowlawn. He gave parties that brought together old Houston, liberals, and any attractive young people he might be grooming for social advancement. The chance presence of the artist Michael Tracy or the Menils' New York

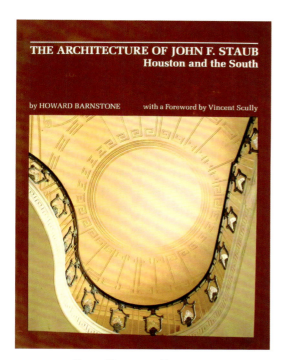

Howard Barnstone, *The Architecture of John F. Staub: Houston and the South*, cover (1979).

publicist, Simone Swan, or the human rights champion Sissy Farenthold added flair to the evening.

Barnstone's social gatherings displayed his gregariousness, conviviality, and imagination. At a surprise birthday party for Eugenia Preston Brooks Richardson, widow of the Episcopal bishop of Texas, J. Milton Richardson, guests were instructed to bring only bottles of Wild Turkey bourbon as gifts. Once when Ima Hogg, then in her nineties, arrived at her apartment at Inwood Manor for a surprise birthday party, she couldn't immediately see her guests, because Barnstone had filled her high-rise glass-walled living room with balloons, floor to ceiling.[69]

It was not simply temperament but also sensibility that distinguished Barnstone from his architectural peers. As he did with Jermayne MacAgy, Barnstone resonated with the sensibilities of his sometime collaborator Sally Sherwin Walsh (1926–1992), a Houston interior designer, and Marti Franco, his client and stepmother. He shared with each an "eye," "taste," a "magic touch," and an imagination unconstrained by inhibition and convention, which enabled all three to compose, orchestrate, and choreograph the arrangement of objects in space in ways that those occupying such spaces found surprising, delightful, even revelatory. Sally Walsh, for instance, painted the thin Miesian reveals in the master bedroom of Bolton & Barnstone's Aaron Farfel House gold and installed a graceful chaise longue to punctuate one of the bedroom's modernist wall planes.[70] Barnstone designed Marti Franco's specialty store, Marti's in Nuevo Laredo, Mexico (1972), to function as a theater of display, which he organized around a broad, irregularly angled spiral staircase wide enough to accommodate not only exhibitions of Mexican crafts, laid out as in a street market, but also a diminutive, elderly indigenous musician who sat in a rustic chair and played traditional music on a lap harp that echoed hauntingly through the space.[71] Sally Walsh's, Marti Franco's, and Howard Barnstone's ability to animate the places where people lived, worked, and traded imbued modern spaces with sensations of the extraordinary that gave them a "magical" aura.

Intimacy and spontaneity were attributes that Barnstone could reproduce spatially. He played intimacy and spontaneity off against each other so that spontaneity was never experienced as messy or disorienting, and intimacy was always open ended rather than confining. Two complexes that Barnstone designed and developed himself, the Vassar Place Apartments (1965) and the Graustark Family Townhouses (1972), embody his skill at orchestrating intimacy, spontaneity, and

Aaron Farfel House (1955, Bolton & Barnstone), 18 Westlane Place, Houston, bedroom, showing gold painted reveals.

surprise to structure spaces that are small in scale but expansive in feeling. Barnstone was also masterly at organizing objects; his dwellings gave ample evidence of that ability.[72] But these assemblies were grounded in simplicity and spatial clarity, represented by the admission of sunlight through walls of glass, which also afforded views of outdoor greenery. Barnstone, perhaps surprisingly, considering his milieu in Houston, was not deeply engaged with art, music, or literature. But he loved plants, whether outside or inside. At a time when Jerry MacAgy and Jim Sweeney often included plants in their exhibition installations and when Sally Walsh introduced them to office workplaces, Barnstone incorporated plants among the interior furnishings he repeatedly used—Thonet bentwood chairs, sisal carpets, white marble-topped steel-framed worktables that he designed, and antique American country pieces (textured wood trestle tables, Windsor chairs)— in order to construct settings that occupants experienced as subtle yet energizing.

Marti's, a specialty store (1971, Howard Barnstone), Calle Victoria 2923, Nuevo Laredo, Tamaulipas, Mexico.

He was able to expand on this sense of spatial intimacy and spontaneity and translate it from the scale of houses to the scale of office workplaces, as his spaces and buildings for Schlumberger demonstrate.

In place of consistent architectural practices, Barnstone substituted a consistent sensibility. Barnstone followed Philip Johnson in his conviction that architects should not be afraid to experiment and change. Some of Barnstone & Aubry's buildings of the 1960s and 1970s, such as the gable-roofed P. G. Bell House (1970), alluded to historic architecture, usually vernacular models. Yet, like other modernists, Barnstone resisted postmodernism until Johnson endorsed it on the cover of *Time* magazine in January 1979. The one architectural movement for which Barnstone felt disdain was regionalism. Barnstone seemed to equate regionalism with parochialism, which he countered with what he considered to be cosmopolitan architecture. That Philip Johnson and Peter Blake set up modern regionalism as an ideological adversary, against which they championed an architecture of "freedom"—the architecture of Mies—in the late 1940s, perhaps explains Barnstone's professed aversion to the idea of regionalism.[73]

Lillian G. and Gerald S. Gordon House (1953–1955, Bolton & Barnstone), 2307 Blue Bonnet Boulevard, Braeswood, Houston, after the addition of the swimming pool in 1980.

Despite his declarations against regionalism, he was repeatedly attracted to regionalist practices, beginning with his earliest work. Bolton & Barnstone's house for Alice Boyd Lindsay (1958) is fitted with an immense solar screen fabricated of cast iron, the material associated with the decorative balconies of nineteenth-century New Orleans. The Owsley House (1961), Bolton & Barnstone's only all-glass house, is surrounded by two-story steel-framed galleries, which Barnstone likened to the decks of a Mississippi River paddle wheeler.[74] Barnstone & Aubry's Rice Museum Building (1969), better known as the Art Barn, launched a trend in Houston architecture (thanks to Aubry's subsequent work, independent of Barnstone), the "tin house" movement, that is as close as Houston architects in the second half of the twentieth century came to achieving consensus on a regionalist practice grounded in Houston.[75] Barnstone's ambivalence about the architecture of regionalism triggered a stress response whose source remains obscure. He was fascinated with doing regionalism, but he could not countenance talking about it.

Barnstone was provocative. Rather than offering answers, he constantly raised more questions. His oppositional nature made him ready to reverse course just to demonstrate that his actions and reactions could not be predicted. That he specialized in producing architectural spaces that were simple, serene, and undemonstratively sensual means that even his architecture countered his personal inclination to polemic and argumentation.

Barnstone killed himself in 1987 by taking an overdose of sleeping pills, ending a second extended period of depression. Phillip Lopate eulogized Barnstone in the *Texas Observer*, writing of his "personal intelligence and integrity," his professional role as a "decent, complex alternative" to Houston's infatuation at the time with star architects, and his "enthusiastic defense of the new Houston." Lopate credited Barnstone with forging "an unapologetic aesthetic for a city meant to serve cars."[76] Barnstone could at times be a monster, but he was a *monstre sacré* who, from the 1950s, lived out a modern life in Houston unburdened by externally imposed or internally adopted clichés about what constituted a Texan identity or by midcentury middle-class American conformity. He redefined what people knew and thought about architecture in Texas and Houston and externalized what went unsaid, and consequently unthought, in public discourse. Barnstone's instinct for mobilizing the dangerous, explosive energy that accrues from not acknowledging contradiction made him seem, as Benjamin Moser observed of the Brazilian modernist writer Clarice Lispector, both fascinating and disturbing to others.[77] He sought to spatially redefine the patrician gentry in modern terms in Houston, using architecture as his instrument to shape new settings for domestic life and work that affirmed, confusingly but often persuasively, liberal individualism and elite class superiority. It is the social contradictions that Barnstone chose to explore spatially, not to resolve but to hold in perennially unstable equilibrium, that imbue his buildings with their paradoxical combination of spatial calm and emotional intensity.

NOTES

1. The title echoes the title of an exhibition, *Why Houston Why?*, that Howard Barnstone's onetime student, colleague, and lifelong friend Burdette Keeland organized with François Ceria and students from the University of Houston's College of Architecture for the opening of the American Center in Paris in 1984. It also reflects the title of Benjamin Moser's biography of the Brazilian modernist writer Clarice Lispector: *Why This World? A Biography of Clarice Lispector*. See also "From Coast to Côte: Houston Architects on Display," *Cite 8: The Architecture and Design Review of Houston* 8 (Winter 1984): 3; the journal is hereafter cited as *Cite*.

2. A review of *The Architects Index* for the years 1951–1954, 1958, and 1961 suggests that Barnstone's national peers included architects whose work was also being publicized at this time: John M. Johansen of New Canaan, Connecticut, son-in-law of Walter Gropius (1916–2012); Alfred L. Aydelotte of Memphis (1916–2008); Alfred Browning Parker of Miami (1916–2011); I. M. Pei of New York (1917–2019); Paul Rudolph of Sarasota and New York (1918–1997); Paolo Soleri of Scottsdale (1919–2013); Romaldo Giurgola of Philadelphia and Canberra (1920–2016); Ulrich Franzen of New York (1921–2012); Charles R. Colbert of New Orleans (1921–2007); Craig Ellwood of Los Angeles (1922–1992); Victor Lundy of Sarasota, New York, and Houston (b. 1923); Mark Hampton of Sarasota and Miami (1923–2015); Gyo Obata of St. Louis (b. 1923); John C. Portman, Jr., of Atlanta (1924–2017); Arthur Erickson of Vancouver (1924–2009); Pierre Koenig of Los Angeles (1925–2004); Gunnar Birkerts of Detroit (1925–2017); Robert Venturi of Philadelphia (1925–2018); Charles W. Moore of Berkeley, New Haven, Santa Monica, and Austin (1925–1993); César Pelli of New Haven (1926–2019); Evans Woollen of Indianapolis (1927–2016); Phyllis Lambert of Montreal (b. 1927); Herb Greene of Houston, Norman, Lexington, and Berkeley (b. 1929); and Hugh Newell Jacobsen of Washington, DC (b. 1929). Barnstone's Texas peers included his partner Preston M. Bolton; E. G. Hamilton of Dallas (1920–2017); Anderson Todd of Houston; John Zemanek of Houston (1921–2016); Alan Y. Taniguchi of Harlingen and Austin (1922–1998); Enslie O. Oglesby, Jr., of Dallas (1925–1993); William R. Jenkins of Houston; John S. Chase of Houston; Robert E. Allen of Longview (b. 1926); Robert D. Garland, Jr., of El Paso and Fort Worth (1926–2008); David E. Hilles of El Paso (1926–1997); Burdette Keeland of Houston; Kenneth E. Bentsen of Houston; J. Victor Neuhaus III of Houston; Harwood Taylor of Houston; Frank D. Welch of Midland and Dallas (1927–2017); James Reece Pratt of Dallas (1927–2018); and Hal Box of Dallas and Austin (1929–2011).

3. Architects of Texas regionalism included Harwell Hamilton Harris of Austin and Dallas (1903–1990); Howard R. Meyer of Dallas (1903–1988); Arthur Fehr (1904–1969) and Charles Granger (1913–1966) of Austin; Milton A. Ryan (1904–1991) of San Antonio; O'Neil Ford of San Antonio (1905–1982); Donald Barthelme of Houston (1907–2006); Richard S. Colley (1910–1983) of Corpus Christi; William W. Caudill (1914–1983) and his firm, Caudill Rowlett Scott (CRS), of Houston; and John G. York of Harlingen (1914–1980).

4. Louis J. Marchiafava, Steven R. Strom, and Denise Wilson, "John S. Chase: Architect and Innovator," *Houston Review* 19, no. 2 (1997): 1–18.

5. W. Barnstone, *We Jews and Blacks*, 9–10, 215–219.

6. Jim McDonald, personal communication to Stephen Fox.

7. Eugene Aubry, interview by Stephen Fox and Michelangelo Sabatino, May 5, 2010, Galveston, Texas.

8. Buñuel directed the film *The Discreet Charm of the Bourgeoisie* (1972).

9. McComb, *Houston*, 170–257.

10. Andrew C. Baker, "From Rural South to Metropolitan Sunbelt: Creating a Cowboy Identity in the Shadow of Houston," *Southwestern Historical Quarterly* 118 (July 2014): 1–22; see also "Booming Houston," *Life*, October 21, 1946, 108–17; George Sessions Perry, "Cities of America: Houston," *Saturday Evening Post*, November 29, 1947, 22–23; Hamilton Basso, "Three Rivals: Fort Worth, Dallas, Houston in a War of Cattle, Culture, Chemistry," *Holiday*, October 1948, 40–55; Fuermann, *Houston*; James Street, "Houston U.S.A.," *Holiday*, April 1952, 98–108; and Stanley Walker, "Houston, Texas, a 'Yes, But—' Town," *New York Times Magazine*, August 1, 1954, 16–17.

11. See Robert S. Thompson, "The Air-Conditioning Capital of the World: Houston and Climate Control," and Tom Watson McKinney, "Superhighways Deluxe: Houston's Gulf Freeway," both in Melosi and Pratt, *Energy Metropolis*, 88–104, 148–172.

12. Pratt, *Growth of a Refining Region*. That the chairman of the Reconstruction Finance Corporation was the Houston banker, newspaper publisher, and real estate developer Jesse H. Jones indicated how Houston's business elite facilitated the city's extraordinary growth and profitability in the twentieth century by turning natural opportunities (Houston's proximity to the Gulf of Mexico and Texas's oil reserves) and historical opportunities (the federal government's response to the Great Depression and to war) to their advantage to construct platforms for systemic and systematic economic expansion; see Fenberg, *Unprecedented Power*.

13. Carleton, *Red Scare!*

14. Bruce J. Weber and Charles Orson Cook, "Will Hogg and Civic Consciousness: Houston Style," *Houston Review* 2 (Winter 1980): 20–36; see also Barry J. Kaplan and Charles Orson Cook, "Civic Elites and Urban Planning: Houston's River Oaks," in Rosales and Kaplan, *Houston*, 22–33; Ferguson, *Highland Park and River Oaks*.

15. Kirkland, *Hogg Family and Houston*; see also David B. Warren, "Ima Hogg: Collector," *Antiques*, January 1982, 228–243.

16. Maas, *Jews of Houston*.

17. Elizabeth Fagan, "Building Walls of Light: The Development of Glass Block and Its Influence on American Architecture in the 1930s," thesis for master of science in historic preservation, Graduate School of Architecture, Planning, and Preservation, Columbia University, May 2015.

18. Scott Reagan Miller, "The Architecture of MacKie & Kamrath" (MArch thesis, Rice University, 1993).

19. Koush, *Donald Barthelme*.

20. Karl Kamrath, "Architectural Impressions," in *Houston: Text by Houstonians*, 110–111. Such stolid, late-modernistic buildings as the City National Bank Building

(1947) and the Ezekiel W. Cullen Building at the University of Houston (1950), both by Alfred C. Finn; the Fondren Library at Rice University by Staub & Rather (1949); the Cullen Building of the Baylor College of Medicine in the new Texas Medical Center by Hedrick & Lindsley (1948); the new Hermann Hospital, also in the Medical Center, by Kenneth Franzheim and Hedrick & Lindsley (1949); and, most notorious of all, the eighteen-story 1,100-room Shamrock Hotel (1949) by Wyatt C. Hedrick bore out Kamrath's assessment. The Shamrock, the largest hotel built in the United States in the 1940s, coupled Texan excess with Houston architectural complacency; see "New Hotel: A Shamrock Grows in Texas," *Architectural Forum* 90 (April 1949): 11; "$21 Million Hotel Opens," *Life*, March 28, 1949, 27–31; "Shamrock Opens with a Bang," *Newsweek*, March 28, 1949, 64; "Big Time in Houston," *Fortune*, May 1949, 80–82.

21. Kathleen Bland, "Glass House Builder Expands on Ideas," *Houston Post*, January 11, 1950.

22. Welch, *Philip Johnson and Texas*; "Art Collection and Home of the John de Menils in Houston's River Oaks," *Interiors*, November 1963, 84–91; see also James Johnson Sweeney, "Collectors' Home: In the John de Menil House, a Great Ranging Art Collection," *Vogue*, April 1, 1966, 184–191.

23. Welch, *Philip Johnson and Texas*; see also "The University of St. Thomas, Houston," *Architectural Record* 122 (August 1957): 137–138, 142–143; "First Units in the Fabric of a Closed Campus," *Architectural Record* 126 (September 1959): 180–182; Michelangelo Sabatino, "Breaking the Egg: The Transformations of the University of St. Thomas Campus," *Cite 73* (Winter 2008): 10–17.

24. "2: House in Houston, Texas," *House and Home*, August 1958, 101, 106–107.

25. "Medical Towers," *Progressive Architecture* 38 (June 1957): 192–95; see also Kevin Alter, "SOM in Houston," *Cite 40* (Winter 1997–1998): 34–37.

26. C. Adams, ed., *Museum of Fine Arts, Houston; Bulletin*, Museum of Fine Arts, Houston, 1992.

27. "Parochial School Attains a Fine Warmth and Scale through Careful Adjustments," *Architectural Forum* 92 (June 1950): 102–105; see also "St. Rose of Lima," *Liturgical Arts* 20 (November 1951): 14–15.

28. "Department Store, Houston, Texas," *Progressive Architecture* 29 (July 1948): 49–59; see also Bruce C. Webb, "The Incredible Shrinking Store: Foley's Department Store, Downtown Houston," *Cite 22* (Fall 1989): 10–11.

29. Michelangelo Sabatino, "Heat and Light Thematised in the Modern Architecture of Houston," *Journal of Architecture* 16 (October 2011): 703–726; see also Ben Koush, "Hope for Growth and Community: The Development of the Texas Medical Center, 1945–2012," *Cite 89* (Summer 2012): 18–23.

30. The July–August 1985 issue of *Texas Architect* was devoted to modern architecture of the 1950s in Texas.

31. Scott Reagan Miller, "The School of Frank Lloyd Wright," *Cite 40* (Winter 1997–1998): 25–26.

32. John Kaliski, "The Wright Stuff: Houston's Natural House," *Cite 7* (Fall 1984): 16–18.

33. Ben Koush, "Houston Lives the Life: Modern Houses in the Suburbs, 1952–1962" (MArch thesis, Rice University, 2002), 141–202.

34. Henry-Russell Hitchcock, introduction to *Ten Years of Houston Architecture*; see also Mark A. Hewitt, "Neoclassicism and Modern Architecture, Houston Style or the Domestication of Mies," *Cite 7* (Fall 1984): 12–15; Koush, *Hugo V. Neuhaus*; Koush, *Booming Houston*; J. Smith, *High Style in the Suburbs*; Witte, *Counting*.

35. Hunter's Creek Village, Hedwig Village, and Bunker Hill Village were incorporated in 1954, and Spring Valley Village, Hilshire Village, and Piney Point Village in 1955.

36. Michael Brichford, "Where the '50s Were Fabulous: A Driving Tour of Memorial Bend," *Cite 57* (Spring 2003): 10–11. The architect William Floyd was one of the developers of Memorial Bend; see also Michael Brichford, "Remembering William Floyd," *Cite 64* (Summer 2005): 11.

37. Bolton & Barstone's Rottersman and M. G. Rosenthal Houses were built in Riverside Terrace, their Ming and Lindsay Houses in Memorial, their Farfel House in River Oaks, their Winterbotham and Owsley Houses in Briar Hollow, and Barnstone's Mermel House in Meyerland.

38. Holmes, *Alley Theatre*; see also Brutvan, *In Our Time*.

39. "Triangular Steel Framework for an Art Museum," *Architectural Forum* 93 (September 1950): 137.

40. Koush, "Houston Lives the Life," 84–86.

41. Robert V. Haynes, "Black Houstonians and the White Democratic Primary, 1920–45," in Beeth and Wintz, *Black Dixie*, 205–207.

42. Cary D. Wintz, "Texas Southern University," *Handbook of Texas Online*, June 15, 2010, modified on July 19, 2017, tshaonline.org/handbook/online/articles/kct27. The State of Texas created TSU soon after Sweatt first filed his case, in 1946 in Austin, well before the US Supreme Court's ruling.

43. Barry J. Kaplan, "Race, Income, and Ethnicity: Residential Change in a Houston Community, 1920–1970," *Houston Review* 3 (Winter 1981): 178–202.

44. Cole, *No Color Is My Kind*, 26–34.

45. Carleton, *Red Scare!*

46. Gereon Zimmerman, "Lady Stirs Her City's Conscience," *Look*, September 21, 1965, 66–71; see also Ronald Moskowitz, "Big City Schools V—Houston: Education and Politics in Boomtown; Factions, Feuds, and the Clouded Educational Future of Space City," *Saturday Review*, February 17, 1968, 51–52; Gertrude Levy Barnstone, oral history interview by Sarah C. Reynolds, June 9, 2006, OpenStax CNX, http://cnx.org/content/m16152/latest; Gertrude Barnstone, oral history interview by Jane Ely, March 25, 2008, Houston Public Library, http://digital.houstonlibrary.org/oral-history/gertrude-barnstone2.php.

47. Stephen James, "Donald Barthelme: Architecture and the Road to La Mancha, *ARRIS: Journal of the Southeast Chapter of the Society of Architectural Historians* 16 (2005): 56–68; George, *O'Neil Ford*; Dillon, *Architecture of O'Neil Ford*. On Hugo Neuhaus, see Koush, *Hugo V. Neuhaus*.

48. Welch, *Philip Johnson and Texas*, 161–208.

49. "Planning, Not Zoning, Needed, UH Architectural Professor Says," *Houston Post*, March 27, 1962. Thanks to Meredith H. James, Jr., for bringing this article to the authors' attention.

50. Esther McCoy, "Young Architects in the United States: 1963," *Zodiac* 13:164–167, 186–190. In a sidebar to an article on transportation planning in Houston by another author, Barnstone asserted that the money required to construct a mass transit system would be better spent on a fleet of Mercedes-Benz jitneys, to be driven by retirees, that would convey passengers anywhere they wanted to go in Houston—for free ("A Modest Proposal," *Cite 3* [Spring 1983]: 16). One Houston architect was so outraged by Barnstone's piece that he resigned from *Cite*'s editorial committee.

51. The Rice Design Alliance symposium "City Houses: Options for Urban Living," April 1977.

52. "UT Symposium Considers Dimensions of Texas Architecture," *Texas Architect* 31 (November–December 1981): 88.

53. Nicholas Lemann, "The Architects," *Texas Monthly*, April 1982; see also Howard Barnstone, "Obit: John de Ménil," *Architecture Plus* 1 (August 1973): 71.

54. Johnson, *Writings*, 206.

55. Philip Johnson, "The Seven Crutches of Modern Architecture," *Perspecta* 3 (1955): 40–45.

56. Kazys Varnelis, "Philip Johnson's Empire: Network Power and the AT&T Building," in Petit, *Philip Johnson*, 120–135.

57. Jermayne MacAgy, "Exposures and Enticements," *Art in America* 46 (Spring 1958): 40–43; see also Lynn M. Herbert, "Seeing Was Believing: Installations of Jermayne MacAgy and James Johnson Sweeney," *Cite* 40 (Winter 1997–1998): 30–33.

58. Eleanor C. Munro, "Totems and Taboos: Art Out of Anthropology," *Art News* 58 (April 1959): 28–29; "Two Ways of Looking at Art in Houston: II. The Gallery of Fine Arts, University of St. Thomas," *Interiors*, November 1963, 92, 96–98; Herbert, "Seeing Was Believing."

59. MacAgy, "Exposures and Enticements."

60. Toni Ramona Beauchamp, "James Johnson Sweeney and the Museum of Fine Arts, Houston, 1961–1967" (MA thesis, University of Texas at Austin, 1983).

61. H. Barnstone, *Galveston That Was*.

62. Smart, *Sacred Modern*.

63. Brennan, *Curating Consciousness*; James Johnson Sweeney, "Le Cullinan Hall de Mies van der Rohe à Houston," *L'Oeil* 99 (March 1963): 38–43; Dore Ashton, "Sweeney Revisited," *Studio Art* 166 (September 1963): 110–13; "Two Ways of Looking at Art in Houston: I. The Museum of Fine Arts," *Interiors*, November 1963, 92–95.

64. Barnes, *Rothko Chapel*; see also Nodelman, *Rothko Chapel Paintings*, 72–75; Dominique de Menil, "Rothko Chapel," *Art Journal* 30 (Spring 1971): 249–251.

65. Anne Schlumberger Brown, interview by Barrie Scardino Bradley and Stephen Fox, September 28, 2018, Houston, Texas.

66. Kacmar, *Victor Lundy*; Zemanek, *Being . . . Becoming*; Turner, *Open Plan*.

67. H. Barnstone, *Architecture of John F. Staub*; Wendy Haskell Meyer, "John F. Staub: A New Book about Our City's Eclectic Architect," *Houston Home and Garden*, October 1979, 55–60.

68. Wendy Haskell Meyer, "Provincial Living: A Contemporary Architect Lives in the Past," *Houston Home and Garden*, February 1979, 90–95.

69. Bernhard, *Ima Hogg*, 130.

70. Judith Kugle, "Sally Walsh: Inside Modern Houston" (MArch thesis, University of Houston, 2013); see also Gretchen Fallon, "Design Innovators: Three Houstonians Who Create Classic Looks," *Houston Home and Garden*, October 1983, 142–143.

71. Laura Sánchez, "Celebran Vida de Marti Franco," *El Mañana Cultura* (Nuevo Laredo, Tamaulipas, Mexico), April 30, 2014, http://avisos.elmanana.com.mx/noticia/31228/Celebran-vida-de-Marti-Franco.html. Despite his disdain for regionalism, Barnstone pursued a regionalist approach in designing the landmark Nuevo Laredo specialty store for Marti Franco on Avenida Guerrero in 1971. Barnstone designed the shop by using vernacular Mexican prototypes in a way that is expressive and purposefully playful.

72. Karleen Koen, "Best of '77: Nine Architects and Their Projects Win Residential Honors," *Houston Home and Garden* (February 1978), 54–55, 60–61; Meyer, "Provincial Living," 90–95.

73. Peter Blake and Philip Johnson, "Architectural Freedom and Order: An Answer to Robert W. Kennedy," *Magazine of Art* 41 (October 1948): 228–231.

74. McCoy, "Young Architects," 186.

75. "Machine Shop for Art," *Architectural Forum* 131 (July–August 1969): 95; see also Cyndy Severson, "The House That Art Built," *Texas Monthly*, September 1977, 100–103; Susan Freudenheim, "Shock of the New," *Texas Homes*, October 1986, 58–63; Neal I. Payton, "Tin Houses," *Cite 8* (Summer 1986); Joseph Giovannini, "Showing Their Metal," *Metropolitan Home*, July–August 1995, 97–101; Terzah Ewing, "The Home Front: Houston Takes a Shine to Metal," *Wall Street Journal*, April 25, 1997; Donna Paul, "Homes of Metal: Great Shining Hope?," *New York Times*, May 14, 1998.

76. Phillip Lopate, "Elegy for Houston," *Texas Observer*, May 29, 1987, 10.

77. Moser, *Why This World*, 2.

I

HOWARD BARNSTONE'S ARCHITECTURE

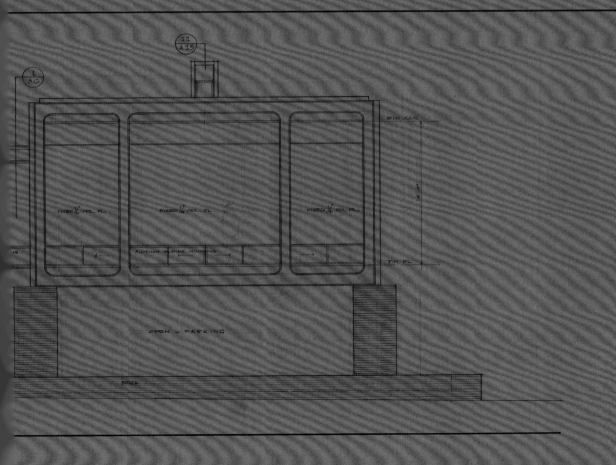

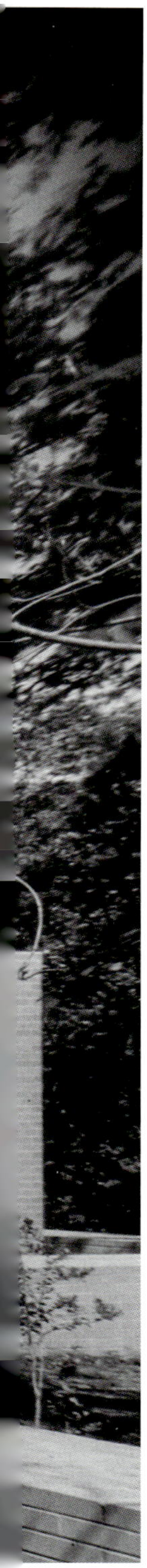

CHAPTER ONE

BARNSTONE'S PRACTICE

STEPHEN FOX

HOWARD BARNSTONE was an architectural auteur.[1] In formulating his architectural designs, he directed, but also depended on, his draftsmen. In an examination of Barnstone's architectural practice from 1949 until 1987 to understand how he interacted with his partners—Preston M. Bolton from 1952 to 1961 and Eugene Aubry from 1966 to 1969—as well as the young men and women he employed as draftsmen, what emerges is the penetrating power of Barnstone's subjectivity: his ability to infuse the buildings that his office produced with phenomenal attributes that persisted over the three and a half decades of his professional activity, even though the formal influences the designs display changed. Like other ambitious American architects of his generation, Barnstone rejected the notion of interdisciplinary collaboration, with which Walter Gropius sought to identify the practice of modern architecture in the 1930s and 1940s, as Anthony Alofsin has shown.[2] Yet even though Barnstone understood significant architecture to be the product of a personal vision, he nonetheless practiced architectural design collaboratively. An exploration of the contradiction between Barnstone's ideology and his practice discloses what others brought to the design of his buildings. It also emphasizes how Barnstone worked to shape the designs produced in his studio to conform to his architectural predilections.

STYLES OF PRACTICE

Houston architectural firms of the 1950s, 1960s, and 1970s represented a range of attitudes toward practice. Caudill Rowlett Scott (CRS), the largest architectural

(LEFT TO RIGHT) Preston M. Bolton and Howard Barnstone c. 1960.

firm in Houston from 1959 until it was merged into Hellmuth, Obata & Kassabaum (HOK) in 1994, externalized the ways architecture might be practiced to develop what the firm's charismatic founder, William W. Caudill, called "architecture by team."[3] CRS's transition between 1948 and 1970 from a partnership to a corporation to a publicly traded company indicates the efforts that Caudill and his partners made to achieve maximum financial profitability from their professional work, efforts that, as the historian Paolo Tombesi has demonstrated, proved so unsatisfactory that the architecture firm was eventually sold off.[4]

Neuhaus & Taylor, the Houston firm founded by J. Victor Neuhaus III and Harwood Taylor in 1955, followed the trajectory of Caudill Rowlett Scott, reorganizing itself as a multidisciplinary practice, 3D/International, in 1972 and also becoming a publicly traded company.[5] Houston architectural firms founded in the 1930s—Lloyd, Morgan & Jones and Wilson, Morris, Crain & Anderson—likewise moved from partnerships to professional corporations as they sought financial stability amid cycles of economic expansion and contraction. Ben Koush, in his book on Lloyd, Morgan & Jones, documents the principals' acquisition of stock in Century Properties, their major client and a formidable Houston real estate developer, in lieu of fees, which imperiled the firm when Houston's economy crashed in 1982 as a result of a sharp downturn in the price of oil.[6] John Wiegman's memoir, *His Story: A Personal History of Morris Architects*, charts the moves that S. I. Morris, Jr., made after firing his partners of thirty-five years in 1972 in order to position his new firm, S. I. Morris Associates, to take advantage of the expansionary phase in which CRS and 3D/International became publicly traded companies.[7]

BARNSTONE'S PRACTICE

Caudill Rowlett Scott (CRS) architects designing by team for the Olin Hall of Science at Colorado College in Colorado Springs. Bill Caudill (with pointer) leads the team.

Barnstone was affected by the ups and downs of the economic cycle. But he had no interest in strategizing styles of practice to achieve professional advantage. While not averse to profitability, he remained engaged with architectural design and production rather than aspiring to move onward, and financially upward, to the management and marketing of design "services."

Aside from his two partnerships, Barnstone practiced as a sole proprietor. While fashioning himself as a gentleman architect—like the Houston architects William J. Anderson, Jr.; Lavone Dickensheets Andrews; Kenneth E. Bentsen; Raymond H. Brogniez; R. H. Donnelley Erdman; John H. Freeman, Jr.; Thomas E. Greacen II; Robert F. Lent; Hugo V. Neuhaus, Jr.; Anderson Todd; and B. Magruder Wingfield, Jr.—Barnstone pursued a practice that was more akin to those of his architecture faculty colleagues: Donald Barthelme, William R. Jenkins, and Burdette Keeland at the University of Houston, and William T. Cannady Caudill, Erdman, and Todd at Rice University. His University of Houston professorship provided Barnstone with a steady income independent of his practice. It also enabled him to recruit talented students to work in his office. Additionally, teaching gave Barnstone the opportunity to engage with ideas, people, and places in ways that he might not have been able to do had practice been his only forum.[8]

Lillian Guberman and Gerald S. Gordon House (1953–1955, Bolton & Barnstone), 2307 Blue Bonnet Boulevard, Braeswood, Houston, on the cover of *Architectural Record*, Record Houses of 1956.

Barnstone keenly understood the value of networking and publicity in constructing a profile of professional leadership locally and nationally. He entered Bolton & Barnstone's buildings in design awards programs sponsored by the American Institute of Architects, Houston Chapter; the Texas Society of Architects; and the American Institute of Architects nationally. Beginning in 1952, the firm's buildings were regularly profiled in *Architectural Forum*, *Architectural Record*, *Arts and Architecture*, *Art in America*, *House and Garden*, *House and Home*, *Progressive Architecture*, and *Texas Architect* as well as in Houston's daily newspapers, the *Post* and the *Chronicle*. Nationally circulated architectural journals and house and garden magazines discovered a new market in Texas in the 1950s, in part because of the efforts of Texas architects such as Barnstone to keep editors and their correspondents abreast of new developments. For Barnstone, these efforts paid off. Among Texas firms, only Caudill Rowlett Scott was published more frequently than Bolton & Barnstone in the national and regional architectural press during the 1950s and early 1960s. It was through publication that Bolton & Barnstone's affiliation with the architecture of Ludwig Mies van der Rohe and Philip Johnson in the 1950s was broadcast nationally.

Eugene Aubry (b. 1935), who began work in the office in 1959, recalls that Bolton & Barnstone's draftsmen produced these designs. Aubry likened this process to the relationship that Philip Johnson had with his chief draftsman, John Manley (1925–2013). Because Johnson, like Barnstone, was not proficient at drawing, Johnson relied on Manley to translate his notes and diagrams into architectural designs. Aubry identified Adrian S. Rosenberg and Donald M. Palmer as the draftsmen who produced Bolton & Barnstone's classic Miesian designs. With access to Johnson's construction drawings for the Menil House, the office could precisely replicate Johnson's system of Miesian details. Aubry laughed about how some details became so ingrained in the firm's practice that even after architectural models had changed, the detailing did not: "We spent hours chasing quarter-inch reveals around houses," he remembered.[9]

Yet Barnstone assimilated Miesian design hesitantly. Bolton & Barnstone's earliest houses in Houston, such as the Dan Bloxsom House (1952) and the Edwin C. Rottersmann House (1953), were not based on Miesian-Johnson prototypes.

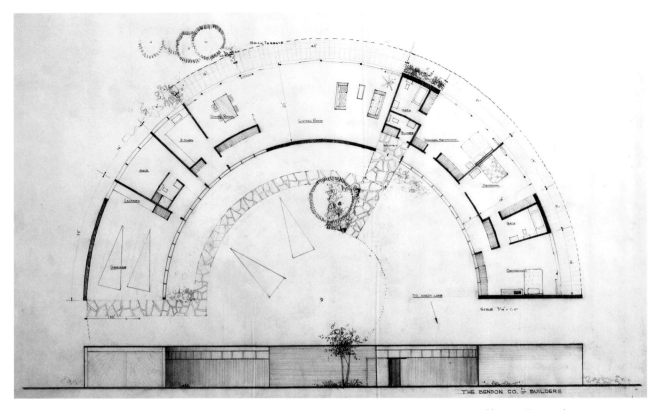

Bloxsom House, plan.

Even so, the Bloxsom House demonstrates one of Barnstone's methods of conceptualizing a design. The house was his version of a Solar Hemicycle house, the Usonian house type originated by Frank Lloyd Wright in 1944 for the second Herbert Jacobs House.[10] Barnstone's cheeky method—appropriating the master's design and, literally, turning it inside out—was one way to generate new designs. Barnstone was quite candid about his source for the Lillian Guberman and Gerald S. Gordon House (1955): Ray and Charles Eames's Case Study House No. 8 (1949), which he aggrandized, formalized, and Miesianized. The house for Dorothy Brookner and Dr. Harris Hosen in Port Arthur, Texas (1957), where site conditions led Barnstone to place the living room on the second floor, was inspired by Johnson's Robert C. Wiley House in New Canaan, Connecticut (1953). Bolton & Barnstone's house for Louise Harbour and W. Gordon Wing (1960) was extrapolated from the house that Johnson designed for Dominique de Menil's sister and brother-in-law, Sylvie Schlumberger and Eric H. Boissonnas (1956), in New Canaan.[11] Barnstone's appropriation of formal models transgressed the ethics of modern architecture, which asserted that modern buildings should be designed to respond rationally and economically to program (functionalism); to site, orientation, and

Dan Bloxsom House (1952, Howard Barnstone, demolished), 22 East Shady Lane, Houston.

locale (regionalism); and to the materials and processes of construction (structure). In "The Seven Crutches of Modern Architecture," a talk that Philip Johnson gave at the Harvard Graduate School of Design in 1954, Johnson derided this earnest, moralistic approach. In place of ethical precepts, Johnson advanced art as the sole standard of judgment: "Art has nothing to do with intellectual pursuits—it shouldn't be in a university at all. Art should be practiced in gutters—pardon me, attics. You can't learn architecture any more than you can learn a sense of music or of painting. You shouldn't talk about art, you should do it."[12]

Barnstone did practice in an attic. Aubry recalled that Bolton & Barnstone's office occupied a two-story early-twentieth-century house at 811 Lovett Boulevard in the Montrose Addition and that Barnstone's attic office, inadequately cooled by a single window-unit air conditioner, was where his draftsmen came to confer with him while he dictated to the firm's secretary, Virginia Hess. Because Aubry had been a student of Barnstone's for two years at the University of Houston and because Miesian architecture was the only architecture sanctioned in

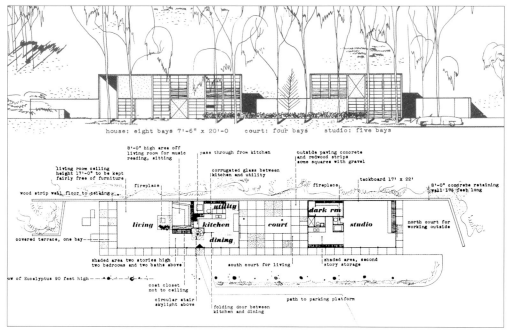

ABOVE Gordon House, with original landscaping by Thomas D. Church (1902–1978), Houston.

LEFT Charles and Ray Eames House (Case Study House 8, 1945–1949, Charles and Ray Eames), Pacific Palisades, California.

W. Gordon Wing House (1959–1960, Bolton & Barnstone), 33 East Rivercrest Drive, Houston.

the architecture program, it came as a shock to Aubry to discover that Barnstone designed through intermediaries rather than generating the firm's designs himself.[13] Reflecting on the working relationship he developed with Barnstone, Aubry said he found he could do what Barnstone wanted done, in the way he wanted it done, without Barnstone having to tell him explicitly what to do.[14]

In writing about the houses designed by Hugo Neuhaus's firm, Cowell & Neuhaus, Ben Koush noted the disparity between Neuhaus's domestic planning and Bolton & Barnstone's planning. Whereas Neuhaus (as well as Anderson Todd) sought to resolve the conflicts between the Miesian imperative to construct flowing, unpartitioned interior spaces in glass-walled houses and the countervailing middle-class expectation of domestic privacy, Bolton & Barnstone's houses tended to rigidly compartmentalize private spaces (especially bedrooms, bathrooms, and closets) in order to create the illusion of free-flowing spaces in the houses' reception rooms.[15] The English critic Colin Rowe, who taught at the University of

Houston in 1957, alluded to the pragmatic, un-Miesian planning of Bolton & Barnstone's house for Germaine de Verteuil and Marc Demoustier (1955), which he illustrated in his essay on the contradictions that modern architecture exhibited as it became the dominant trend in the United States in the 1950s.[16] Bolton & Barnstone's earliest Miesian house, for Faye Byer and Lawrence H. Blum in Beaumont (1954), cleverly dissembled Miesian symmetry by balancing the solid wall panel to the right of the central entrance bay with the overhead door of the double garage to the left. An even more serious infraction of the ethical precepts of the modern movement occurred when photos of the Blum House published in *Architectural Record* and *Arts and Architecture* were airbrushed to make it look as if the house had a flat roof, when in fact it had a shallowly pitched hipped roof.[17] Bolton & Barnstone's large, elegant house for Esther Susholtz and Aaron J. Farfel (1956) in Houston's elite River Oaks neighborhood is a wood-framed brick-veneer house plated with steel channels to imply its steel-framed construction.[18] In the all-glass house for Barbara Robinson and Alvin M. Owsley, Jr. (1961), wall partitions in bedrooms and bathrooms die into the mullions of the perimeter curtain wall as unobtrusively as possible.[19]

Eric H. Boissonnas House (1956, Philip C. Johnson Associates), New Canaan, Connecticut.

Had Bolton & Barnstone's sleights of hand been detected, it is unlikely that the firm would have received the recognition it did through publication and design awards. What won it these accolades was the precision, assurance, and refinement of the firm's houses. The Blum House is a marvel of spatial economy. The Gordon House entranced not only the editors of *Architectural Record*, *Arts and Architecture*, and *House and Garden*, but also the historian and critic Henry-Russell Hitchcock, who visited the house and extolled its spatial originality.[20] Barnstone integrated his houses and clients into broader modernist networks linking Houston with East and West Coast centers of architectural culture. He persuaded Mr. and Mrs. M. L. Cook, Mr. and Mrs. Demoustier, and Mr. and Mrs. Gordon to retain the Knoll Planning Unit of New York to furnish their houses.[21] He got the Demoustiers, Farfels, and Gordons to hire the San Francisco landscape architect Thomas D. Church to design their gardens.[22] Barnstone reinforced local modernist networks too through his collaboration with Houston design professionals. Sally Walsh, a former Knoll employee, designed the interiors of the Farfel House, and Herbert Wells (1924–2010) those of the Owsley House.[23] Whether the interiors were entirely modern—as in the Knoll installations—or an eclectic mixture of the new and

Howard Barnstone in his office, 811 Lovett Boulevard, Houston, c. 1955.

the antique, they reinforced the aura of "magic" that Bolton & Barnstone houses emitted: the perception of scintillating spatial brilliance. Seated in the Owsley's double-height glass-walled living room on upholstered antique furniture set on an Oriental rug, guests experienced the surreal sensation of being suspended amid the dense canopy of evergreen woodland vegetation that surrounds the house. Barnstone mobilized the modern technologies of steel framing, wall-size sheets of plate glass, and central air-conditioning to induce this hallucinatory feeling.[24] In Bolton & Barnstone's practice of Miesian architecture, "art" (as Philip Johnson would have it) decisively triumphed over the "crutches" of ethical imperatives.

STYLES OF CHANGE

Gene Aubry, who became Barnstone's design amanuensis in the 1960s, describes the other instructors at the University of Houston during the second half of the 1950s as "high school teachers" when compared with Barnstone and Donald Barthelme, the architecture school's charismatic (but profoundly antagonistic) stars. Aubry aligned himself with Barnstone and Barnstone's former student and protégé, Burdette Keeland. Aubry described Barnstone as teaching through conversation. According to Aubry, Barnstone possessed an uncanny intuitive judgment for what was right, what would work architecturally.[25] Aubry said that Barnstone never

ABOVE LEFT Marc Demoustier House (1955, Bolton & Barnstone, demolished), 608 Little John Lane, Houston.

ABOVE RIGHT Demoustier House, interior design by the Knoll Planning Unit (1955, Bolton & Barnstone, demolished).

simply directed him to pursue a specified design direction. The buildings that Howard Barnstone & Partners produced in the 1960s looked different from those Bolton & Barnstone had designed, a contrast that Aubry accounts for by observing that as people in the office changed, so did the "styles" of Barnstone's buildings, a dynamic that prevailed throughout the rest of Barnstone's career.[26] One change that marked Aubry's appearance in the office was his production of large-scale perspective drawings, especially interior perspectives. These were not produced as client presentation drawings but as working design studies. Aubry's arrival also corresponded with the firm's new interest in angular geometry, initially the incorporation of octagonal spaces, as in the Freeman House in Houston and the Challinor House in New Haven, Connecticut.[27]

This paradoxical method of subliminal transmission separated Barnstone's practice from the division of labor common in large architectural firms, in which principals get the jobs and manage them and "designers" produce the architecture. Barnstone's buildings demonstrate amazing consistency in their spatiality, proportions, scale, indoor-outdoor relationships, use of transparency, and details. Barnstone's insistence that light-switch plates be aligned at doorknob level rather than at shoulder height is a telling instance. This detail captivated not only architects who worked for Barnstone, but also other Houston architects who came into contact with his work. Horizontally aligned drawer and cabinet pulls, globular doorknobs, railings and tables fabricated of one-inch-square steel bar, and

Lawrence H. Blum House (1954, Bolton & Barnstone), 1030 23rd Street, Beaumont, Texas.

retractable canvas awnings above windows were other identifying details. Aubry said that the common denominator among these details was their unobtrusiveness: visually, they went away.

The work of Howard Barnstone & Partners between 1961 and 1966 and of Barnstone & Aubry from 1966 to 1969 moved away from Miesian models. Barnstone & Partners' house for Ann Rauch and Irving Mermel in Meyerland (1961) exemplifies the firm's rejection of what Colin Rowe described as the formal "conventions" of Miesian architecture in favor of a design that sought to make strengths out of the limitations of the house's awkward site on the flat, treeless coastal plain of southwestern Houston. Dividing the house into two pavilions (a motel-like bedroom wing facing a swimming pool, plus a thirty-foot-square glass-walled pavilion with a truncated hipped roof that rose to an interior height of twenty-five feet) and working with narrow, fenced courtyards to both construct and contain outdoor views, Barnstone with Aubry transformed the site's disadvantages into architectural advantages.[28]

The firm's skill in cleverly exploiting the limitations of compressed size to produce sensations of spatial discovery and intimacy was evident in the ten-unit Vassar Place Apartments (1965), for which Barnstone was his own client.[29] A published description of the Mermel House characterized the relationship of interior space to its walled courtyards as "Japanese." Although Barnstone never sought to reproduce a Japanese-style landscape, his ability to work with small and often confined planted spaces, and to visually and spatially connect these with interior spaces, displayed a profoundly Japanese sensibility.[30] Barnstone's gift

California. Paint steel to blend or contrast.

Pennsylvania. Steel can be "tailored" to any shape.

 Steel

For Strength
... Economy
... Beauty

Oregon. No site is too steep for steel.

Texas. Slender steel members are attractive.

Connecticut. Wide overhangs are no problem with steel.

Why your new house should have a steel frame

It should have a steel frame... if you like contemporary designs... spacious interiors you can easily rearrange... a strong frame that lets you build on any site. Your architect can tell you more. So can we.*

PERMANENCE. Steel frame withstands earthquakes, hurricanes, landslides. It won't rot or burn. It can't shrink, warp, creep, or sag. And termites hate steel.

WIDE-OPEN SPACES. Steel is so strong that even slender beams can provide column-free interior areas of 30, 40 or more feet... and wide overhangs outside for shade and protection.

CURTAIN WALLS. Roof and floors are supported by the steel frame, not by walls. Exteriors can be floor-to-ceiling glass, sliding doors, any other material. Interiors can be completely flexible.

STEEL SOLVES SITE PROBLEMS. Build on a steep hillside. Over rocks. Even over a ravine! Pick up an "impossible" building lot at a bargain price, with no need for costly grading or excavation.

Steel frame lets you enjoy the view. No interior columns .... floor-to-ceiling glass walls.

BETHLEHEM STEEL

*Send for new booklet "The Steel-Framed House." Write Publications Department, Bethlehem Steel Co., Bethlehem, Pa.

for shaping intimate spaces is more evident in his domestic projects of the 1960s than in Bolton & Barnstone's work.

Barnstone and Aubry's houses tended toward external self-effacement; composure and proportion rather than formal assertiveness characterized their work. Their grandest house, built in the Homewoods section of River Oaks for Lois Lasater and John F. Maher (1964), is faced with windowless planes of pink St. Joe brick bracketed with advancing chimney stacks that asymmetrically frame a recessed glass entrance bay.[31] The house's rear-facing living room and dining room occupy a raised pavilion, fifty-five feet by thirty feet in plan and fourteen feet high, walled with glass-filled steel Vierendeel trusses. Barnstone and Aubry tempered the spatial magnificence of the Maher House with austerity and wit. They took advantage of the site's downslope to Buffalo Bayou to insert the children's bedrooms beneath the main floor level. The carport below the living room pavilion is accessible by a driveway that descends beneath the house's broad entrance deck and then turns to cut between the children's bedrooms. Barnstone and Aubry inserted long, narrow slot skylights in the library and John Maher's dressing rooms to bring natural light in from unseen sources and animate these windowless spaces. The house's essential austerity was foregrounded when its second owner, Mary Ralph Lowe, dialectically challenged austerity with her eighteenth-century French furniture and collection of gilt-framed paintings by the nineteenth-century academic artist William-Adolphe Bouguereau.

External self-effacement characterized the Houston Area Teacher's Credit Union Building (1964), a two-story office building on the edge of downtown; the pavilion-like studio building that Barnstone, Aubry, and Burdette Keeland built for their own use in the historic Sixth Ward neighborhood (1964); houses for Agnes Arnold and Dr. Joseph Barnhart at the Texas Corinthian Yacht Club in Kemah, Texas (1968), for Helen Hill and I. H. Kempner III in River Oaks (1968), and for Edna Seinsheimer and Dr. William C. Levin in Galveston (1968); and Guinan Hall, the student dormitory at the University of St. Thomas (1971). Wit was evident in their design of the internally glazed "wiggle wall" office floor at 277 Park Avenue (1966) in New York for Schlumberger Ltd., the jaunty but economical six-story tower they added to a two-story house for the Institute for Storm Research at the University of St. Thomas (1968), and the shed-like Rice Museum at Rice University (1969), better known as the Art Barn.[32] Austerity marked the design of the firm's concrete-framed institutional buildings: Piney Point Elementary School (1962) for the Houston Independent School District; the Galveston County Publishing Company Building in Galveston, commissioned by the Houston newspaper publisher and communications corporation owner Oveta Culp

OPPOSITE Alvin M. Owsley, Jr., House (1960, Bolton & Barnstone), 65 Briar Hollow Lane, Houston, featured in a Bethlehem Steel advertisement. The Owsley House is labeled "Texas. Slender steel members are attractive."

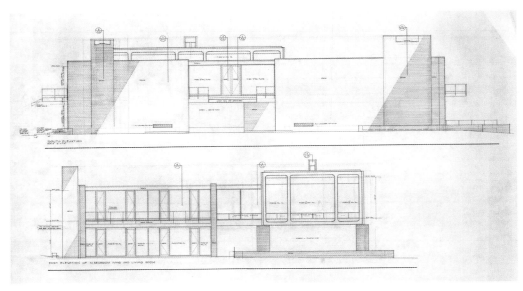

Maher House, elevations.

Hobby; and Barnstone & Aubry's biggest commission, the Harris County Center for the Retarded (1966), a six-building complex occupying an undulating five-acre site facing Buffalo Bayou Park just outside the gates of River Oaks.[33]

Gene Aubry recalls that Barnstone became so dysfunctional during his depression in 1968–1969 that Aubry was left to carry out the firm's work on his own. In late 1969, Aubry dissolved their partnership. After consulting with John de Menil, Aubry accepted an offer from S. I. Morris to join Wilson, Morris, Crain & Anderson as design partner in April 1970.[34] Aubry produced a revised scheme for the gabled house of Sue Ledbetter and Gervais Bell; the Media Center at Rice University (1970), a companion to the Art Barn; and the Doherty Library at the University of St. Thomas (1971), all built after the dissolution of the firm.[35]

Barnstone returned to practice in 1970 in an unsettled emotional state that was exacerbated by the financial consequences of months of professional inactivity and the dissolution of both his marriage and partnership. Remarkably, he began to receive architectural commissions and, with the assistance of a new generation of students from the University of Houston, to reconstruct his practice. Anthony E. Frederick, a graduate of the College of Architecture, carried out three notable designs while working for Barnstone between 1971 and 1975: extensive alterations and additions to a house designed in 1956 by Frank D. Welch that had been purchased by Doreen Wolfson and Frank C. Herzog (1971); a seasonal house in Scottsdale, Arizona, for the chairman of Schlumberger, Jean Riboud, and his wife, Krishna Roy (1974); and Marti's, the specialty store that Barnstone's stepmother, Marti Franco, and her second husband, Earl L. Suneson (1971), operated

OPPOSITE, TOP John F. Maher House (1964, Howard Barnstone & Partners, altered), 2930 Lazy Lane, Houston.

OPPOSITE, BOTTOM Maher House, living-dining room wing.

in the Mexican border city of Nuevo Laredo, Tamaulipas. The Herzog House experimented with layers of transparency, achieved by replacing solid interior walls with internal glass partitions and inserting concealed skylights to illuminate windowless spaces.[36] The Riboud House is embedded in its undulating site. Irregularly angled interior walls internalize the contours of the landscape, producing a sense of enclosure that is played against simple interior finishes and framed views of the desert.[37] Marti's involved remodeling three adjoining buildings with different floor heights and construction systems. Taking advantage of flexible Mexican building codes, Barnstone and Frederick fashioned an irregular interior, hinted at in the store's entrance patio, where arched display windows penetrate the bounding walls with playful randomness. Humor, allusiveness, spontaneity, and intimacy were mobilized to craft a building that exploits contingency and limitation with imaginative exuberance.

Barnstone worked with another draftsman, Jim Powers, on the Graustark Family Townhouses (1972), a set of three row houses built in the backyard of a 1930s duplex in the Museum District, to which Barnstone moved his office in 1971.[38] Each house is sixteen feet wide, the width of a single garage stall flanked by an entrance hall and stair. The design compensates for each house's narrow width with a stepped section in which a second-story dining room overlooks a two-story living room. A glass garage door and an interior glass wall between the garage and entrance hall not only promote transparency and the transmission of daylight, but also enable cars to live with their owners, a domestic arrangement that Barnstone extolled.

Ted B. Gupton, a graduate of the University of Texas at Austin, took Frederick's place when Frederick left to begin his own practice. Gupton worked on Barnstone's major projects of the 1970s: the Menil-Carpenter Houses in East Hampton; the Menil-Carpenter Apartment in New York; the unbuilt Congregation Am Echad Synagogue in Auburn, Maine; and the Schlumberger-Doll Research Center in Ridgefield, Connecticut.[39] The Schlumberger-Doll Research Center project was of sufficiently long duration and required so much travel that Barnstone hired Robert T. Jackson (an Austin architect), Robert Morris (a Houston architect), and Anthony Di Sunno (an architectural intern from East Hampton, Long Island) to supplement his small staff, which by the late 1970s also included Shawn McFarland, an architecture student at the University of Houston. Gupton recalled that he and Barnstone worked together on producing designs; Barnstone would propose a concept that Gupton would then develop under his guidance. "Howard would come and go, mentally and physically, during design, but he was always 'present' in the sense that he would drop in on the work on what seemed

Howard Barnstone & Partners and Burdette Keeland office building (1963, Howard Barnstone & Partners and Burdette Keeland), 1914 West Capitol, Houston.

like a random schedule and have a look at what I was doing," Gupton observed. Although Barnstone was unpredictable and could at times be verbally abusive, he was also humorous, fun, and charming, traits that, according to Gupton, outweighed the emotional impact of his darker moods.[40]

In 1979, Barnstone briefly employed Doug Michels, cofounder of the design collective Ant Farm.[41] Michels produced a scheme for the Menil Foundation's art storage building, an office building in Austin for Robert Barnstone, and a house in Houston for Carolyn Grant and Ernest Bel Fay, none of which was built. Michels's persona as a comic book superhero was radically at odds with Barnstone's projection of gentlemanly understatement; Barnstone's method of editing Michels's science-fiction-like designs was to have another draftsman selectively erase them. Yet Barnstone was not deterred by what, in retrospect, seemed like a predictable collision of architectural cultures. He was willing to try a collaboration with Michels, even though the likelihood that it would succeed was minimal.

By the 1980s, Roger Dobbins, Edward Rogers, and Rudolph Colby had become the office's primary design associates. This period was marked by Barnstone's transition to his subdued version of postmodernism. The De Saligny townhouse complex in Austin for Robert Barnstone (1981) and the Houston houses of Beth Carson and Robert S. Bramlett (1983) and Nancy Girling and George Peterkin, Jr. (1984), display formal postmodern attributes.[42] Yet they are also charged with Barnstone's sense of spatial buoyancy. For the Menil Foundation's unbuilt photo archives building (1981), Barnstone reverted to his earlier use of models: its vaulted roof structure was derived from Louis Kahn's Kimbell Art Museum in Fort Worth. An unbuilt design for a midrise tower for the Webb County Administration Building in Laredo, Texas (1981), engaged the local architectural-historical "context" with a giant-scale postmodern appropriation of the cupola of the adjoining 1909 county courthouse. This commission gave Barnstone's office a rare chance to propose an urban design scheme, tying the county government complex together with a network of open spaces in the only Texas city to preserve its eighteenth-century Spanish colonial town plan. The office's last big project, the Schlumberger Austin Systems Center (1987), a seven-building office complex occupying a 438-acre site in what was then rural north Austin, also relied on an architectural model: Batey & Mack's Holt House in Corpus Christi (1982). But at Schlumberger Austin, the use of a formal model was almost irrelevant. The complex was designed to be experienced in spatial and visual fragments keyed to specific landscape settings rather than as a set of freestanding buildings. As associated architect (rather than an employee), Robert Jackson shared design credit for Schlumberger Austin with Barnstone; J. Robert Anderson of Austin was the landscape architect.[43]

Barnstone adhered to Philip Johnson's predilection for embracing the dynamics of change—the ongoing construction of difference—rather than formulating an architectural ethic based on searching for truths that, once clarified, did not require reformulation. Protagonists of different strands of the modern movement—Wright, Mies—were drawn to the truth paradigm, as were the Houston architects MacKie & Kamrath, Donald Barthelme, and Barnstone's peers Anderson Todd and John Zemanek. Barnstone's practice was to engage change. His method for doing so was to work with young draftsmen, appropriating their skill, enthusiasm, and imagination to give varied form to his visions of space, light, and nature.

IDENTIFYING STYLE

As an architectural auteur, Barnstone drew liberally on the talents of the draftsmen and technicians he directed in order to achieve a look and feel that consistently identified his architecture. Barnstone's authorial prerogative is evident in his ability to infuse his buildings with subjective attributes—proportion and scale relationships, preferred dimensions, distinctive use of daylighting as both sidelight and skylight, intimate interactions with the landscape, and a sense of spontaneity—even when these buildings were designed by other people and based on models originated by other architects. Barnstone publicly represented himself, as the Chicago design critic Nory Miller described him, as a "lone star."[44] But he also managed to make use of the agency of others to expand his design vision. Gene Aubry observed that Barnstone exercised authority by telling stories that amused and captivated his listeners, either in support of a proposed course of action or to dismiss a competing alternative (usually with clever and subversive sarcasm). Barnstone's facility for mythmaking compensated for his weakness in portraying his ideas through drawing. He managed the contradiction between his projected image of liberal individuality and his reliance on the talents of others by weaving myths—word pictures—with his stories, marshaling wit, humor, intuition, and insight to ensure that his directives proved memorable and compelling. The San Antonio architect O'Neil Ford (1905–1982), professionally a generation older than Barnstone, and the Houston architect Charles Tapley (1931–2015), professionally a generation younger, shared his method of directing the efforts of their employee-collaborators.[45] Barnstone, like Philip Johnson, had a flair for assembling networks of clients, architects and artists, politicians and journalists, academics and clerics, and socialites to people his imagined community of liberal Houston modernity. Dominique and John de Menil were his archetypes. His architecture, its formal variations notwithstanding, was meant to identify this community to its constituents ("our crowd," as Bruce Webb recalls Barnstone saying) and to differentiate them from competing camps: not only conservatives, but especially those affiliated with lesser, middlebrow modernities in Houston.[46] Barnstone's practice of architecture constructed a community of modernity by rewarding its constituents with access to his distinctive flair for modern subjectivity.

Barnstone relied on personal charisma to establish his claim to originality. He mobilized bravado and charm to deflect potential challenges and developed a social-cultural network that could be called on to defend his position as architectural arbiter.[47] This imagined liberal community was how Barnstone conceptualized "team," in contrast to Caudill's (and Gropius's) exclusively disciplinary conception. Barnstone's architectural practices were an extension of his personal practices. His agenda was to use architecture to build a community of belonging in which he would feel at home. And as a team builder (though rarely a team player), Barnstone sought talented collaborators who could be persuaded to invest their energy and imagination in constructing, one building at a time, the mythical realm of enlightenment symbolized for him by modern architecture.

NOTES

1. "Auteur" (French for "author") is a term associated with French filmmaking of the 1950s and 1960s, which ascribed artistic authority to a film's director rather than its actors or screenwriter.

2. Alofsin, *Struggle for Modernism*, 136, 222, 240.

3. "Architectural Firm to Center in Houston," *Houston Chronicle* (February 8, 1959), 3; Caudill, *Architecture by Team*; King and Langdon, *CRS Team and the Business of Architecture*. CRS was founded in Bryan, Texas, in 1948; it moved to Houston in 1959.

4. Paolo Tombesi, "Capital Gains and Architectural Losses: The Transformative Journey of Caudill Rowlett Scott (1948–1994)," *Journal of Architecture* 21 (June 2016): 540–563.

5. Nory Miller, "Moving Up to the Big Leagues," *Inland Architect* 21 (July 1977): 12–13.

6. Koush, *Constructing Houston's Future*, 25.

7. Wiegman, *His Story*, 10–12, 23, 26–27.

8. Only a few of these architects have had their careers documented; see Koush, *Hugo V. Neuhaus*; Witte, *Counting* [Anderson Todd]; Stephen James, "Kenneth Bentsen's Pan American University: Regionalist Architecture and Identity in the Borderlands," *ARRIS: Journal of the Southeast Chapter of the Society of Architectural Historians* 28 (2017): 46–67; Stephen James, "Donald Barthelme: Architecture and the Road to La Mancha," *ARRIS* 16 (2005): 56–68; Koush, *Donald Barthelme*; J. Smith, *High Style in the Suburbs* [William R. Jenkins]; Cannady, *Four Houses*; Kacmar, *Victor Lundy*.

9. Eugene Aubry, interviews by Stephen Fox and Michelangelo Sabatino, May 5, 2010, and May 9, 2011, Galveston, Texas.

10. J. M. Syken, "Solar Hemicycle: Frank Lloyd Wright's Herbert Jacobs II Passive Solar House," 2014, PDH Online, accessed August 30, 2018, https://pdhonline.com/courses/c683/c683slideshow.pdf.

11. "Record Houses of 1956: Disciplined Elegance Marks House Design," *Architectural Record* 119 (mid-May 1956): 134–138; see also "Rectangular Houses: 6, Port Arthur, Texas: Dr. and Mrs. Harris Hosen, Owners; Bolton & Barnstone, Architects," *Architectural Record* 122 (November 1957): 162–163; Esther McCoy, "Young Architects in the United States: 1963," *Zodiac* 13:188–189. On the Wiley and Boissonnas Houses, see Payne, *Architecture of Philip Johnson*, 66–67, 72–73.

12. Philip Johnson, "The Seven Crutches of Modern Architecture," *Perspecta* 3 (1955): 41. Johnson identifies the "crutches" as history, pretty drawing, utility, comfort, cheapness, serving the client, and structure.

13. Aubry describes Preston Bolton's role in the firm as that of office manager (Aubry interviews). He remembers that by the time he arrived, in 1959, Barnstone and Bolton were not on good terms. Barnstone objected so strongly to a house that Bolton designed for Carol Sue and Jack Finkelstein in 1961 that he dissolved the

partnership. As part of the dissolution process, Bolton and Barnstone divided the office records. The agreement regarding that division makes it possible to determine which were Barnstone's jobs and which were Bolton's jobs (see the Catalogue Raisonné). Aubry remembers that Adrian Rosenberg designed both partners' buildings, which explains why there is no formal disparity in the firm's work, at least among the projects that were published. Aubry said that during the time he worked for Bolton & Barnstone, he worked only with Barnstone.

14. Aubry interviews.

15. Koush, *Hugo V. Neuhaus*.

16. Colin Rowe, "Neo-'Classicism' and Modern Architecture I," in Rowe, *Mathematics of the Ideal Villa*, 120, 137; see also "Colin Rowe, RIBA, Visiting Critic at University of Houston," *Texas Architect* 7 (May 1957): 14. On the Demoustier House, see "Strong Emphasis on Privacy," *Architectural Record* 123 (April 1958): 199–202.

17. "South Central: Lawrence H. Blum House, Beaumont, Texas, Bolton and Barnstone, Architects," *Architectural Record* 117 (May 1955): 182–183; see also "Small House Designed for the Gulf Coast Region of Texas," *Arts and Architecture* 72 (March 1955): 28–29.

18. "Record Houses of 1957: Design Expressing Dignity," *Architectural Record* 121 (mid-May 1957): 164–167.

19. McCoy, "Young Architects," 187; see also "Steel and Glass House on Buffalo Bayou," *Interiors* 123 (November 1963): 72–79.

20. "New Scale for Living: This House Sets Trends with 2-Story Rooms, 2-Part Plan," *House and Garden*, January 1958, 32–35; see also Henry-Russell Hitchcock, introduction to *Ten Years of Houston Architecture*, "New Talent USA: Architecture," *Art in America* 48, no. 1 (1960): 156–157.

21. Bobbye Tigerman, " 'I Am Not a Decorator': Florence Knoll, the Knoll Planning Unit and the Making of the Modern Office," *Journal of Design History* 20 (Spring 2007): 61-74.

22. Ben Koush, "Organic Gardens: The Houston Landscape Designs of Thomas Church," *Cite* 73 (winter 2008): 32-35.

23. Judy Kugle, "Inside Modern Houston: The Life and Design of Sally Walsh," *Cite* 95 (Fall 2014): 26–31.

24. "Steel and Glass House on Buffalo Bayou."

25. Aubry was not impressed with Barnstone's knowledge of structure, a critique also made by other draftsmen.

26. Aubry interviews.

27. "Architects Design Eight-Sided Home," *Houston Chronicle*, December 6, 1959; see also R. E. Connor, "Wide Interest Shown in Houstonians' Plan," *Houston Chronicle*, February 7, 1960; "Here Are Two New Experiments in Geometric Form," *House and Home* 17 (January 1960): 136–137.

28. McCoy, "Young Architects," 190; see also Mary Rice Brogan, "Home Designing in for Revolution: 'Togetherness' on Wane, New Separate Living Areas Seen,"

Houston Chronicle, January 31, 1960; "'House of Light' Attracts Visitors," *Houston Chronicle*, June 18, 1961.

29. "Village-Like Garden Apartment Addition Coordinates Parking, Outdoor Living, and Privacy on a Limited Half-Round Site," *Architectural Record* 143 (January 1968): 152–153; see also "Thirteen Award-Winning Apartments and Townhouses," *House and Home* 29 (August 1966): 73.

30. McCoy, "Young Architects," 190. John Zemanek, Barnstone's faculty colleague at the University of Houston, was the Houston architect most identified with an affinity for Japanese landscape and architecture; see Carlos Jiménez, "The Light between Gardens," *Harvard Design Magazine*, Summer 1997, 65–67, and Zemanek, *Being . . . Becoming*.

31. "Record Houses of 1965: 'Treetop' Living Pavilion of Steel and Glass," *Architectural Record* 137 (mid-May 1965): 66–69.

32. "The Architect's Own Office: Showplace and Workspace," *Progressive Architecture* 47 (September 1966): 129; see also "Record Houses of 1973: House, Galveston," *Architectural Record* 153 (mid-May 1973): 60–61; "New St. Thomas Dormitory," *Houston Chronicle*, September 2, 1969; "New Angles on the Executive Floor," *Fortune*, June 1966, 169; C. Ray Smith, "Wiggle Walls," *Progressive Architecture* 47 (August 1966): 160–163; "Angling the Rectangle . . . The Park Avenue Offices of Schlumberger, Ltd.," *Interiors* 126 (September 1966): 132–133; C. Smith, *Supermannerism*, 103; "Machine Shop for Art," *Architectural Forum* 131 (July–August 1969): 95.

33. "Houston School," *Architectural Forum* 116 (June 1962): 52; see also "Industrial Buildings: Building Types Study No. 366: Publishing Company Building, Galveston, Texas," *Architectural Record* 141 (January 1967): 158–159; "Advanced Center for the Retarded," *Architectural Forum* 127 (December 1967): 48–53.

34. Aubry interviews; see also Wiegman, *His Story*, 26.

35. "New England Comes to Houston," *Texas Architect* 23 (November–December 1973): 22–24.

36. "Texas Architecture 1974: The Herzog Residence, Houston," *Texas Architect* 24 (November–December 1974): 35; see also Frances Stamper, "Houston: Artistic Renovations," *Texas Homes* 1 (March–April 1978): 40–43.

37. Nory Miller, "Lone Stars—Howard Barnstone and Karl Kamrath," *Inland Architect* 21 (July 1977): 16.

38. Karleen Koen, "Best of '77: Nine Architects and Their Projects Win Residential Honors," *Houston Home and Garden* (February 1978): 54–55, 60–61; see also Gary McKay, "Architectural Honors," *House Home and Garden* 11 (July 1985): 60–61.

39. "Schlumberger-Doll Research Center, Ridgefield, Conn.," *Texas Architect* 31 (March–April 1981): 40.

40. Theodore B. Gupton to Stephen Fox, August 6, 2018.

41. Ken Johnson, "Doug Michels, Radical Artist and Architect, Dies at 59," *New York Times*, June 21, 2003.

42. Jeffrey Karl Ochsner, "Bramlett House," *Texas Architect* 33 (May–June 1983): 46–47; see also Mark Alan Hewitt, "Barnstone's Benchmarks," *Ultra* 4 (February 1985): 56–61.

43. "Schlumberger Austin Systems Center, Austin, Texas, 1987," *A+U* 206 (November 1987): 31–38; see also Joel Warren Barna, "Bridgelike Walking System Links a Set of Five Office Pavilions: Schlumberger Company, Austin, Texas, Systems Center," *Architecture* 77 (January 1988): 87–91; "Austin Systems Center: Research Center for Schlumberger Company, Joint Venture by Howard Barnstone and Robert Jackson," *Baumeister* 85 (April 1988): 50–57; Joel Warren Barna, "High Tech Office Center Fits One of a Kind Site," *Texas Architect* 38 (November–December 1988): 36; Peter Davey, "Texas Nature," *Architectural Review* 981 (September 1989): 67–70; Michael Leccese, "Hill Country Headquarters," *Landscape Architecture* 86 (April 1996): 56–63.

44. Miller, "Lone Stars," 16.

45. For the uncanny parallels in temperament and working habits between Ford and Barnstone, who, architecturally, had an adversarial relationship, see George, *O'Neil Ford*.

46. The term "our crowd" is taken from the title of Stephen Birmingham's book *Our Crowd: The Great Jewish Families of New York*.

47. In *Sacred Modern* (48), Pamela Smart writes about the formation of an imagined community; that term was coined by Benedict Anderson in *Imagined Communities: Reflections on the Origin and Spread of Nationalism* (1983).

CHAPTER TWO

TRANSLATING MIES

Barnstone and Houston Modernism

MICHELANGELO SABATINO

DURING the English architectural critic Reyner Banham's last visit to Houston, to write about the Menil Collection by Renzo Piano (with Richard Fitzgerald, 1987), he observed the interrelationships among three generations of architects—Ludwig Mies van der Rohe, Philip Johnson, and Howard Barnstone—who all left an indelible mark on modern architecture in Houston:

> Locally the echoes are of Mies van der Rohe, which may sound strange, but one should remember that, next to Chicago itself, Houston must be the most Miesian city in North America. Quite apart from Johnson's works for the de Menil/St. Thomas connection, and Mies's own extensions to the Museum of Fine Art, there is also the work of . . . Howard Barnstone himself, Anderson Todd, and a small host of their pupils, partners, and followers. Almost anywhere, it seems, in the rambling, unzoned dystopia that makes Houston an urbanist's nightmare, one may stumble with relief on neat steel-framed structures with "made-at-IIT" written all over them, and as often as not the exposed I beams of their exteriors are painted white against their gray walls.[1]

The German émigré Mies had a considerable impact on Chicago, where he taught at the Illinois Institute of Technology (until 1940, the Armour Institute of Technology) for two decades after arriving in 1938. He designed a significant number of buildings in Chicago and trained students who would go on to successful careers of their own. The same can be said of his impact on booming Houston during the 1950s and 1960s, the decades that marked the height of his

Across the U.S. from New York to Texas, a stern but stunning new architecture has begun to tower on city horizons. Boldly rectangular, with skeletons of steel sheathed in sheets of glass, it is the inspiration and accomplishment of one of the great architects of the 20th Century, Ludwig Mies van der Rohe.

"MASTERPIECES BY MIES," LIFE, MARCH 18, 1957

professional prestige, in part because of the extensive media coverage that he and his work received in both the professional and mainstream press in the United States.[2] Yet Banham's and *Life* magazine's observations need some qualification. Most examples of architecture realized in Houston by Mies and his followers were cultural institutions or houses rather than skyscrapers, the building type with which Mies was most associated in Chicago. While his house for Dr. Edith Farnsworth in Plano, Illinois (1951), was highly influential for generations of architects, only two other house designs of his were built in the United States: the Isabella Gardner and Robert Hall McCormick III House in Elmhurst, Illinois (1952), and the Rose and Morris Greenwald House in Weston, Connecticut (1956).[3] While the Farnsworth and McCormick Houses are now accessible to the public, architects, for several decades had to rely on photographs instead of in situ visits. Only a handful of Houston high-rises, such as the thirty-two-story First City National Bank Building (1961), by the New York office of Skidmore, Owings & Merrill, and the thirty-three-story Tenneco Building (1963), by the San Francisco office of Skidmore, Owings & Merrill, can claim a Miesian genealogy.[4]

Mies's Cullinan Hall (1958) and Brown Pavilion (1974), his two additions to the Museum of Fine Arts, Houston; Philip Johnson's Dominique and John de Menil House (1951) and University of St. Thomas campus (1957–1959); and Bolton & Barnstone's Barbara and Alvin M. Owsley, Jr., House (1960) all represented a radical intervention in the cultural and domestic fabric of Houston, reflecting Miesian tectonics, materiality, and spatial clarity. The aura of cosmopolitan elegance and glamour associated with Miesian architecture that they emitted stood in contrast to the ordinary buildings of developers.[5] This intervention signaled

ABOVE LEFT First City National Bank Building (1961, Skidmore, Owings, & Merrill), 1001 Main, Houston.

ABOVE RIGHT Tenneco Building (1963, Skidmore, Owings & Merrill), 1010 Milam, Houston.

shifts in postwar modern architecture as young, US-trained architects translated the experiments of European modernism to significantly different political and cultural frameworks.

Houston's (and Barnstone's) Miesian episode is paradoxical because it took place within a laissez-faire, market-driven, populist cultural economy not known for its adherence to standards of rigor, austerity, and refinement. Barnstone's contribution to postwar architecture in Houston is best understood by examining the buildings that he and his collaborators produced in response to the genius loci of Houston, a city on the flat Gulf Coast plain of Texas. Defined by heat and humidity, Houston has long been in thrall to automobiles, air-conditioning, and the absence of zoning.[6] Barnstone's design trajectory can be divided into phases: his partnerships with Texas A&M–trained Preston M. Bolton (1952–1961) and with his former University of Houston student Eugene Aubry (1966–1969) stand out distinctly.

The process of translation—whether linguistic or architectural—implies shifting a concept from one language or place to another without substantially changing its meaning, allowing the concept to be understood by those who do not know the language in which it was first articulated. What matters in the relationship

Cullinan Hall, Museum of Fine Arts, Houston (1958, Ludwig Mies van der Rohe and Staub, Rather & Howze), 1001 Bissonnet.

between translation and architecture is the meaning that this process carries for architects. Translation requires creativity, flexibility, and a thorough understanding of both languages. Although some authors believe that translation undermines the authenticity of expression and meaning, others see it as an important challenge for granting the broader public access to unfamiliar ideas and helping it understand them. The translation of Mies's architecture—shifting the tectonic and spatial language that he generated in Chicago and, before that, Berlin—to postwar Houston was not an expression of center-periphery time lag (Barnstone aspired to align his practice with his peers in New York) or a derivative phenomenon typical of teacher-pupil dependency; Barnstone trained at Yale, not IIT.

In architectural practice and discourse, translation also can be understood as the transfer of principles and techniques across successive generations of architects who aspire to interpret creatively a language in climatic, cultural, economic, and social contexts significantly different from those in which it was first articulated. If Miesian architecture can be understood as a language of construction, then the act of translating presents the author (i.e., the architect) who engages with this work with a series of options and tools.[7] Mies explained this concept:

Brown Pavilion, Museum of Fine Arts, Houston (1974, The Office of Ludwig Mies van der Rohe).

"I'm not working on architecture, I'm working on architecture as a language, and I think that you have to have a grammar in order to have a language. You can use it, you know, for normal purposes, and you speak in prose. And if you are good at that, you speak a wonderful prose. And if you are really good, you can be a poet."[8] The translation of architectural language reflected the experiences of European émigré architects in the United States.[9] Geographic, climatic, and social differences played an important role in shaping this process of translation in cities throughout the Americas.

While teaching in Austin and Houston between 1954 and 1957, the English architect, critic, and historian Colin Rowe wrote about the phenomenon of translating Miesian principles, which he describes as a "mutation," in his essay "Neo-'Classicism' and Modern Architecture." Rowe discusses and illustrates Bolton & Barnstone's Demoustier House (1955, demolished 1995) as an example of American Miesian architecture displaying neo-Palladian overtones:

More generally the contemporary neo-"Palladian" building presents itself as a small house equipped with Miesian elevations and details. Conceptually a pavilion and usually a single volume, it aspires to a rigorous symmetry of exterior and (where possible) interior. If not Mies's Resor House, then Philip Johnson's Oneto House at Irvington-on-Hudson may be considered a forerunner of the type, of which John Johansen's house in Fairfield County, Connecticut, and Bolton & Barnstone's Demoustier House in Houston represent more elaborate examples.[10]

Two years after Rowe penned his observations, Henry-Russell Hitchcock wrote the introduction for the catalogue of *Ten Years of Houston Architecture*, an exhibition that Barnstone and Burdette Keeland organized at the Contemporary Arts Museum in March 1959.[11] In his introduction, Hitchcock discusses the impact of Mies and the proliferation of courtyard houses in Houston during the previous ten years, referring to "vocabulary" and thus reinforcing notions of language and translation:

> The plan characteristics of Mies's "court" house projects of before the war, for example, are emulated with notable variety and amplitude in Cowell & Neuhaus' Neuhaus house of 1951; and, with a two-story block not envisaged by Mies, in Bolton & Barnstone's Gordon house of 1953. This permits the luxury of upward as well as two-dimensional extension in the principal living-space. If the "vocabulary," so to put it, of the design of the Neuhaus house is Miesian—or perhaps, even more specifically, Johnsonian—the "zoned" plan goes back to Wright's Johnson house in Racine of 1936 or even to his Coonley house in Riverside, Illinois, of 1908; while the patio is of Californian origin.[12]

Translation requires understanding fundamental concepts before they can be transformed. In Barnstone's sidebar accompanying Esther McCoy's article for the Italian magazine *Zodiac*, he declared: "The average architect is usually not a great designer and, when he has a book to go by, whether it be colonial, Georgian, or Mies, the design had a certain built-in insurance—in that a vocabulary was being copied. Now with no vocabulary the door is wide open."[13]

The architect and critic Peter C. Papademetriou wrote apropos of Houston: "A comparison between some of the more noteworthy architectural landmarks of the last two decades [1960s and 1970s] and certain occasionally unrelated knock-offs in Houston may help us understand the dilemma. Because of their individuality, the 'originals' may be rather easily identified; this very individuality prevents their synthesis into more general categories of form."[14] Among the "knock-offs" Papademetriou cites is the diminutive Bank of Houston (1967) by Wilson, Morris, Crain & Anderson. Its design is based on Mies's New National Gallery in Berlin (1969).[15]

The three architects identified by Banham, Rowe, and Hitchcock as shaping Houston modernism were separated by generational intervals of twenty years: Mies van der Rohe, Philip Johnson, and Howard Barnstone. When called upon to work in Houston, Mies understood that each project presented distinct conditions. Cullinan Hall and the Brown Pavilion (the latter completed four years after Mies's death) are the only constructed projects in Mies's body of built work designed to extend an existing building and geometrically accommodate a nonorthogonally defined site.[16] Some continuities existed: during the mid-1950s, Bolton & Barnstone, following the Farnsworth House precedent, painted the steel frames of the Gordon and Demoustier Houses white. Mies used a luminous white paint for Cullinan Hall to reflect the Houston light. Decades later, Renzo Piano did the same thing with the exterior structural elements of the Menil Collection. Remarkably, for the Owsley house Barnstone chose to paint the steel elements a spring foliage color, a greenish yellow.

Johnson's single-story Menil House is a translation of Miesian principles to accommodate a house for a family with five children on a flat site in a neighborhood where deed restrictions required that the house be faced with brick. The interior courtyard, replete with tropical plants, bears witness to Dominique de Menil's nostalgia for the time she spent in Caracas, Venezuela, in the 1940s. Johnson's spatial format conforms to Miesian practices and produces a condition justifying an exterior brick wall plane while also incorporating floor-to-ceiling glass walls.[17] Johnson's designs for single-family Miesian houses completed in 1951—besides the Menil House, the Geraldine and Richard Hodgson House (New Canaan, Connecticut) and the George J. Oneto House (Irvington, New York)—demonstrate how the translation of domestic programs, site conditions, and budget considerations can produce glass houses that are distinctly different.[18]

BRINGING MIES'S VISION TO HOUSTON

A significant example of the translation of Miesian practices to Houston is Philip Johnson's master plan for the University of St. Thomas (1956–1957) and the first three campus buildings (1957–1959), to which Bolton & Barnstone contributed as associate architects. Johnson organized two-story buildings designed according to Mies's material, constructional, and spatial practices at IIT. Rather than siting

Bank of Houston (1967, Wilson, Morris, Crain & Anderson), 5115 Main Street, Houston.

them as freestanding pavilions in a verdant planar landscape, Johnson connected them with two-story canopied steel walkways that frame garden courts and, as the system was expanded in the 1980s, the university's central lawn.[19] Johnson understood that Houston's coastal climate offered opportunities for year-round use that Chicago's cold and lengthy winters did not. At the University of St. Thomas, Johnson translated Miesian construction practices not only to shape shade- and breeze-enhancing walkways but also to spatially evoke associations with monastic cloisters and the columned walkways of Thomas Jefferson's Academical Village at the University of Virginia, historical resonances that were meaningful to Johnson in ways they were not to Mies. Over time, Johnson's attitude toward translation—the selective adaptation and transformation of Mies's constructional practices and space-shaping operations—changed as he continued to emphasize associational references and de-emphasize tectonic clarity.[20]

Emblematic of Barnstone's translation of Miesian architecture is the Owsley House, designed during the Bolton & Barnstone partnership for a lawyer and his family. It reproduces the steel frame and glass walls of Johnson's Glass House

(1949), but in a three-story spatial configuration. Built on the bank of Buffalo Bayou, the house's site possesses more topographic variation than is customary in flat Houston. In place of the free plan of the Glass House, Barnstone substituted a compartmentalized spatial organization, adapting the Glass House format to the requirements of a family with three children.[21] The only free-planned space in the Owsley House is the double-volume living room. Barnstone further translated Johnson's Miesian practices by adapting the outdoor walkways of the University of St. Thomas to completely surround the perimeter of the Owsley House, which Barnstone likened to the decks of a nineteenth-century Mississippi River steamboat. Asked to summarize the challenges of the commission, Barnstone stated, "The problem was to search for a form which would make the glass box an easily adaptable solution to the near-tropical sun exposure, waterproofing of doors and openings (an extremely difficult problem even in our age of superb synthetic waterproofing mixtures) and the problems of night lighting and breaking through the 'glass barrier.'"[22]

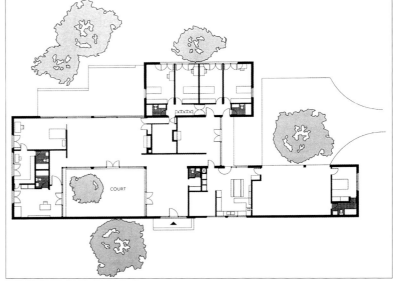

TOP Dominique and John de Menil House (1951, Philip C. Johnson Associates with Cowell & Neuhaus), 3363 San Felipe, Houston. This photograph was taken before Howard Barnstone added a canopy in 1961 over the interior courtyard.

BOTTOM Menil House, plan (1951, Philip C. Johnson Associates with Cowell & Neuhaus).

The Houston architect Hugo V. Neuhaus, Jr., Johnson's supervising architect for the Menil House and his Harvard classmate, was also committed to translating Miesian architecture to Houston during the 1950s and 1960s.[23] Neuhaus and his associate David Haid (an IIT College of Architecture graduate and former employee of Mies's) translated the Farnsworth House to Friendswood, Texas, in the rustic Letzerich Ranch House (1962–1963; demolished).[24] Neuhaus and Haid's translation consisted of an elevated platform replete with outdoor decks, but replaced the free interior plan with articulated rooms. The house was built with post-and-beam wood construction rather than steel framing. A generous overhang on all sides provided shading

Welder Hall, University of St. Thomas (1957–1959, Philip Johnson with Bolton & Barnstone), 3812 Yoakum, Houston.

Barbara and Alvin M. Owsley, Jr., House (1960, Bolton & Barnstone), 65 Briar Hollow, Houston.

from the unrelenting Texas sun. Whereas Johnson's Glass House and the Farnsworth House were weekend retreats, each designed for a single person, the Houston translations were almost always designed as permanent residences for families, who required degrees of privacy.

Barnstone's students at the University of Houston (Burdette Keeland, William R. Jenkins, Kenneth E. Bentsen, and Harwood Taylor) and other Houston architects trained at elite US universities, such as Anderson Todd, translated Miesian modernism to Houston by way of the courtyard house.[25] Examples were the Nina Cullinan House (1953) by Cowell & Neuhaus[26] and the Todd House (1961) by Anderson Todd on Shadowlawn Circle.[27] Johnson mischievously described the Todd House as "more Mies than Mies" because of its rigorous conception

Louis Letzerich Ranch House (1963, Cowell & Neuhaus, David Haid, Associate, demolished), 302 East Viejo, Friendswood.

and execution and its material and spatial amplitude and precision.[28] A period photograph of an elegantly dressed woman posing in front of the entrance of the Cullinan House speaks volumes about the association of Houston's elite with Miesian modernism. A period photograph of Howard and Gertrude Barnstone in the living room of the Lois Lasater and John F. Maher House (1964; extensively remodeled) also conveys an aura of cosmopolitan elegance.

In addition to translating Mies's vocabulary, a number of architects in Houston translated Le Corbusier, whom they merged with Mies, so to speak. The one-story suburban office building, raised above grade on *pilotis* to make room for automobile parking on the ground level, emerged as a distinctive Houston building type during the 1950s. The Fred Winchell Photography Studio and Apartment (1954), designed by Burdette Keeland and Harwood Taylor, was the prototype. It was followed by a series of office buildings on Richmond Avenue that Harwood Taylor and his partner, J. Victor Neuhaus III, designed for the developer Gerald D. Hines in the early 1960s.[29]

Miesian rationalism brought some semblance of order and human scale to Houston's sprawling, formless cityscape. This was also true in Los Angeles, where a group of architects working in light-steel construction—Charles and Ray Eames, Craig Ellwood, Pierre Koenig, and Raphael Soriano (none of whom trained with Mies)—participated in the Case Study program, which was initiated by John Entenza, an admirer of Mies. The Arlene and Gerald Rosen House (1962), designed by Texas-born Craig Ellwood in Brentwood, California, extends and privatizes the traditional multiunit courtyard house of Mediterranean origin, much as Johnson did at the Menil House.[30] The individually distinctive houses of this group of architects displayed attitudes about translation that differentiated them from those of the Houston school.[31] For instance, when compared with Mies's use of steel and glass, Ray and Charles Eames's Case Study House No. 8 (1949) in Pacific Palisades exhibits a playful ad hoc attitude toward the use of industrially produced construction materials, in contrast to the laconic solemnity of even Mies's smallest US buildings.

Barnstone, like Johnson, understood that translating modernism required nondogmatic interpretation. Whereas Anderson Todd and Hugo Neuhaus were more rigorous in articulating the constructional language of Mies, Barnstone was interested in translating its cosmopolitan associations, which pertained more to Johnson's interpretation than to Mies's work itself.[32] This affinity speaks to the freedom for which Barnstone yearned. When faced with choosing between Louis I. Kahn or Edward Durell Stone as his thesis adviser at Yale, Barnstone chose the charming, debonair Stone, architect of the Museum of Modern Art, who allowed students to forge paths of their own, rather than Kahn, the intense, obscure, mystical Jewish immigrant.[33]

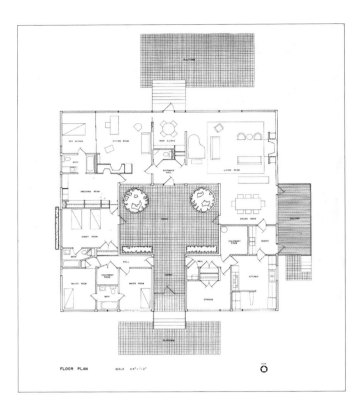

Nina Cullinan House, plan.

Paul Rudolph, who trained under Walter Gropius at Harvard, offers a parallel example to Barnstone's approach to translation.[34] A southerner, Rudolph spent the early years of his career in subtropical Sarasota on Florida's Gulf Coast before moving to New York City, where he translated the post-and-beam tectonics characteristic of the Sarasota school into reinforced concrete.[35] The translation of the thin post-and-beam construction of his Walt Walker Guest House (1953) on Sanibel Island to the massive reinforced-concrete pier-and-beam construction of the University of Massachusetts Dartmouth Campus (1963) indicates Rudolph's trajectory. His transition from small-scale domestic buildings to large-scale institutional ones was registered in the structural, scale-related, and programmatic changes of his architecture.

Although Barnstone's years at Yale as an architecture student occurred a decade before Rudolph joined the faculty there, Barnstone's design process and work were attuned to the polemic that Rudolph expressed in his seminal essay "Regionalism in Architecture," published in *Perspecta: The Yale Architectural Journal* in 1957: "The great architectural movements of the past have been precisely formulated in a given area, then adapted and spread to other regions suiting

OPPOSITE Nina Cullinan House (1953, Cowell & Neuhaus), entrance, with her nephew's wife, Alison Prescott (Mrs. Craig F., Jr.) Cullinan, Houston.

themselves more or less to the particular way of life of the new area. If adaptations, enlargement, and enrichment of basic principles of twentieth-century architecture were carried out, always relating it to the mainstream of architecture and the particular region, the world would again be able to create magnificent cities. Unfortunately, this has not yet come to pass. We continue to ignore the particular."[36]

For Barnstone, Rudolph's "adaptation, enlargement, and enrichment" defined this process as translation instead of copying. Barnstone's approach to design can be read as reflecting a deeper existential condition formed by his social identity as an outsider, as a Jew, and as a man who struggled to define his sexual orientation. Barnstone was a restless, experimental modernist who developed architecture in response to the tangible and intangible spaces of his adopted city. He translated Miesian architectural ideas to Houston's brand of mid-twentieth-century American liberalism, the local subculture in which he found his friends, associates, and clients. Perhaps because of his acute awareness of his outsider/outlier status, Barnstone excelled as an architect of domesticity, displaying a rare ability to relate to and interpret the psychological and spatial desires of his clients.[37]

Barnstone came of age architecturally just as Mies began to exert enormous influence on the American architectural profession, which was first evident in the Museum of Modern Art's retrospective exhibition *The Architecture of Mies van der Rohe* (1947), designed and installed by Mies with an accompanying catalogue by Philip Johnson.[38] Firsthand access to Mies's buildings became increasingly easy for American architects because of the number of his buildings constructed during the postwar years; in addition, they received extensive exposure in print media. Although Barnstone embraced the rigor of Miesian details, he embraced a critique of functionalism, too, by way of spatial complexity. In this he was like Frederick Kiesler, an architect whom he met through Johnson and came to admire.[39] Kiesler criticized "pseudo-functionalism" in an essay published in 1949 and celebrated "magic architecture" in a manifesto published in 1947: "Magic Architecture is the expression of the creativeness of man. It is an architecture of contact, not of separation (resignation). . . . Magic Architecture is not dream architecture, like that of temples or castles; it is the architecture of every-day, every-night reality."[40] In speaking about Kiesler to Esther McCoy, Barnstone touched indirectly on the role of translation: "New thought always seems to come from young revolutionaries who are followed by a generation of Madison Avenuers who make cash out of the thoughts and hopes of the innovators. . . . Our present giants are marketing contributions made by Mies, Neutra, and Kiesler when they were young."[41]

ABOVE Lucie and Anderson Todd House (1961, Anderson Todd), 9 Shadowlawn Circle, Houston.

RIGHT Howard and Gertrude Barnstone in the living room of the Maher House, June 25, 1965.

REGIONAL BUT NOT REGIONALIST

Barnstone's admiration for Miesian precision coexisted with his Kiesler-like fascination with the "magical" (even melancholic) qualities he observed in the atmosphere of Galveston. A once-great city fifty miles from Houston, full of effusive Victorian architecture, Galveston failed to rebound after the hurricane of 1900. Barnstone's admiration should come as no surprise. Nearly two decades after arriving in Houston, Barnstone maintained the ability to see his adoptive city (and surrounding cities of the Gulf Coast) with the eyes of both an insider and an outsider. In the foreword to Barnstone's book *The Galveston That Was* (1966), James Johnson Sweeney, director of the Museum of Fine Arts, Houston, highlights the dialectical possibilities of regionalism and cosmopolitanism: "Regionalism can no longer be expected to dominate any expression of contemporary art. But where it survives, dominated by the broader international discipline, it can give vitality to our art, as individualism can to our lives."[42] Perhaps Barnstone understood that Galveston's vitality relied on a balance between its "international" buildings by Galveston's Victorian architect N. J. Clayton and his contemporaries in its "regional" (i.e., local) alleys and back buildings.[43]

With the publication of *The Galveston That Was* (1966) and *The Architecture of John F. Staub: Houston and the South* (1979), for which the Yale historian and critic Vincent Scully (1920–2017) wrote the preface, Barnstone stimulated the historic preservation movement in Texas. John Staub, who began his practice in 1923, was the first Houston architect to move beyond the simple accommodation of climate to creatively translate the historical models he typically employed, by registering the effects of climate on the shaping of habitable dwelling space in Houston.[44] Barnstone's emphasis on Staub's relationship to the South is also worth noting, especially as it applied to professional and cultural frameworks. Lewis Mumford addressed the topic in his book *The South in Architecture* (1941). Mumford identifies adaptation to climate as key: "Take for example a capital matter: adaptation to our trying American climate, with the extremes of temperature that prevail in the North and the sub-tropical conditions that exist in large portions of the South. . . . The forms of building that prevail in any region reflect the degree of social discovery and self-awareness that prevails there."[45]

Several years after writing this, Mumford defended modern regionalism against Philip Johnson, among others, in a heated debate at the Museum of Modern Art.[46] A survey of modern architecture, Elizabeth and Edward Waugh's *The South Builds: New Architecture in the Old South* (1960), included Rudolph's seminal Riverview High School in Sarasota, Florida. Taking a cue from Mumford,

Mies van der Rohe exhibition catalogue, cover (Museum of Modern Art, 1947).

Charles W. Moore subsequently defined "southernness" as "a kind of scaled-down urbanity that seems to me, a Northerner, the most powerful Southern image."[47] Southernness, regionalism, and magic were architectural categories unrelated to Mies's discourse on how to architecturally construct modernity. Barnstone, the rebel and nonconformist, persistently carried these phenomena across the bounds of discursive insularity in order to expand that discourse.

Barnstone's translations of Mies for Houston clients were based on a strategy of design that rejected the complacency of parochial regionalism. Barnstone was interested in language, not dialects. He consistently avoided materials that in Houston connoted regionalism, such as fossilized Texas limestone used by his peers. Instead, he selectively and critically assimilated Houston's location through an idiosyncratic reinvention of place and materiality. If the situation required it, he was as adept at building in steel and glass as in deploying wood cladding. Such translational flexibility reduced the estrangement from place that can result from strictly formalist approaches. Because Houstonians tend not to think of themselves in relation to their city's past, even the most talented architects learn to conceive of their contributions to the city fabric as "islands" in a dynamic and restless sea. Houston's relatively low density means that even today it possesses plenty of vacant real estate. Houston is a moving target of a city. Barnstone was defiantly proud of preferring deed restrictions (i.e., contractual agreements regulating land use within subdivisions) to a comprehensive zoning ordinance, as if to cast off any sense of temporal or spatial limitations by which to measure himself.[48]

Barnstone's preference for difference over consensus (i.e., parochial regionalism) was perhaps reinforced by the fact that the houses he designed were most often built in established neighborhoods rather than new, edge-of-town subdivisions. Thus, he was never a mass-housing producer, but rather an expert in designing one-off dwellings for the well-to-do liberal clientele in Houston with which he identified. Barnstone passionately embraced Houston with the curiosity of an outsider seeking to make sense of a new physical and social environment.[49]

Ludwig Mies van der Rohe with Philip Johnson (Museum of Modern Art, 1947).

Reliance on the automobile and the hubris of bigness had become synonymous with Houston before the 1960s, when the Astrodome (1965) was hailed as the eighth wonder of the world and Space City came of age with the opening of NASA's Manned Spacecraft Center (now the Lyndon B. Johnson Space Center) in nearby Clear Lake City (1964). Barnstone countered architecturally with precision, refinement, discretion, and intimacy. His Houston was focused on luminous, expansive interiors; transparency that highlighted broadleaf and evergreen woodland vegetation; and proportioned but undemonstrative exteriors.

For Barnstone, the material economy, tectonic rectitude, and spatial transcendence of Miesian architecture embodied a modern world of imagined cosmopolitan community that, throughout his life, he longed to be part of. Miesian architecture materialized a modern subjectivity that was so compelling that alternative modern subjectivities, and their corresponding architectures, seemed deficient by comparison. Barnstone felt the egalitarian styles identified with Usonian modernism and Texas regionalism were insufficiently cosmopolitan. As he put it in 1963: "The regionalism or vernacular buildings in Texas were all designed to catch the breeze in the summer with wide open porches and for small, easy-to-heat interiors during the short winter months. Today with the climate-controlled interiors and our continued desire to wear suit jackets no matter what the weather, none of this makes sense. I find nothing immoral in a complete change of architecture once you control the interior temperature efficiently."[50] Even more unappealing to Barnstone was the subjectivity identified by the flamboyant contemporary houses of Riverside Terrace, Houston's upper-income Jewish neighborhood, in the 1950s. In this dialectical confrontation of contending modern prejudices, it was the architecture of Mies and Johnson that embodied the restraint, clarity, generosity, and order that Barnstone identified with elite, liberal, cosmopolitan subjectivity.[51]

Barnstone's interiorized, sometimes aloof architecture reimagined Houston with poetically complex spaces that enhanced the "magic" of southern dwellings, characterized by a balance of formal and informal qualities in planning, siting, and materiality, and offsetting the ugly beauty of Houston, where the dialectical tension between "spontaneous" (i.e., popular) and pedigreed architecture occasionally made for exciting contradictions but more often reinforced the acute disparities visible in Houston's urban landscape.[52] Barnstone's architecture, like that of Staub, stressed interiority and containment.[53] These attributes were also characteristic of such Houston enclaves of planned pastoral order as Rice University and the neighborhoods of Shadyside and River Oaks.[54] Today these places are experienced as "islands." But they were constructed with the expectation that they would serve as models for Houston's subsequent development into a modern garden city. The social and economic realities of Houston as it actually developed affected attitudes toward architecture in a city where individual achievements trump collective action and where even the most significant architectural contributions, such as the Menil Collection, can be viewed as "domestic" sites more closely identified with their patrons than with the institutions for which they were built.

GOOD-BYE TO MIES

In contrast to the translation of Miesian architecture typical of Bolton & Barnstone's houses, the domestic architecture that Howard Barnstone & Partners produced in the first half of the 1960s abandoned Miesian identity while adhering to post-and-beam construction practices. The Lois Lasater and John F. Maher House (1964) is a linchpin between the Bolton decade and the Aubry decadedf. It combines assertive steel-framed construction with thick brick *pilotis* and translates the distinctive curved contours of Philip Johnson's East Wing addition to the Museum of Modern Art (1964) to a Houston domestic setting.[55] Barnstone, as Le

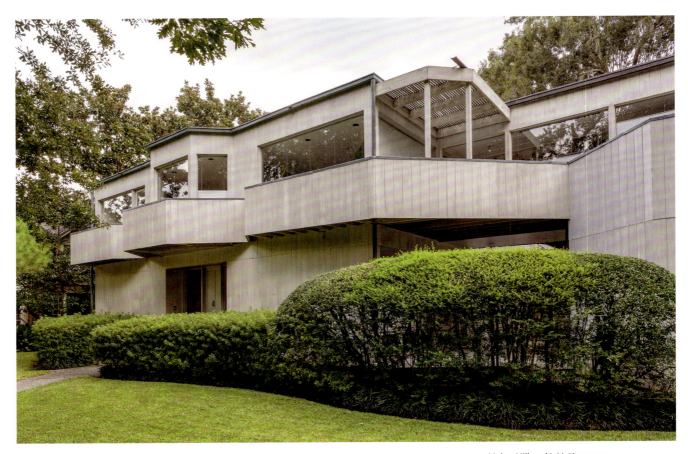

Helen Hill and I. H. Kempner III House (1969, Barnstone & Aubry), 3811 Del Monte Drive, Houston.

Corbusier had done, irreverently raised the Maher House to allow cars to park in its underbelly.

    Barnstone & Aubry's house for Helen Hill and I. H. Kempner III (1969) translated the confrontational assertiveness of the New Brutalism to a two-story house, framed and sheathed in wood, constructed in a section of River Oaks developed in the 1940s with modestly scaled, architecturally conventional two-story houses. Barnstone & Aubry translated their defiance of convention not as architectural aggrandizement but as self-effacement. Those entering the Kempner House are rewarded with a sequence of magical interior spaces culminating in a glass-walled living and dining room facing the backyard. To compensate for the fact that the house takes up so much of the backyard, Barnstone densely planted the remaining open space with a grove of trees. This grove gives the illusion of being a forest, which prevents the Kempner House from intruding on its neighbors. Barnstone's gift for conjuring intimacy is evident in the master bathroom. He positioned the vanity as a floating horizontal plane in front of a projecting bay window. A

Kempner House, rear.

floating circular mirror above the vanity screens the bay window from view while enabling it to backlight the composition of floating planes, horizontal and vertical, solid and reflective. A concealed slot skylight brings natural light down in front of the vanity, creating the ethereal sensation of spatiality that Barnstone called the "divine float."

Barnstone's partnership with Aubry also included nonresidential work. For many of their institutional buildings, the new material of choice was reinforced concrete. Unlike Harwood Taylor, whose move from domestic to civic architecture led him to use reinforced concrete in a variety of applications (as in the monumental Houston Independent School District Headquarters Building [1969, Neuhaus & Taylor; demolished]), Barnstone & Aubry embraced post-and-beam tectonics translated into concrete.[56] Barnstone & Partners designed its only public school building, Piney Point Elementary School (1962), for the Houston Independent School District in a rural African American community subsequently engulfed by Houston's suburban sprawl.[57] Photographs emphasize the building's isolation and austerity and juxtapose the scale of its interlocked precast components and exposed conduits, grilles, and concrete block partitions with that of its diminutive students. Barnstone's translation of the New Brutalism seemed to register a shift in liberal consciousness, away from the images of glamour and style associated with Johnson's interpretation of Mies and toward engagement with such social issues as the struggle for racial justice.

Barnstone & Aubry pursued this essentialist tectonic approach in the Galveston County Publishing Company Building in Galveston (1965) and in their largest commission in Houston, the six-building Harris County Center for the Retarded (1966).[58] The precast concrete piers and beams of the Galveston County Publishing Building confer a modest monumentality on this utilitarian building. Like Rudolph's Forestry Building at Yale University (1959), which the Galveston building seems to translate, it rejects refinement in favor of rugged materiality. Rudolph had questioned the myth of Miesian purity: "You can talk about the purity of Mies's structure till the cows come home. It's not pure. It rises far above that. Well, in my own way, I try to do the same thing."[59] The sculptural drama of the Center for the Retarded's cast-in-place concrete roof slabs and columns, the buildings' subtle spatial adjustments to the sloping five-acre site, the unobtrusive warmth of the buildings' rose-colored St. Joe brick facing, and the center's generously proportioned, simply finished interiors make this complex, built under rigid cost constraints, seem remarkable today. Rather than minimize the complex architecturally, Barnstone & Aubry's design monumentalized the center as an imagined liberal community encompassing its clients, professional staff, and elite donors and trustees, a design decision to which Louis Kahn took such emphatic exception that, after visiting the center, he sought out Barnstone to deliver a critique.

In his sidebar to McCoy's *Zodiac* article, Barnstone wrote: "Architecture has a new freedom. The restraints of the Academy—Mies and FLW—are now dead. With this new freedom comes the possibility of an entirely new expression in our time, the era of the car."[60] Indeed, modern architecture in the United States in the 1960s increasingly asserted monumentality through aggressive size, scale, and profiling—exemplified by Skidmore, Owings & Merrill's Lyndon B. Johnson Presidential Library in Austin (1970), which, against the backdrop of political disillusion and civil disturbance, came to seem hollow and oppressive.[61] Barnstone & Aubry's buildings of the late 1960s, especially their nonresidential buildings, experimented with architectural assertiveness while also exploring alternatives. Yet as the political contradictions of modern American liberalism became less and less susceptible to harmonious resolution, Barnstone & Aubry found their practice repositioned by external events. The identity and subject positions that their buildings represented were not compatible with the radical communitarian rejection of standards, form, and taste that erupted in the late 1960s. When

OPPOSITE, TOP Piney Point Elementary School (1962, Howard Barnstone & Partners, demolished).

OPPOSITE, BOTTOM Galveston County Publishing Company Building (1965, Barnstone & Aubry), Galveston, Texas.

OPPOSITE Harris County Center for the Retarded (1966, Barnstone & Aubry, demolished 2019), 3550 W. Dallas Avenue, Houston.

compared with the radicalism of Southcoast Team Number 1, a design collective of young instructors and students at the University of Houston's College of Architecture; Ant Farm, also active in Houston and the University of Houston; and SITE, the New York–based multidisciplinary collaborative that designed the Best Products *Indeterminate Façade* store in Houston (1975), Barnstone & Aubry's buildings were unthreatening and nonsubversive, firmly identified with establishment institutions and practices.[62]

In 1968–1969, when Barnstone fell victim to his inner contradictions and suffered a prolonged depression, his marriage and his partnership with Aubry fell apart. Barnstone resumed practice in 1970 with a succession of new collaborators, many of them talented graduates of the University of Houston. Some buildings, such as the three Graustark Family Townhouses (1974), which he designed and developed as infill in a 1920s Houston neighborhood, retained the introverted strategy of the 1960s that abandoned the transparency of Mies. Spatially inventive inside, the townhouses are self-effacing externally.[63] Barnstone's ability to imaginatively sidestep the complacency of the corporate modernism that came to define much of American architecture in the 1950s and 1960s charted an alternative track for repairing the damaged liberal consensus.

With the exception of the Rothko Chapel, a design by Philip Johnson that Barnstone & Aubry modified to satisfy Mark Rothko (1971), Barnstone's work never entered the canon of iconic Houston modern buildings. Yet as a professor at the University of Houston's College of Architecture, an author of important books of architectural history, and the principal of a small, experimental firm, Barnstone was an influential participant in Houston's contribution to post–Second World War architecture in the United States and beyond.

A rebel and a nonconformist, an intellectual and a pragmatist, Howard Barnstone translated Miesian architectural ideas to brand Houston's mid-twentieth-century American liberalism, the local subculture in which he found his friends, associates, and clients, as refined and aristocratic. In contrast to the stereotype of a politically conservative Texas broadcast by the national media, Houston was home to a small yet lively community of cosmopolitan and liberal patrons of modern art and architecture. Barnstone's architecture reveals an alternative interpretation of Houston from the 1950s to the 1980s as both gentler and more magical, an interpretation to which Barnstone substantially contributed.

NOTES

1. Reyner Banham, "In the Neighborhood of Art," *Art in America* 75 (June 1987): 124–129; reprinted in Banham, *A Critic Writes*, 270–275.

2. Stephen Fox, "Framing the New: Mies van der Rohe and Houston Architecture," in Scardino, Stern, and Webb, *Ephemeral City*, 252–265.

3. Susan Benjamin and Michelangelo Sabatino, *Modern in the Middle: Chicago Houses, 1929–1975* (New York: Monacelli, 2020).

4. Kevin Alter, "SOM in Houston," *Cite 40* (Winter 1997–1998): 34–37. Some of these tall buildings, especially those by Skidmore, Owings & Merrill, introduced climate-specific solutions to reduce heat and glare; see Michelangelo Sabatino, "Heat and Light Thematised in the Modern Architecture of Houston," *Journal of Architecture* 16 (Fall 2011): 703–26; N. Adams, *Skidmore, Owings & Merrill*.

5. Friedman, *American Glamour*.

6. Lerup, *One Million Acres*; see also Kamps and Goldsmith, *No Zoning*.

7. A number of English and American critics have developed the idea of architecture as language, with repercussions for post–Second World War architecture; see Summerson, *Classical Language of Architecture*, and Jencks, *Language of Post-Modern Architecture*.

8. Quoted in Phyllis Lambert, "Mies Immersion," in Lambert, *Mies in America*, 192–330; Neumeyer, *Artless Word*, 327.

9. Jordy, *American Buildings and Their Architects*.

10. Colin Rowe, "Neo-'Classicism' and Modern Architecture I," in Rowe, *Mathematics of the Ideal Villa*, 119–138. This essay was written in 1956–1957 but first published in the journal *Oppositions* in 1973. Rowe wrote: "In the United States, regionalism, by attempting to set up the spirit of the province as a check to the spirit of the age, provided one characteristically American solution. But this form of architectural states' rights could scarcely exist without the complement of a central authority; and, as a version of this central authority, the present neo-'Classical' [i.e., Miesian] mutations must appear to any dispassionate observer to be no less typically American" (132). The Demoustier House was first published in the article "House in the Southwest: Gulf Coast Region of Texas," *Arts & Architecture* 74 (December 1957): 22–23; and in "Strong Emphasis on Privacy," *Architectural Record* 4 (April 1958): 199–256.

11. Brutvan, *In Our Time*. The Contemporary Arts Museum was established in 1948. In 1972, the Gunnar Birkerts–designed building was inaugurated as its new permanent home.

12. *Ten Years of Houston Architecture*.

13. Esther McCoy, "Young Architects in the United States: 1963," *Zodiac* 13:186.

14. Peter C. Papademetriou, "Aspects of a New Urban Vernacular," *Harvard Architecture Review* 1 (Spring 1980): 122–135.

15. In parallel with his own design work, S. I. Morris served as the architect of record for SOM's First City National Bank Building, One Shell Plaza, and Two

Shell Plaza, as well as Johnson/Burgee's Pennzoil Place; see Barry Moore, "Building a Houston Practice: The Career of S. I. Morris," *Cite* 43 (Winter 1999): 30–34.

16. C. Adams, *Museum of Fine Arts, Houston*; see also Lange, *Ludwig Mies van der Rohe*. For the silk industry in Krefeld, Germany, Mies designed a wedge-shaped building for an irregular site in 1937.

17. Bruce C. Webb, "Living Modern in Mid-Century Houston," *Journal of Architectural Education* 62, no. 1 (September 2008): 11–19; see also Stephen Fox, "Dominique and John de Menil as Patrons of Architecture, 1932–97," in Helfenstein and Schipsi, *Art and Activism*, 199–234.

18. Hitchcock, *Philip Johnson Architecture*; Philip Johnson, "House at New Canaan, Connecticut," *Architectural Review* 108 (September 1950): 152–159; Whitney and Kipnis, *Johnson: The Glass House*.

19. "The University of St. Thomas," *Architectural Record* 122, no. 2 (August 1957): 138, 142–143; see also "First Units in the Fabric of a Closed Campus," *Architectural Record* 126 (September 1959): 180–182; Welch, *Philip Johnson and Texas*, 61–65; Michelangelo Sabatino, "Cracking the Egg: The Transformation of the University of St. Thomas Campus," *Cite 73* (Winter 2008): 10–17.

20. Welch, *Philip Johnson and Texas*; see also Petit, *Philip Johnson*; Bjone, *Johnson and His Mischief*.

21. "Steel and Glass House on Buffalo Bayou," *Interiors* 123 (November 1963): 72–79; see also McCoy, "Young Architects," 164–167, 186–190.

22. McCoy, "Young Architects," 186.

23. Anderson Todd, "Hugo V. Neuhaus, Jr., 1915–1987," *Cite 19* (Winter 1987): 19–20; see also Koush, *Booming Houston*; Koush, *Hugo V. Neuhaus*.

24. "Hugo V. Neuhaus, Jr., Architect," *Arts and Architecture* 82 (October 1965): 12–13.

25. Stephen Fox, "Honor," in Witte, *Counting*, 53. Todd met Mies van der Rohe (and David Haid) during the design and construction of Cullinan Hall (1954–1958).

26. Todd, "Hugo V. Neuhaus, Jr., 1915–1987," 19–20.

27. Todd followed his first courtyard house with another one on Bolsover Road in 1995; see Frank Welch, "At Home with Anderson Todd," *Cite* 34 (Spring 1996): 48–49.

28. Welch, *Philip Johnson and Texas*, 61.

29. Barry Moore and Anna Mod, "The Richmond Corridor: Where Developer Gerald Hines Went to Graduate School," *Cite 57* (Spring 2003): 14–15; see also Seal et al., *Hines*.

30. N. Jackson, *California Modern*; see also Polyzoides, Sherwood, and Tice, *Courtyard Housing in Los Angeles*.

31. McCoy, *Modern California Houses*; E. Smith, *Blueprints for Modern Living*.

32. Michelangelo Sabatino and Stephen Fox, "Howard Barnstone: Mid-Twentieth-Century Architecture in Houston and the Crises of American Liberalism," *ARRIS: Journal of the Southeast Chapter of the Society of Architectural Historians* 25 (Spring 2015): 48–63.

33. Hunting, *Edward Durell Stone*.

34. On the role that both Mies and, later, Rudolph played in Barnstone's architecture, see Stephen Fox, "Howard Barnstone (1923–1987)," *Cite 18* (Fall 1987): 18–24. The Bass House (1971) in Fort Worth, Texas, is Rudolph's most explicit homage to Mies.

35. Howey, *Sarasota School of Architecture*.

36. Paul Rudolph, "Regionalism in Architecture," *Perspecta 4* (1957): 12–19, reprinted in Rudolph, *Writings on Architecture*, 30–38.

37. Reed, *Not at Home*.

38. Johnson, *Mies van der Rohe*. A copy of this book was in the Bolton & Barnstone office library. Thanks to George Barnstone for allowing me to view the books he inherited from his father's library.

39. Kiesler was a visiting lecturer at the University of Houston in March 1960. For the audio recording of his (undated) lecture, see Burdette Keeland Architectural Papers (Series 5 Audio recordings, 1953–1968), University of Houston Libraries, Special Collections.

40. Frederick J. Kiesler, "Magic Architecture" (1947), in Kiesler, *Selected Writings*, 34; Kiesler, "Pseudo-Functionalism in Modern Architecture," *Partisan Review* (July 1949): 733–742, reprinted in Sonzogni and Krjci, *Friedrich Kiesler*, 29–49. In a dedication dated March 29, 1967, in a copy of Kiesler's *Inside the Endless House*, Lilian Kiesler wrote: "Homage to the Barnstones. They CAN and DO make everyday life an exciting event! Love Lilian Kielser."

41. McCoy, "Young Architects," 164.

42. James Johnson Sweeney, foreword to H. Barnstone, *Galveston That Was*; Brennan, *Curating Consciousness*.

43. Scardino and Turner, *Clayton's Galveston*; see also Beasley, *Alleys and Back Buildings*.

44. H. Barnstone, *Architecture of John F. Staub*, 52–53.

45. Mumford, *South in Architecture*, 3–44.

46. For a broad overview of the debates surrounding regionalism, see Canizaro, *Architecture Regionalism*.

47. Charles W. Moore, "Southerness: A Regional Dimension," *Perspecta* 15 (1975): 9–17, reprinted in Stern, Deamer, and Plattus, *Re-reading Perspecta*, 328–334.

48. The adjective "ephemeral" was used to describe Houston in Scardino, Stern, and Webb, *Ephemeral City*.

49. Stephen Fox, "The Stars Are Big and Bright—Deep in the Heart of Texas," *Cite 78* (May 2009): 48.

50. McCoy, "Young Architects," 167.

51. W. Barnstone, *We Jews and Blacks*. Howard Barnstone's rejection of Riverside Terrace's contemporary ranch-house architecture cohered with his effort to forge a liberal, modern position that embodied the patrician restraint he materialized in his architecture.

52. It is worth recalling that this disparity extends beyond Houston to the rest of Texas. For example, Lady Bird Johnson played a leading national role in securing passage of the Highway Beautification Act, in 1965. It was signed by her husband, President Lyndon B. Johnson.

53. After the dissolution of his marriage, Barnstone bought and lived in a Staub-designed house at 17 Shadowlawn Circle.

54. In a very different way, the automobile architecture of strip malls, which has dominated Houston from the 1960s, shares a dimension of interiority insofar as all the "action" and spatial complexity, if any, happen once you cross the parking lot and enter the interior of the shop or restaurant.

55. "Record Houses of 1965: 'Treetop' Living Pavilion of Steel and Glass," *Architectural Record* 137 (mid-May 1965): 66–69; see also Gary McKay, "Architectural Honors," *Houston Home and Garden* 11 (July 1985): 60–64.

56. Ben Koush, "Light Touch: The Work of Harwood Taylor," *Cite 64* (Summer 2005): 14–15.

57. "Houston School," *Architectural Forum* 116 (June 1962): 52.

58. "Advanced Center for the Retarded," *Architectural Forum* 127 (December 1967): 48–53; see also "Industrial Buildings: Building Types Study No. 366: Publishing Company Building, Galveston, Texas," *Architectural Record* 141 (January 1967): 158–159.

59. Cook and Klotz, *Conversations with Architects*, 90–124.

60. McCoy, "Young Architects," 186.

61. Mildred F. Schmertz, "In Praise of a Monument to Lyndon B. Johnson," *Architectural Record* 150 (November 1971): 113–120.

62. C. Ray Smith, "The House Built on Its Side," *Progressive Architecture* 50 (June 1969): 104–109; see also "Ant Farm: Jost, Lord, and Michels: House of the Century," *Progressive Architecture* 54 (January 1973): 95; "House of the Century," *Progressive Architecture* 54 (June 1973): 126–134; "An 'Indeterminate Façade' for Best Products Company, Houston," *Architectural Record* 161 (March 1977): 124–125; Turner, *Open Plan*, 20–22; Michelangelo Sabatino and Bruce C. Webb, eds., "Sixties and Seventies Sites of Counter Culture: Space City Subversion," *Cite 82* (Summer 2010).

63. Karleen Koen, "Best of '77: Nine Architects and Their Projects Win Residential Honors," *Houston Home and Garden*, February 1978, 54–55, 60–64.

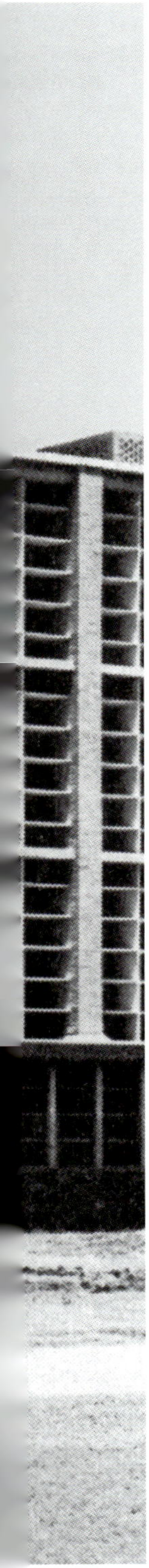

CHAPTER THREE

TO BE MODERN IN TEXAS

Lone Star Avant-Garde

KATHRYN E. HOLLIDAY

HOWARD BARNSTONE'S fascination with the history of Texas architecture is a central theme of his modernist practice. As the author of the sweeping *The Galveston That Was* (1966) and the admiring *The Architecture of John F. Staub* (1979), Barnstone extended his analytical thinking beyond the making of new architecture and into the traditions that informed its past.[1] As an architect of modern, postwar Houston, Barnstone explored in historical narratives the designers and strategies that formed its foundations. He began *The Galveston That Was* with the assertion "This book is about the Galveston that *was*. It is not about the Galveston that is; nor is it about the Galveston that will be." It is an unpretentious statement that seems to focus on documentation, lacking an agenda beyond intellectual curiosity. Scholars have explored the purpose of Barnstone's writings in light of his modern design sensibility and the development of his subtle manipulations of space and structure to adapt to the climatic and cultural particularities of Houston and the Texas Gulf Coast.[2]

Barnstone's embrace of history places him directly in line with other avant-garde modernist architects. It is well established that the heroic figures of the modern movement did not abandon or reject history in their architectural thinking, contrary to what was suggested in the first histories of the era. Walter Gropius did not, in fact, throw away the history books at the Harvard Graduate School of Design, and Mies van der Rohe's radical simplicity drew on his study of nineteenth-century neoclassicism and Karl Friedrich Schinkel. The Texas Rangers, the young architecture instructors recruited by Harwell Hamilton Harris to teach at the University of Texas in the mid-1950s, may have rejected the Beaux Arts design curriculum of the previous generation, but they embraced the formalist study of urban history as an integral part of contemporary practice. The uses and meaning of history changed for modern architects, but did not disappear.[3]

Barnstone's embrace of history raises questions that point to the distinct cultural context for modernist practice in the Lone Star State. As Stephen Fox pointed out, the construction of an architectural identity for Texas was challenging. As national discussions of regional architectural identities gained strength in the early twentieth century, Texas "seemed to possess no historical architecture that could be revived and 'developed' to serve as the origin of an authentic regional architecture."[4] Texas architecture thus drew on a variety of sources, from the language of Spanish colonial mission architecture, to pioneer cabins, to Mexican border churches. The most powerful strand of Texas regionalism emerged in the late 1920s in the work of the Dallas architect David R. Williams (1890–1962), who explored the limestone cabins of German and Alsatian immigrants to the Hill Country as honest expressions of local climate and materials. Williams's position continued to evolve through succeeding generations of architects that included O'Neil Ford, Frank Welch, and Lake|Flato.[5]

What these disparate ideas of Texas regionalism have in common is their pre-urban context. Texas was a state known for its hinterlands, its prairies and cowboys, its position on the frontier. J. Frank Dobie's *The Mustangs* (1952), John Graves's *Goodbye to a River* (1960), Larry McMurtry's first novel, *Horseman, Pass By* (1961), all helped solidify this image in the public imagination in the postwar decades. The epic film *Giant* (1956), with its empty landscapes, oil wells, and chiseled loner James Dean in a cowboy hat, provided the popular imagination with a

The iconic image of James Dean as Jett Rink, a hardscrabble Texas antihero, in the movie *Giant* (1956), a modern parable of family, land, and oil.

compelling modern antihero. Sam Rayburn's nearly twenty-year rule as Speaker of the US House of Representatives (1940–1961) made chili and tamales a centerpiece of Washington, DC, social life; Lyndon Johnson's ascent to the presidency transformed his family ranch outside Johnson City into the Texas White House, a potent symbol of Johnson's persona as a "modern cowboy" and a firebrand man of the people.[6] The literary, artistic, and cultural traditions of Texas were rooted in a mythology of independent male conquests of an unforgiving and endless wild terrain, and that view engaged the national imagination in the 1960s.[7]

To be modern in Texas—as an architect—required grappling with notions of regional identity that had long been attached to romanticized images of the West and the frontier, and adapting them to the exploding postwar Sunbelt cities. Houston, Dallas, San Antonio, and Corpus Christi changed radically in the decades after World War II, annexing new suburban land and reconstructing (or deconstructing) downtowns. Much of their growth was fueled by technical industries associated with oil production and the military-industrial complex.[8] NASA in Houston, Texas Instruments in Dallas, General Dynamics in Fort Worth, and Lackland Air Force Base in San Antonio typified the tension between the old Texas and the new, pitting the cowboy against the rocket scientist. The image of

Barnstone in a cowboy hat and Brooks Brothers shirt, evoked by Bruce Webb, embodies this tension, deliberately deconstructing the frontier image and combatting the identity of the "professional Texan" as a hick in dusty cowboy boots.

Barnstone's rhetorical strategy was to establish a history for urban Texas that would be particularly suited to the postwar years. Barnstone and a handful of other Texas architects demonstrated an interest in their local city landscapes as the source languages for Texas architecture. They used their local research and design projects as defining features of the state's avant-garde small-scale practices. Barnstone, along with O'Neil Ford in San Antonio, Richard S. Colley in Corpus Christi, and Pratt, Box and Henderson in Dallas, provided variations on the theme of the Texas city as the new frontier, highlighting the tension between a mythologized Texas and the realities and politics of rapid postwar urbanization. The construction of local architectural and urban history in Galveston and Houston gave Barnstone an intellectual foundation for his performative modernist practice. It also

The classic mythology of the cowboy confronting the reality of booming cities and technology in postwar Texas.

provided a foil for his attacks on Houston's careless and rapacious development and conservative politics. By creating a narrative of Texas architecture focused on its urban contexts, Barnstone and his peers provided a means to critique large-scale commercial practice, explosive and thoughtless developer-driven urban growth, and weak civic governance.

HISTORY AS CRITIQUE

The Prairie's Yield was published as a guidebook for the American Institute of Architects' national convention in Dallas in 1962. The architects Hal Box and James Pratt were the primary authors, working with a team of collaborators who

1521
CORTEZ CONQUERS AZTECS

1546-1878
PALACE OF THE LOUVRE
Paris/Lescot, Lemercier, et al

1558-90
DOME OF ST. PETER'S
Rome/Michelangelo

1559-84
ESCORIAL
near Madrid/Bautista and de Herrara

c. 1567
VILLA CAPRA
Vicenza/Palladio   6

The appearance of the Texas prairie before European settlement.

assembled photographs and provided the layout. Box and Pratt were imbued with different, though complementary, strands of modernist theory that used history in contemporary practice. Box graduated from the School of Architecture at the University of Texas at Austin after working in O'Neil Ford's studio. Pratt had graduated from the Graduate School of Design at Harvard and spent a year traveling in Europe, where he stayed in the home of Carola Giedion-Welcker and Sigfried Giedion in Switzerland and visited Nikolaus Pevsner in London.[9] *The Prairie's Yield* was Box and Pratt's argument for a sophisticated understanding of an unsophisticated city such as Dallas and a justification for their choosing to settle and practice in a land of opportunity outside the traditional seats of architectural power.

The book, with its running time line and chronologically thematic chapters, like Barnstone's treatments of Galveston and Staub, was presented in an ostensibly documentary format. Moving from Dallas's origins on the prairie in the 1840s through the development of the railroads in the 1880s to the oil boom of the 1920s, *The Prairie's Yield* offered a narrative of a city created by "simple pioneering people" with "a will to create something from nothing."[10] The authors' agenda, though, was more complex than simple documentation. Box and Pratt heroized

the "utilitarian" agenda of Dallas pioneers, celebrating their lack of aesthetic pretension and their necessary "self-reliance."[11] While architectural developments were often "fifteen years late" in reaching Dallas, which lagged behind such progressive centers as New York and Chicago, it shared with other American cities a tendency to ignore the urban environment as a whole: "Most buildings put on blinders to face the world; like ostriches they seem unaware that their backsides also face the world."[12]

The Prairie's Yield remains today an impressive feat of historiography, a history of Dallas architecture establishing a canon of its greatest architectural moments (though unfortunately, true to the pragmatic character the book evokes, many of those landmarks have been demolished). More importantly, though, the book positioned a new generation of Dallas architects to take on the project of shaping the city intentionally as advocates for reforming the market-driven, laissez-faire practices of previous decades: "Current data show enormous increases in the magnitude of city problems. . . . No Authority has yet been organized to encompass planning for the entire Dallas–Fort Worth urban region. The need for full-time creative design planning with greatly increased city plan staff has not yet become evident to city leaders."[13]

The Prairie's Yield amplified a central message of Pratt and Box's partnership, founded in 1958. (Philip Henderson joined them as partner in 1962.) One of Pratt and Box's first collaborations was an exhibition at the Dallas Museum of Art in Fair Park in 1957, put together with the support of the museum's director, Jerry Bywaters. The exhibition was a critique of Dallas and its urban core, designed to provoke public conversation about how to make the city a better place. Bywaters wrote an impassioned letter to the *Dallas Morning News*: "We have been too prone to claim that Dallas is a civic and cultural leader without backing up our words with enough actions. Now the entire city is on trial as to whether it can make its fine dreams come true."[14] Pratt and Box took this critique of Dallas on the road as a slideshow, which was later featured in *Texas Architect*. It was a prime example of the new generation's engagement with urban design. They used the image of

TEXAS ARCHITECT

OFFICIAL PUBLICATION OF THE TEXAS SOCIETY OF ARCHITECTS

DECEMBER 1958

SEE PAGE 5
A proposed plaza development for Dallas, by architects John Harold Box and James Reece Pratt, TSA-AIA of Dallas.

▶ Robert P. Woltz Named TSA President

▶ "Look Into The Future" Is Convention Topic For AIA President

▶ "Are We Still Building Log Cabins?"

The "Dallas Tower," a proposal by Pratt, Box & Henderson for an eighty-story skyscraper topped with an amusement park and Ferris wheel.

frontier architecture, the log cabin, to diagnose the problem of building singular objects divorced from their urban context. They lampooned traditional architectural and planning practices in a series of caricatures and placed the architect at the forefront of the conversation about abandoning the Texas tradition of isolated "log cabins" and moving toward a connected urban fabric.[15]

The Prairie's Yield provided sweeping arguments for Dallas to develop "a more human downtown" (46), a clear housing policy (58), and a better approach to school design (67). An activist history hidden within a convention guidebook, it propelled the firm's forays into speculative urban reforms. Their proposal for "The Dallas Tower," an eighty-story skyscraper topped by an enclosed Ferris wheel and amusement park, must be understood in this context as a provocative critique of developer-driven commercial designs that isolated downtown sidewalks and removed human interaction from the street. Their efforts to reinvigorate Fair Park through a series of joyful master plans sponsored by Angus Wynne, the developer of Six Flags Over Texas, was a more direct attempt to bring life to the neglected civic realm of the state fairgrounds.[16] The project's failure, and the city's decision to instead fence off the fairgrounds from the surrounding African American neighborhood, continued to position Pratt, Box and Henderson as an open critic of Dallas's planning and development culture.

On the surface, Barnstone's books appear less polemical than *The Prairie's Yield*. But like Pratt and Box, Barnstone used a conventional format—in this case, the architectural monograph—to pursue a complex agenda. While ostensibly a book about a city, *The Galveston That Was* is more accurately about the city's architects and the ways they responded to the rigors of designing in the isolated and idiosyncratic context of the Gulf Coast and its "uncultured flats," bringing moments of transcendent wonder to the time-forsaken city streets.[17] Barnstone's interpretation of the minutest architectural details ascribes poetic intention to the quirks of decaying chimneys, shutters, and bricks and casts an enthralling spell over the city and the ghosts that haunt its neighborhoods. His detailed description of the Henry Landes House (1887) and its eclectic juxtaposition of mansard tower, "tiny turrets," oriels, and cornices leads to an appreciative declaration of affection: "The Landes House is not much appreciated architecturally today. The first reaction is disappointment. But if looked at more keenly, it is seen to be a handsome structure,

OPPOSITE Pratt and Box's proposed plaza for Dallas, *Texas Architect*, December 1958, cover.

TO BE MODERN IN TEXAS   105

Henry A. Landes House (1887, George E. Dickey and D. A. Helmich, architects), 1604 Post Office Street, Galveston.

dignified, and lyric."[18] The cast-iron columns of the Block-Oppenheimer Building (1881–1882), designed by the architect Nicholas J. Clayton, who emerges as the hero of the book, "are beautified articles of utility."[19] Barnstone trains our eyes to see the quixotic flourishes of architectural art in unexpected places and ultimately makes an argument for their collective urbanity.

The photographs by Henri Cartier-Bresson and Ezra Stoller provide equally important editorial commentary on the architectural precision and human dimension of Galveston culture and its slow, humid pace.[20] The pairing of the more clinical Stoller and the atmospheric Cartier-Bresson heightens the narrative tension between the importance of architecture as a precise physical setting and its role as a backdrop for the social theater of the city.

Critique of and engagement with Barnstone's local urban environment informed his stance on the meaning and uses of history, as it did that of Pratt and Box. By studying Staub, Barnstone made a case for the operative nature of his own modernist practice, which was likewise responsive to the climate and culture of Texas cities. Barnstone admired the Gartner House (1929–1930) in Fort Worth, designed with a nearly blank wall facing the street, a seemingly hostile gesture that in fact graciously blocks the western sun. The house's "intricate and

OPPOSITE Block-Oppenheimer Building (1882, Nicholas J. Clayton), 2314 Strand, Galveston.

Ashton Villa, J. M. Brown House (1858–1859, architect unknown), 2328 Broadway, Galveston.

circumstantial" plan "trickily" responds to its site and solar orientation, defying convention to deliver a house suited to its particular locale. By interpreting Staub through clever manipulations of form, scale, and space, Barnstone successfully abstracts from a historicizing form a template for modern practice.[21] Bolton & Barnstone's Winterbotham House (1964), designed for the grandson of a client of one of Clayton's spectacular Galveston houses, was a modernist variation, with a solid brick wall facing the street, behind which private spaces looked onto the landscape.

That attention to small-scale localized practice was a hallmark of Barnstone's critique of Houston's architecture and planning culture. In a city best known in design circles for its anarchic lack of zoning, Barnstone publicly spoke out against a proposed 1962 zoning ordinance. "Zoning is for the Zeckendorfs and land speculators," Barnstone said, suggesting that zoning provided advantages for large-scale developers over individual property owners and provided incentives

Elizabeth Reynolds and Herman Gartner House (1930, John F. Staub), Rivercrest, Fort Worth.

Wandy Renfert and John M. Winterbotham, Jr., House (1960, Bolton & Barnstone, demolished 2000), 54 Briar Hollow Lane, Houston.

for corruption among city officials.[22] In an interview with the libertarian magazine *Reason* twenty-one years later, Barnstone ascribed the survival of historic buildings like the Antioch Missionary Baptist Church, an anchor for the Fourth Ward, one of Houston's historic African American neighborhoods, to the city's lack of zoning. The survival of Antioch at the base of the sleek glass postmodern towers is a disjunctive symbol of Houston's developer-driven planning, which haphazardly leaves fragments of the city's original fabric and texture in place. Barnstone fought zoning in Houston to protect the interests of low-income property owners with little influence—a counterintuitive argument that pitted him against developers and landowners as well as progressive, liberal advocates for zoning.[23]

Antioch Missionary Baptist Church after remodeling (1879, Richard Allen, builder; remodeled 1889–1890, Robert Jones), 500 Clay, Houston.

As documented throughout this volume, Barnstone was an outspoken critic of city policy, using his position as an architect to suggest a complete reform of city planning and civic governance, paralleling the political engagement of his wife, Gertrude, with issues of equity and access to public education (see chapter 8). This combative relationship with the city, based in progressive politics and avant-garde architectural ideas, fueled his design practice as a critique of the venal and commercial world that surrounded the serene oases he created for his clients, connecting him with the wise practices of Staub and Clayton before him.

That heroic sense of an architect at war with a city he loved also drove O'Neil Ford's relationship with San Antonio.[24] Ford was a talker, a charismatic producer of lectures that persuaded and inspired. In 1968, in a lecture at the University of Texas at Arlington, he railed against the "dreadful uglification of America" as a symptom of a political and cultural system that failed to fulfill its citizens' needs for a beautiful and authentic world. "If I as an architect," he said, "fight the building of a garage on the river in San Antonio (this poor little river carries a terrible responsibility), this is important because it is visible evidence of what a planner has done . . . In San Antonio, they're not alarmed at driving to Austin and seeing one long slum called US 81."[25] Of all the vanguard Texas architects with a penchant for history, Ford was the most enthralled. His explorations of the

Hill Country in the 1930s had become a full-fledged encyclopedic appreciation of Texas and the world by the 1960s. But his biggest passion was local: he spoke of the need to teach "a child what's under his eye, what's in his own home town."[26]

Ford had a direct line to local history in San Antonio through preservation and his lifelong engagement with La Villita, a small piece of a vibrant residential neighborhood in the direct path of San Antonio's urban renewal.[27] Ford would later recall that when he left Dallas to begin work at La Villita in 1939, "this changed the whole direction of my life. I was in the place I loved—San Antonio—with all the surrounding old towns we knew so well."[28] Ford's painstaking work of restoration and reconstruction, a project spearheaded by San Antonio mayor Maury Maverick and funded by the National Youth Administration, became the first stage in a lifelong engagement with preservation and development along the historic banks of the San Antonio River.[29]

Like Barnstone's studies of Galveston and Houston, though, Ford's work on La Villita was strictly about preserving its historical forms. At La Villita, Ford worked with a team to survey and document what remained of the nineteenth-century houses and the details of their doors and woodwork. But he balanced this work with the construction of new facilities, especially Bolivar Hall (1940). Ford carefully set it apart from the nineteenth-century fabric by using an exposed concrete frame and floating steps that linked it with the modernist language he would use on the Trinity University campus ten years later rather than with the limestone and wood of the surrounding neighborhood.

When San Antonio chose the Villita area as the site of HemisFair, the 1968 world's fair, Ford was initially at the helm of the design process as coordinating architect, in collaboration with Allison Peery, who covered site planning. Ford's vision once again involved mixing the adaptive reuse of historic structures with the construction of new pavilions scattered throughout the site. Ironically, the only exposition building actually designed by Ford and his firm, Ford, Powell, & Carson, was the Tower of the Americas, a "useless" signature building that Ford had argued against building. After conflicts and arguments, Ford withdrew from the planning process, leaving his partners to complete the design of the tower.

It is disjunctive to compare the intimate, small urban scale of La Villita with the HemisFair tower. Though they were designed under the guidance of the same architectural hand, what truly binds them is a continued exploration of the possibilities of concrete construction and the underlying typology of the tower as a place-making device. Trinity University's Murchison Tower, later echoed by Ford, Powell & Carson's tower at the University of Dallas, abstracted the bell towers of medieval campuses into a modern engineered form. That form was blown

up to the scale of HemisFair for the Tower of the Americas, which became a lonely, futuristic symbol, disconnected from the fair and the city below. Its rotating restaurant and cocktail lounge offered the possibility of space-age pleasures, but enjoying them was dependent on elevators, not the monastic endurance of hundreds of stairs to climb. In 1980, Ford wrote disparagingly of development in what is now called Uptown Dallas, where he had worked in the 1920s and 1930s. He highlighted the contrast between its historic fabric and everything that had grown up around it: "I am sure you would all get a jolt if you saw Maple and McKinney and Cedar Springs—it is ugly in an ugly city—only the Stoneleigh Hotel—and Maple Terrace remain."[30] Ford's vision of a city that integrated new construction with old, that blended progress with the past, was one that remained elusive anywhere in Texas.

The promotion of local practice and local history in publications was crucial to the creation of modern architecture—its aesthetics, its construction, and its social role in redefining modern urban society. Local histories were only first steps. Although prone to error, they emphasized the heroic role of architects as the uniquely inspired form givers of cities. None of that distracts from the importance of these texts and designs as documents that positioned avant-garde Texas architects as intellectuals on the urban frontier.

While not as literary as his peers, the Corpus Christi architect Richard S. Colley succeeded in implementing his vision of an urban Texas, whereas Barnstone, Ford, Pratt, Box, and Henderson did not. Colley was a passionate, often polarizing advocate for modern design as a way to change the civic culture of the Gulf Coast port city, particularly through a "broad, long-range city-planning program."[31] Because Corpus Christi was a case-study city for the National Resources Planning Board's program to develop civic planning tools that could be translated for use by others in the 1940s, Colley was able to use his city as a laboratory for modernist ideas about urban design and architecture. Colley first designed a city hall with an adjoining exhibition hall and chamber of commerce (1952), followed by a massive redevelopment of the waterfront, anchored by the Memorial Coliseum (1954) and the Sheraton Marina Inn (1966). Colley built civic designs on a scale that other Texas modernists did not achieve. These projects, because they were an outgrowth of the NRPB program, had a didactic intention as demonstrations that could educate other cities about the virtues of modern design, construction, and materials.

Colley's first project was the city hall complex at the heart of the city. It was part of a massive superblock project for such a small city as well as an

OPPOSITE, TOP La Villita, San Antonio, 1939.

OPPOSITE, BOTTOM La Villita, San Antonio, 1941, after O'Neil Ford's restoration and reconstruction. Bolivar Hall (1940) is at the top right of the square.

ambitious statement about the reinvention of modern civic government. The concrete-and-masonry office tower dramatically announced the presence of city government, contrasting it with the hierarchy of state governance symbolized by the classical portico of the Nueces County Courthouse a few blocks away. In keeping with postwar discourse on efficient city management, Colley's city hall stripped away the traditional trappings of civic symbolism in favor of a progressive minimalism that focused on lighting and space for the expression of its programmatic goals. The "ample daylight" and strategically placed *brise soleil* were intended to reduce the need for electric lighting and to minimize costs for air-conditioning, aspects of the building repeatedly emphasized to the public in tours of the new building and in features in the local newspaper.[32]

Colley's reinvented civic core for Corpus Christi lasted less than fifty years. The city hall, exhibition hall, and coliseum became unloved and unused within two generations. They all fell to the wrecking ball despite efforts by architects and preservation advocates to reinvigorate discussions about the importance of avant-garde modernist ambition in Texas. As we continue to lose the built record of midcentury design, we may begin to find that these architects' books and essays provide the firmest foundation for understanding their vision of a new Texas.

Ford's biographer Mary Carolyn Hollers George pointed out that he was an articulate and passionate critic of the city, "vulgarians," and mediocre architecture, but lacked the "efficient pragmatic" approach necessary to achieve his vision on a large scale, an assessment that can be equally applied to all the architects discussed here.[33] Ultimately, the image of the modernist avant-garde architect

HemisFair Tower (1968, Ford, Powell & Carson) with Sharon Gillette, Bell System Pavilion hostess.

Corpus Christi City Hall (1952, Richard S. Colley, architect, demolished 1988). Colley focused on environmental conditions as a rational justification for form and space.

remained entangled with that of the hardscrabble independent pioneer of the West. It was a potent mix of intellectual bravado, aesthetic adventurism, and cultural activism that defined the increasingly urban context of Texas architecture in the 1960s and 1970s but left a gap between rhetoric and implementation. It is no accident that Ford was fired by the mayor of San Antonio, Colley was fired by Corpus Christi's planning department, Barnstone was sometimes at odds with the University of Houston, and James Pratt spent a career pursuing thoughtful and visionary planning schemes for Dallas with no success. Each of these architects saw the pulsing, growing cities around them as a subject of investigation and critique and staked a purist's claim, a "hero's solo role," to his unique vision of how to guide raw, young Texas cities into the future.[34]

TO BE MODERN IN TEXAS   115

NOTES

1. H. Barnstone, *Architecture of John F. Staub* and *Galveston That Was*.

2. Fox, *Country Houses of John F. Staub*; see also Stephen Fox, "Howard Barnstone (1923–1987)," *Cite 18* (Fall 1987): 18–24; Peter Brink, afterword to H. Barnstone, *Galveston That Was*, 212–213; Scardino and Turner, *Clayton's Galveston*, 199–200; Vincent Scully, foreword to H. Barnstone, *Architecture of John F. Staub*, ix–x.

3. Alofsin, *Struggle for Modernism*; Riley and Bergdoll, *Mies in Berlin*; Caragonne, *Texas Rangers*; see also Sarah Williams Goldhagen, "Something to Talk About: Modernism, Discourse, Style," *Journal of the Society of Architectural Historians* 64, no. 2 (June 2005), 144–167.

4. Stephen Fox, "Regionalism and Texas Architecture," in Canizaro, *Architectural Regionalism*, 206.

5. David R. Williams, "Toward a Southwestern Architecture," *Southwest Review* 16, no. 3 (April 1931): 301–313; see also Welch, *On Becoming an Architect*. On the more recent exploration of Williams's regionalism, see Gerald Moorhead, "Lone Stars: Regional Portfolio, Texas," *Architectural Record* 179, no. 2 (February 1991): 84–93; Joel Barna, "New Texas Houses and Redefined Regionalism," *Texas Architect* 39, no. 3 (May 1989): 23–37.

6. Vera Norwood, "Natives' Return: LBJ's Texas White House and Lady Bird's Wildflowers," in Miller, *Cities and Nature*; see also Rothman, *LBJ's Texas White House*; Dulaney and Phillips, *Speak, Mister Speaker*.

7. Graham, *Cowboys and Cadillacs*; Dobie, *The Mustangs*; Graves, *Goodbye to a River*; McMurtry, *Horseman, Pass By*. For competing images of Texas in Dobie and McMurtry, see Don Graham, "J. Frank Dobie: A Reappraisal," *Southwestern Historical Quarterly* 92, no. 1 (July 1988): 1–15.

8. The concept of the Sunbelt continues to be elastic, but is well discussed in Rachel Guberman, "Is There a Sunbelt After All? And Should We Care?," *Journal of Urban History* 41, no. 6 (2015): 1166–1174; see also Bernard and Rice, *Sunbelt Cities*. For Texas cities in the Sunbelt, see Fairbanks and Underwood, *Essays on Sunbelt Cities*.

9. James Pratt, interview by the author, June 14, 2013, at the Pratt residence, Dallas, Texas, Oral History of Texas Architecture Collection, Special Collections, University of Texas, Arlington; and Philip Henderson, interview by author, October 20, 2011, at the Henderson residence, Dallas, Texas, Oral History of Texas Architecture Collection.

10. American Institute of Architects, Dallas Chapter, *Prairie's Yield*, 14, 16.

11. Ibid., 17, 20.

12. Ibid., 28, 46.

13. Ibid., 56.

14. "Leaders in the Field Agree—Dallas Needs a Face-Lifting," *Dallas Morning News*, December 8, 1957.

15. James Reese Pratt and John Harold Box, "Are We Still Building Log Cabins?," *Texas Architect*, December 1958, 5–6.

16. Pratt interview and Henderson interview; both projects are also documented in the James Pratt Papers, Dallas Public Library.

17. H. Barnstone, *Galveston That Was*, 154. Barnstone asked rhetorically, "Could Stanford White, the designer, have felt that on the uncultured flats of Galveston there should be one last utterly romantic building?"

18. Ibid., 139.

19. Ibid., 81.

20. Beasley, *Alleys and Back Buildings*; see also Aubry, *Born on the Island*; Hardwick, *Mythic Galveston*.

21. H. Barnstone, *Architecture of John F. Staub*, 142–144; see also Fox, "Howard Barnstone," 18–21.

22. Barnstone quoted in "Architect Says Zoning May Lead to Land Speculation, Hurt Growth," *Houston Chronicle*, March 27, 1962; see also "Zoning Debate Next Tuesday," *Houston Chronicle*, March 4, 1962. William Zeckendorf, Sr., was a well-known New York real estate developer.

23. Thomas Winslow Hazlett, "They Built Their Own Highway and Other Tales of Private Land-Use Planning," *Reason*, November 1, 1983. Barnstone's reading is echoed in Lerup, *One Million Acres*.

24. On Ford, see George, *O'Neil Ford*; Dillon, *Architecture of O'Neil Ford*.

25. O'Neil Ford, "Remarks at the Planning Versus or For the Individual Conference, University of Texas at Arlington," in Ford, *O'Neil Ford on Architecture*.

26. Ford, "Culture—Who Needs It?" in Ford, *O'Neil Ford on Architecture*.

27. Lydia Magruder, "La Villita," *Handbook of Texas Online*, June 15, 2010, modified on June 12, 2018, tshaonline.org/handbook/online/articles/hpl01. La Villita was the site of a Coahuiltecan Indian village from about 1722. Later, families of soldiers attached to the San Antonio de Bexar Presidio lived there, followed by German, Swiss, and French immigrants in the mid-nineteenth century. The area was restored in 1939, used as a Red Cross camp during the Second World War, and afterward restored again to preserve early Texas and Spanish culture. In 1972, twenty-seven buildings in the area were listed in the National Register of Historic Places.

28. O'Neil Ford, foreword to *David R. Williams, Pioneer Architect*, reprinted in Ford, *O'Neil Ford on Architecture*.

29. George, *O'Neil Ford*, provides a thorough recounting of the La Villita projects, especially in chapters 7 and 12.

30. O'Neil Ford to Crystal and Lewis and Zerílda, c. 1980, David Dillon Papers, Special Collections, University of Texas at Arlington.

31. Colley as quoted in Lessoff, *Where Texas Meets the Sea*, 235.

32. "Manner of Lighting Played Major Part in City Hall Plans," and "New Tax Office Convenient, Spacious and Practicable," *Corpus Christi Caller-Times*, March 23, 1952; "Plans for New City Hall to Go to Council Today," *Corpus Christi Caller-Times*, May 9, 1950; "Civic Buildings: Corpus Christi," *Progressive Architecture* 34 (February 1953): 83–92. A few clippings related to these projects are held in the Colley Papers, Alexander Architectural Archives, University of Texas at Austin.

33. George, *O'Neil Ford*, 172.

34. Ibid., 181.

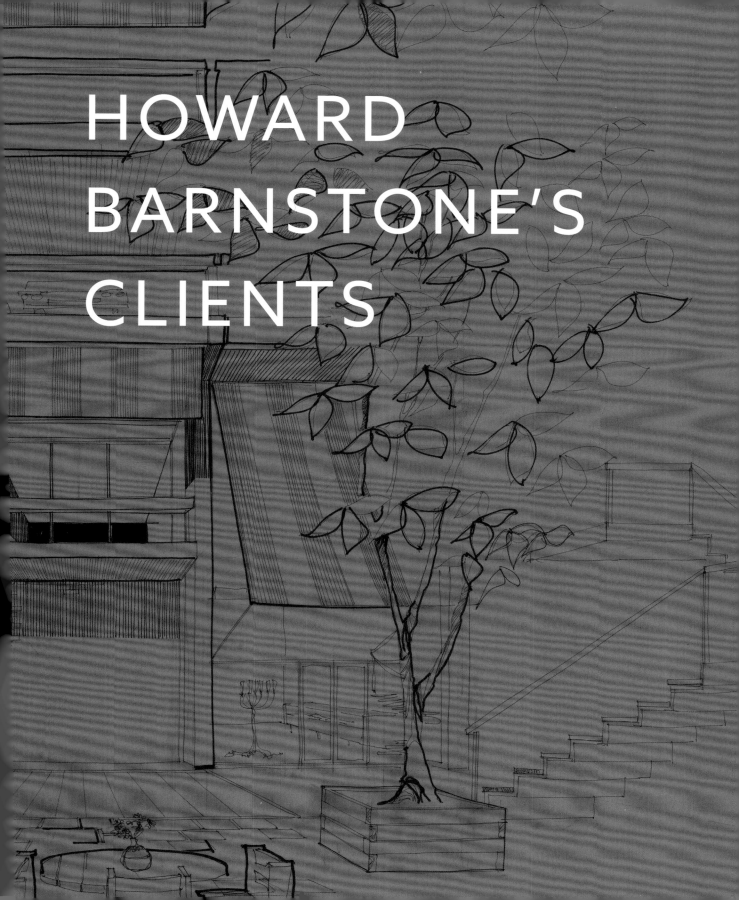

HOWARD BARNSTONE'S CLIENTS

CHAPTER FOUR

A CONSTRUCTIVE CONNECTION

Barnstone and the Menils

BARRIE SCARDINO BRADLEY

DOMINIQUE SCHLUMBERGER and John de Menil were French émigrés who settled in Houston during the Second World War. John de Menil headed two divisions of Schlumberger, one of the largest oil field services companies in the world. Dominique de Menil was rigorous and disciplined, and exhibited a pronounced religious vocation. She became an exhibition curator and, with her husband, a proponent of liberal social consciousness. Together they assembled an exceptional private art collection. Howard Barnstone essentially became the Menils' in-house architect. He provided architectural services for the Schlumberger corporation as well as the Menils, their extended family, and friends throughout the United States, South America, and Europe. The opportunities that Barnstone gained as a result of these commissions broadened his architectural palette, gave him an opportunity to work on historic buildings, and allowed him to form relationships with sophisticated individuals, which he relished doing. There is no particular architectural link among the Menil-related projects; they include relatively simple and contextual South American farmhouses, the interiors of high-rise office buildings and condominium apartments, and modern houses. The Menils' patronage provided a lucrative career for Barnstone and, perhaps more importantly, gave him the opportunity to construct the kind of world in which he wanted to live.

Howard Barnstone met Dominique and John de Menil at a dinner party given by Mary Wood and Hugo V. Neuhaus, Jr., in the elegant modern house that Neuhaus had completed for his family in River Oaks in 1950.[1] Neuhaus was Philip Johnson's associate architect for the construction of the Johnson-designed house for Dominique and John de Menil in Houston. The occasion for the dinner party

John de Menil, Andy Warhol, Simone Swan, Fred Hughes, Dominique de Menil, and Howard Barnstone in Buckminster Fuller's US pavilion for Expo 67, Montreal, 1967.

was to introduce the Menils to Barnstone, whom Neuhaus had recommended as the architect to manage alterations and repairs to the Menil House. One can easily imagine the stimulating evening in the glamorous River Oaks setting. Howard Barnstone and the Menils experienced an immediate mutual attraction. Dominique and John de Menil became Barnstone's most generous and enduring clients and patrons.

Jean-Marie-Joseph Menu de Ménil (1904–1973) was the son of Marie-Madeleine Rougier and Georges-Auguste-Emmanuel Menu de Ménil, members of a Roman Catholic military family ennobled by Napoléon I. Jean Menu de Ménil graduated from the University of Paris in 1922 and in 1925 received an advanced degree in political science from the same institution. While working as a banker in Paris from 1932 to 1938, he completed a law degree. He married Dominique Schlumberger in Paris in 1931, and she converted to Roman Catholicism. In 1938, at the behest of her uncle, Marcel Schlumberger, Jean joined the Société de Prospection Électrique, the oil field services corporation that Marcel and his brother Conrad, Dominique de Ménil's father, founded in 1926.

During the Second World War, Jean Menu de Ménil served as an intelligence officer in the French Army in Bucharest. After the fall of France, in June 1940, he escaped to the United States to help restructure Schlumberger. Dominique and Jean, their three children, and other members of the Schlumberger family made their way to Houston, where the headquarters of the company's North

American division, the Schlumberger Well Surveying Corporation, had been located since 1934. From 1941 to 1957, Jean headed two divisions of the company: Schlumberger-Surenco, the Latin American division, and the Schlumberger Overseas Company, the Middle Eastern division, both headquartered in Houston.[2] Marcel Schlumberger, in Paris, retained control of the company's European division, and Pierre Schlumberger (1914–1986), Marcel's son and Dominique's first cousin, administered the US division from Houston.[3]

In the United States, Ménil dropped his family name (Menu) and took his toponym (Menil) as his American surname, leaving off the acute accent mark but retaining the noble predicate "de." He Anglicized his given name to John and became a naturalized US citizen in 1962. John de Menil loved Houston for its potential. In a chapter that he contributed to *Houston: Text by Houstonians*, provocatively titled "Provincial Town," Menil exhorted Houstonians to think in bold, cosmopolitan terms rather than to acquiesce resentfully in ascriptions of provincial inferiority.[4] Menil delighted in confounding expectations. As early as 1957, he challenged racial segregation in Houston by getting the Shamrock Hilton Hotel to admit African American guests when the American Federation of Arts held its national conference in Houston at the Shamrock.[5] The conference also gave Menil the opportunity to display his legendary expansiveness: for one of the conference tours, he had a Schlumberger plane fly participants to Dallas and Fort Worth to tour private art collections.[6] Menil could be curt and dismissive to those who tried his patience, but he was alert and encouraging to talent and promise, especially when displayed by young people such as Howard Barnstone.

Dominique Schlumberger (1908–1997) grew up in Paris and Val-Richer, her family's country estate near the Normandy coast.[7] She was the privileged daughter of Louise Delpech and Conrad Schlumberger. Her father, a professor of physics at the École des Mines in Paris, was born into an Alsatian industrial family. Conrad and Marcel, a mechanical engineer, invented an electromagnetic sounding device to identify minerals according to their degree of electrical resistance. With financial support from their father, Paul, they opened an office in Paris in 1920. That enterprise, the Société de Prospection Électrique, steadily grew into the international oil services firm Schlumberger Ltd., which produced tremendous wealth for the Schlumberger family and, in the next generation, executive positions for Marcel's son, Pierre, and Conrad's sons-in-law, Henri-Georges Doll, John de Menil, and Eric H. Boissonnas.[8]

Dominique Schlumberger possessed an intellect commensurate with her distinguished lineage. She received a BA from the University of Paris in 1927 and did postgraduate work in mathematics and physics. Although her formal education was not in the field of art history or exhibition design, she possessed an unerring eye and educated herself in art; Barnstone wrote that she could have been a great architect.[9] She and her husband began to collect art in 1945, after they came to the United States. In 1964, she was appointed chair of the Art Department at the University of St. Thomas in Houston, after the death of her mentor and friend, Jermayne MacAgy. Dominique de Menil excelled in organizing provocative and imaginatively installed art exhibitions.[10] She had enormous energy but was calm and reserved. Although she and Barnstone became friends, their professional relationship was at the core of their friendship. Barnstone had a different sort of relationship with John de Menil, whose manner was commanding, charismatic, and expansive. He promoted Barnstone for large and small Schlumberger commissions. Simone Swan, the first executive vice president of the Menil Foundation, stressed that John loved Howard and completely trusted his design decisions.[11] What may have held the three together beyond personal affinity and a love of architecture was that each was a perfectionist. Every project the Menils sponsored was completed to the highest degree of detail and excellence. They, like Barnstone, were liberal Democrats who championed racial integration and social justice. The three found in one another a broadmindedness and intellectual curiosity that each valued and admired.

John's passion for art matched Dominique's. In 1954 they established the Menil Foundation to "support [the] advancement of religious, charitable, literary, scientific, and educational purposes," primarily through art.[12] Architecture was integral to the Menils' vision. Their patronage of Howard Barnstone brought him major commissions throughout his career.

THE MENIL HOUSE

The Barnstone-Menil relationship blossomed when the Menils turned to Barnstone, as Hugo Neuhaus had suggested, for repairs, alterations, and additions to their house. Johnson stepped out of the picture on completion of the house; for a long time he declined to publish it with his other work.[13] He was chagrined that the Menils had turned to the couturier Charles James (1906–1978) to design the interiors of their house.[14] James filled the house with sumptuous antique furniture and covered the walls in luscious dark fabric instead of composing the interior with Miesian austerity, which Johnson favored. Dominique de Menil also insisted, despite Johnson's objections, that two elongated windows be inserted

Dominique and John de Menil House (1951, Philip C. Johnson Associates with Cowell & Neuhaus), living room interiors by Charles James, 3363 San Felipe.

into Johnson's long unbroken (but for the flush glass entrance) brick entrance elevation, in order to bring natural light into the kitchen.

From 1952 to 1975, Barnstone made many minor alterations to the Menil House, supervised repairs, and provided services (such as designing and installing the Menils' Christmas decorations).[15] In 1960 he designed a modest, two-bedroom guesthouse that fit unobtrusively into the treed lawn behind the rear-facing driveway.[16] Barnstone's most visually significant alteration was occasioned by the brown, wilted condition of the tropical plants in the interior patio. An ice storm in February 1960 killed the tree that had shaded the patio, and the unprotected vegetation, scorched by the Texas sun, presented a dismal spectacle from the entrance hall and living room. In 1961, Barnstone designed what he called a "barrel vaulted

Menil House with "barrel-vaulted canopy" designed by Howard Barnstone (1962).

canopy" over the courtyard, which changed the look of the house by breaking the plane of the flat roof.[17] In 1965, he produced plans for an addition off the master bedroom wing on the east side of the house; it would be used to store the Menils' burgeoning art collection.[18] Instead of building this addition, the Menils decided to convert the garage into an office and collection storage area, using plans supplied by Barnstone's office.[19]

SCHLUMBERGER-SURENCO

From 1941 to 1957, John de Menil was responsible for the operations of Schlumberger-Surenco, a subsidiary of Schlumberger Overseas that undertook contracts in South America. Menil hired Barnstone to remodel and furnish the offices of Schlumberger Overseas (including Surenco) in Schlumberger's headquarters, located in a modernistic building at 2720 Leeland Avenue in the East End of Houston (1938, Russell Brown Company).[20] This job, from 1952, was the first in which Barnstone specified the use of Knoll furniture supplied by the

Drawing of the Menil House in Caracas, Venezuela, by Dominique de Menil for her children.

Knoll Planning Unit in New York.[21] John de Menil must have been pleased with the modern furniture designed by Florence Schust Knoll, Harry Bertoia, Eero Saarinen, and others, for he signed off on the truckloads of it that Barnstone specified for Schlumberger offices and apartments and housing for Schlumberger employees in South America. After the Leeland building was decommissioned, Bolton & Barnstone remodeled executive offices for Schlumberger in the Bank of the Southwest Building (1957) at 910 Travis Street in downtown Houston and remodeled the sixteenth floor of the Commerce Building (1958) at 914 Main Street downtown for Schlumberger-Surenco's offices.[22]

To organize Surenco's operations, John and Dominique lived in Trinidad and then in Caracas, Venezuela, during the Second World War, leaving their children in Houston with relatives. At that time, John coined the phrase "Wherever the drill goes, Schlumberger goes," which became Schlumberger's motto.[23] As the productive oil fields of Venezuela and other Latin American countries were developed, Schlumberger was indeed there. The company established "camps," not unlike the earlier oil and lumber camps in Texas, where workers and supervisors lived close to their company's operations. Dominique and John de Menil worked together during their time in South America. Dominique was especially involved in establishing Schlumberger's camps in the mid-1940s, designing and furnishing houses there before they commissioned Barnstone to continue that work.[24] She sent drawings to their children illustrating their life in South America, including one of the farmhouse in Caracas where they lived.

The earliest drawings in the Howard Barnstone Collection, archived at the Houston Metropolitan Research Center of the Houston Public Library, for the Surenco South American projects date from the summer of 1952. They are labeled "Howard Barnstone, Architect," indicating that John de Menil hired Barnstone for the Surenco projects before Barnstone began his partnership with Preston M. Bolton in late 1952. Maracaibo, Venezuela, on Lake Maracaibo in the northwestern corner of the country, was, like other towns where Schlumberger operated, a center of the country's oil and gas industry. Barnstone's three-bedroom house in Maracaibo set the style for those that followed in other camps. The similarity between the Menil's Caracas house and the Barnstone houses is striking, perhaps indicating Dominique de Menil's influence on Barnstone's work for the Schlumberger-Surenco projects. The vernacular aspect of the Surenco houses acknowledged local traditions and materials: one-story structures, shallow peaked roofs, patios, enclosed gardens, and multiple exposures in every room for cross-ventilation. Barnstone outfitted them with stylish modern furniture from Knoll and other North American vendors, and light fixtures that were shipped, often by air, from the United States.

Between 1952 and 1958, Bolton & Barnstone designed ten camps in Trinidad, Argentina, and Peru, but primarily in Venezuela, where producing oil fields were discovered one after another during the late 1940s and 1950s. At the time, the Surenco camps, labeled Camp A through Camp J, generally consisted of offices for personnel and garages for Schlumberger vehicles, often combined in one building; workshops; several two- or three-bedroom houses; a larger house for the manager; a dormitory for bachelors; a mess hall and, in some cases, a club; and recreational facilities such as tennis courts. Surenco's larger camps had a residential area next to, but separate from, the work area. Most of the camps were established on unimproved property where infrastructure, as well as new construction, was needed. Site plans for each camp depended on the size of the property and the number of personnel. These plans identified ancillary structures that

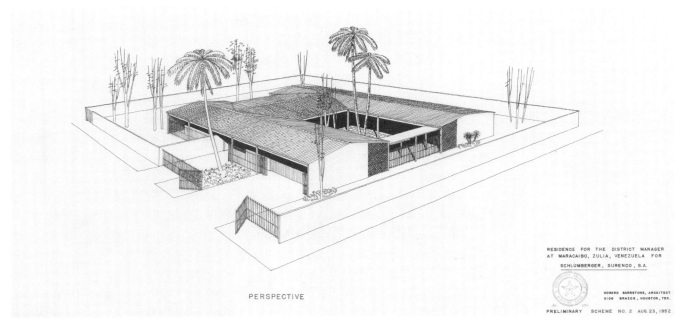

Schlumberger-Surenco District Manager's House (1952, Howard Barnstone), Maracaibo, Zulia, Venezuela.

Bolton & Barnstone designed, including perimeter walls and entrance gates, gas stations, pump houses, water wells and towers, wash racks for vehicles, schools, cable houses, radio towers, and generator houses.

Both Barnstone and Bolton made trips to South America to supervise and troubleshoot between 1952 and 1958. Barnstone sometimes stayed more than a month, visiting camps and working out of Schlumberger's regional offices in Caracas or Buenos Aires. These lucrative projects kept Bolton & Barnstone busy; everything from preliminary sketches to working drawings were produced in Houston and then translated into Spanish for local supervising architects and construction managers.[25]

Camp A, located on a steep hill in San Fernando, Trinidad (now Trinidad and Tobago), was planned with Colin Laird, the local supervising architect. A modern company-house prototype, decidedly different from the houses in other Surenco camps, was completed in 1957 and published in *Arts & Architecture*.[26] The ground floor, cut into the slope of the site, contained a parking bay, three patios, a dining room, a kitchen, a servant's room, and a bathroom. The street-level entrance, on the second floor, adjoined an open well containing a tight circular stair, with the living room, master bedroom, and bath to one side and two children's or guest bedrooms on the other side of the entry bay. The *Arts & Architecture* article noted, "Every room in the structure opens up completely to the easterly breeze." The overhanging screen of wooden louvers over the second floor was a practical device

Schlumberger Trinidad Company House (1957, Bolton & Barnstone with Colin Laird), San Fernando, Trinidad, British West Indies.

that could be closed to protect the house from wind-driven horizontal rains and to direct views to the hills in the distance. The article closes: "This house reflects considerable credit on a company that was willing to experiment and unwilling to accept the local, standard, expensive solution." With the exception of the misplaced "expensive," which should have been placed before "house" at the beginning of the sentence, this assertion is characteristic of Schlumberger's projects: the company never accepted standard solutions and thereby provided an environment that was innovative, beautiful, and functional—and designed by Bolton & Barnstone.

The Schlumberger-Surenco projects were complicated, challenging, and time consuming, but they provided Barnstone, the partner most responsible for them, with the kind of fast-paced life he enjoyed: one full of meaningful work that he could design by directing his staff, incessant travel, and the camaraderie of interesting international colleagues. During construction of the Surenco camps, Schlumberger projects directed by John de Menil and commissions based on his recommendation began to flow continuously to Bolton & Barnstone.

NEW YORK RESIDENTIAL WORK

Schlumberger's headquarters were moved from Paris to Houston in 1940 so that Schlumberger could continue to operate in the United States and Latin America despite the war in Europe.[27] For social and cultural as well as business reasons, the company's top executives, including John de Menil, maintained residences in New York, where an office remained after the war. In 1954, Dominique and John de Menil began renting four apartments in a wide redbrick Georgian townhouse just off Fifth Avenue at 120 East 80th Street. They occupied apartments 2A and 2B (the entire second floor) at the top of a graceful curving stair. Barnstone combined, reconfigured, and furnished the apartment. He also ordered furnishings from Knoll for the two one-bedroom apartments, 3B and 4B, which were kept for visitors, family, or Schlumberger personnel.[28] Barnstone's modifications included "modernizations"—removing moldings, wainscots, and a mantel. He added a bathroom and closets and installed a walk-in vault.[29]

In 1961, when the Menils were ready to move to a nearby townhouse on East 73rd Street that they had purchased before their lease on 80th Street expired, Barnstone went to New York to negotiate with the landlord, who was unhappy about changes made to the apartments.[30] Barnstone apparently succeeded, probably by agreeing that the Menils would pay the balance of the lease and continue to lease 3B, for the Menils moved out on their schedule.

Simone Swan remembered another incident in which Barnstone was called on for nonarchitectural services: "One morning John called to say he had summoned Howard to their townhouse on East 73rd Street because there was a bad smell—a stench throughout all five floors. By the afternoon, I learned that Howard had flown in from Houston and solved the problem by removing a dead rat from the air-conditioning system. That night we all walked to a Turkish restaurant, gave a toast to the rat, and Howard was off the next morning back to Houston."[31] Even outside of Houston, Howard had become indispensable to the Menils.

Barnstone remodeled the Menil Townhouse at 111 East 73rd Street, including the courtyard, which was terraced and laid out as a garden to exhibit their Max Ernst sculptures.[32] The street front of the five-story limestone-clad house was austere and unusually narrow. A series of plans with existing conditions laid out next to a new plan for each floor showed that Barnstone's remodeling primarily consisted of rearranging secondary spaces to obtain more closets, including a generous area for storing paintings under the stair, and installation of a central air-conditioning system that later harbored the infamous rat.[33]

Barnstone secured a number of residential architectural commissions in New York through John de Menil. In 1955, he remodeled an apartment for Germaine du Verteuil (1917–2001) and Marc-Marie-Joseph Demoustier (1913–1967), a Schlumberger-Surenco executive with whom Barnstone had worked in South America. Bolton & Barnstone also designed the Demoustiers' house in Houston at 608 Little John Lane (1955).[34]

In 1961–1962, Bolton & Barnstone remodeled the apartment of Dominique's sister Annette Schlumberger (1905–1993) and her husband, Henri-Georges Doll (1902–1991), an inventor and engineer who headed research and development at

Schlumberger.[35] According to his obituary in the *New York Times*, Doll was "credited with many of the advancements that elevated Schlumberger to pre-eminence in oil exploration."[36] For the Dolls' New York residence, Barnstone combined three apartments on the thirty-first floor of the thirty-three-story Ritz Tower (built in 1931 as the St. Moritz Hotel, Emery Roth) at 50 Central Park South on the corner of Sixth Avenue. The combined apartments filled the floor that had housed a dinner-dance club and "sky garden" near the top of the setback skyscraper. The generous terrace, with stunning views of Central Park, would have been a significant attraction to the Dolls. Barnstone's changes included replacing perimeter oak flooring throughout where wall-to-wall carpeting nails had split the wood; reconfiguring and eliminating redundant kitchens; rewiring and adding new lighting; installing air-conditioning; and applying three coats of paint, "due to the large amount of new plaster patching required." The cost of the remodeling was approximately $43,500 (including Barnstone's $6,200 fee).[37]

In 1967–1968, with his next partner, Eugene Aubry, Barnstone remodeled the third-floor apartment at 211 East 49th Street for Krishna Roy (1926–2000) and Jean Riboud (1919–1985). Jean Riboud became president and chief executive officer of Schlumberger in 1965, a position he held for twenty years, until six months before his death from cancer.[38] The Ribouds' choice of neighborhood was not surprising, since their friends were artists, politicians, and writers rather than businessmen.[39] The four-story townhouse was one of eleven houses purchased and remodeled by Charlotte Sorchan in 1919; she combined all the backyards into a common garden that became known as Amster Yard. The sculptor Isamu Noguchi, the designer Billy Baldwin, and other celebrities and artists lived in Amster Yard (211–215 East 49th) and shared the garden during the time the Ribouds lived there.[40] A plan of the Ribouds' small apartment, drawn in the Barnstone office, specifies modern and antique furniture in all the rooms. Barnstone sought to control the furniture in spaces he designed. He regularly ordered furniture for his clients and indicated exact locations within rooms. In 1978, the Ribouds moved to the ninth floor of the Carlton House at 680 Madison Avenue and 61st Street. Barnstone recovered pieces from their 49th Street apartment and ordered new furniture for the much larger apartment.[41]

Adelaide de Menil (b. 1935), a photographer and the daughter of Dominique and John de Menil, and her husband, Edmund Snow Carpenter (1922–2011), an anthropologist known for his work with the Inuit people, purchased a townhouse at 163 East 69th Street in 1970.[42] The house had been chopped up into apartments, so Adelaide de Menil and Ted Carpenter engaged Barnstone to restore it to a single-family house. After four years of planning, they abandoned this project.

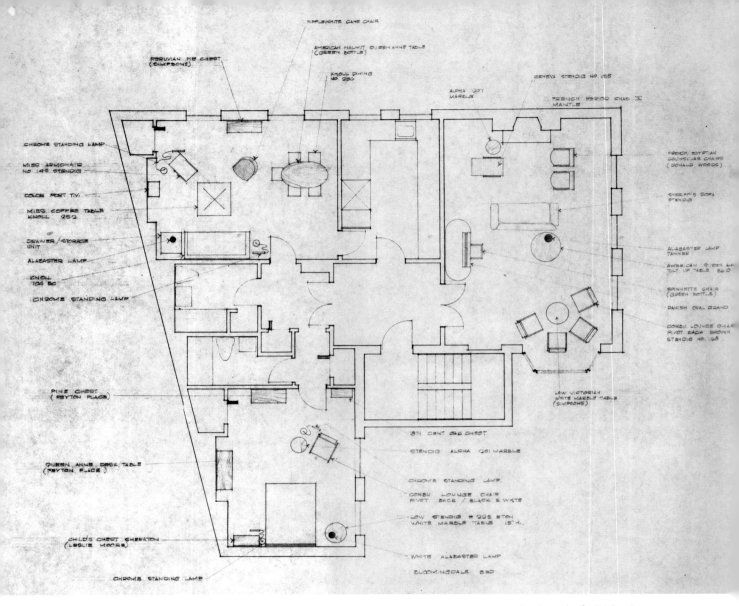

Furniture plan for Krishna Roy and Jean Riboud apartment (1968, Barnstone & Aubry), 211 East 49th, New York City.

Adelaide later wrote to Howard: "The most serious problem with 163 East 69th is that everything took so long. When we decided to abandon that project, we decided never to work with you again. The trouble is that you are so damned talented."[43]

Adelaide and Ted Carpenter moved instead to a co-op apartment in the distinctive sixteen-story Gainsborough Studios (1908, Charles W. Buckham) at 222 Central Park South, and despite Adelaide's misgivings, they hired Barnstone to remodel two apartments into one.[44] The building, designed as an artists' cooperative with only two apartments per floor, had eighteen-foot-tall studios and double-height windows that provided northern light on the front of the sixteen-story (eight double-height stories) building overlooking Central Park.[45] Glenn Heim, a former Basilian scholastic who took courses at the University of St. Thomas taught by Dominique de Menil, found his true calling as an artist and a carpenter. Heim constructed the apartment for Adelaide and Ted in the Gainsborough and installed a stone floor in the living room from an old French monastery.[46]

Howard Barnstone worked with the physicist and Schlumberger vice president for research Michel-Marie Gouilloud (1930–1997) in another distinguished New York apartment building. Gouilloud's co-op was in midtown Manhattan's Murray Hill on the top floor of a nine-story building at 34 East 30th Street.[47] It was with such clients as the Demoustiers, Dolls, Ribouds, Carpenters, and Gouilloud that Barnstone loved to work. They were, like the Menils, sophisticated, cosmopolitan patrons who respected his modern vision and did not quibble about the high cost of his ideas. Barnstone hated budgets; the Menil projects usually had none.

NEW YORK COMMERCIAL WORK

Barnstone's commercial work in New York was also the result of his Menil-Schlumberger connections. The projects included Schlumberger Ltd. offices in the J. Paul Getty Building at 660 Madison Avenue (1958, Emery Roth & Sons); new corporate headquarters for Schlumberger at 277 Park Avenue (1965, Emery Roth & Sons); offices for Istel, Lepercq & Co. in the Wall and Hanover Building at 63 Wall Street (1929, Delano & Aldrich); offices for Lepercq de Neuflize & Co. at 345 Park Avenue (1967–1969, Emery Roth & Sons); and the Alexandre Iolas Sculpture Gallery at 15 East 55th Street (demolished in 1980 for Johnson/Burgee's AT&T Building).[48]

In 1961, when Schlumberger's corporate headquarters were still in Houston, Barnstone redesigned the ten-room New York offices of Schlumberger's small technical and advisory staff on the fifteenth floor of the Getty Building. He did not reconfigure the conventional office floor plan but instead turned what he called "modern Chinese Chippendale" décor into a sleek modern space.[49] Barnstone's specifications called for all ceilings to be painted flat black, horizontal

Library for Schlumberger Ltd. (1961, Bolton & Barnstone), 660 Madison Avenue, New York City.

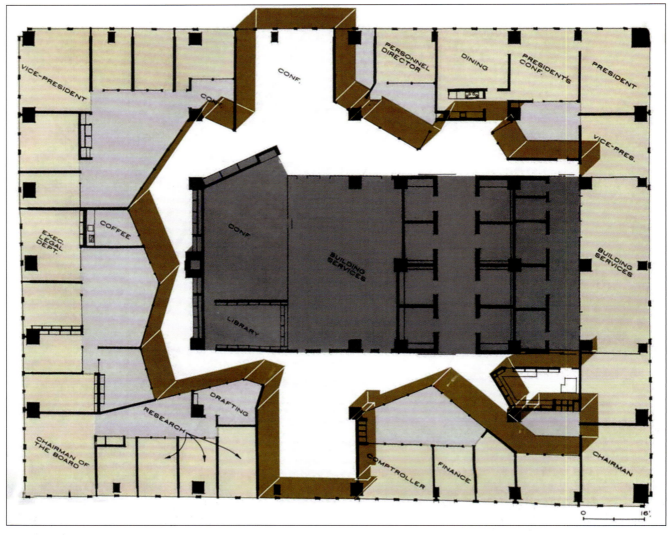

Schlumberger Ltd., "wiggle walls" office plan (1966, Barnstone & Aubry), 277 Park Avenue, New York City.

trim painted gloss black, and everything else painted stark white. He even specified that the conventional black telephones be exchanged for white ones. All new furniture and draperies were ordered from Sally Walsh in Houston, who, after leaving Knoll, became an independent interior designer.[50]

Barnstone became the de facto architect for Schlumberger when Jean Riboud and John de Menil decided to move the Schlumberger headquarters to New York from Houston in 1965 after Pierre Schlumberger retired and Riboud took his place as president.[51] The company moved to the forty-third and forty-fourth floors of 277 Park Avenue in 1966 after a remodeling of the space by Barnstone & Aubry that was "very minimal in detailing and spatially active in plan," as

Schlumberger Ltd., office corridor with "wiggle wall" (1966, Howard Barnstone & Partners) 277 Park Avenue, New York City.

Robert A. M. Stern, Thomas Mellins, and David Fishman describe it.[52] What distinguished these offices were the zigzag "wiggle walls" of angled glass that produced a dynamic sense of movement and provided openness, an innovative concept in office design before the popularization of the office landscape.[53] Barnstone & Aubry revealed that the idea for these unconventional walls came from a "squiggly doodle," no doubt drawn by Barnstone.[54] Barnstone covered the floors in sisal, painted the walls at the core dark brown but white everywhere else, and installed modern furniture, including pieces from Schlumberger's former office. In addition to the imaginative architectural interiors, John de Menil lent paintings and other works of art that were spotlighted throughout the Schlumberger offices to create a sense of drama and of excellence in a workaday environment.[55]

Jean Riboud had come to New York in 1946 to open the American branch of André Istel & Co., a French investment bank owned by Istel, a friend of Riboud's father. Schlumberger was Istel's major client, and Riboud so impressed the Schlumbergers that Marcel persuaded Riboud to join Schlumberger Ltd. in 1951.[56] This connection to what became Istel, Lepercq & Co. and then Lepercq de Neuflize & Co. provided Barnstone with two more office-remodeling projects in New York. The first was on the fourteenth floor of a venerable Wall Street building. Istel, Lepercq had been in the building since the early 1950s. In 1960, Bolton & Barnstone received the commission to remodel it. One plan shows the

A CONSTRUCTIVE CONNECTION

Istel suite on the corner of the building overlooking Wall and Hanover Streets. A letter from Istel's Bruno Desforges outlined the project: repaint the whole office; improve the lighting and the ceiling; carpet the whole office; improve and perhaps relocate the reception and switchboard; and build a new guest office.[57] Such changes were similar to those undertaken for most office remodelings, but Barnstone's sense of space and his affinity for crisp, modern solutions made his projects stand out.

In 1968, Barnstone & Aubry remodeled the Lepercq de Neuflize & Co. offices on the twenty-third floor of 345 Park Avenue, across 52nd Street from the Seagram Building (1958, Ludwig Mies van der Rohe and Philip Johnson).[58] A *New York Times* article lauded the remodeled offices as an outstanding example of the "new practices" of "office landscape" (open planning). Paul A. Lepercq (1922–1999) said that he wanted "the kind of place where one can walk around with pleasure—hallways bore me. I did not want the feeling of one desk after another boom, boom, boom."[59] In a corporate history of Schlumberger that is primarily a biography of Riboud, Ken Auletta described Riboud's office, furnished and designed by Barnstone: "His New York office is a snug corner—sixteen feet by twenty—with beige walls. . . . [It] has a single telephone with just two lines, and no private bathroom; there are white blinds on the windows, and a simple beige sisal carpet on the floor. His desk is a long, rectangular teak table with chrome legs."[60] Barnstone's invoices corroborate this description of what is labeled "conference room number 1" on the plan.[61] A huge custom-made octagonal table served as the partners' desk. The conference room was configured as a modified octagon, and even the stands on the trading floor were arranged as an octagon.[62] The staff area behind the entrance was divided into separate cubicles with low, movable partitions.

In 1975, Philippa de Menil (b. 1947), the youngest child of Dominique and John, and her fiancé, Heiner Friedrich, consulted with Barnstone about remodeling a former fire station at 155 Mercer Street in Lower Manhattan into a Sufi mosque, the Masjid Al-Fara, for their Dia Art Foundation.[63] The mosque opened in 1980 with a Dan Flavin light installation and quarters for Sheikh Muzaffer Ozad, an Istanbul-based dervish and Philippa's spiritual adviser. When Philippa and Heiner married there in a Sufi ceremony in 1979, before the mosque officially opened, she changed her name to Sheikha Fariha Fatima al-Jerrahi. Some writers have suggested that in her spirituality and dedication to art, Fariha de Menil is the sibling most like her mother.[64] Adelaide and Fariha worked with Howard Barnstone, but their siblings did not. For Christophe de Menil (b. 1933), Frank Gehry remodeled an East 69th Street apartment in the late 1970s, and Charles Gwathmey designed a house for François de Menil (b. 1945) in East Hampton,

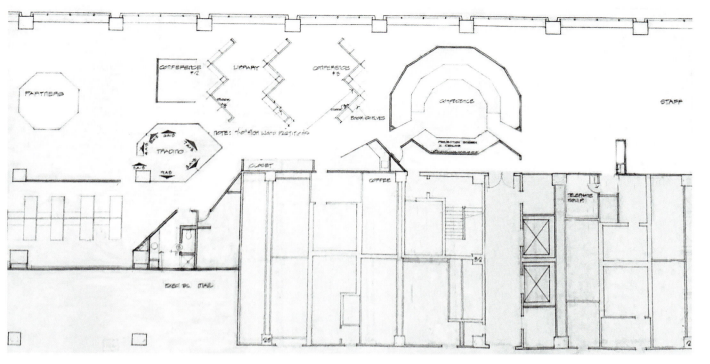

Lepercq de Neuflize & Co., office plan (1968, Barnstone & Aubry), 345 Park Avenue, New York City.

completed in 1982, and remodeled houses for him in Houston and Santa Monica before François himself became an architect.[65] Georges de Menil (b. 1940) lived in Paris. Each of the five Menil children had a trust fund worth approximately $57 million in the early 1980s.[66] Each, like their parents, used those resources to invest in art and architecture.

AT HOME IN HOUSTON

Barnstone, alone and with partners, is perhaps best known for his residential projects in Houston. Bolton & Barnstone produced Miesian houses, including the house for Germaine and Marc Demoustier and their five daughters on a three-acre wooded site in the Sherwood Forest subdivision, off Memorial Drive.[67] The pink brick elevation of the symmetrical house was framed in white-painted steel with large black-painted steel-framed windows facing the rear of the property, where a private sitting room and terrace were built on the sloping site below the master bedroom suite. Typical of Barnstone's Miesian houses, the Demoustier House had an interior courtyard. The house was designed and constructed between 1953 and 1955. After the Demoustiers moved to New York, they sold the house in 1958 to

A CONSTRUCTIVE CONNECTION

Anne Schlumberger and C. Leroy Melcher, Jr., House, before renovation (1949, Hamilton Brown), 13 Tiel Way, Houston.

Grace McMillan and Henry David, who engaged Barnstone to modify it. When it was sold in 1965 to Lawrence Marcus, vice president of Neiman-Marcus, Barnstone was again consulted about remodeling.[68]

Two of Pierre Schlumberger's five children by his first marriage lived in Houston: Pierre M. Schlumberger, Jr. (b. 1941) and Anne-Marie Louise Schlumberger Brown (b. 1939). Barnstone remodeled residences for both of them. Pete Schlumberger and his wife, Lesley, lived at 528 West Friar Tuck Lane in Memorial, a house originally designed by Hamilton Brown. Barnstone designed a pool pavilion for them in 1967.[69] Anne Schlumberger, who became an architect, engaged Barnstone for several projects in the 1960s and 1970s. In 1962, she and her husband, C. LeRoy Melcher, Jr. (1938–1981), bought a house at 13 Tiel Way and had Howard Barnstone & Partners extensively remodel it, doubling its size. Barnstone removed walls on the interior to create larger spaces and added an angled two-story wing at the northwest corner of the house, where a striking rear façade of full-height windows and a wide balcony on the second floor looked onto a patio and new circular swimming pool.[70] Gene Aubry said of this project

Melcher House, after alterations and additions (1965, Howard Barnstone & Partners).

that it was the most "typically Howard" of all the domestic projects produced by their office.[71]

LeRoy Melcher continued the family loyalty to Barnstone, even after he and Anne were divorced. In 1967, Barnstone added to a townhouse for him at 4527 West Alabama Avenue in Afton Oaks and designed a boathouse and pavilion for him in Seabrook, Texas.[72] Anne and her second husband, Dr. Jules Bohnn, bought the Robert W. Wier House in Broadacres at 1411 North Boulevard (1928, Birdsall P. Briscoe) and engaged Barnstone to remodel it in 1972. As in the Tiel Way house, Barnstone added a glassed breakfast room off the kitchen, overlooking the back garden, and orchestrated minor remodeling of the original house.[73]

The Schlumberger and Menil families commissioned Barnstone to remodel or add to their Houston houses, but he never designed a new house for any of them. Anne's parents, Pierre Schlumberger (1914–1986) and Claire Simone Schwob d'Héricourt (1917–1959), moved to a house in River Oaks at 2970 Lazy Lane (1934, James C. Mackenzie with Charles W. Oliver; Birdsall P. Briscoe, consulting architect), an unusually planned neo-Georgian house.[74] After Claire Schlumberger's sudden death and Pierre's subsequent marriage to Maria da

Diniz Conceição, Barnstone remodeled the library of the Lazy Lane house in 1961 and, the following year, added a dressing room and bathroom to the house. As he did for the Menils, Barnstone supervised Christmas decorations for the Schlumbergers.[75]

SWEENEY AND GALVESTON

Bolton & Barnstone remodeled the Houston apartment of Laura Harden and James Johnson Sweeney on the fifteenth floor of 1400 Hermann Drive in 1961, the year John de Menil brought Sweeney, former director of the Guggenheim Museum, to head the Museum of Fine Arts, Houston.[76] Sweeney revolutionized the Houston art scene with his dramatic exhibitions. Sweeney and Barnstone became friends as a result of Sweeney's support and encouragement for Barnstone's first book, *The Galveston That Was* (1966). The book was made possible by John de Menil's financial backing and Sweeney's arrangement to have the Museum of Fine Arts sponsor its publication by Macmillan.

Barnstone discovered the blocks upon blocks of remarkable Victorian buildings on excursions to the seaside city of Galveston, fifty miles southeast of Houston, in the 1950s. He especially remembered one tour he led for Dominique and John de Menil and their guest, the art critic Alfred Frankenstein, which concluded with lunch at the Staub-designed house of Katherine Risher and Dr. Edward Randall after a stop at Commodore Bob Sealy's house, The Open Gates (McKim, Mead & White, 1891). At the time of Sealy's death in 1979, the house was virtually untouched except for a redecoration in 1915 by Elsie de Wolfe. Seeing many of these historic houses in a dilapidated condition, Barnstone felt compelled to compile a written and visual record before they disappeared. He sought help from the Guggenheim Foundation and Galveston's Moody Foundation in 1960, but both turned him down because they did not award grants to individuals. After talking to Sweeney, who had proposed documenting Galveston's nineteenth-century architecture to the museum's trustees, Barnstone's project came alive. The two approached John de Menil, who was enthusiastic and willing to finance the project. Menil, who insisted that the production be of the highest caliber, engaged his friend Henri Cartier-Bresson, also a lifelong friend of Jean Riboud's, to take photographs for the book. Before Barnstone even knew of this arrangement, Cartier-Bresson was on his way to Houston. Barnstone, who had already spoken to the American architectural photographer Ezra Stoller, had the embarrassing task of disinviting Stoller to take photographs for the book because Cartier-Bresson refused to have another photographer involved. This was an example of the control that came with Menil largesse. Cartier-Bresson's photographs were beautiful, soulful, and evocative of Galveston's aging neighborhoods, but they were not architectural. John de Menil was able to convince Cartier-Bresson to allow the Stoller pictures in the book, and Stoller graciously agreed to come back into the project.[77]

Peter Brink, in *"The Galveston That Was*: Requiem or Inspiration?," a conference paper delivered in 1989, observed: "Howard loved the architecture. The romantic allusions throughout the designs fitted perfectly with his love of the nostalgic . . . Howard also loved the drama associated with the old wealthy families of Galveston and the leading roles they played in the intrigue of Galveston's economic and political life. For him it was high theater and only added to Galveston's allure."[78] Gene Aubry, in acknowledging, as many have done, that this book spurred the preservation of Galveston's historic building stock, said that writing *The Galveston That Was* should be considered one of Howard Barnstone's greatest accomplishments.

HOUSES ELSEWHERE

The gallery owner Alexandre Iolas, a friend and art adviser of the Menils', engaged Barnstone to remodel his house in Athens, Greece, in 1961. The nature of any remodeling by Barnstone is unknown, but he did make at least one trip to Athens with Iolas to look at the house and discuss the project.[79]

Simone Swan asked Barnstone to design a summerhouse for her in Peconic, New York, on Long Island Sound, but she was disappointed with his plans and eventually turned to Charles W. Moore to design her house.[80] The Barnstone-designed house was to have been built of unpainted redwood siding with a black composition roof.[81] In a letter to Barnstone written just after she received the plans in October 1972, Swan wrote: "The drawings turn me off because: very little attention was paid to my desires (four bedrooms! separate study! all upstairs; the locker-room was to replace closets, now there are both closets & locker-room; I wanted my bedroom-study downstairs, etc.). The elevation shows a kind of Bay area townhouse with townhouse balconies. In other words, it's all very neat, very resellable but it's not me. I just want to cool it right now."[82]

For a brief time, Barnstone must have convinced Swan to move forward with the project. A letter in December 1972 to the surveyor for the Swan House, James P. Knowles, reveals that Barnstone was not well:

> I had a very slight mania siege some weeks ago. . . . After a few disastrous encounters, and lots of money spent, one Sunday morning as I put down the phone to a friend in Trinidad, I realized that it had been a totally unnecessary call, and I had taken two serious steps backward. I have this all under control by having doubled the dose [of lithium] and will continue that for another three or four days. What is interesting, is that while the illness is totally chemical, events in one's life, and there were a few disappointing ones and one that was elative, seem to water down the lithium and require adjustment of the dose based on events.[83]

This account concerning his bipolar disorder seems to indicate that Barnstone was adjusting his medication on his own. Even with his talented assistant, Tony Frederick, managing projects at the time, when Barnstone suffered from depression (or mania), he apparently was not able to conjure his best ideas. Nevertheless, his practice continued apace with the help of Frederick and others in his office.

Barnstone's most impressive residential project outside Houston, the Krishna and Jean Riboud House in Scottsdale, Arizona, was designed and built at this time. The commission dated to late 1961 but was not completed until 1974. Although he was in partnership with Bolton at the time the project began, Barnstone worked with Tony Frederick on the design that was built.

Krishna Roy Riboud was born into a wealthy family in Dhaka, India. After her father died, when she was ten, her maternal uncle Soumyendranath Tagore, a Marxist revolutionary leader, raised her in Calcutta. Through the sponsorship of Lois and Spencer Kellogg, Jr., Krishna Roy enrolled in 1943 at Wellesley College (with letters of introduction from John Dewey and Albert Einstein), and during her years in college, she spent winter vacations at the Kellogg House in Scottsdale.[84] She came to love the Sonoran high desert, and her longing for it prompted the Ribouds to build their winter house there.

Because they planned to use the Scottsdale house for only a short time each year, the Ribouds asked for a secure, low-profile house with a two-bedroom guest suite separated from the master bedroom suite and a large open space for living, dining, and cooking.[85] The one-story adobe-like house is nestled into the side of a hill and undulates with the topography on a 5.9-acre site. The buff stucco exterior and interior were finished simply. Views of the surrounding landscape were framed by windows on the east (back) side of the house. In the interior, Navajo blankets and rugs, which Barnstone collected, decorated the white walls.[86] This house, like those in South America, shows that even though he disparaged

OPPOSITE, TOP Krishna and Jean Riboud House (1975, Howard Barnstone, FAIA, Architect), 38850 North Spanish Boot Road, Scottsdale, Arizona.

OPPOSITE, BOTTOM Riboud House, Scottsdale, Arizona, plan.

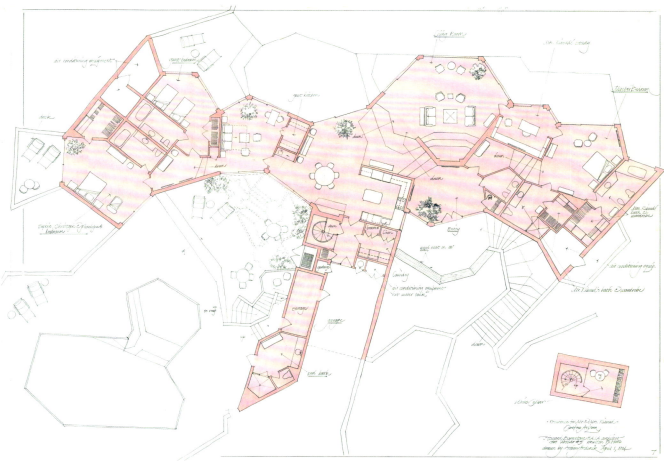

regionalism, Barnstone could be very sensitive to the natural and cultural landscapes of the places where he worked.

While Barnstone was working with Adelaide de Menil and Ted Carpenter on their apartment in the Gainsborough Studios, he was also involved with them in an extraordinary project on Long Island. Around 1970, wandering around East Hampton, Adelaide de Menil was struck by the many seventeenth- and eighteenth-century structures falling into ruin along Route 27A, a busy highway. No one seemingly wanted to restore and live in such small, antiquated houses. She decided to preserve them by moving them from the highway to another site. She and Carpenter bought a forty-acre beachfront potato farm in East Hampton and began working with the New York architect William P. Chafee and then with the local firm Morey & Hollenbeck. Adelaide de Menil looked for deteriorating structures within twenty miles of their potato farm. She ultimately moved seven structures—two barns and five houses—which she bought for prices ranging from $1,000 to $60,000. Barnstone became involved in the project in 1974. Morey & Hollenbeck remained as associate architects after Barnstone took charge.

The Baker Barn became a drive-through entrance gate. Next to it, the Erwitt House (also called the Phoebe House, after a ghost story of a long-ago resident named Phoebe who died there) was restored as a caretaker's cottage. The main house was assembled from the Purple House (which was not purple), the Bridgehampton Barn (which became the living room), and a greenhouse structure designed by Barnstone to connect the two. Three other houses—the Peach House, Hand House, and Cutchogue House—became guesthouses. They were assembled in a village-like configuration that the *Houston Chronicle* critic Ann Holmes described as "vintage New Englanders in architectural dialog with one another."[87]

The sturdy buildings were restored with integrity, using original or hand-hewn wood of the same vintage obtained from other places, plaster (not sheetrock), milk paint, and original seventeenth- and eighteenth-century hardware throughout the structures. The thick shingles of the Purple House were removed and turned inside out. Because they were extra-long, additional shingles needed for it and the other houses had to be hand cut in Maine. Holmes considered these simple, unadorned buildings "elegant in their proportions and ascetic plainness." The project, in addition to local and state design awards, won a national American Institute of Architects Honor Award in 1978, the AIA's highest distinction for design excellence. The awards jury commented: "This project exhibits a level of care about the whole project that is amazing and wonderful. In detail after detail the issues have been faced and thoughtfully dealt with. The sense of oldness of the buildings comes through clearly, while the underground inclusion of new and

OPPOSITE Adelaide de Menil/Ted Carpenter Complex (1974–1981, Howard Barnstone, FAIA, Architect with Morey & Hollenbeck, associate architects), Further Lane, East Hampton, Long Island, New York.

technical areas insures extended use."[88] Indeed the interiors, all white and natural wood, were serene in their simplicity and comfortably modern in their sparse furnishings and the latest technology.

Barnstone must have immensely enjoyed working on the East Hampton buildings. In writing *The Galveston That Was*, according to Michelangelo Sabatino, he explored his nostalgia and despair by documenting the "ghostly charm" of the mostly uncared-for Victorian houses of a bygone era of wealth and accomplishment. In East Hampton, Barnstone was able to do something other than contemplate ruin. He meticulously restored and rehabilitated seven buildings as if they had undergone rigorous psychoanalysis. The decade of the 1970s was a productive time for Barnstone. He became immersed in the Menils' Houston world of the Rothko Chapel, Rice University, and Do-ville, the Menil Foundation's Montrose domain, where he produced plan after plan for art storage facilities and museum buildings that were never built.

UNIVERSITY OF ST. THOMAS

In 1956, Dominique and John de Menil convinced the Basilian Fathers, who administered the Roman Catholic University of St. Thomas in Houston, to commission Philip Johnson to produce a master plan and design buildings for a three-block campus site in Houston's Montrose neighborhood adjacent to the J. W. Link House (1912, Sanguinet, Staats & Barnes), which the religious order had purchased as the university's initial building in 1947. This relationship alerted the Menils to the Montrose area, where they would buy more than fifty houses and vacant lots, engaging Barnstone for multiple remodeling projects there.[89] The Menils helped St. Thomas procure property to expand its campus, and they paid Johnson's architectural fees for the master plan of 1956–1957. John de Menil suggested Bolton & Barnstone as Johnson's associate for construction of the first three buildings at the university. Thus, Barnstone became involved with Houston's Catholic university.

In 1966, Barnstone & Aubry were commissioned to design the first non-Johnson building on the University of Virginia–like academic mall, M. D. Anderson Hall, for the biology department. The first building on the west side of the mall, Anderson Hall was directly across from Strake Hall (1958, Philip Johnson). Along with Strake, Johnson's original buildings—Jones Hall (1958) and Welder Hall (1959)—provided the template for Barnstone & Aubry's building as well as others that eventually filled out Johnson's master plan: the Doherty Library (1971, Eugene Aubry and Wilson, Morris, Crain & Anderson), Cullen Hall (1979, S. I. Morris Associates), Robertson Hall (1994, Merriman Holt), and Malloy Hall (2001, Ziegler Cooper). Anderson Hall has a central bay of black steel-framed double-height glass flanked by solid two-story walls of rose-colored St. Joe brick. It is set behind a continuation of Johnson's portico of black steel columns and decks.[90] Barnstone & Aubry were commissioned in 1967 to design the university's first dormitory, named for Father Vincent J. Guinan, the first president of the university. Guinan Hall, completed in 1971, was demolished for a new, larger dormitory of the same name in 2003. Aubry followed the Johnson template in designing the university library at the south end of the mall, the site where Johnson had proposed placing the university chapel.

ROTHKO CHAPEL

Howard Barnstone readily admitted that he had little to do with the design of the Rothko Chapel. In a lecture to his architecture students in the chapel, he said: "In all of the magazines . . . I am credited along with my former partner, Eugene Aubry, as the architect for this building, and technically I guess that's true. But to be honest with you and history and myself, I can claim little for the design and plan of this building."[91]

The Rothko Chapel is the result of a six-year saga involving the donors, Dominique and John de Menil; the architect Philip Johnson; and the artist Mark Rothko. In 1964, following the sudden death of Jermayne MacAgy, Dominique and John de Menil commissioned Rothko to paint a series of canvases for a Catholic chapel to be built at the University of St. Thomas.[92] Inspired by the Chapel of the Rosary in Vence, France (1951), with stained-glass windows and murals by Henri Matisse, Dominique de Menil wanted the St. Thomas chapel to be a simple structure containing the work of a great artist. Rothko had been captivated by his visit in 1950

Howard Barnstone lecturing to architecture students, October 21, 1971, in the Rothko Chapel (1971, Barnstone & Aubry), 3900 Yupon, Houston.

to the Basilica of Santa Maria Assunta on the island of Torcello, Italy, where the portentous fourteenth-century mosaic at the entrance (*The Last Judgement*) is juxtaposed with a luminous mosaic of the Madonna and Child set in the apse amid a field of radiant gold, a confrontation Rothko said he tried to duplicate in the Houston chapel.[93] The needs of the Basilian Fathers and the university receded in importance. As Johnson's efforts to satisfy Rothko's criticisms took on more monumental form, the university administration responded by moving the chapel off the axis of the academic mall to a site alongside Barnstone & Aubry's Anderson Hall. Barnstone, as Johnson's associate architect and confidant of the Menils, was involved with the dozen or so schemes that Johnson presented, all rejected by Rothko or the Menils.

Rothko wanted a simple frame for his work, not an architectural statement. The Menils sided with Rothko rather than Johnson over Rothko's critique of Johnson's design of the towering chapel skylight. Johnson bowed out of the project in 1967. The next year, the Basilian Fathers withdrew from the chapel project. The Menils considered building the chapel, now conceived of as an ecumenical chapel rather than a Roman Catholic church, in the Texas Medical Center in 1969.[94] Instead, they settled on a site they owned three blocks west of the university's academic mall. As Barnstone told it, when Johnson said he would have nothing

A CONSTRUCTIVE CONNECTION   149

more to do with the project, Mark Rothko said, "Please have Howard Barnstone who is your partner [associate] . . . deal with me."[95] The Menils would no doubt have asked Barnstone & Aubry to take over the chapel, but it is interesting that Barnstone wanted the record to indicate that it was Rothko who chose him. Even so, Barnstone and Aubry found the collaboration with Dominique de Menil and Rothko trying. Aubry said: "We drove ourselves to distraction over it. We made about eight miniature chapels, each time incorporating some new scheme Dominique came up with. She would have us set up these models, and then she would call in architects from all over the world to give her ideas on how to make it work. What a circus!"[96]

The Rothko Chapel, containing fourteen monumental dark paintings by Rothko, became a contemplative space for all religions. Rothko never saw the paintings installed in the chapel; he committed suicide on February 25, 1970, two days after approving Aubry's final plans for the building and the placement of the paintings. Between 1965 and 1968, Howard Barnstone frequently met with Rothko in his New York studio. Barnstone usually arrived from Houston around two in the afternoon, after Rothko had already consumed half a bottle of scotch. The two of them sat around the studio, contemplated the chapel and Rothko's work, drank, and commiserated.[97]

Dominique de Menil spoke of how shocked she was when she first saw the completed paintings. She had expected "bright colors."[98] Although she and many others saw deep spirituality and transcendence in the paintings, the art must also have been born of considerable pain and brooding, which Barnstone's angst may have added to. After suffering a major episode of depression in 1968 that left him unable to work, Barnstone was hospitalized at the University of Texas Medical Branch in Galveston. Aubry finished the chapel design, with Philip Johnson consulting on the design of the entrance and the location of the reflecting pool, which became the site of Barnett Newman's (1905–1970) sculpture *Broken Obelisk*, an integral part of the chapel experience.[99]

THE MENILS AND RICE UNIVERSITY

Dominique and John de Menil supported the University of St. Thomas by underwriting salaries and professional fees for the art and art history department and, at the end of each year, writing a check to cover the university's deficit. In return, they expected the support of the board of trustees, the authority to recruit new faculty members for the art department, and commitment to the construction of

OPPOSITE Rothko Chapel (1971, Barnstone & Aubry), exterior, with *Broken Obelisk* (1963–1967, Barnett Newman).

a university chapel. Their relationship with the St. Thomas administration was tested when it and the university's board of trustees chose not to endorse John de Menil's proposal to expand the board and appoint more non-Catholic members. After months of negotiation, the Menils withdrew from the University of St. Thomas in 1968, buying back almost all the art, books, equipment, and real estate they had given to the school.[100]

At the time, Rice University was struggling to establish an art program. John de Menil negotiated an agreement with Rice to bring art and art history instructors from the University of St. Thomas and establish the Institute for the Arts, where the Menils could continue programs they had initiated at St. Thomas.[101] Although they gave the art library to Rice, all the artwork bought back from St. Thomas rejoined the Menils' collection.

In January 1969, while Barnstone was hospitalized, the Menils invited Aubry to dinner. As the meal concluded, John de Menil mentioned that in ten weeks they would need a 6,000-square-foot building for an exhibition that the institute was bringing to Rice from the Museum of Modern Art in late March, and he wanted Gene "to draw it." The exhibition, *The Machine as Seen at the End of the Mechanical Age*, would close in New York on February 9 and was then scheduled to travel to Houston. The three sat around the dinner table discussing possibilities that could be constructed in eight weeks. Aubry came up with the idea of cladding a shedlike wood-framed building with galvanized sheet iron. The catalogue for the New York exhibition, which was bound in "tin-can steel," perhaps served as inspiration for Aubry's cladding plan.[102] Galvanized sheet iron could be put up cheaply and quickly. And in its subversive rejection of durability and stylishness, it symbolized American modernism's countercultural turn at the end of the 1960s. John de Menil was elated. He got up from the table and called the general contractor Gervais Bell. Bell responded: "We will be there in the morning." According to Aubry, staff people from the P. G. Bell Construction Company arrived at Rice the next day to begin negotiations. As Aubry observed: "That's the way Mr. D. worked."[103] Rice, understanding that this was to be only a temporary building, provided a site at the edge of the campus in one corner of the stadium parking lot. The building, affectionately known as the Art Barn, stood for forty-five years, until its demolition in 2014. In 1970, a second component of the Menils' Institute for the Arts, the Rice Media Center, also designed by Aubry, was constructed next to the museum; it was still standing at the time of this writing. In 1969, Barnstone & Aubry also drew plans for the Rice art department offices and library on an upper floor of the new Allen Center office building (1967, Lloyd, Morgan, & Jones) on the Rice campus.[104]

Rice Art Museum, known as the Art Barn (1969, Barnstone & Aubry, demolished 2014), Rice University, Houston.

Howard Barnstone, Eugene Aubry, and Philip Johnson were not the Menils' only architects. Dominique de Menil was captivated by Louis I. Kahn (1901–1974) and his esoteric, poetic approach to architecture.[105] She and John de Menil pledged two million dollars toward construction of a performing and visual art center at Rice. Rice's board of trustees hired Kahn in October 1969 at the behest of the board chair, H. Malcolm Lovett. Kahn's multibuilding complex for Rice, designed for a site behind the Fondren Library, would have been brilliant, had it been built. It never proceeded past schematic design, though, because the estimated cost for the project was astronomical, far beyond what the university had budgeted for a single building. Moreover, the Menils' relationship with Rice was unsteady. Stephen James, in his comprehensive discussion of Kahn's Rice project, concluded that its quiet termination in 1970 is what led the Menils to begin their own institution instead of trying to work with Rice.[106] In light of this decision, the Menils asked Kahn to plan an art storage building for property they owned next to the Rothko Chapel. Nevertheless, they continued to support the Institute for the Arts at Rice until the Menil Collection museum opened in 1987.

A CONSTRUCTIVE CONNECTION   153

GRAY IS THE COLOR

AN EXHIBITION OF GRISAILLE PAINTING
XIIIth-XXth CENTURIES
ORGANIZED BY THE INSTITUTE FOR THE ARTS
RICE UNIVERSITY

RICE MUSEUM, HOUSTON, TEXAS
OCTOBER 19, 1973 to JANUARY 19, 1974

LEFT Frontispiece and title page of *Gray Is the Color: Catalogue of an Exhibition of Grisaille Painting, XIIIth–XXth Centuries*, Rice Museum, Houston, Texas, October 19, 1973, to January 19, 1974, organized by the Institute for the Arts, Rice University.

BELOW Menil Foundation houses painted gray with white trim at Barnstone's recommendation, 1400 block of Branard, Houston.

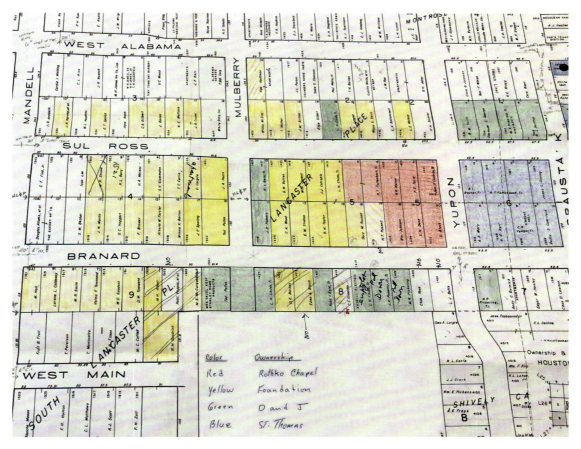

Color-coded map of Lancaster Place (Do-ville).

DO-VILLE

Although the Menils asked Kahn to plan one building on their property in the Lancaster Place subdivision, he produced sketches for a multiblock, multibuilding campus during 1973–1974. These called for the clearance of nearly eight blocks of neighborhood bungalows.[107] Kahn did not present his preliminary scheme until after John de Menil died, in June 1973. The project was put on hold after Kahn died unexpectedly, in March 1974. This pause gave Dominique de Menil the opportunity to explore alternative designs for an art storage building to be produced by Barnstone's office.

A 1973 color-coded plat map of the area shows fifty-eight of the seventy-one lots that the Menils and the Menil Foundation eventually owned.[108] Barnstone's fingerprints were already all over the area. Block 6 of Lancaster Place, owned by the University of St. Thomas, was the site of Barnstone & Aubry's Guinan Hall. The Rothko Chapel occupied six lots on Block 5 across Yupon Street from Guinan

A CONSTRUCTIVE CONNECTION 155

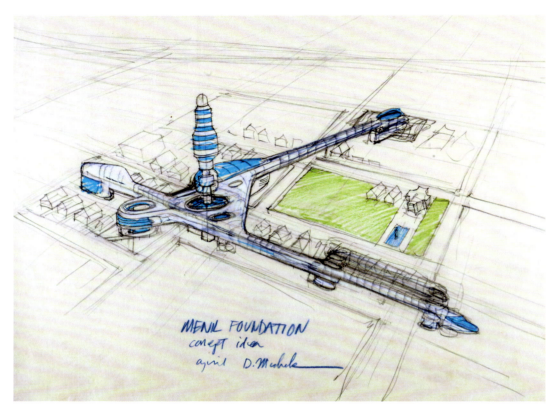

Doug Michels, concept for the Menil Museum, c. 1980. The Rothko Chapel is at the center right of the drawing.

Hall. Inspired by an exhibition held in the Art Barn, *Gray Is the Color*, mounted in the fall of 1973 under the auspices of the Institute for the Arts, Barnstone suggested to Dominique de Menil that she paint all the Menil-owned bungalows the same gray color with white trim.[109] Dominique de Menil wrote to Howard from Belgium: "After having wanted to see Bruges for 50 years, I have finally come here. The modest size of the houses is what makes it so human. You were the first one to advocate keeping the houses around the Rothko Chapel. Their human scale will have a prevailing influence."[110] The small act that unified the Menil neighborhood—dubbed Do-ville (for Dominique) by Karl Kilian—has had a lasting effect on the area, and it has become one of Howard Barnstone's most significant contributions to Houston.[111]

Barnstone's office produced multiple schemes for the proposed Menil art center, which would house art storage primarily, along with offices, a conference room, and a small public gallery. The program grew to include a library for 3,700 volumes of "spiritual and philosophical" books, a workshop, and a small theater. Of the plans that emerged from Barnstone's office, the most outrageous was a museum–art storage building designed by Doug Michels that was probably

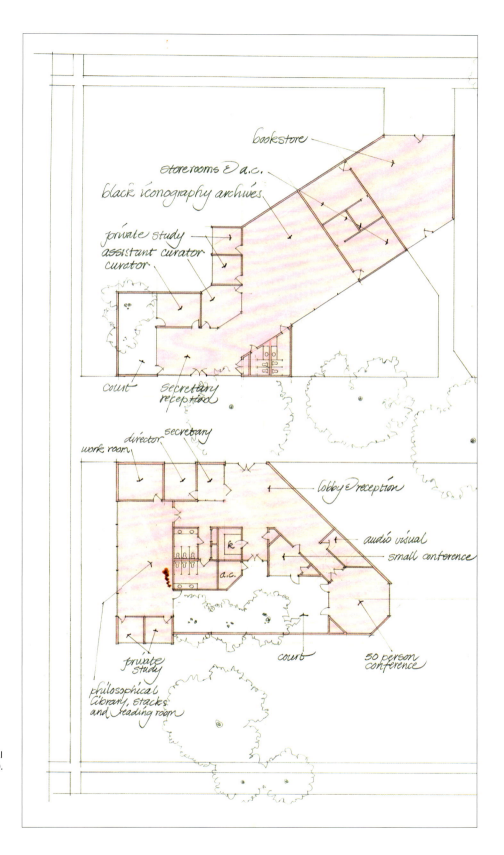

Howard Barnstone, proposal for a Menil museum, c. 1980.

never shown to Dominique de Menil. It zoomed across the Menil-owned blocks like some futuristic transportation system, emanating from a central hub with a striped "tower." In Michels's scheme, buildings for different purposes (museum, auditorium, offices) touched down among the bungalows, with the large storage facility at the hub. This drawing (one among many for this project) demonstrates that Barnstone did not discourage design exploration; instead, he treated his employees as if they were students in his University of Houston design studio, encouraging them to search for innovative solutions, even if they were unlikely to be built.

A more modest Barnstone proposal among those prepared between 1975 and 1979 called for two buildings, probably connected by a tunnel, as in other schemes. Different sites were considered for different proposals. This project was designed for the site where the Menil Collection museum eventually would be built, bound by Sul Ross, Mulberry, Branard, and Mandell. As in Renzo Piano's Menil Collection museum, art storage would have occupied the second story in both buildings. Unlike Piano's plan, Barnstone's included a bookstore, conference rooms, study areas, and libraries, but essentially no exhibition space. One similarity, though, was the courtyards. When Dominique de Menil finally awarded the commission to Renzo Piano in 1981, it was a significant disappointment for Barnstone, who had spent four years working on plans while Mrs. de Menil sorted out her intentions.[112]

SCHLUMBERGER-DOLL RESEARCH CENTER

While Barnstone was designing alternative storage and museum buildings to contain the Menils' art collection, he was also working on the largest project of his career. The differing outcome of these two projects may indicate the relative strengths of Barnstone's relationship with John and Dominique de Menil. The last two major projects of Barnstone's career can be attributed to John de Menil's influence at Schlumberger, which lived on after his death. By that time, Barnstone had developed strong working relationships with Jean Riboud and Michel Gouilloud, with whom he worked directly on the Schlumberger-Doll Research Center.[113] Dominique de Menil found in Renzo Piano's methodical, detail-oriented, problem-solving ethos a more sympathetic sensibility than Barnstone's expansive, intuitive esprit, even though they enjoyed each other's company. John de Menil's support of and generosity to Barnstone were constant.

Schlumberger-Doll Research Center conference room and interior courtyard after restoration (1952, Philip Johnson; 2018 restoration by Craig Bassam), 36 Old Quarry Road, Ridgefield, Connecticut. This was Philip Johnson's first nonresidential project and the first building of the SDRC.

In the 1940s, Annette Schlumberger and Henri Doll had settled in Ridgefield, Connecticut. When Schlumberger decided to build a research center that Doll would manage, he convinced the board of directors that Ridgefield was an ideal location. The first research lab was constructed on a forty-five-acre site there in 1948. When more space was needed, John de Menil recommended Philip Johnson as architect for the small administration building. The one-story Schlumberger Building, Johnson's first commercial project, was completed in 1952 and won a Merit Award from the American Institute of Architects in 1956. It was a one-story flat-roofed steel-framed Miesian building with dark glass windows and a facing of glazed gray brick. In 1967, when Doll retired, the complex, by then expanded to four buildings, was named the Schlumberger-Doll Research Center (SDRC) in recognition of his technical contributions to Schlumberger.[114]

By 1976, the complex of buildings needed updating, and the center required more sophisticated laboratories. Barnstone got the commission for "an entire renovation and expansion of SDRC," as his contract specified.[115] The Johnson-designed

A CONSTRUCTIVE CONNECTION

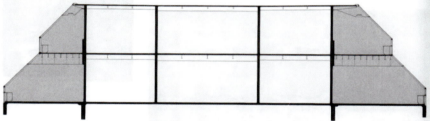

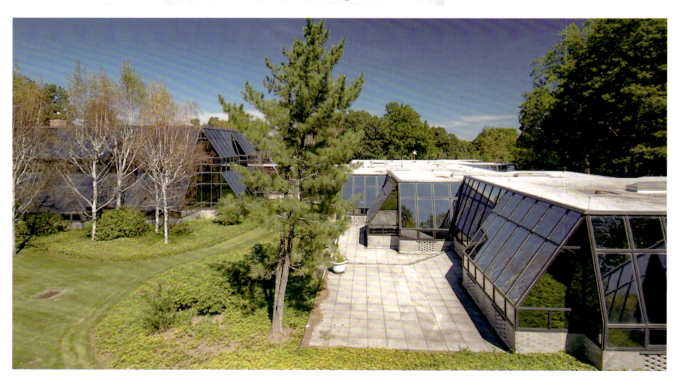

office building received a new roof, a remodeled basement, and some interior changes, but the exterior was left untouched. The two-story 1948 building and two other architecturally inconsequential buildings were dramatically altered by adding what Barnstone called a glass "tent," with sloped bay windows projecting outward from the floor plates of the existing buildings, increasing the square footage of each building. Materials used in the remodeling and in a new laboratory building were extrapolated from the Johnson building: steel framing, dark glass, glazed gray brick. The unified result was a series of stunning, faceted glass buildings that economically incorporated their mundane predecessors. The Schlumberger-Doll Research Center was one of Barnstone's most beautiful and imaginative projects.[116] In 2006 Schlumberger moved its research center to Cambridge, Massachusetts, and the Ridgefield facility was closed.[117] To save the property from overdevelopment, the City of Ridgefield bought it in 2014 for $7 million. All the buildings except the Johnson building were demolished in 2015.[118] In 2018, the Johnson building became the home of A Contemporary Theater (ACT) of Connecticut.[119]

SCHLUMBERGER AUSTIN SYSTEMS CENTER

Barnstone's last major project was the Austin Systems Center for Schlumberger Well Services, which he designed in a joint venture with the Austin architect Robert T. Jackson. Despite Schlumberger's satisfaction with and pride in the Ridgefield research center, Barnstone had to compete against Emilio Ambasz and other contenders to win the Austin commission in June 1984.[120] Barnstone's association with Jackson (who had worked on the SDRC job as Barnstone's employee) was important because Jackson's office in Austin took the lead in completing the project after Barnstone experienced a recurrence of depression in 1985. During 1986, the joint venture's average billings were $24,000 a month: $7,000 for Barnstone and $15,000 for Jackson, with an additional $2,000 for office associates.[121] In correspondence between Barnstone's Houston office and Jackson, it is clear that working drawings were produced in Houston, whereas site visits, change orders, and other matters were handled by Jackson in Austin. But at the groundbreaking on April 15, 1985, Barnstone, not Jackson, spoke, along with Schlumberger officials Kerry Schoenberg, Jim Baker, and Ian Strecker. Daniel Construction Co. was general contractor for the $20.5 million complex.

The Schlumberger property in Austin was a wooded 438-acre site in the hills northwest of Austin, overlooking Lake Travis in the distance. Schlumberger made

OPPOSITE, TOP Schlumberger-Doll Research Center entrance (1980, Howard Barnstone, FAIA, demolished), Zion & Breen, landscape architects.

OPPOSITE, CENTER Schlumberger-Doll Research Center, elevation, tentlike section (c. 1977, Howard Barnstone, FAIA, Architect).

OPPOSITE, BOTTOM Schlumberger-Doll Research Center, one- and two-story buildings. All of the SDRC buildings were demolished except for the Philip Johnson building and the Schlumberger auditorium that was remodeled for ACT (A Contemporary Theater) of Connecticut in 2018.

Schlumberger Austin Systems Center, pergola called the "Broad Way" by Howard Barnstone (c. 1981, Howard Barnstone, FAIA, Architect, with Robert Jackson; J. Robert Anderson, landscape architect), I-35 and Yager Lane (current address, 11400 Concordia University Drive).

the decision to develop only twenty acres and mandated that the buildings be sensitive to the environment and preserve the native landscape. Schlumberger asked that the buildings face east along a bluff at the highest point of the property in order to provide morning light and the best views.[122] Seven buildings snaked along the irregular ridge, as Barnstone's Riboud House in Arizona had done on a much smaller scale. The connections between buildings were imagined as a long greenhouse, like the greenhouse with which Barnstone connected the buildings in Adelaide de Menil and Ted Carpenter's East Hampton complex. This skylit walkway widened and narrowed as it wove through the buildings, providing places for chance encounters and conversations among the engineers who worked there. Joel Warren Barna described the central walkway: "[It] goes into the tree tops, spans ravines, and passes through each of the office buildings as 'the Broadway.' A circulation corridor under dark-glazed skylights provides the only way into or out of the offices and laboratories. Informal meeting areas where corridors meet the broadway (with interiors designed by ISD, Inc. as were the individual offices; J. Robert Anderson of Austin was the landscape architect) provide places to sit and converse."[123] Stephen Fox compared this Broadway, as Barnstone nicknamed it,

162   HOWARD BARNSTONE'S CLIENTS

Schlumberger Austin Systems Center, presentation rendering (c. 1981, Howard Barnstone, FAIA, Architect, and Robert T. Jackson).

with the wiggle walls in Schlumberger's New York offices.[124] The Schlumberger Austin Systems Center is now the campus of Concordia University Texas.[125]

The buildings of the Schlumberger Austin Systems Center, completed in 1987, are magical in the way that so much of Howard Barnstone's work was. They sparkle. They weave up and down, in and out, with a sense of adventure amid lush vegetation. And they hold constant surprise.

Howard Barnstone's architectural practice relied on three client groups: the Menils, Houston's Jewish community, and himself and his family. Of these, the Menils unquestionably provided him with the most work and the largest fees. As extraordinary as some of these projects were at the time of their execution, most of them have turned out to be ephemeral. The New York projects in high-rise buildings disappeared as the ownership of condos and offices passed to others, who redecorated and remodeled, obliterating Barnstone's work. The East Hampton village he created for Adelaide de Menil and Ted Carpenter has been dismantled, and the property sold off in parcels. In Houston, the Demoustier House has been demolished, and the Melcher House has been significantly remodeled, as have others of Barnstone's Houston buildings. The Art Barn at Rice has been

A CONSTRUCTIVE CONNECTION 163

demolished. Although the Ribouds' Arizona House is standing, recent photographs show that it has weathered and no longer has the allure it once did. And perhaps more lamentably, the Schlumberger-Doll Research Center buildings that Barnstone designed and remodeled have all been torn down. The Schlumberger Austin Systems Center buildings have been remodeled; the building and walkway skylights were replaced with solid green roofs, taking away much of their spontaneous charm.

These circumstances do not diminish Barnstone's work. Surviving drawings, plans, and photographs show that he was given incredible opportunities and that his talent rose to meet the expectations of the time. Of all his clients, he was closest to John de Menil; the two might have created a very different Montrose ensemble than the memorable configuration of gray cottages that he and Dominique accomplished. Barnstone's legacy in the Menil-Schlumberger world is the graying and unification of Do-ville, a special place in Houston, and the publication of *The Galveston That Was*, widely accepted as the catalyst for preservation in historic Galveston.

NOTES

1. Howard Barnstone, "Biographical Sketch of Dominique de Menil," typescript, 1985, accompanying the nomination of Dominique de Menil for honorary membership in the Texas Society of Architects and AIA Houston, 1986, Barnstone Collection, HMRC. This nomination was subsequently withdrawn, probably at the request of Dominique. Barnstone dated their first meeting to 1948 and claimed, "The impression which she and her husband made upon me was so strong that I stopped my trip across the country and decided to settle in Houston." In fact, the reason why Barnstone moved to Houston in 1948 was to teach at the University of Houston. The date of the Neuhaus dinner party is unknown, but it probably occurred in 1951 or early 1952. Neuhaus, who had a conflict with Johnson over interpretation of construction details, did not want to be involved with the Menil House once the initial construction was complete.

2. See the entries "de Ménil, John" in *Who's Who in America, 1964–1965*, 33:504, the first year he was listed, and in *Who's Who in America, 1974–1975*, 38:773, the last year he was listed; Allaud and Martin, *Schlumberger*, 214–215; Gruner-Schlumberger, *Schlumberger Adventure*, 119–120, 123–124.

3. Linda Peterson, "Menil, John de," *Handbook of Texas Online*, June 15, 2010, modified on September 12, 2017, tshaonline.org/handbook/online/articles/fmeny.

4. John de Menil, "A Provincial Town," in *Houston: Text by Houstonians*, 127.

5. Jonathan Marshall, "The A.F.A. Convention," *Arts* 31 (May 1957): 10–11.

6. Ibid. Marshall describes this in the *Arts* article as an "art air-left."

7. Middleton, *Double Vision*, 30–47. François Guizot (1787–1874), a French historian, philosopher, and statesman, was Dominique's great-great-grandfather who bought Val-Richer, once part of a twelfth-century Cistercian monastery. It was abandoned during the French Revolution. The house that remained at Val-Richer was a twenty-room limestone mansion that Guizot restored as the family's country estate. Guizot, one of postrevolutionary France's most prominent figures, was well known throughout Europe.

8. "Our History," Schlumberger website, accessed August 1, 2018, https://www.slb.com/about/history.aspx; Jon Kutner, Jr., "Schlumberger," *Handbook of Texas Online*, June 15, 2010, tshaonline.org/handbook/online/articles/dzsxg. Paul Schlumberger and his brother Léon married the sisters Marguerite and Jeanne de Witt. Marguerite and Paul (Dominique's grandparents) inherited Val-Richer from her mother, Henriette, the daughter of François and Elisa Dillon. Conrad's sons-in-law, John de Menil and Henri-Georges Doll, who married Annette Schlumberger and became the chairman of the Schlumberger board of directors, were both powerful within the company. Pierre Schlumberger, Marcel's only son, became president of Schlumberger from the time of Marcel's death, in 1953, until 1965. European operations were run by René Seydoux, Marcel's son-in-law.

9. H. Barnstone, "Biographical Sketch of Dominique de Menil."

10. Ibid. Dominique de Menil organized twelve successful art exhibitions at the University of St. Thomas between 1964 and 1967. At the Rice Museum, she

organized twenty-two exhibitions from 1969 to 1982, including *Gray Is the Color* in the fall of 1973.

11. Simone Swan, interview by the author, July 13, 2018, Houston.

12. Ibid.; Diana J. Kleiner, "Menil Foundation," *Handbook of Texas Online*, June 15, 2010, modified on September 12, 2017, tshaonline.org/handbook/online/articles/vrm04.

13. Middleton, *Double Vision*, 335.

14. Philip Johnson to Mrs. Jean de Menil, May 2, 1950, Menil Collection Archives 2001–2002 (folder 01/01–9). Johnson wrote: "That other point in your letter that bothered me is the appointment of Charles James as the consultant on the interior. I admire his work as a dress designer enormously but you can imagine the disappointment of an architect when someone else finishes his work"; Susan Sutton, exhibition notes for *A Thin Wall of Air: Charles James*, 2014, Menil Archives; Coleman, *Genius of Charles James*.

15. Barnstone Collection, HMRC. There are ten projects for the Menil House, 3633 San Felipe Road, with correspondence or drawings. Job #533 in 1953, the first, encompassed initial small projects.

16. Barnstone Collection, HMRC, box 10:12.

17. Ibid., box 18–4.

18. Ibid., drawings.

19. Ibid.

20. "Schlumberger Well Surveying Corporation Building," National Register of Historic Places Nomination form, October 2017, Texas Historical Commission website, accessed May 28, 2019, https://atlas.thc.state.tx.us/NR/pdfs/100002601/100002601.pdf. This first Schlumberger industrial campus in the United States consisted of eighteen buildings on a three-block site. Only the office building is extant. In 1953, Mackie & Kamrath completed (at the behest of Pierre Schlumberger, president at the time) a new campus located on the Gulf Freeway. By 1956, the entire company had left the Leeland Avenue campus. Schlumberger Overseas and Schlumberger-Surenco offices moved to the Bank of the Southwest and the Commerce Building. In the 1990s, Schlumberger moved to Sugar Land; the Gulf Freeway location became a business park, and then it was purchased by the University of Houston in 2008 for its Energy Research Park.

21. Barnstone Collection, HMRC, boxes 1:8–10 and 2:1–4; drawing online 178–3093; photos 178–1052 to 178–1059.

22. On the Bank of the Southwest offices, see Middleton, *Double Vision*, 380; on the Commerce Building offices, see Barnstone Collection, HMRC, box 10:4 and photos 178–1052 to 178–1059.

23. Middleton, *Double Vision*, 283.

24. Ibid., 270–272. Middleton notes that John de Menil organized the camps, determining the number of buildings, and Dominique took over their construction, working with a contractor from Caracas. Dominique described her work in her letters.

25. Statement of Account from Bolton & Barnstone to Schlumberger Overseas Company, April 17, 1957, Barnstone Collection, box 2:9. This monthly statement, for one example, totaled $8,133.52 and included time on the Surenco project ($10 an hour for draftsmen), Barnstone's travel (at $80 a day between February 21 and March 25, when he visited Los Morochas, El Tigre, Caracas, Maracaibo, and Mata), plus reimbursable expenses (telephone calls, blueprints).

26. "Company House in Trinidad, B.W.I.," *Arts & Architecture*, April 1957, 28–30.

27. "1940s: New Frontiers," Schlumberger website, accessed August 1, 2018, https://www.slb.com/about/history/1940s.aspx. The first Schlumberger offices in Houston, occupied in 1937, were located downtown in the Niels Esperson Building.

28. Barnstone Collection, HMRC, box 2:4.

29. Blueprint of the second floor of 120 East 80th Street, Barnstone Collection, HMRC, drawings.

30. Barnstone Collection, HMRC, box 3:9. The lease for 4B was terminated in 1959, and at that time Barnstone went to New York to solve disputes with the owner of the building, Mendel Haskelloward. R. D. "Bob" Ford, general manager of the Venezuelan operations, occupied 3B for a time, even after the Menils left.

31. Swan interview.

32. Barnstone Collection, HMRC, drawings and model photographs 178–326 to 178–390; Stephen Fox, "Dominique and John de Menil as Patrons of Architecture 1932–97," in Helfenstein and Schipsi, *Art and Activism*, 206.

33. The Menil Townhouse in New York was sold in 1996, a year before Dominique died. It is now part of the Buckley School, a K–9 private school for boys founded in 1913; François de Menil attended it. The school moved in 1917 to 74th street directly behind the Menil Townhouse, which it acquired in 2014. Today the school occupies several other adjacent townhouses as well.

34. Barnstone Collection, HMRC, box 2:8.

35. "Ritz Tower," Barnstone Collection, HMRC, drawings and box 17:9–11.

36. "Henri-Georges Doll; Ex-Engineer Was 89," *New York Times*, July 28, 1991; see also "Henri-Georges Doll: 1902–1991," *Oilfield Review* 4, no. 1 (January 1992): 4–7, available on the Schlumberger website, accessed August 2, 2018, https://www.slb.com/resources/oilfield_review/en/1992/or1992_jan.aspx. Doll held more than seventy international patents.

37. Patricia and Edward Shillingburg, "S. Gregory Taylor: 1888–1948, A Greek Patriot and Hotel Magnate," 2006, Shelter Island website, accessed August 2, 2018, https://www.shelter-island.org/Summer_Series_2006/taylor_one.html. Taylor was manager of the St. Moritz Hotel. When the hotel opened, a dinner-dance club decorated with Omar Khayyam murals occupied the thirty-first floor, with a "sky garden" on the large terrace created by the form of the setback skyscraper. The hotel was completely redecorated in 1950, and the thirty-first-floor club was converted to three apartments; see also Robin Finn, "A Hint of Versailles on Central Park South," *New York Times*, May 15, 2017. Today the thirtieth and thirty-first floors make up a duplex apartment that sold in 2014 for $70 million. There are twelve condos above the Ritz-Carlton hotel today.

38. Middleton, *Double Vision*, 426–427. Pierre Schlumberger was forced out as president of Schlumberger, and Riboud received John de Menil's support as the next president; Barnstone Collection, HMRC, drawings and box 27:4–9.

39. Auletta, *Art of Corporate Success*, 44–45; see also Todd S. Purdum, "Jean Riboud Dies in Paris at 65; Headed Schlumberger Company," *New York Times*, October 22, 1985.

40. Nicole Saraniero, "Amster Yard in Turtle Bay, One of NYC's Most Beautiful Hidden Courtyards," March 29, 2018, Untapped Cities website, accessed August 2, 2018, https://untappedcities.com/2018/03/29/amster-yard-in-turtle-bay-one-of-nycs-most-beautiful-hidden-courtyards. In 1944, the houses on 49th were redeveloped by the interior decorator James Amster, who created a lush garden in the long courtyard created by Sorchan. The gardens and houses were designated the Turtle Bay Gardens Historic District in 1966. As the glamour of Amster Yard faded, commercial tenants moved in. In 1999, the New York Landmarks Conservancy approved plans for the Instituto Cervantes, which offers Spanish classes and cultural programs, to make Amster Yard its New York base. This institution, which still occupies the property, purchased all the buildings and restored the area.

41. Barnstone Collection, HMRC, drawings and box 67:1, 7.

42. Ibid., box 33:6–10.

43. Adelaide de Menil to Howard Barnstone, July 2, 1976, Barnstone Collection, HMRC, box 78:10. This letter was written out of frustration at how slow things were moving on the project in East Hampton, where Adelaide and Ted were assembling and restoring a group of historic barns and houses on an old potato farm.

44. Barnstone Collection, HMRC, drawings and box 50:5–13. Adelaide and Ted occupied the whole second floor of the Gainsborough Studios.

45. Virginia Kurshan, "Gainsborough Studios," New York Landmarks Preservation Commission nomination, designation list 200, LP-1423, February 16, 1988, Neighborhood Preservation Center website, accessed August 4, 2018, neighborhoodpreservationcenter.org/db/bb_files/Gainsborough-Studios.pdf. The narrow Gainsborough Studios building was one of the early cooperative apartments in New York, and it has a distinctive façade decorated with colorful glazed tiles on the top, two double-height floors, and a striking bas-relief frieze by the Austrian-born Isidore Konti, which separates the first floor from those above; see Stern, Gilmartin, and Massengale, *New York 1900*, 296, 298.

46. Helen Fosdick and Glenn Heim, "Ephemeral Space: The Seminarian and the Student Chapels at the University of St. Thomas," *Cite* 74 (Spring 2008): 10–13.

47. Barnstone Collection, HMRC, box 68–12. Correspondence indicates that Gouilloud bid $81,808 for this apartment, but it is unclear whether the sale went through. No drawings or further information on this project is in the Barnstone Collection. In 2018, the 3,000-square-foot apartment on the sixth floor was sold for $2.8 million.

48. Ibid., box 23:5. Barnstone remodeled the entire first-floor space and attended the opening on October 15, 1963.

49. "Contemporary at Its Best: A Renovation of a Renovation by Houston Architect Howard Barnstone, AIA; see also Designer in Charge Eugene Aubry, AIA," *Interiors*, April 1963, 98–101.

50. Barnstone Collection, HMRC, box 14: 7–11.

51. Middleton, *Double Vision*, 427–428.

52. Stern, Mellins, and Fishman, *New York 1960*, 566.

53. C. Ray Smith, "Wiggle Walls," *Progressive Architecture* 47 (August 1966): 160–163; see also "Angling the Rectangle . . . The Park Avenue Offices of Schlumberger, Ltd.," *Interiors* 126 (September 1966): 132–133; Barnstone Collection, drawings and box 25:9–13.

54. Smith, "Wiggle Walls," 162.

55. Barnstone Collection, HMRC, box 26:28; 1972, 43rd floor, drawings and box 38:1; 1980–82, box 81:10–13; 1984, Michel Gouilloud Office, drawings: 10 sheets. Barnstone continued to make modifications to the Schlumberger offices on Park Avenue until 1984.

56. Auletta, *Art of Corporate Success*, 39.

57. Bruno Desforges to Howard Barnstone, November 7, 1960, Barnstone Collection, HMRC, box 66:1.

58. "Lepercq de Neuflize & Co.," Lepercq website, accessed August 5, 2018, lepercq.com. Paul Lepercq began his investment-banking career with Andre Istel (1888–1996), whose company, Istel, Lepercq, managed France's finances during the Second World War. Lepercq de Neuflize was established in New York in 1948 as the American investment arm of Banque Schlumberger, a family-owned French bank.

59. Carter B. Horsley, "New Ideas Change Office Landscapes," *New York Times*, May 14, 1972.

60. Auletta, *Art of Corporate Success*, 19–20.

61. Barnstone Collection, HMRC, drawings: 3-sheets and box 67:1.

62. Ibid., drawings and box 91:22.

63. Ibid., drawings and box 51:12.

64. Bob Colacello, "Remains of Dia," *Vanity Fair*, April 30, 2008.

65. Joseph Giovannini, "An Amicable Parting or Man and Home," *New York Times*, April 26, 1988.

66. Colacello, "Remains of Dia."

67. "House in the Southwest: Gulf Coast Region of Texas," *Arts & Architecture* 74 (December 1957): 22–23. The Demoustier House was featured on the Contemporary Arts Association Tour VI, April 13–14, 1957; see also Barnstone Collection, HMRC, drawings and box 2:3 2:8. Barnstone also was involved in furnishing a house for the Demoustiers in Caracas, Venezuela (Barnstone Collection, HMRC, box 9:8).

68. David Bucek, "David House, Landmark Designation Report," 2014, City of Houston website, accessed August 6, 2018, https://www.houstontx.gov/planning

/HistoricPres/landmarks/14L302_David_House_1807_Wroxton.pdf. Henry David was a drilling-mud pioneer, and his wife, Grace McMillan, was a Houston bonne vivante who, with her children Dorman and Grace, owned The Bookman bookstore and the David Gallery. Charles Tapley designed the Wroxton House for Grace David after she sold the Demoustier House. Grace David was Larry McMurtry's model for Aurora in his novel *Terms of Endearment*. Lawrence Marcus was the son and nephew of the founders of Neiman-Marcus and managed the Houston store. The Demoustier House was demolished in 1995 for a new 7,000-square-foot house.

69. Barnstone Collection, HMRC, drawings and box 27:3.

70. Kate Gurwell, "House Tour," *Houston Post*, December 1, 1964. The Melcher House, which was featured on the 1964 AIA Houston / CAA annual tour, was the primary subject of this article; see also Barnstone Collection, HMRC, drawings and boxes 19:3–10, 26:7. The house was extensively remodeled again in 2001–2002.

71. Eugene Aubry, interviews by Stephen Fox and Michelangelo Sabatino, May 5, 2010, and May 9, 2011, Galveston, Texas.

72. Barnstone Collection, HMRC, drawings.

73. Fox, *AIA Houston Architectural Guide*, 177; see also Barnstone Collection, HMRC, drawings and boxes 39:19–21, 40:3. Anne Schlumberger Brown also had Barnstone add closets and a skylight to a temporary apartment at 4727 Graustark in 1971–1972; see Barnstone Collection, HMRC, box 37:12.

74. Fox, *AIA Houston Architectural Guide*, 403.

75. Barnstone Collection, HMRC, drawings and boxes 18:2–3, 19:2. Pierre, who was in charge of the Houston headquarters from 1940, commissioned MacKie & Kamrath, not Bolton & Barnstone, to design the Schlumberger Well Services complex on the Gulf Freeway, completed in 1953, when Barnstone was remodeling the Schlumberger-Surenco offices in the Leeland Building. It is probable that Pierre Schlumberger felt the more experienced firm would be better for such a large project.

76. Barnstone Collection, HMRC, box 16:16. The Sweeneys' apartment number was 15G.

77. Peter Brink, "The Galveston That Was: Requiem or Inspiration?," dedicated to Howard Barnstone, October 1, 1989, written for the North American Print Conference, November 1988, typescript, 7–10, Barnstone Collection, HMRC. A version of this paper was published in 1993 as the afterword to the second edition of *The Galveston That Was*.

78. Brink, "Galveston That Was," 7.

79. Barnstone Collection, HMRC, box 16:14.

80. Swan interview. Swan said the architectural historian Thomas S. Hines told her the Swan House was one of Moore's best houses; see Mildred Schmertz, "Two Houses by Charles Moore," *Architectural Record* 161 (June 1977): 109–116, and "Swan House, North Fork, Long Island, New York," *GA Houses* 7 (1980): 78–81.

81. Tony Frederick to Simone Swan, October 12, 1972, Barnstone Collection, HMRC, box 39:5.

82. Simone Swan to Howard Barnstone, October 18, 1972, Barnstone Collection, HMRC, box 39:5. This collection contains letters from other dissatisfied clients, particularly concerning invoices, but none (with the exception of the Swan letter) was from a Menil-related client. John de Menil paid Barnstone's invoices for the Swan project.

83. Howard Barnstone to James P. "Jim" Knowles, December 8, 1972, Barnstone Collection, HMRC, box 39:5. Apparently, Barnstone shared this medical information with Knowles because Knowles too was taking lithium: "Delighted you are both so well, and the lithium is so doing wonders."

84. Auletta, *Art of Corporate Success*, 42–43.

85. Barnstone Collection, HMRC, drawings and boxes 17:17, 67:1, 40:18–19, 41:1–6; 51:13.

86. "Ribouds' Vacation Home Super," *Houston Post*, December 10, 1975. The Zillow website, accessed August 7, 2018 https://www.zillow.com/homedetails/38850-N-Spanish-Boot-Rd-Carefree-AZ-85377/8032100_zpid, shows that the house last sold for $785,000 in 2013, and posted photographs indicate it has been extensively remodeled.

87. Ann Holmes, "New Environment for New Houses," *Houston Post*, October 23, 1979.

88. *Houston Post*, April 21, 1978.

89. Barnstone was constantly involved in remodeling one or another of the bungalows for offices, storage, a film archive, and the like.

90. Michelangelo Sabatino, "Cracking the Egg: The Transformation of the University of St. Thomas Campus," *Cite 73* (Winter 2008): 10–17. In this article, three plans of the St. Thomas campus drawn by Serge Ambrose illustrate three phases of development.

91. Howard Barnstone, October 21, 1971, transcript of a lecture to architecture students in the Rothko Chapel, Barnstone Collection, HMRC. The chapel was dedicated on February 27, 1971.

92. Two books and numerous articles have illustrated and analyzed the construction of the Rothko Chapel; see Barnes, *Rothko Chapel*, and Nodelman, *Rothko Chapel Paintings*.

93. Nodelman, *Rothko Chapel Paintings*, 9.

94. Barnstone Collection, HMRC, box 28:9. The Menils explored the idea of putting the chapel in the medical center under the auspices of the Institute of Religion there.

95. Barnstone, Rothko Chapel lecture.

96. Dominique Browning, "What I Admire I Must Possess," *Texas Monthly*, April 1983.

97. Barnstone, Rothko Chapel lecture.

98. Nodelman, *Rothko Chapel Paintings*, 9.

99. John de Menil purchased *Broken Obelisk* and planned to give it to the City of Houston. In the aftermath of the assassination of Martin Luther King, Jr., in 1968,

he stipulated that the sculpture be dedicated to Dr. King, which caused the city to refuse it. In 1970, it was installed in the reflecting pool on axis with the entrance to the Rothko Chapel. There have been four fabrications of *Broken Obelisk*. The others are at the Museum of Modern Art, New York City; the University of Washington, Seattle; and the Storm King Art Center, New Windsor, New York.

100. Browning, "What I Admire."

101. Ibid. The Menils donated their art library to Rice and paid the salaries of the art history professors who left St. Thomas to teach at Rice; see Marguerite Johnston, "The Institute for the Arts Comes to Rice," *Rice University Review* 6 (Summer 1971): 6–11.

102. Hulten, *Machine as Seen*. The acknowledgments in this catalogue close with: "On behalf of the Trustees of the Museum of Modern Art, The University of St. Thomas, and the San Francisco Museum of Art, I wish to express thanks to all the lenders listed here as well as to several who preferred to remain anonymous." Planning for the exhibition began in 1965, so it is obvious that the Menils planned to bring it to St. Thomas, and they probably financed it in the name of St. Thomas.

103. Eugene Aubry, interview by Catherine Essinger, October 30, 2012, University of Houston, for the American Institute of Architects, Houston Chapter, oral history project, audio recording, accessed May 28, 2019, https://av.lib.uh.edu/?f%5Bcollection_ssim%5D%5B%5D=Building+Houston&f%5Bgenre_sim%5D%5B%5D=interviews.

104. Barnstone Collection, HMRC, drawings.

105. Stephen James, "The Menil Connection: Louis Kahn and the Rice University Art Center," *Journal of the Society of Architectural Historians* 69, no. 4 (December 2010): 561.

106. Ibid., 571–572.

107. Stephen Fox, "A Clapboard Treasure House," *Cite 1* (August 1982).

108. Ann Holmes, "Rothko Chapel Park Expanding," *Houston Chronicle*, July 30, 1974. For the Lancaster Place map, along with others, see Barnstone Collection, HMRC, box 42:3.

109. "Grisaille Exhibition Opens at Rice Museum," Institute for the Arts newsletter, Rice University (Fall 1973); Harris Rosenstein, oral history interview, 1992, Houston Public Library website, accessed August 20, 2018, http://digital.houstonlibrary.org/oral-history/harris-rosenstein_OHJL16.php.

110. Dominique de Menil to Howard Barnstone, Barnstone Collection, HMRC, private correspondence.

111. Howard Barnstone designed signage for the area, arranged for street lighting, and buried the electric and phone lines—all of which enhanced the neighborhood and helped it stand out from other additions and subdivisions of similar age.

112. Reed Karaim, "How the de Menils and Their Art Museum Changed Houston," *Architect*, June 19, 2013. In 2013, the Menil Collection won the national 25-Year Award from the American Institute of Architects. This article outlines the history of the building that was ultimately built. Howard Barnstone was not involved in the design or construction of the completed museum.

113. Gouilloud signed all contracts and invoices for this project.

114. "Schlumberger-Doll Research Center," Schlumberger website, accessed August 28, 2018, https://www.slb.com/about/rd/research/sdr.aspx.

115. Barnstone Collection, HMRC, box 61–8.

116. Ibid. Rudimentary sketches made by Barnstone indicate that he formulated the idea of the "tents," for which measured drawings were made by others in the office, as was his general practice. Time sheets and correspondence with the contractor indicate that Ted Gupton (who was often on-site), Robert Morris, Robert Jackson, Ronald Smith, and Paul Gloriod worked on this project.

117. Robert Miller, "Vacant Schlumberger Buildings in Ridgefield Might Be Razed," *Danbury (CT) News-Times*, July 20, 2011, accessed August 27, 2018, https://www.newstimes.com/local/article/Vacant-Schlumberger-buildings-in-Ridgefield-might-1474164.php#photo-1114377.

118. Anna Quinn, "Ridgefield Nearing End of Schlumberger Projects," *Danbury (CT) News-Times*, July 27, 2017, accessed August 28, 2018, https://www.newstimes.com/local/article/Ridgefield-nearing-end-of-Schlumberger-projects-11399365.php.

119. Kerry Anne Ducey, "Former Schlumberger Property Will Soon Be Alive with the Sound of (Broadway) Music!," Ridgefield's Hamlethub, January 23, 2018, accessed August 28, 2018, https://news.hamlethub.com/ridgefield/places/58794-former-schlumberger-property-will-soon-be-alive-with-the-sound-of-broadway-music.

120. The unsuccessful Emilio Ambasz project for Schlumberger Austin was published in Martin Filler, "The Architecture of Emilio Ambasz," *A + U* 8 (August 1983): 29–82; see also Peter Buchanan, "Laboratory Landscape: Laboratories, Austin, Texas," *Architectural Review* 174 (November 1983): 64–67; and Douglas Brenner, "Et in Arcadia Ambasz," *Architectural Record* 172 (September 1984): 120–133.

121. Robert Jackson to Howard Barnstone, September 2, 1986, Barnstone Collection, HMRC. This letter, in anticipation of the project winding down, concerned final billings, along with a recounting of past billings.

122. "Design Elements: Austin Engineering Center, Schlumberger," n.d., Barnstone Collection, HMRC.

123. Joel Warren Barna, "High-Tech Office Center Fits One-of-a-Kind Site," *Texas Architect* (November–December 1988).

124. Stephen Fox, "Howard Barnstone," in Scardino, Stern, and Webb, *Ephemeral City*, 239.

125. Landan Kuhlman "Schlumberger Consolidating National Headquarters to Sugar Land," *Houston Chronicle*, October 16, 2015. In 2015, Schlumberger consolidated its research operations at its headquarters in the Houston suburb of Sugar Land. In 2006, the Austin Schlumberger property was sold to Concordia University Texas, which relocated its campus from central Austin to the Schlumberger site in 2008 and now uses the Barnstone-Jackson buildings as academic buildings; see the Concordia Master Plan, Concordia University Texas website, accessed February 16, 2019, https://www.concordia.edu/resources/facilities-management/master-plan.html.

CHAPTER FIVE

AN ARCHITECTURAL FAMILY PORTRAIT

ROBERT BARNSTONE AND
DEBORAH ASCHER BARNSTONE

DURING the winter break of 1979–1980, in Robert Barnstone's first year of studying architecture at Bennington College, in Vermont, he was offered an apprenticeship in the Houston office of his uncle Howard. Robert's teachers at Bennington were from the Architectural Association in London, known for its innovative approaches to design but not for inculcating technical prowess. Because of this, and because he had only just started drafting, Robert was worried he would not be able to perform adequately, so he asked Howard whether he should take an architectural drafting class at a community college. Howard retorted, "Anything you learn about architecture in a community college, you will have to unlearn!" If Robert wanted to learn to draft well, he should "sign up for a course in structural steel drafting," Howard asserted. "They draft well." Naturally, Robert followed this advice. Learning to draft the hard-to-read, precise steel profiles trained him to read drawings carefully. He learned more than just drawing, however. The course taught Robert the tectonic significance of steel connections, basic structural types, framing patterns for floors and vertical structures, and a host of clean, utilitarian construction details. Like so many other modernist architects of his generation, Howard Barnstone strove to achieve immaculate detailing in every project. He recognized that an academic architectural education did not school students in the know-how required to detail well.

At another point, Robert asked Howard to recommend books on architecture that he considered indispensable to a novice. The younger Barnstone was stunned when his uncle handed him Bernard Rudofsky's *Architecture without Architects* (1964). Really? No Mies, Le Corbusier, or Aalto?[1] But the immense beauty of the structures that Rudofsky documented and the unparalleled lessons one could learn from studying work that emanated from the rudiments of world building practices were apparent. These experiences demonstrated Howard's insistence on understanding architecture profoundly, its material options and its construction methods. Howard's genius lay in his passionate interest in, and willingness to explore and exploit, all aspects of architecture, regardless of style.

From a practicing architect's perspective, there were three strengths in Howard's work: versatility and range, evident in his ability to synthesize elements from different architectural traditions into a coherent whole; sensitivity to site and nature; and a fascination, even obsession, with the automobile as a constituent element of modern design. The thread connecting these strengths was Howard's ability to imbue every aspect of his work with what he called "magic," engaging the occupants of his buildings emotionally, whether because of the architecture's stunning relationship to the natural environment or because of his mesmerizing treatment of interior and exterior spaces. Howard declared in a sidebar to Esther McCoy's *Zodiac* article in 1963 that architecture had been freed from the restraints of the old guard (Mies van der Rohe and Frank Lloyd Wright), and with this freedom came risks: "There is also the possibility of anarchy. There is also certainly due a new generation of horrors. . . . The new expression, however, should certainly be that of the 'car in urban society.'"[2] Howard's dual interest in the natural environment and the automobile may seem oxymoronic. But for Texans in the second half of the twentieth century, the automobile was the indispensable mode of transport in a suburban society wedded to an idealized relationship to nature.[3] In addition, rapid postwar expansion opened up opportunities for young architects to build.

Howard's body of work spanned a forty-year period. During that time, he designed and constructed an impressive array of buildings of every type and scale, from single-family houses to apartment blocks, from an intimate chapel to a university campus. He received support from family members both close and distant. Among Howard's first commissions was a house for his Texas cousin, Evelyn Fink Rosenthal, a project that helped him establish his practice in Houston. Although it is not unusual for architects to begin their careers by designing houses for relatives, Howard continued to engage with family throughout his professional life.

Evelyn Fink and Morris G. Rosenthal House (1954, Bolton & Barnstone), 4506 North Roseneath Drive, Houston.

Howard Barnstone was one of three children by his father's first wife: his siblings were his older sister, Beatrice, and his younger brother, Willis. His father subsequently had two more sons, Ronald and Robert, by his second wife, Marti Franco. The siblings and Howard's stepmother, along with other, more distant relations, were sources of emotional support for his professional choice and the source of many commissions. In addition, Howard acted as a developer, which meant he was his own client. Because of their number and scope, the projects that Howard designed for the family provide a lens through which to view the breadth of his architecture.

EVELYN AND MORRIS ROSENTHAL HOUSE

The first project that Howard designed for a family member was the Rosenthal House in Houston, completed with his partner Preston Bolton in 1953. As Stephen Fox asserts, the house was one of Bolton & Barnstone's first forays into Miesian aesthetics, but Howard combined Miesian ideas with his interests in nature and the automobile to create his own language.[4] The house is a tightly planned 4,600-square-foot single-family house on a triangular suburban lot. From Mies, Howard borrowed the house's structural rationalism, its square façade grid, and its overlapping planes. These were combined with a sensitivity to the house's site and the Texas climate. The entry, covered for protection from the sun, is offset to one side of the front façade, which is divided into five square bays, a geometric regularity that echoes Mies's work. The façade departs from Mies's material palette: the lower half is exposed brick and the upper half is white stucco, with a long narrow rectangular window separating top and bottom. At the base of the front wall is a

Elli Tzalopoulou and Willis Barnstone House, interior (1964 remodeling, Barnstone & Aubry), 4930 East Heritage Woods Road, Bloomington, Indiana.

planting bed, which allows the house to be framed in nature and protected by it. Because Howard understood modern living, the house is approached by car: the car turns to enter the garage, situated to the left of the main entry and disguised as a blank wall from the street. In this way, the car has pride of place yet is still subordinate to the house.

The Rosenthal House is squeezed on its long narrow site. Therefore, it has no windows on the sides, and only a tiny window facing the public street, but it then opens onto a generous rear garden. Howard turned the house inward to face a substantial skylit space, bringing light into the interiors and creating the illusion of an interior courtyard. The kitchen and living room open onto a true, planted exterior courtyard near the front of the house, a space that also acts as a light well. The third side of the living room has the enormous floor-to-ceiling glass walls that Howard loved and looks out to the private rear garden. Thus, the living room is surrounded by green: Howard was able to create the illusion of living in an Edenic garden.

ELLI AND WILLIS BARNSTONE HOUSE

In 1964, Howard visited Bloomington, Indiana, to discuss designing a house for his brother, Willis. Howard was not impressed with the local architecture. After riding around Bloomington and its outskirts, he declared that the traditional wood-framed Indiana barns were the only buildings of architectural merit. Howard discovered an abandoned rough-sawn hardwood barn sitting in the midst of a new subdivision in the process of development. The barn was going to be demolished to make way for tract housing. The contractor was willing to give it away as long as the barn was removed. From the start, Howard's vision was to take advantage of the beauty of the Indiana vernacular barn, using its structure and roof as the core of a modern house. He listened carefully to what Elli Barnstone envisioned for the house. She wanted a low-maintenance house with three bedrooms for the children, a painting studio for herself, and a study for Willis, a poet, writer, and university professor. Howard integrated different architectural languages into a new synthesis. At the house on Heritage Woods Road, Howard married vernacular and modern tropes, man-made structures and the landscape, interior and exterior living.

Howard asked a real-estate agent to take him to the neighborhood where the bankers lived, since he reasoned that would be in the upscale part of Bloomington. At the time, Bloomington bankers lived on East Heritage Woods Road in the rolling hills four miles outside the center of town. As its name suggests, Heritage Woods Road runs through an Indiana hardwood forest. Large maple, oak, hickory, and poplar trees spread out with canopies one hundred feet high. By 1962, the road had been extended along the ridge of a hill. Tracts for development ran on either side, but there were no city services. The plot that Howard liked was a wooded south-facing site of three and a half acres that sloped down to a creek below. Howard placed the house in the woods on a slight plateau situated two hundred yards or so down the hill.

The barn was typical of those seen in early-twentieth-century Indiana. It has the usual plan dimensions of about thirty by forty feet, a long-span roof that made an enormous open space inside, and a large gambrel roof over the hayloft. The structural timber used for the roof trusses and the walls is oak, as is the rough-hewn exterior cladding. The braced timber-framed construction is distinct in that it is light and delicate and lacks the massive mid-bracing beam ring that many gambrel barns possess. This system of trusses is fabricated by sandwiching rough-cut two-by-six-foot rafters at the joints with a one-by-six-foot gusset plate stiffening the moment connection between the rafters and shortening the span. The trusses are clad above with white prepainted tongue-and-groove decking. The braced truss vault spans nearly 30 feet. The roof construction was like the framing and bracing of a seafaring vessel, turned upside down.

The barn was disassembled and the framing members were numbered before being moved to Heritage Woods Road. Measurements were taken of the existing barn and sent to Howard in Houston so that he could prepare the construction drawings. His concept was to insert a modern house into and underneath the

Barnstone House, Bloomington, Indiana, exterior.

old barn, thereby merging the language of traditional architecture with a modern idiom.

Along with the stunningly beautiful timber frame and impressively shaped roof, the barn had two enormous façades, which Howard exploited. He used one side as the main entrance and the other as a passive solar collector. To that end, he oriented the house to the south and replaced the wooden siding with large double panes of transparent glass. He constructed the ground floor as a concrete slab so that it could act as heat storage and be easy to clean. In summer, the solar façade is shaded by the decks and the tree canopy.

Visitors enter the site on a gravel driveway that gently drops from the ridge plateau above and then splits into a large circular drive spanning the width of the house. The passage moves through a dense old-growth forest of huge hardwood trees dappled with sunlight. The wood is bisected by a clearing and a path leading directly to the house, so that visitors driving in get a glimpse of the house on axis at the turn to enter the circular drive. Once down the hill and deep in the forest, the barn springs into view. To its left is the garage. The entry to the house divides the volume in two: it sits at the juncture of a low-lying volume on the right and the main body of the barn.

An open wooden-lattice pergola made of squares connects the house to the door of the garage and doubles as a porte cochere. The flat black color of the pergola dematerializes the wood, making it appear abstract, and acts as a visual contrast to the graying wood siding of the house. Not only does the pergola unify the compound, but it also lends importance to the automobile and makes entry from the car ceremonial, recalling the carriage entries of earlier centuries. The canopy is a precise modern foil to the barn vernacular.

Howard detailed the parapet flashing and the garage door facing the house in hard-line flat black to contrast with the dull gray of the natural wood siding and to frame the soft vernacular wall planes with precise modern lines. The exterior vertical board-and-batten barn siding is a combination of poplar battens and rough-sawn oak boards prepared at local sawmills and left untreated, resulting in a sun-bleached gray finish. The boards and battens give the façades vertical consistency.

Howard was interested in spatial sequences and transitional spaces that are unexpected and elegant. From the moment when visitors walk over the threshold, nature is part of the architectural experience. One enters the house through full-light double doors into an oak mezzanine. Stepping inside the monumental, fifteen-foot-high reception foyer, the view is split into two. On the right, it is possible to see up into the light-filled living room and former hayloft above, to a vast expanse of glass framed with timber posts, and to the forest canopy beyond. To the left, it is possible to look down into the family room and, again, to the woods beyond. To the hard right is the passage to the artist's studio, which is the only room on the entry level.

Downstairs, visitors enter a large open-plan kitchen, dining, and living area. The room has a low ceiling, concrete floors, and sliding glass doors across the forest side, which open onto a deck and make it possible to open the living space to the outdoors. Storage and a bathroom are located against the slope in the plan's dark space. To the left are three bedrooms for the children and a second bathroom. Upstairs, visitors enter a room with an enormous vaulted ceiling. The framing of the gambrel roof is like an umbrella opened over the living room, covering the thirty-five-foot span. Here, the floors are wood, which softens the space. At the back of the space, Howard placed the master bedroom and a stair to a loft above. The loft, which has views out to the driveway and woods in front of the house as well as down into the living room, was designed as Willis's study. As below, a balcony spans the south-facing façade, offering the possibility of indoor-outdoor

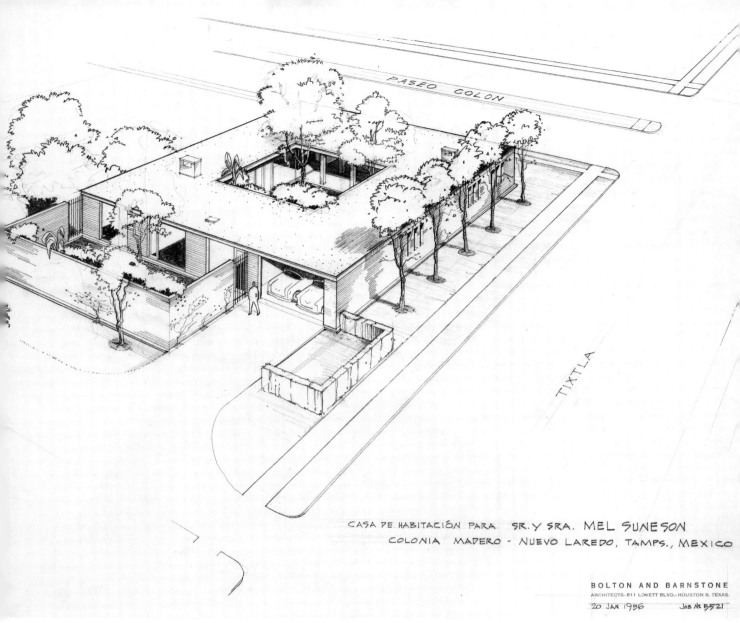

Marti Franco and Mel Suneson House, axonometric drawing (1955, Bolton & Barnstone), Nuevo Laredo, Tamaulipas, Mexico.

living while shading the lower room in summer. The entire house is surrounded with balconies and terraces, which make possible a close connection between the house and nature.

PROJECTS FOR MARTI FRANCO

Howard's stepmother, Marti Franco, is a tiny force of nature. Standing about five feet tall, full of energy, she was an early and loyal patron of Howard's, commissioning projects of all kinds from him for sites in Mexico and Texas. These buildings show Howard's range as well as the evolution of his design thinking.

The first project that Howard designed for Marti and her second husband, Earl L. "Mel" Suneson, was a house in Nuevo Laredo, Tamaulipas, Mexico (1956), to accommodate their family. The house was a modern interpretation of a traditional Mexican courtyard house.[5] Like the type it adapted, the single-story building was a fortress against the outside world, arranged around a central outdoor patio garden, which made it possible to blur the boundaries between interior and exterior. In contrast to most of Howard's American designs, he relegated cars to the rear of the house, tucked away behind other functions and adjacent to the servants' quarters.

Casa de Piedras, Marti Franco and Mel Suneson House (1967, Barnstone & Aubry), Puerto Vallarta, Jalisco, Mexico.

A rendering of the house shows a cleanly detailed flat-roofed structure with no roof overhangs. It is flanked by tall trees on one side and a walled garden at the back. Surfaces are not divided into a grid, as they are at the Rosenthal House, but are continuous planar surfaces, occasionally punctuated by openings. In keeping with the protective architecture typical of Mexico, the outer walls have only thin vertical windows. In contrast, the façades to the inner patio feature floor-to-ceiling glass, as do the openings facing the enclosed rear yard, which was to be a "jungle-like garden—rich, tropical and heavy," planted with jasmine, sago palms and hibiscus.[6] In this way, nature was part of the private domestic experience as well as a partial shield against the public domain.

A decade later Howard designed another house for Marti and Mel Suneson, one that contrasts with the first design in almost every way. Located in Puerto Vallarta, Jalisco, Casa de Piedras (House of Stones) is one of Howard's most unusual designs. It draws heavily on Ezra Stiles College by Eero Saarinen at Yale (1961). In a radical departure from the rational, orthogonal design of the Nuevo Laredo house, the Puerto Vallarta house has no right angles or regular geometries whatsoever. Instead, it consists of irregular angular shapes. It is closed to the street but open on two sides to the Pacific Ocean. The house in Nuevo Laredo was a

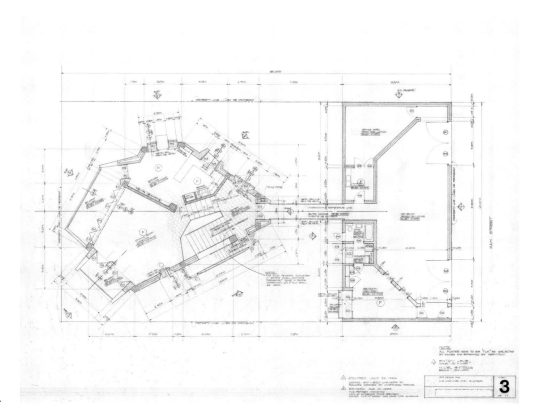

Casa de Piedras, plan.

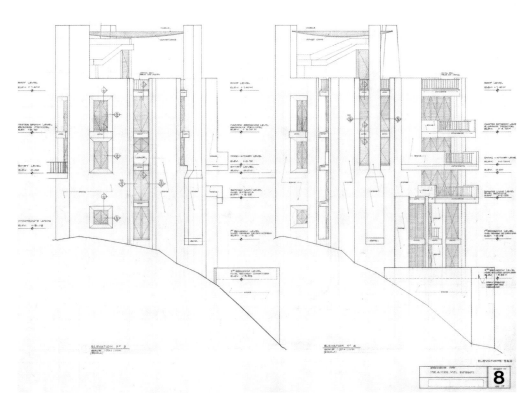

Casa de Piedras, elevation.

single-story building whose strengths lay in its plan; the Puerto Vallarta house is a multistory exercise in sectional space. Nuevo Laredo turned inward; Puerto Vallarta looks outward.

Built on a sloped site facing the ocean, the house is a prismatic tower. Spaces are dispersed over five stories in a dynamic set of sectional relationships. Just as the car's movement informed many of Howard's designs, here the human body moving vertically through space while engaging with interior and exterior views determines the experiential sequence. Visitors enter the house at street level by driving into the garage, where the view to the sea is obscured. Leaving the garage, visitors must cross a suspended bridge to the fourth floor, where the kitchen and dining room are located. The spatial magic reveals itself via the architectural promenade. The first space is a small foyer off axis and higher than the dining room. The sea, not visible at first, gradually comes into view as visitors descend into the space and approach the two large balconies, which have floor-to-ceiling windows set on either side of the room. The main living areas are one floor below the entry level and only partially visible. Howard divided the living space into winter and summer living rooms. The winter living room is tucked at the back of the plan, protected by the outer walls from cold and wind, and the summer living room is in front, flanked by balconies on either side that can be opened to make a seamless inside-to-outside connection.

The house is connected by a series of stairs varying in tread height and width and winding their way through the spaces. Views shift constantly from the sea, to the interior, and then back again while one ascends and descends the stairs. The house was constructed with a concrete structural frame that radiates from a central column out to the peripheral walls. Other than the central column, most of the vertical structure is not revealed on the exterior, whereas all the stair slabs are prominently accentuated on the façade. Since the stairs vary in pitch, they read with a modicum of abstraction. Between and embedded into the radiating beams are exposed wooden floor joists and decking coated with dark stain. The exterior stone walls read as a bearing wall envelope accented by the concrete structure within. On the interior, Howard applied white stucco to intermittent surfaces such as the banister or wall partitions to contrast with and mitigate the stone envelope.

Among the projects Howard designed for Marti was the specialty store she opened in Nuevo Laredo, Mexico, in 1955. From a series of drawings made by Tony Frederick, it is apparent that from the start Howard intended to combine elements of traditional Mexican architecture with more contemporary planning. In each version of the project, Howard inserted exterior arched windows reminiscent of those in a traditional Mexican house or mission church into an equally

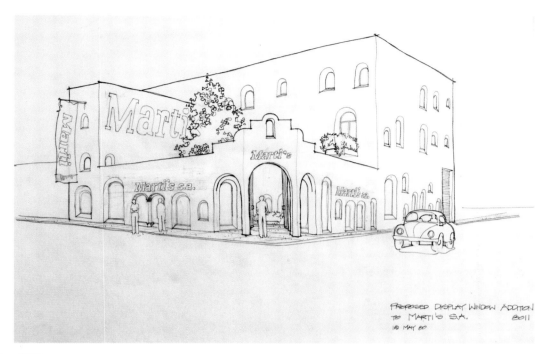

Marti's specialty store (1980 additions, Howard Barnstone, FAIA, Architect), Nuevo Laredo, Tamaulipas, Mexico.

traditional wall of stuccoed masonry. But instead of the relentlessly uniform arrangement found in traditional buildings, Howard created a playful array of windows of many sizes disposed in a seemingly random configuration across the façades. In 1980, he walled in the entrance forecourt, adding an arched entrance portal that recalls the frontispiece of a Mexican mission church. He also borrowed the Mexican architect Luis Barragán's use of brilliant color to paint the stucco façades henna, giving them a deep rich rose color.

The plans for the store, which entailed combining and reconfiguring several existing buildings, are spatially complex and original, a complete departure from the Miesian box with which Howard was identified in the 1950s. With the exception of outer walls that follow the property line, there are no parallel or perpendicular walls. Instead, walls radiate in a fractal manner to create spatial dynamism as well as intimate moments.

Howard wanted to create the spatial experience of looking through physical spatial layers from the street as a way to entice shoppers into the store. To accomplish this, he designed a double-layered façade. The outer façade is the henna stucco surface; the inner façade, a volume in sheet glass. Looking through that glass, passersby could see, framed inside, Marti's elegant wares.

Customers entered the store under the arched portal at the corner of Avenida Guerrero and Calle Victoria, passing through the entrance patio and into a glass passage made from fractured surfaces, behind which were merchandise displays. The store's interior was multilevel and open to views. It possessed a measure of the dynamism of the Puerto Vallarta house in a more modest configuration.

MOTELS

In a series of designs for motor hotels from 1962, Howard pursued his love of automobiles while experimenting with some of his more daring formal and spatial ideas. The projects were all for a site in Nuevo Laredo, where Marti introduced Howard to the brothers Octaviano L. and Eduardo Longoria-Therot, who, among their many business enterprises, owned automobile dealerships. Howard believed that the car had not been adequately considered in relation to contemporary architecture and lifestyles, that no "top-notch architect . . . has really concerned himself with the car and an office building; the car and a home; or the car and store—only one, Le Corbusier, and his thoughts of 1921 are archaic, out-of-date, and the wrong things are extracted from his schematics."[7] In the motel schemes, Howard explored many different ways that the car could interact with motel architecture in plan and in section.

In one design for the Highway Motel, he anticipated architects like SANAA by proposing a transparent glass box filled with independent spaces. In plan, such individual rooms as the kitchen, bar, and offices were enclosed by wavy walls that occasionally broke through the orthogonal building envelope. The two very different formal systems were in tension with one another, which charged the design with spatial variety and interest.

One version of the site plan for the Highway Motel shows a series of cruciform pavilions arranged around a central garden, squeezing the architecture between the automobile and nature. Cars can park on two or three sides of each building, and a road rings the site. The rendering of this design is drawn from above: the complex is a series of flat-roofed one-story structures connected by an outdoor covered walkway, similar to the one at the University of St. Thomas. The central garden is a lush tropical landscape with an enormous multi-kidney-shaped pool. Tellingly, although a handful of human figures appear in the drawing, it is crowded with cars—parked in front and at the side and circulating around the edges.

In another version of the same project, the residential pavilions are designed quite differently. The entire outer wall is a series of waves sitting underneath a rectangular roof, with orthogonal rooms for the bedrooms and bathrooms inside, inverting the tension between orthogonal and curvilinear from the

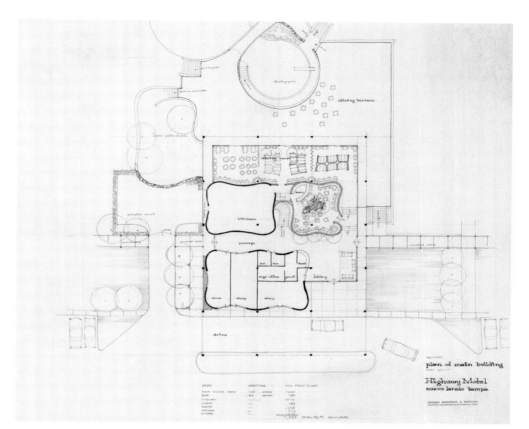

Highway Motel (also called Longoria Motel), site plan (1962, Howard Barnstone & Partners), Nuevo Laredo, Tamaulipas, Mexico.

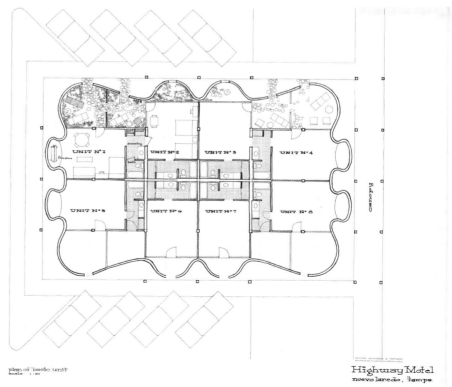

Highway Motel, Nuevo Laredo, first-floor plan.

earlier exploration. In this version, the space between orthogonal interior and curvilinear exterior becomes either a built-in fireplace or a private garden with landscaping and lounge furniture. Here, car parking is located on two sides of the building.

The Motor Hotel scheme is a more radical departure from motel design conventions. Howard proposed to stagger car parking and residential spaces in sections. A circular ramp at the side of the building allows cars to ascend to the appropriate level. Rooms were arranged around a central patio that had stair access to a central court and parking below. The design contributes a new inflection to the word "park."

A rendering of the proposal drawn from the central patio shows a car ascending through the building, with two parked cars sandwiched between two residential sections. Another view has café tables with chairs and potted trees framing the view of the motel building beyond. An open book and two martini glasses sit on one table, suggesting that this space will be one for relaxation and enjoyment. The juxtaposition of these symbols of middle-class luxury with gardens, domestic space, and the automobile creates an idealized vision of auto-centric modernity while willfully ignoring the exhaust fumes and noise that would permeate such a space. None of these motels was ever constructed.

PROJECTS FOR ROBERT BARNSTONE

Marti's son and Howard's half brother Robert Barnstone (1946–2008) was an economist, a progressive urban thinker, a city councilman in Austin, Texas, and an important Austin developer. The partnership between Howard and Robert resulted in some of the most significant and transformative buildings in Austin's contemporary resurgence. Examples include the Encinal condominium complex (1979) and the De Saligny townhouse complex (1983). The work for Robert was critical for Howard's career in other ways as well. It was through these projects that Howard met the Austin architect Robert T. Jackson, with whom he collaborated on the Schlumberger Austin Systems Center.

For the Encinal, Robert purchased a challenging hillside site on West Sixth Street near downtown in Old West Austin, a neighborhood known for its pedestrian-friendly design and village-like character.[8] The site, which rises nearly thirty feet from south to north, is roughly 150 feet wide by 200 feet deep and bounded by old-growth trees. Howard sited the buildings to preserve the trees and surrounded the architecture with steep garden landscapes infused with

OPPOSITE, TOP Highway Motel, Nuevo Laredo, rendering.

OPPOSITE, BOTTOM Highway Motel, Nuevo Laredo, "view in center court."

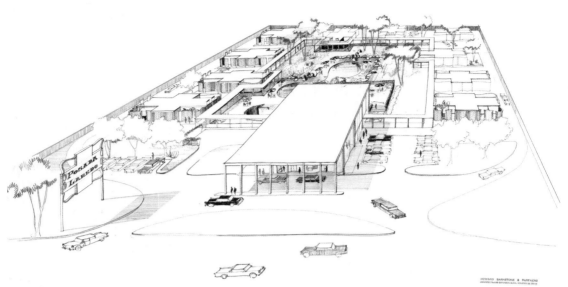

Highway Motel
nuevo laredo, tamps

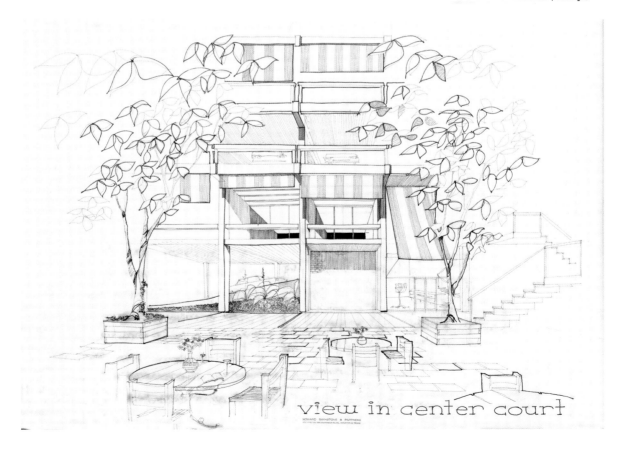

view in center court

De Saligny Condominiums (1982, Howard Barnstone, FAIA, Architect, and Robert T. Jackson), 1111 West Twelfth Street, Austin, Texas.

multilevel stairs. He looked to Italian hill towns for inspiration, even though the architectural expression is modern. He took advantage of the sloping site to lay out a set of dynamic pathways, passages, and elevated walkways and bridges that thread through the landscape and the architecture. The series of crisscrossing blackened steel bridges and stairs cuts through the building in a way reminiscent of the Piranesi *Carceri* etching that hung in Howard's living room.

The Encinal demonstrates Howard's conviction that the automobile should be integrated into contemporary living as an essential part of the modern condition. The site plan is configured by placing seventeen units on the top and east side of the site while joining the five remaining units to the west with a canted bridge that spans the driveway below. Parking is clustered in groups spread across the site and tucked under the buildings and bridges. The parking is surrounded by a series of complex landscape maneuvers that arrange cars in discrete locations and mask the parking from view. Thus, the Encinal appears to float dramatically in and above the natural landscape, accented with black steel bridges and stairs and

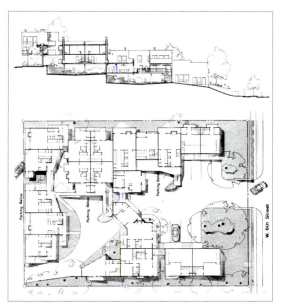

LEFT Encinal Condominiums, plan (1977–1979, Howard Barnstone, FAIA, Architect, with Allan Nutt), 1106 West Sixth Street, Austin, Texas.

RIGHT Encinal Condominiums.

wooden lattice awnings. Each unit has a fireplace and exterior terrace, all looking into the multilevel courtyards woven through the project.

SELF-COMMISSIONED PROJECTS

Two of Howard's more daring designs were for his own office—a small building at 1914 West Capitol in Houston that was completed in 1964, and an unbuilt scheme. The first was a collaboration between Howard, Eugene Aubry, and Burdett Keeland; the unrealized project was designed by Howard and Keeland.

The completed studio is a modest one-story building. Rectangular in plan, built on a concrete slab on grade, it plays with the geometric language that Mies favored, albeit with Howard's inflections. Two spaces anchor the plan: the reception area at one end and the drafting room at the other. A series of square offices line either side of a passage between the end spaces. When a compass is laid over the plan, each office forms a golden section when the circulation space is included in the measurement. The elevation is also a series of repeating golden sections. The project's innovation, however, was its use of transparent floor-to-ceiling sliding glass doors for the entire building envelope, with retractable canvas awnings on the exterior to prevent undue solar gain. These canvas awnings became a Barnstone & Aubry signature. Howard pointed to the façade treatment as an inexpensive solution to enclosing habitable space.[9] By making all four façades see-through

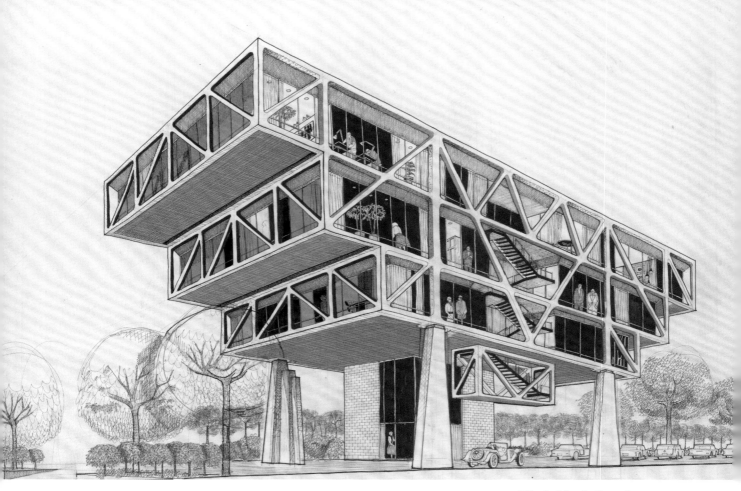

Office building for Howard Barnstone and Burdette Keeland, 1962, unbuilt project.

glass, and by building on a slab-on-grade foundation that kept the floor and ground outside on a continuous plane, Howard and his partners created a more direct relationship between the pavilion and nature than was the case with either Mies's Farnsworth House (1951) or Philip Johnson's Glass House (1949).

The scheme that was never built was a daring cantilevered structure that recalls El Lissitzky's *Wolkenbügel* (Cloud Irons, 1924) and other Futurist and Constructivist proposals, anticipating work by MVRDV and OMA.[10] Drawings show a multilevel structure suspended on enormous, tapered, reinforced concrete columns and cantilevered in three steps on the two short sides. The entrance is underneath the building, at its center. The main volumes are held in three giant steel box trusses visible on the building's exterior. The façades are floor-to-ceiling transparent glass panels inset slightly from the slab's edge in order to create wrap-around balconies. In this way, even a structure suspended above nature maintained a relationship to the outside, beyond views.[11]

OPPOSITE, TOP Vassar Place Apartments, second-floor plan (1965, Howard Barnstone & Partners), 1301–1305 Vassar, Houston.

OPPOSITE, BOTTOM Vassar Place Apartments, Houston.

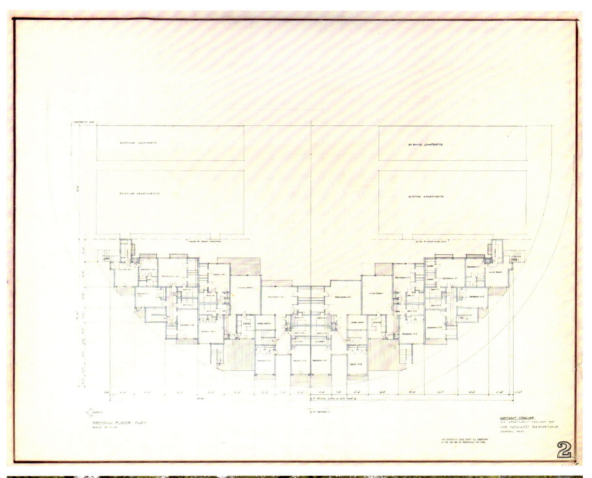

The Vassar Place apartment complex in Houston was one of many projects Howard designed as a personal investment.[12] He purchased the site in October 1962. It had two apartment blocks on it and room to expand; it is the expansion that is of interest. Like the Encinal, Vassar Place floats above the ground over a series of projecting volumes. It reflects Howard's integration of nature and architecture, and the automobile and architecture. The site plan is a carefully arranged semicircular form with an outer ring of small garden spaces, each with a tree, grass, and hostas, placed directly in front of the pathways to the units. The placement creates a green screen around the crescent-like street front. The half-round configuration screens a collective rear garden accessible from individual rear gardens. In this way, Howard created two realms, an unprotected outer realm and a protected inner realm. The buildings are lifted above the shadowed carport spaces: carport volumes and balconies above are staggered spatially. They push and pull to construct a dynamic series of solids and voids along the curved street front of the complex. Nature penetrates the interiors of the apartments in clever internal courtyard spaces that bring natural light into the middle of the living space.

Vassar Place, interior first floor.

For much of the 1970s, Howard's architecture office occupied one of the two-story three-bedroom units at the center of the complex. The reception area, conference room, and office were downstairs in the living-dining space, and the drafting studios occupied the three bedrooms upstairs. At the time, the office was working on a variety of projects. Some were for buildings with curvilinear forms of reinforced concrete, like his unconstructed proposals for highway motels. Other designs were seemingly far more traditional in their form and materiality, like the pueblo-inspired store he built for Marti in Nuevo Laredo. Howard's ability to work across a range of aesthetic approaches to architecture tied his architecture to that of other twentieth-century modern architects such as Gunnar Asplund, Willem Dudok, and Bruno Taut, who rejected narrow definitions of the modernity and modernism for a more inclusive way of designing. Common to them all was an appreciation for sophisticated space, for materiality and the inventive detail, and for composition at every level as well as reverence for every kind of architecture, from the vernacular to modern.

Vassar Place Apartments, entrance.

NOTES

1. Rudofsky, *Architecture without Architects*.

2. McCoy, "Young Architects," 186.

3. See, for instance, Kenneth T. Jackson's *Crabgrass Frontier*, in particular the chapters "Romantic Suburbs," "The New Age of Mobility," and "The Drive-in Culture of Contemporary America"; see also Duany, Plater-Zybek, and Speck, *Suburban Nation*; and Wells, *Car Country*.

4. Stephen Fox, "Howard Barnstone (1923–1987)," *Cite 18* (Fall 1987): 18–24; see also "Houses on Difficult Sites: An Almost-Triangular Lot, Wide End to Street," *Architectural Record* 116 (October 1954): 170–171; "Residence of Mr. and Mrs. M. G. Rosenthal," *Texas Architect* 5 (December 1954): 12.

5. "Modern Home, yet Mexican in Styling," *Houston Chronicle*, February 19, 1956.

6. Ibid.

7. McCoy, "Young Architects," 186.

8. "Encinal Condominiums," *Texas Architect* 31 (March–April 1981): 40; see also Katherine Liapi and Charles W. Moore, "Court Living," in "Ah Mediterranean! Twentieth-Century Classicism in America," special issue, *Center: A Journal for Architecture in America* 2 (1985): 86, 88.

9. Gene Aubry noted that although it was an inexpensive solution, the sliding doors made the building more accessible to burglars.

10. See, for example, Perloff and Reed, *Situating El Lissitzky*; Tupitsyn, *El Lissitzky*; Cooke, *Russian Avant-Garde*; and projects such as the MVRDV's WoZoCo Housing in Amsterdam and OMA's Shenzhen Stock Exchange.

11. "Houston Offices," *Architectural Forum* 118 (May 1963): 59.

12. "Thirteen Award-Winning Apartments and Townhouses," *House + Home* 29 (August 1966): 73; see also "Village-Like Garden Apartment Addition Coordinates Parking, Outdoor Living, and Privacy on a Limited Half-Round Site," *Architectural Record* 141 (January 1967): 158–159.

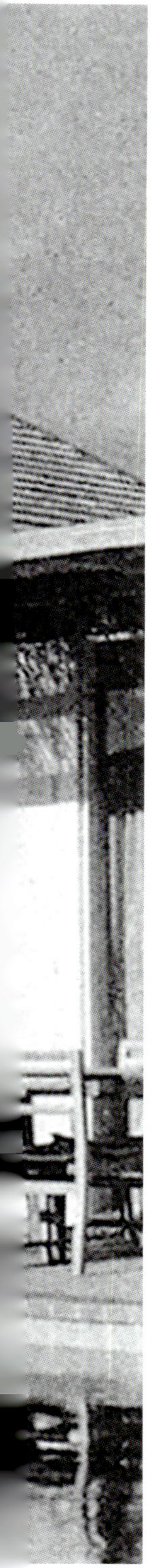

CHAPTER SIX

BARNSTONE'S JEWISH HOUSTON

JOSHUA J. FURMAN

IN 1948, when Howard Barnstone arrived in Houston, the city's Jewish community was on the cusp of a dramatic transformation. As the 1940s drew to a close, the Jews of Houston numbered approximately 13,000, and most of their homes and institutions were rooted in and around Riverside Terrace, a scenic neighborhood located southeast of downtown and east of Main Street. Jews first settled there in the 1930s, in palatial mansions constructed along the banks of Brays Bayou. They were among the city's wealthiest families, titans of retail and commerce such as the Weingartens and Sakowitzes. Unable to purchase houses in River Oaks because of gentlemen's agreements that rigidly maintained the white Christian character of Houston's premier neighborhoods, the city's Jewish elite laid claim to large plots of land along North and South MacGregor Ways. Before long, the neighborhood was known around town as the "Jewish River Oaks."[1]

Jews of more modest means took up residence in Washington Terrace, a subdivision just north of Riverside Terrace. By 1950, the South End was home to most of Houston's synagogues, including Congregation Beth Israel. Founded in 1859, the city's first Jewish house of worship and the oldest Jewish congregation in Texas stood at the corner of Austin and Holman Streets in a majestic building constructed in 1925. Across from Beth Israel, at 1300 Holman, was San Jacinto High School, where two generations of Houston Jewish teenagers received their secondary educations. Along Almeda Road, the neighborhood's primary commercial artery, Jews shopped for kosher meat and baked goods. The neighborhood was by no means exclusively Jewish; Jews lived, studied, and worked side by side with their white non-Jewish neighbors in Riverside Terrace, who constituted most of its residents. The dense concentration of Jewish families and institutions

OPPOSITE Houston map, 2017, with Jewish settlement patterns, several houses, and Jewish congregations delineated.

HOUSES

A Rosenthal House - 4506 N. Roseneath Drive
B Gordon House - 2307 Blue Bonnet Boulevard
C Farfel House - 18 West Lane
D Mermel House - 5043 Glenmeadow Drive
E Herzog House - 21 Robinlake Lane

INSTITUTIONS

1 Congregation Beth Israel (1925) - 3517 Austin Street
2 San Jacinto High School - 1300 Holman Avenue
3 Congregation Emanu El - 1500 Sunset Boulevard
4 Jewish Community Center (1950) - 2020 Hermann Drive
5 Congregation Beth Yeshurun - 4525 Beechnut Street
6 Jewish Community Center (1969) - 5601 S. Braeswood Boulevard
7 Alfred's Delicatessen - 2408 Rice Boulevard
8 Congregation Beth Israel (1967) - 5600 N. Braeswood Boulevard

in a relatively small pocket of the city, however, gave the neighborhood a distinct feel and reputation.

Between 1950 and 1970, that nucleus of Jewish communal life in Riverside steadily disintegrated, in large part as a consequence of racial integration and white flight. A similar Jewish concentration ultimately re-formed in the suburbs of southwestern Houston. An influx of African Americans coming to Houston during and after World War II in search of economic opportunity created a housing crunch in the deeply segregated city. African Americans began moving into the section of Houston's Third Ward adjacent to Washington Terrace as early as 1940, when Cuney Homes, public housing for low-income African Americans, was built just across the railroad tracks. In 1947, Texas State University for Negroes (later renamed Texas Southern University) opened its doors on a fifty-three-acre campus in the neighborhood. TSU enrolled more than two thousand students in its first year, intensifying the demand for housing near Washington Terrace.[2]

Jews and other white residents of Washington Terrace and Riverside Terrace left the neighborhood for a variety of reasons, and they left quickly. Between 1940 and 1960, the white population of Washington Terrace declined from 98 percent to 21 percent. Similarly, in Riverside Terrace the percentage of white residents plummeted from 97 percent in 1950 to 25 percent by 1960. While racist attitudes and social mores certainly influenced individual decisions to leave, the twin pernicious forces of redlining and blockbusting placed intense financial pressure on those who might otherwise have chosen to stay in an integrated neighborhood. Despite the noble grassroots efforts of residents of both races to organize resistance to predatory real estate agents, the area fell into steady decline. Developers turned single-family dwellings into rental properties and apartments; the frequency and quality of city services to the neighborhood dropped off as its racial makeup changed. Most notoriously, in 1953 the home of the first black family to settle in Riverside Terrace was bombed by a disgruntled white neighbor who hoped to scare away African Americans. Fearing their new black neighbors, as well as crime, violence, and the deterioration of property values, white Houstonians fled the community in droves.[3]

To examine a selection of the houses that Howard Barnstone designed or remodeled for Jewish clients in Houston between 1953 and 1974 is to examine the postwar dispersal of Houston's Jewish community throughout the city, out from Riverside to destinations as varied as Meyerland, Memorial, and even River Oaks. Stories of these families and the houses they lived in offer vivid portraits of where and how prominent and successful Jewish Houstonians lived during the decades in question, and how they turned to one of their own to design the living quarters of their dreams.

EVELYN AND MORRIS G. ROSENTHAL HOUSE

The house that Bolton & Barnstone designed for Morris "M. G." Rosenthal and his wife Evelyn in 1953 stands at 4506 North Roseneath Drive, a short walk from scenic MacGregor Park in the heart of the affluent Riverside neighborhood. A native Houstonian, Rosenthal served as assistant district attorney and then city attorney between 1937 and 1942, when his military service began. While stationed at Fort Custer in Michigan, Rosenthal married the former Evelyn Fink (Howard Barnstone's cousin), also of Houston, in the post chapel on July 2, 1943. Fink grew up attending religious services and classes at Beth Israel, where she was confirmed in 1931, and graduated from the Rice Institute in 1937, where she served as a reporter for the campus newspaper.[4]

As a married couple, the Rosenthals were active at Congregation Emanu El, Houston's second Reform Jewish institution, which was established in 1944 when a faction of Beth Israel members resigned their memberships in the wake of a bitter communal dispute over Zionism and support for a Jewish state in British Palestine. At Emanu El, Evelyn chaired a sisterhood interfaith committee that welcomed members of an Assembly of God church for Sabbath services in 1957, and Morris served as treasurer and member of the board of trustees. After the war, Morris went into private law practice for a time and then organized the Southern Title Company and Southern Title Guaranty Company in 1948. The Rosenthals had one son, Gary.[5]

The Rosenthal House was introduced to readers of *Architectural Record* in October 1954 in an article headlined "Houses on Difficult Sites." Measuring 4,600 square feet, the house was laid out on a semitriangular lot with bedrooms at the front of the house, facing the street, and the living room at the back. "The shape and size of the lot were the governing

Evelyn Fink and Morris G. Rosenthal House site plan (1953, Bolton & Barnstone), 4506 North Roseneath Drive, Riverside, Houston.

BARNSTONE'S JEWISH HOUSTON 203

factors in the planning of this Texas house," the magazine explained. Difficulties presented by geography, as well as the presence of close-in two-story structures on either side, were solved by "a plan straddling the lot and extending to the allowable building lines on front and sides." To create privacy for the family, the house was designed with almost no windows except in the rear of the structure, which was heavily glazed to maximize natural light. Elsewhere in the house, skylights brought the sun into the children's playroom and an interior garden area. To comply with deed restrictions requiring the house to have a second floor, servant's quarters were added on top of the carport.[6]

The Rosenthal House, certainly a symbol of achievement and prosperity for the family, received an Award of Merit for Bolton & Barnstone in a statewide 1953 competition sponsored by the Texas Society of Architects.[7] This house went up in Riverside just as the neighborhood was experiencing tumultuous change to the north of the bayou. That same year, Barnstone began work on another house for a Houston Jewish family in a different neighborhood, Braeswood, an area that would become a destination for some of the city's most prominent Jewish families when they left the Riverside area behind.

Rosenthal House, entrance.

LILLIAN AND GERALD S. GORDON HOUSE

Braeswood was developed in the late 1920s by George F. Howard, president of Houston's San Jacinto Trust Company. Howard enlisted the Kansas City landscape architects Hare and Hare to design what he hoped would become "the South End's response to the upstart River Oaks," a neighborhood "bounded to one side by a public parkway along Brays Bayou, its broad, gently curving streets fanning out from Main Boulevard and lined with widely spaced, amply sized 'country houses' designed in the eclectic architectural styles so popular in the 1920s."[8] Main Boulevard served as the western boundary of the neighborhood, providing access to nearby Hermann Park and the Rice Institute. Braeswood attracted a middle- and upper-middle-income clientele; former Texas governor William P. Hobby and W. W. Fondren, Jr., were among its earliest notable residents. The neighborhood was formally annexed to Houston in 1937. A number of important Houston Jewish families were drawn to Braeswood in its first decades, including the Gordons, Rauchs, Brochsteins, Battelsteins, and Kaufmans, and they often employed Jewish architects such as Joseph Finger, Irving Klein, and Lenard Gabert, as well as Barnstone, to design their houses.[9]

The two-story house at 2307 Blue Bonnet, designed by Bolton & Barnstone for Lillian and Gerald S. Gordon and completed in 1955, fit this pattern. The design was inspired by the work of Ludwig Mies van der Rohe, with minimalist styling and an extensive use of steel and glass. Photos of the house were featured on the covers of *Architectural Record* (mid-May 1956) and *House and Garden* (January 1958), and the Gordon House earned design awards in 1956 from the Houston Chapter of the American Institute of Architects and the Texas Society of Architects.[10]

Reflecting on the Gordons in an interview with *Architectural Record*, Barnstone commented, "It isn't often that we find clients who are so anxious to get a good house, that they slow you up, to give you the opportunity to reflect on what's been drawn on paper."[11] Gerald Gordon, an attorney, married Lillian Guberman in 1939. The family attended Congregation Beth Israel, where Gerald taught Sunday-school classes, and they were members of the Westwood Country Club, founded in 1929 by prominent Jewish families who were not welcomed at the River Oaks Country Club and other elite gentile social clubs.[12] The Gordon House was celebrated in *Architectural Record* for its elegant simplicity, a "disciplined and understated" approach to home design that exuded an "impression of considerable luxury." The Gordons told *Architectural Record*, "We feel we are living in a piece of sculpture, unique in that it is spacious, comfortable, sparkling, and above all—beautiful."[13]

ESTHER AND AARON J. FARFEL HOUSE

While Braeswood was not alien territory to Jewish families such as the Gordons in the 1950s, River Oaks was another matter. Prejudice against Jews remained in force into the 1940s, as in other elite Houston neighborhoods such as Shadyside.[14] When Aaron and Esther Farfel sought to purchase a parcel of land on West Lane, to the west of Willowick Road, in River Oaks, they were not sure that the property owner would sell to a Jewish couple. The Farfels' friend and business associate

Lillian Guberman and Gerald S. Gordon House entrance (1953–1955, Bolton & Barnstone), 2307 Blue Bonnet Boulevard, Braeswood, Houston.

Gordon House, double-height living room.

John Maher, who lived nearby, offered to purchase the property and sell it to them if needed; fortunately, that was not necessary.[15]

Aaron Joseph Farfel was born in Lithuania and came to New York City in 1910, where he grew up. After graduating with an accounting degree from New York University, he went to work for the IRS, which offered him a post in Houston in 1935. Shortly after arriving, he met and married Esther Susholtz. They raised two children, and Aaron eventually left accounting to become a private investor, finding success with such prominent companies as Evenflo, Spaulding, and the parent company of Houston's KTRK television station. The Farfels were active philanthropists and community leaders, most notably at the University of Houston, where Aaron served as chairman of the board of regents and where a faculty award was dedicated in Esther's name in 1979.[16]

The Farfels were introduced to Howard Barnstone by their close friends Dominique and John de Menil. The house that Barnstone designed for them at 18 West Lane, a masterpiece of brick and glass, was built to hold three generations of the Farfel family, including Ben Susholtz (Esther's father) and Esther's sister, Ida. Lois Farfel Stark, the daughter of Esther and Aaron, stated that the house was built to maximize privacy from the outside, and light and warmth from within. Each room had a glass wall and private courtyard so that nature and sunlight could reach every corner of the house. The wide entry corridor served as a staging ground for large group meals, including Passover Seders, and the Farfel House was open to guests on the Jewish New Year in a time-honored family tradition. Members of Houston's art community, along with prominent businessmen and academics, were also frequent visitors.

The Farfel House garnered accolades from the Texas Society of Architects, which named it the best residential design of 1957, and *Architectural Record*, which featured it as one of the twenty-five most notable houses of the same year. The *Houston Chronicle* noted that the house's "unusual . . . solid black walnut paneling" revealed walls that appeared to float, magically untethered from the floor. *Architectural Record* praised the house's clever "binuclear plan," which provided "maximum ease of traffic flow" for its multigenerational residents. Bolton & Barnstone situated the bedrooms, the library, and the children's den close together in one part of the house so that parents would have easy access to children and other family members needing assistance. The dining room, kitchen, activity room, and maid's quarters filled the second, rectangular wing of the structure.[17] In Lois Farfel Stark's words, her childhood home "set the mind to the widest questions, allowed the imagination to take forms that were not previously manifest, and linked humanity's deepest connections from the familial to the universal." The

ABOVE Esther Susholtz and Aaron Farfel House (1955, Bolton & Barnstone), River Oaks, Houston.

RIGHT (*left to right*) Aaron Farfel, Esther S. Farfel, and Gail Farfel sitting under *La Fin du Monde*, 1963, by René Magritte.

ceiling in her bedroom was painted a deep, dark blue, "as if it opened to your dreams, allowed you to expand your mind, and live without limits."[18]

ANN AND IRVING MERMEL HOUSE

Following the Farfel House in River Oaks, a neighborhood where for decades Jews had not been welcome, Howard Barnstone's next significant project for a Jewish client took him to Meyerland, the suburban development in southwestern Houston that had become the new focal point for the city's Jewish community by the mid-1960s. Meyerland was developed on 1,200 acres of farmland originally owned by Joseph F. Meyer, a non-Jewish German immigrant who arrived in Houston after the Civil War. Near the turn of the century, Meyer invested some of the profits from his successful hardware business into shrewd real estate purchases beyond Houston's city limits, believing that in time the metropolitan area would come out to meet him. He died before this vision could be realized, but his sons capitalized on their inheritance. One of them, George Meyer, developed his share of the family's landholdings into Meyerland, a subdivision that debuted in 1955 with great fanfare: a Parade of Homes exhibition that featured then–vice president Richard Nixon at the ribbon-cutting ceremony and drew more than 75,000 people in two weeks to see the state-of-the-art modern houses.[19]

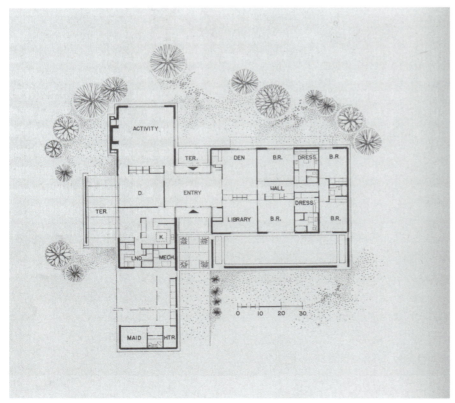

ABOVE Farfel House, interior.
LEFT Farfel House, floor plan.

ABOVE Meyerland houses, Parade of Homes.

RIGHT Levittown, Long Island, New York, c. 1956.

As a suburb, Meyerland was designed to be the opposite of Levittown, the classic cookie-cutter postwar American neighborhood with prefab structures and rigid aesthetic restrictions. Twenty-three builders constructed the thirty model homes on display during the Parade of Homes, testifying to the diversity of styles available to prospective Meyerland homeowners. In this spirit, a colorful half-page advertisement for Meyerland in the real estate section of the *Houston Chronicle* proclaimed, "We're a bunch of individuals in Meyerland. For example, if a Meyerland man likes a double-breasted suit, chances are he will damn the ivy, full speed ahead in a peppy double-breasted job. You see, we're not slaves to conformity in Meyerland. The entire concept of Meyerland is opposed to the monotony of sameness."[20]

Jewish families were initially attracted to Meyerland because it offered modern homes, good public schools, and convenient commuting access to downtown Houston. By the end of the 1960s, most of the city's Jewish institutions had relocated from the Riverside area to southwestern Houston, including the Jewish Community Center, the Jewish Home for the Aged, Congregation Beth Israel, and Congregation Beth Yeshurun. The area around Alfred's Delicatessen on Stella Link Road near South Braeswood Boulevard became known as the "Borscht Belt" because of its high concentration of Jewish residents, shops, and institutions.[21]

Howard Barnstone left his imprint on Meyerland in the form of 5043 Glenmeadow, the home he designed for Irving Mermel and his family in the early 1960s. Mermel, an accountant, grew up in Chicago and married Houston native Ann Rauch in 1945, following his army service in Africa and Italy during the war.[22] In January 1960, the *Houston Chronicle* published a sketch of the Mermel House above the title "Sketch of Houston Home of Tomorrow," offering it up as a prime example of the trends that Houston home builders would follow in the decade to come. In an article accompanying the drawing, Barnstone predicted that design styles in the 1960s would turn away from minimalism and uniformity, returning to older types of building materials, such as roof shingles and wood paneling, and older schematic models of room arrangement, with defined separate quarters for living, dining, and cooking. "Contemporary architecture and furnishings have gone about as far as possible in terms of simplicity and starkness," he noted. "The pendulum will start swinging back to other forms."[23]

By June 1961, however, it was clear that Barnstone's vision for the Mermels would incorporate only some of these anticipated design trends, owing mainly to the need to maximize space within the constraints of the Meyerland lot. Their new 2,500-square-foot "house of light," as the *Chronicle* called it, featured as its centerpiece a large central room, completely encased in glass, that served as living

Ann and Irving Mermel House (1959, Howard Barnstone & Partners), 5043 Glenmeadow, Meyerland, Houston.

room, kitchen, dining room, and playroom all at once—a perfect space for entertaining. In other ways, the newspaper explained, "the house breaks rules previously thought sacred." Despite the west wall of the house being made of glass, a row of magnolia trees strategically placed outside provided the necessary shade to prevent overheating of the house. The main room of the Mermel House was lit from the outside, using lamps installed under the eaves to brighten both indoors and outdoors at night. An eight-foot wall surrounded the house as a privacy shield, but to a limited effect. Ann Mermel reported to the newspaper that the sight of passersby scaling the wall for a peek into the glass house was an all-too frequent occurrence.[24]

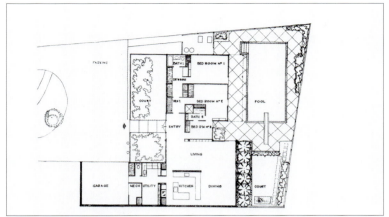 

LEFT Mermel House, plan.

RIGHT Mermel House, interior.

DORENE AND FRANK HERZOG HOUSE

Even as Meyerland became the primary destination for Houston Jewish families in the 1960s and 1970s, with about two-thirds of the city's Jewish population concentrated in two zip codes in southwestern Houston, about 10 percent of Jews lived in River Oaks, Memorial, and Highland Village, according to data collected by Elaine Maas at the time. Located west of downtown and to the north of the Meyerland area, the Memorial neighborhood takes its name from Memorial Park, the 1,500-acre greenway situated to the east. It comprises six independent municipalities called villages. Memorial became an attractive destination for some Jewish families of means who wished to escape the so-called Borscht Belt.[25]

Frank and Dorene Herzog were married in 1958 at the Westwood Country Club.[26] The Herzogs moved into the house at 21 Robin Lake in the Sandalwood section of Memorial, designed in 1955 by the Midland architect Frank Welch. By the early 1970s, with three growing children, the family began to think of relocating but despaired of abandoning the verdant woodland setting that surrounded their lot. Ultimately, they decided to hire Howard Barnstone to enlarge and remodel the existing structure.

Committed to preserving the integrity and original vision of Welch's work, but needing to add both space and functionality, Barnstone began by repurposing some of the existing rooms, for example, shifting the dining room away from the living room and into what had been a family living area. This reimagination of the structure, in turn, allowed for the installation of a glass-enclosed sunlit gallery space, more than one hundred feet long, that showcased the house's lush natural surroundings and created a passageway linking the public rooms. Hardwood floors and neutral colors accentuated the woodland atmosphere. Both the Texas

OPPOSITE, TOP Doreen and Frank Herzog House, glazed entrance hall from exterior (1955, Frank Welch; 1972–1974, Howard Barnstone, FAIA, Architect), 21 Robin Lake Lane, Memorial, Houston.

OPPOSITE, MIDDLE Herzog House, glazed living room from exterior.

OPPOSITE, BOTTOM Herzog House, interior.

Society of Architects (1974) and the Houston Chapter of the American Institute of Architects (1975) honored the newly renovated house with awards for architectural excellence.[27]

This "tour" of a selection of the houses that Howard Barnstone built or remodeled for Jewish clients in Houston offers portraits of some of the architect's finest work and a useful map for tracking the migration of Houston's Jewish families from Riverside to other parts of the rapidly growing Sunbelt metropolis in the decades after the Second World War. Meyerland was the most popular and best-known Jewish neighborhood in postwar Houston, but the city's Jewish demographic footprint was nonetheless geographically diverse.

NOTES

1. Maas, *Jews of Houston*, 50–53, 66–67; Barry J. Kaplan, "Race, Income, and Ethnicity: Residential Change in a Houston Community, 1920–1970," *Houston Review* 3 (Winter 1981): 186–187. The population figure is drawn from a Jewish Community Council of Houston study done in 1956, which estimated the city's Jewish population at a figure between 13,500 and 14,850 (Maas, *Jews of Houston*, 66).

2. Kaplan, "Race, Income, and Ethnicity," 187–189; "History," Texas Southern University website, accessed July 25, 2018, tsu.edu/about/history.

3. Kaplan, "Race, Income, and Ethnicity," 190–194. On racial and neighborhood change in Riverside Terrace, see the documentary film *This Is Our Home, It Is Not for Sale* (1987; dir. Jon Schwartz).

4. "Temple Beth Israel Holds Confirmation," *Houston Chronicle*, May 24, 1931; see also "Mrs. Morris G. Rosenthal," *Houston Chronicle*, July 4, 1943; "Local Attorney M. G. Rosenthal Dies; Rites Set," *Houston Chronicle*, June 17, 1959.

5. "Interfaith Program Set by Emanu El Sisterhood," *Houston Chronicle*, February 13, 1957; see also "Local Attorney M. G. Rosenthal Dies." On the Beth Israel–Emanu El split, see Stone, *Chosen Folks*, chap. 6.

6. "Houses on Difficult Sites: An Almost-Triangular Lot, Wide End to Street," *Architectural Record* 116 (October 1954): 170–171.

7. "Residence of Mr. and Mrs. M. G. Rosenthal," *Texas Architect* 5:4 (August 1954): 7.

8. Fox, *Braeswood*, 1.

9. Ibid., 24–28, 39, 51–52.

10. Ibid., 53–54.

11. "Disciplined Elegance Marks Houston Design," *Architectural Record* 119 (mid-May 1956): 135.

12. "Gerald S. Gordon," obituary, *Houston Chronicle*, December 9, 2003. On the Westwood Country Club, see "Work on New Country Club to Be Started," *Houston Chronicle*, October 27, 1929.

13. "Disciplined Elegance Marks Houston Design," 136.

14. Maas, *Jews of Houston*, 58–59.

15. Lois Farfel Stark, telephone conversation with the author, August 20, 2018.

16. "History of the Esther Farfel Award," University of Houston, Office of the Provost, accessed August 29, 2018, https://ssl.uh.edu/provost/faculty/current/awards/farfel/history.

17. Charlotte Millis, "Home Here Wins Design Laurel," *Houston Chronicle*, October 24, 1957; see also "Design Expressing Dignity," *Architectural Record* 121 (May 1957): 164–167.

18. Stark telephone conversation.

19. Melanie Knight, "Dream Merchant," *Bellaire Monthly*, December 1995, 10–13; see also "Family Heritage: Area Acquired 60 Years Ago," *Houston Chronicle*, April 17, 1955; R. E. Connor, "Parade of Homes Impresses Nixon," *Houston Chronicle*,

June 13, 1955; "Houston's Home Builders Lead Off 1955 Parade of Homes," *House & Home* (September 1955): 140–151.

20. "Houston's Home Builders Lead Off," Meyerland Parade of Homes advertisement, *Houston Chronicle*, June 10, 1955; see also "Some Meyerland Residents Like Double-Breasted Suits," advertisement, *Houston Chronicle*, November 10, 1957; Max Apple, "This Land Is Meyerland," in Apple, *Three Stories*.

21. Maas, *Jews of Houston*, 86.

22. "Society," *Houston Chronicle*, March 14, 1945.

23. Mary Rice Brogan, "Home Designing in for Revolution," *Houston Chronicle*, January 31, 1960. See the accompanying sketch of the Mermel House on the same page.

24. "'House of Light' Attracts Visitors," *Houston Chronicle*, June 18, 1961.

25. Maas, *Jews of Houston*, 68–69, 86–91; Fox, *AIA Houston Architectural Guide*, 498–499.

26. "Miss Dorene Faye Wolfson Becomes Bride on Sunday," *Houston Chronicle*, August 18, 1958.

27. "Houston: Artistic Renovation," *Texas Homes* 42 (March–April 1978): 40–42.

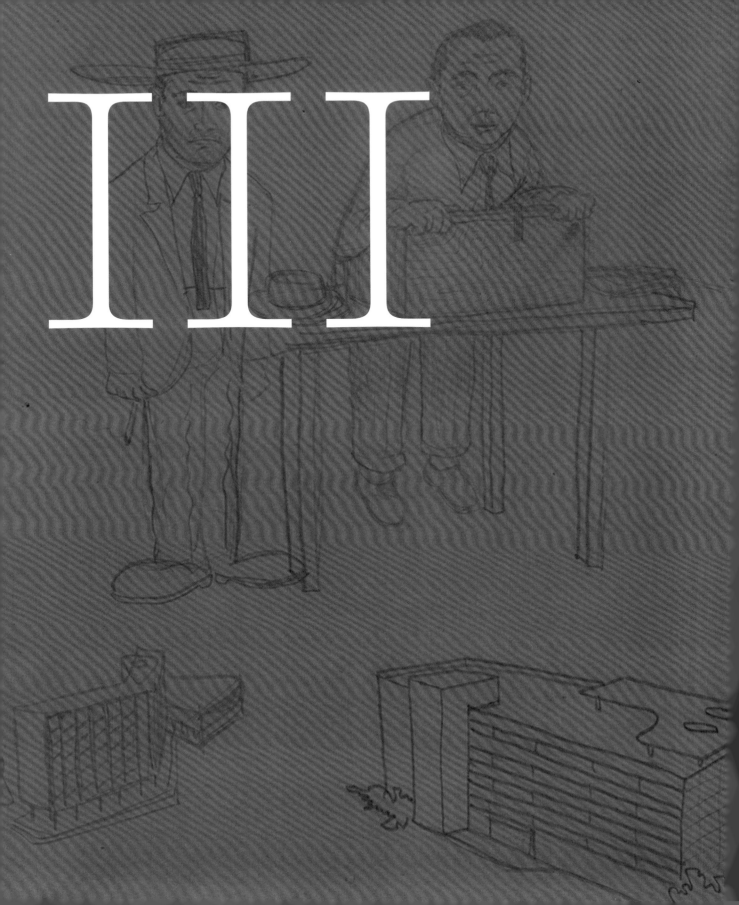

III

HOWARD BARNSTONE'S LIFE

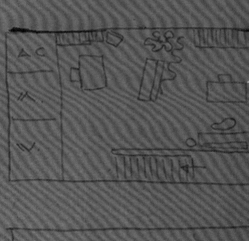
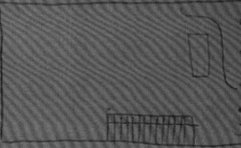

CHAPTER SEVEN

A SHORT BIOGRAPHY

BARRIE SCARDINO BRADLEY AND STEPHEN FOX

HOWARD LEONARD BARNSTONE was born March 27, 1923, in Lewiston, Maine, to Doris Ida Lempert (called Dora, 1894–1955) and Robert Carl Barnstone (1893–1946). The second of three children, he was preceded by a sister, Beatrice Barnstone (1915–2006), subsequently Mrs. Oscar Kammerman, and followed by a brother, Willis Barnstone (b. 1927). Howard was called "Howie" by his family; Beatrice was "Beatsie," and Willis was "Billy." Barnstone's father was the Boston-born son of Russian Jews, Bessie and Morris Bornstein, who immigrated to the United States in 1886. Morris Anglicized the family's surname to Barnstone in 1912 after they moved from Boston to the twin cities of Auburn and Lewiston, Maine.

In 1914, at age twenty-one, Robert married his cousin Dora Lempert, age twenty. Her parents, Sarah Halprin (1863–1939) and Hyman Michael Lempert (1865–1938), were Polish Jews who immigrated to the United States in 1888 and settled in Auburn. Mike Lempert was a leader of the local Jewish community and a founder of Auburn's Beth Abraham Synagogue in 1902.[1]

In 1919, Sarah and Mike Lempert bought an imposing Victorian towered villa house at 18 Laurel Avenue on Laurel Hill in Auburn, overlooking the Androscoggin River.[2] Dora and Robert moved into the house with her parents and lived there for a decade, making it their children's first home. Completed for Francis M. Jordan in 1881, the house was designed by the architect Charles Sumner Frost, then an employee of the Boston architects Peabody and Stearns and subsequently a distinguished Chicago architect.[3] The house and its interiors were described in detail in the *Lewiston Evening Journal* in September 1881.[4] Howard Barnstone's first home, one that he returned to often throughout his childhood, rivaled the

LEFT Dora Lempert and Robert Barnstone, parents of Howard Barnstone, c. 1916.

CENTER Francis M. Jordan House (1881, Charles Sumner Frost), 18 Laurel Avenue, Auburn, Maine. Childhood home of Howard Barnstone.

RIGHT Dora Barnstone with her three children (left to right) Howard, Willis, and Beatrice, in Riverside Park, New York, c. 1929.

Victorian houses of Galveston that later captivated him, tapping into his nostalgia for Maine.

Although Mike Lempert is consistently listed in census records and city directories as a "junk dealer," he paid cash for the house on Laurel Avenue.[5] Morris Barnstone, Howard's paternal grandfather, was a tailor. Robert Barnstone, Howard's father, owned a jewelry store, Barnstone & Co., at 50 Lisbon Street in downtown Lewiston.[6] In 1929, Robert Barnstone moved his family to Manhattan, where he opened a wholesale jewelry business at 5 Maiden Lane, then the center of New York's jewelry district.[7]

In New York, the Barnstones first lived at 54 Riverside Drive at the corner of West 78th Street on the Upper West Side, where many upper-middle-income Jewish families lived. By 1935 they had moved into an even more upscale building at 175 Riverside Drive, designed by J. E. R. Carpenter in 1925, which overlooked Riverside Park and the Hudson River.[8] Howard and Willis attended public schools in Manhattan.[9] Yet Barnstone never identified himself as a New Yorker. He always gave the impression that he had grown up in Maine. He also never used his middle name or initial.

In the early 1940s Robert Barnstone left his wife and moved to Colorado, where he worked for the Colorado Sterling Silver Company. He and Dora were divorced, and he married Matilde Franco-Béjar (b. 1924), an Istanbul-born Sephardic Jew whose family migrated to Mexico in the year of her birth. A year younger than Howard Barnstone, Marti Franco exchanged identities with her elder sister Adela in order to be able to marry and leave Mexico without her parents' permission. Marti and Robert Barnstone's eldest son, Ronald A. Barnstone, was born in

A SHORT BIOGRAPHY 223

LEFT Eighth-grade class B4, PS 166, New York City, 1937. Howard Barnstone is fourth from the right on the second row from the bottom.

RIGHT Dora Lempert Barnstone and Lieutenant (JG) Howard Barnstone in his US Navy uniform, Maine, c. 1945.

Boulder, Colorado, in 1945. Marti was pregnant with the couple's second son, Robert, when her husband, who was bipolar, committed suicide in Colorado Springs in 1946 after experiencing serious financial reversals.[10]

Howard Barnstone spent a year at Amherst College (1942) before enlisting in the US Navy as a lieutenant (JG). He was able to transfer to the Naval Reserves, which allowed him to enroll in Yale University, where he earned an AB in 1944. Barnstone was on active duty in the Mediterranean from late 1944 to 1946. He returned to Yale to earn his BArch in 1948.[11] Barnstone's thesis adviser was Edward Durell Stone (1902–1978), the Arkansas-born New York architect who designed the Museum of Modern Art. Because the Connecticut architectural licensing board did not have an internship requirement in 1948, Barnstone was eligible to take the state's architectural licensing exam immediately after his graduation, which he did and passed.

According to Barnstone, he decided to celebrate his graduation and licensing by driving cross-country to California in the summer of 1948. Car problems in Oklahoma led him to take a side trip to Houston to visit his Texas relatives, Celia Cohen Fink, a widow, and her daughter Evelyn Fink Rosenthal, a graduate of the Rice Institute.[12] Mrs. Fink took Barnstone to the University of Houston, which had initiated an architecture program in 1945. There Barnstone met Richard Lilliott, Jr., the program director. Lilliott was so impressed with Barnstone that he offered him a teaching job on the spot that he accepted.

Barnstone did not gravitate to Houston in isolation; a substantial percentage of Yale's class of 1948 seemed to end up in Texas, its most celebrated member being future US president George Bush. Barnstone would later say that he assumed he would remain in Houston for a year or two and then return to Maine to become a "regional architect." Articles in the *Houston Chronicle* and the University of Houston campus newspaper, the *Cougar*, indicate that by the spring semester of 1949, during his first year of teaching, Barnstone had already begun to demonstrate his leadership aspirations by publicizing his design studio activities and assembling a network of contacts.[13]

Even as Barnstone engaged with Houston's architectural community, he remained connected with his family in New York and Maine. In the summer of 1949, he travelled to Europe with his mother and Celia Fink.[14] Photographs show them visiting Austria, France, and Italy. He and his mother returned to Paris for his brother Willis's wedding in December 1949. Barnstone grew up traveling with his parents and grandparents and never lost his sense of wanderlust. He enjoyed the opportunities that the Menils and other clients provided to work and travel outside Houston. With his engaging personality, Barnstone made close friends in Europe and South America, as his correspondence shows.[15]

TOP Howard Barnstone, seated at right, with fellow students and the instructor Christopher Tunnard at the Yale School of Architecture.

BOTTOM Celia Cohen Fink, Dora Lempert Barnstone, and Howard Barnstone, Pisa, Italy, 1949.

In addition to his teaching career, Barnstone began to attract architectural clients to his office at 3106 Brazos Street in Houston's South End, a building that the architect Bailey Swenson had converted into an architecture studio. Barnstone completed his first house in 1949, for Nona Cook and Dr. Lee E. Hartman in Beaumont, eighty-five miles northeast of Houston. The Hartman House was followed by houses for Jeanne Brookner and Herbert M. Blum (1952), Selma Zuber and Seymour G. Rosenthal (1954), Herbert Blum's sister-in-law and brother, Faye Byer and Lawrence H. Blum (1954), all in Beaumont, and Jeanne Blum's sister and brother-in-law, Dorothy Brookner and Dr. Harris Hosen, in nearby Port Arthur, Texas (1957). These houses track Barnstone's evolving architectural awareness: the Hartman and Herbert Blum Houses were contemporary, the Seymour Rosenthal House exhibits a tentative assimilation of the Miesian architectural practices associated with Philip Johnson, and the Lawrence Blum House was Barnstone's first published example of Miesian modernism. Barnstone's initial clientele of Jewish professional and merchant families represented an enthusiastic constituency for modern architecture in postwar southern cities.[16] The Rosenthal, Lawrence Blum, and Hosen Houses were produced under the auspices of the architectural partnership Barnstone established with Preston M. Bolton in late 1952.

A SHORT BIOGRAPHY

Barnstone gravitated to Preston Bolton because he was a central figure in Houston's mid-twentieth-century modern culture scene.[17] From 1952 to 1957, Bolton was president of the Contemporary Arts Museum. During his tenure, the Contemporary Arts Association inaugurated its annual Modern House Tour and hired Jermayne MacAgy as the museum's first professional director. Bolton subsequently served as president of the boards of the Houston Arts Council, the Alley Theatre, the Houston Ballet Foundation (of which he was a cofounder in 1955), and the Contemporary Music Society, as well as a term as president of the American Institute of Architects, Houston Chapter.[18] Bolton joined Hugo V. Neuhaus, Jr., Anderson Todd, and Ralph A. Anderson, Jr., as one of the architect members of the selection committee that recommended Ludwig Mies van der Rohe as architect for the expansion of the Museum of Fine Arts in 1954.[19] With John de Menil and Stanley Marcus of Dallas, Bolton was a local cochair of the annual meeting of the American Federation of Arts in Houston in 1957.[20] Bolton, who was connected with the modern branch of "old" Houston, possessed the social connections that Barnstone craved.

The year 1952 was also when Barnstone met the couple who became his most important clients, Dominique and John de Menil. This connection facilitated the expansion of his social network, as did his acquaintance, and developing romance, with the Houston actress and artist Gertrude Levy, whom he married in 1955. Because Gertrude had grown up in Houston, she, like Bolton, was acquainted with the people whom Barnstone wanted to know. Clare Fleming and Sam Sprunt, Mary Bates and Kenneth Bentsen, Caroline Staub and Charles Callery, and Diana Stallings and William P. Hobby, Jr., were friends of Gertrude's whom Barnstone absorbed into his social network. Barnstone's marriage to Gertrude Levy, an outspoken advocate for social justice, also identified him with liberal politics in Houston during the civil rights era, a minority position that suited his need to define himself against conventional wisdom, common sense, and received opinion.

The dissolution of Bolton & Barnstone at the end of 1961 occurred at a pivotal moment for Houston architectural practices. Local modern architects—MacKie & Kamrath and Cowell & Neuhaus—who had received corporate and major institutional commissions in the 1950s saw their positions erode as a newer generation of Houston clients turned instead to such well-known out-of-state firms as Skidmore, Owings & Merrill, to whom Cowell & Neuhaus and Wilson, Morris, Crain & Anderson both forfeited major jobs.[21] Houston firms that wanted to compete in this changed environment jettisoned their residential and small-scale institutional commissions in order to concentrate on large-scale building projects. Wilson, Morris, Crain & Anderson; Lloyd, Morgan & Jones; and Neuhaus

Howard and Gertrude Barnstone with Dora and Lily Barnstone, 1961.

& Taylor successfully moved into this new mode of practice in the 1960s, especially by designing speculative suburban office buildings for the emerging developers Gerald D. Hines and Kenneth Schnitzer.[22] Barnstone and Bolton, as they went their separate ways, continued to adhere to residential practices.

Barnstone embarked on preparation of the book that became *The Galveston That Was* in 1962. He and Gertrude enjoyed jaunts to Galveston and its beaches; they and their children, Dora, Lily, and George, sometimes spent weekends there. Collaborating with the French photographer Henri Cartier-Bresson, Barnstone directed him to seek out the "moody aspects of the seaside city," as the *Chronicle* reported in May 1962, from a "telephone-rigged Renault convertible"—the Barnstone touch of insouciant modern style.[23]

Gertrude Barnstone's election to the Houston Independent School District's Board of Education in the fall of 1964 catapulted her into a highly public, controversial, and extremely stressful five-year term (fig 9.9).[24] The board's contentious public meetings were reported in the daily press and televised. During the 1960s, the glamorous Barnstones were highlighted in the social columns of the *Chronicle* and the *Post*, photographed while attending events at the University of St. Thomas Gallery of Fine Arts or the Museum of Fine Arts (often for exhibitions with a Menil connection), entertaining at their house at 1720 North Boulevard, or being feted at one of Gertrude Barnstone's openings at the Louisiana Gallery, where she showed her free-form, curvilinear, molded plastic sculpture.[25] The Louisiana Gallery, one of Houston's foremost contemporary art galleries during the 1960s and 1970s, was owned by Joan Crystal and her partner, the architect Adrian Rosenberg. Rosenberg was a former student of Barnstone's and, subsequently, a draftsman for Bolton & Barnstone during the 1950s.[26]

Barnstone juggled architectural practice and teaching. He helped raise three young children while frequently traveling as his work expanded to New York City (thanks to the Menils); New Canaan (a house for Ruth Ann Hall and Charles Smithers, Jr.); New Haven (a house for Joan Ridder and David Challinor); Nuevo Laredo and Puerto Vallarta, Mexico (thanks to Barnstone's stepmother, Marti Franco, and her second husband, Mel Suneson); and Bloomington, Indiana (thanks to Barnstone's brother Willis and his wife, Elli Tzalopoulou).

In 1968, Barnstone was elected to fellowship in the American Institute of Architects in the categories of design, literature, and education, an unusual circumstance, since most fellows are admitted in only one category.[27] But in September of that year, Barnstone experienced a severe bipolar episode, which coincided with Gertrude Barnstone's filing for divorce.[28] As Gene Aubry remembers, Barnstone simply disappeared. He turned up in New Haven, where Charles W. Moore, Yale's dean of architecture, appointed him a visiting critic. Barnstone's erratic behavior grew worse. Unable to complete the semester, he returned to Texas in November 1968 and admitted himself to the psychiatric wing of John Sealy Hospital in Galveston. His psychiatrists, doctors Martin L. Towler and Eugene McDanald, treated his depression with psychotropic drugs and electroconvulsive therapy (ECT). After his discharge in January 1969, Barnstone continued to take lithium, which he credited with slowly restoring his emotional equilibrium, although he believed that the ECT had had an adverse effect that complicated his recovery.[29]

Aubry dissolved the Barnstone & Aubry architectural partnership in 1969. Barnstone's projects immediately following his hospitalization—an addition to the Menil's guesthouse and a one-story office building in Sixth Ward for Albert Bel Fay—seemed to mirror his dispirited outlook. Barnstone's grief over John de Menil's death from prostate cancer in June 1973 is evident in the long personal tribute he wrote, an edited version of which Peter Blake published in *Architecture Plus*.[30] Barnstone's architecture recovered more rapidly than his spirits. In 1972 he designed and built three narrow four-story row houses. The Graustark Family Townhouses are a marvel of spatial compression.[31] Barnstone moved into the house at 4923 Graustark and relocated his office to one of the large apartments in the Vassar Place Apartments, two blocks away.

In addition to his emotional travails, Barnstone confronted the specter of professional slippage as a younger generation of Houston architects emerged in the late 1960s and early 1970s: Clovis Heimsath, Charles Tapley, William T. Cannady, and W. Irving Phillips, Jr., and his partner, Robert E. Peterson. Buildings designed by these architects explored angular plan geometry, activated sections, and roughly textured wood or masonry finishes (or smooth white-painted stucco) to differentiate their buildings from those with which Barnstone had been identified in the 1950s. Gene Aubry had edged Barnstone & Aubry's work in this direction through the 1960s. After 1970, Aubry emerged as an architect in his own right, designing major institutional and commercial buildings for Wilson, Morris, Crain & Anderson, which after 1972 became S. I. Morris Associates. Aubry's buildings were far larger in scale than any of Barnstone & Aubry's buildings.[32]

Barnstone's response was to submit Barnstone & Aubry's designs for publication, omitting Aubry's name.[33]

Citations in the *Daily Court Review*, which published Houston legal notices, indicate Barnstone's new tendency in the 1970s to initiate litigation. This was the course he pursued in a dispute with Congregation Am Echad, a conservative synagogue in Auburn, Maine. In 1975, Barnstone's mother's sister, Jennie Lempert Lichter (1896–1976), who lived in Cincinnati, made a substantial donation to the congregation to construct a synagogue and community center. Barnstone was commissioned as architect. Because his design exceeded the available construction funds, the congregation terminated the project a year later. Barnstone sued in federal court to collect fees that he asserted were due him under the contract, although representatives of the congregation had never signed it. In June 1977, a federal magistrate in Houston found for Congregation Am Echad, holding that it could not be sued in Texas, a judgment affirmed by the Fifth Circuit Court of Appeals in 1978 after Barnstone appealed the Houston court's judgment.[34] In October 1975, Barnstone sought an injunction to prevent the Internal Revenue Service from seizing property to pay a judgment that Barnstone had contested.[35] Thus, by 1976 he was involved in two lawsuits in federal courts in Houston.

The Galveston That Was identified Barnstone with the historic preservation movement just as it was emerging nationally in the early 1970s. Barnstone's visually sensational rehabilitation of the former Federal Reserve Branch Bank Building (1970–1973) in downtown Houston as offices for the Belgian-born steel trader André Crispin reinforced Barnstone's preservationist profile.[36] Because Barnstone was charming, witty, and articulate, he was sought out by such documentary filmmakers as Lois Stark, the daughter of his clients Esther and Aaron Farfel, for her film on Houston architecture, *We Are What We Build* (1976), and by Robert S. Cozens, then married to Elsian Rooney Davidson, Dominique de Menil's assistant, for Cozens's film *Galveston: The Gilded Age of the Golden Isle* (1977).[37]

The publication of new local and statewide magazines beginning in the 1970s—*Houston Home and Garden*, *Texas Monthly*, *Texas Homes*, and *Ultra*—gave Barnstone access to a broader regional audience than did the professional architectural press.[38] He was last published in *Architectural Record* in 1973, in *Progressive Architecture* in 1975, and in *House and Home* in 1979. (*Architectural Forum* ceased publication in 1974, and Peter Blake's attempted competitor, *Architecture Plus*, lasted only from 1973 to 1974.) *Texas Architect* continued to publish Barnstone's buildings during the 1970s and 1980s, and he was featured in theme issues on Houston and Texas architecture in the Chicago-based *Inland Architect* (July 1977) and the London-based *Architectural Review* (November 1978).[39] Yet when, in 1978, Barnstone won his only national design award from the American Institute of Architects—for the adaptive reuse of the Menil-Carpenter Houses in East Hampton, Long Island—the project was published nationally only in the *AIA Journal* and in *House and Home* (renamed *Housing*), neither of which possessed the prestige of *Progressive Architecture* or *Architectural Record*.[40] Barnstone's most widely published late career work was the Schlumberger Austin Systems Center in Austin (1987, with Robert Jackson), which was not completed until after his death[41].

In 1973, Barnstone was approached by William A. Wareing III, the nephew of Caroline Staub Callery and a recent architecture graduate of the University of Texas at Austin. While a student, Billy Wareing had prepared a report on the architecture of his grandfather, John F. Staub, and he asked Barnstone to consider collaborating on a book about Staub's work. Wareing had been afflicted with polio as a child, which left him with a compromised immune system. While visiting his Staub grandparents in Houston in November 1973, Wareing died in his sleep a week before his twenty-fifth birthday.[42] This event propelled Barnstone into writing his second book, *The Architecture of John F. Staub: Houston and the South*, which he began in 1975 and on which he worked with the historian David Courtwright, the architectural historians Stephen Fox and Jerome Iowa, and the photographers Rick Gardner and Rob Muir. Published in 1979, the book gave Barnstone the opportunity to develop a friendship with Staub. It also caused Barnstone to question his own assumptions about the relationship between eclectic architecture and modern architecture as he grew to respect and admire Staub's skill and sense of style.[43]

In 1976, Barnstone bought a Staub-designed house built in 1926, which he rehabilitated and lived in with his children and, for a time until her death, his mother's widowed sister, Eva Lempert Space (1887–1979).[44] It was at the house at 17 Shadowlawn Circle that Barnstone celebrated the wedding of his eldest daughter, Dora, in 1980 with a memorable garden party that drew the ire of his neighbor, the Algerian-born antique dealer Norbert Choucroun, the only other Jewish resident on Shadowlawn Circle. Choucroun repeatedly called the police to complain about the noise. The police did not make Barnstone aware of the complaints until after Fred Hofheinz, the young, liberal mayor of Houston, had left the party. Thereafter, whenever Barnstone planned to entertain at Shadowlawn, he would offer to pay for a room so that his neighbor could spend the night in the quiet of the Warwick Hotel (now the Hotel Zaza).

Barnstone habitually tested the limits of tolerance. He partitioned his two-lot site in Shadowlawn and built a freestanding house for a client in a sliver of his

LEFT Copley House living room as furnished by Howard Barnstone.

RIGHT George N. Copley House (1926, John F. Staub; 1977, remodeled by Howard Barnstone), 17 Shadowlawn Circle, Houston. Home of Howard Barnstone from 1976 to 1982.

backyard. When Anderson Todd, who lived across the street in a house he had designed for his family, questioned the legality of the partition under terms of the Shadowlawn deed restrictions, Barnstone aggressively countered by threatening to sue Todd, even though Barnstone had been one of Todd's nominators for fellowship in the American Institute of Architects (as he had been for Hugo Neuhaus, Kenneth Bentsen, and Lavone Andrews). In later life, Barnstone's sense of exceptionality outweighed his desire to ingratiate himself with the patrician personalities with whom he kept company. Barnstone partitioned the lot and designed the house at 16 Shadowlawn, completed in 1982 for Beth Carson and Robert S. Bramlett.[45]

The Bramlett House marked Barnstone's first excursion into postmodern design. He said he wanted the compact house to look like the gatehouse to the adjoining Staub house. Barnstone came to the postmodern critique of modern architecture hesitantly, although he had been quoted extensively in C. Ray Smith's book *Supermannerism: New Attitudes in Post-Modern Architecture* (1977).[46] Philip Johnson's flamboyant "conversion" to postmodernism in January 1979 perhaps legitimized the trend for Barnstone, but so too did the recognition that one of his faculty colleagues at the University of Houston, Robert H. Timme, and Timme's partners, John J. Casbarian and Danny Marc Samuels of Taft Architects, began to receive attention in the national and international architecture press. They became Houston's most publicized architects of the 1980s.[47] By relying on talented

A SHORT BIOGRAPHY

recent architecture graduates to work in his office, Barnstone had moved to postmodernism by 1980.

Barnstone's most enthusiastic client during what proved to be the late period of his career was the Schlumberger corporation, for which he designed two multi-building suburban complexes, one in Ridgefield, Connecticut, the other in Austin. In addition, his younger half brother, the Austin entrepreneur (and city council member) Robert Barnstone, provided commissions. Between 1975 and 1978, Barnstone rehabilitated a limestone Victorian cottage for Ann Bauer and Robert Barnstone and their three children in the near-town Old West Austin neighborhood. Barnstone almost doubled the size of the house. Yet by taking advantage of the downslope of the deep backyard, he was able to insert the three-story rear addition so surreptitiously that it is invisible from the street. Barnstone subsequently designed the Encinal Condominiums on West 6th Street (1979) and the De Saligny Condominiums on West 12th Street (1981–1982), both in Old West Austin, for his brother.

In 1982 the international oil market crashed, and then crashed again in 1986. Those shocks sent the economy of Houston and much of Texas into a rapid downward spiral following what had been the heady period of economic expansion that began in the aftermath of the Arab oil embargo of 1973. The recession of the 1980s shook the economy of Houston more severely than the Great Depression of the 1930s. Architects and other building professionals were hard hit. Barnstone had borrowed money to buy real estate. He sold the Staub-designed house at 17 Shadowlawn Circle and moved to the Vassar Place Apartments, maintaining his office in a house at 5200 Bayard Lane near the Contemporary Arts Museum. Designed by the architect William Ward Watkin (1920), the Bayard Lane house was rehabilitated by Barnstone in 1980.

In 1985, Barnstone suffered a major bipolar episode. Barnstone attributed it to the shock he experienced when a Southwest Airlines plane from Las Vegas on which he was a passenger skidded off the runway in Amarillo, Texas, on April 28, 1985. Passengers were evacuated via slides, and Barnstone claimed for months that he had suffered injuries. He threatened, through his attorney, Robert C. Richter, Jr. (who was also on the plane), to sue the airline.[48] Barnstone experienced first a protracted, months-long period of manic elation, followed by an episode of intense depression. During his manic period, Barnstone sought baptism and confirmation as an Episcopalian at Christ Church Cathedral in Houston in June 1985.[49] In November 1986, he secretly remarried Gertrude Barnstone to ensure that she would have access to his health and retirement benefits after his death.[50]

Howard Barnstone, c. 1979.

Once depression set in, Barnstone became calm, subdued, and rational, in contrast to his disturbing, although at times hilarious, conduct during the manic cycle. But he repeatedly spoke of being in pain. He said he felt like he was trapped in a cloud of foreboding, circumstances that he remedied by taking an overdose of sleeping pills on April 29, 1987.[51] In September 1986, the Houston architect Joseph Krakower had committed suicide, which troubled Barnstone.[52] In December 1988, the architect Harwood Taylor killed himself.[53] Like Barnstone, Taylor was bipolar and had experienced professional reversals due to Houston's economic depression.

Barnstone's funeral was held on May 1, 1987, at the Rothko Chapel. Marguerite Johnston Barnes, a friend and the *Houston Post*'s associate editor, stood next to his plain pine coffin and delivered a eulogy. Even in death, Howard Barnstone stirred controversy. At the burial, which followed at Forest Park East Cemetery, Willis Barnstone, after the reading of the burial office by the Very Reverend J. Pittman McGehee, dean of Christ Church Cathedral, leapt up to pray the Shema, insisting to those who had gathered at the grave site that his brother had remained Jewish.[54] Barnstone's death was the subject of articles in the Houston and Austin newspapers and the *New York Times*.[55] Peter Papademetriou's tribute in *Progressive Architecture* focused on Barnstone's professional achievements, and Phillip

Lopate's in the *Texas Observer* focused on his personal attributes.[56] Lopate noted for the first time in print that Barnstone was bisexual.

Burdette Keeland was executor of Barnstone's estate, which was not closed until four years and ten months after his death. Rudolph Colby, Barnstone's last employee, worked for several months to close down Barnstone's office and transfer his drawings, correspondence, and photographs to the Houston Metropolitan Research Center of the Houston Public Library, as Barnstone had directed. In October 1988, the Rice Design Alliance paid homage to Barnstone by organizing a tour of six of his houses.[57]

Barnstone's legacy extends to the architects who once worked for him, Gene Aubry, Tony Frederick, Hossein Oskouie, Ted Gupton, Robert Jackson, Roger Dobbins, Edward Rogers, and Rudy Colby among them. Barnstone's nephew, Robert Barnstone, is an architect, as is Robert's wife, Deborah Ascher Barnstone. Adela Franco Frank's daughter, Viviana Frank, is an architect who practices in Laredo with her husband, Frank Rotnofsky. Following Barnstone's death, his daughter Dora and her husband, Gary Barber, occupied Barnstone's apartment in the Vassar Place Apartments. Gertrude and Howard Barnstone's younger daughter, Lily, a former actress and a writer, and her husband, Clinton Wells, settled just up the street from the Vassar Place Apartments. Gertrude and Howard's son, George Barnstone, a lawyer and eventually a judge in the Harris County civil court system, and his wife, Francine, restored a midcentury house in the Riverside-area neighborhood of Timbercrest, where they display a portion of George's father's folk art collection with consummate Barnstone flair.

Howard Barnstone's suicide disconcerted his family and friends. He acknowledged his bipolar disorder and often talked about the connection between depression and suicide. Yet despite the emotional anguish that Barnstone was experiencing, his friends assumed he would recover, as he had before. The finality of his suicide dissolved the fragile fictions that Barnstone was expert at fabricating, and exposed the melancholy that suffused his ebullience.[58]

NOTES

1. Websites on the history of the Jewish community of Auburn and Lewiston suggest that many of the families were interrelated; see Elliott L. Epstein, "Fitting In and Moving Up: Harris Isaacson in Lewiston-Auburn, 1900–1922," accessed March 6, 2019, https://web.colby.edu/jewsinmaine/files/2011/04/Epstein-Harris-Isaacson-in-L-A.pdf; Phyllis Graber Jensen, "The Jewish Merchants of Lewiston's Lisbon Street," accessed March 6, 2019, http://web.colby.edu/jewsinmaine/files/2011/04/Jensen-Jewish-merchants-of-Lisbon-Street.pdf; Krasne Guestbook Archive, accessed March 6, 2015, http://eilatgordinlevitan.com/krasne/kne_pages/kne_gb_archive.html.

2. The first two buildings for the Beth Abraham congregation burned; the third was erected in 1934 on a new site at 35 Laurel Avenue, just a few doors down from the Lemperts in Auburn, Maine.

3. National Register of Historic Places Registration Form, NRHP ref. #14001088, 2014, US Department of the Interior, National Park Service, accessed March 3, 2019, https://www.nps.gov/nr/feature/places/pdfs/14001088.pdf.

4. *Lewiston Evening Journal*, September 10, 1881.

5. The 1920 US Census shows that the Lemperts had no mortgage on 18 Laurel Avenue.

6. *Lewiston and Auburn, Maine, City Directory*, 1915. The firm was later Barnstone-Osgood and then H. A. Osgood & Sons after Barnstone moved to New York. In city directories of the 1930s, Barnstone is listed as "proprietor" of the store even though he was in New York.

7. Jen Carlson, "A Clock Has Been Embedded in This New York Sidewalk since the 1880s," *Gothamist*, September 29, 2014, accessed May 7, 2019, http://gothamist.com/2014/09/29/sidewalk_clock_nyc.php. The clock embedded in the sidewalk on Maiden Lane by the jeweler William Barthman in 1899 to attract customers still exists.

8. The 173–175 Riverside Drive building has been converted into condominiums. A three-bedroom apartment there now sells for over $2 million. The Barnstones' apartment may have been even larger, since census records show that in addition to their five-member family, two maids or nannies also lived with them.

9. Information on Barnstone's youth and family comes from the entry "Barnstone, Howard," in *Who's Who in America, 1970–71*, 115; see also W. Barnstone, *We Jews and Blacks*, 9–10, 14–15, 18–19, 43, 84; "Short History of the Jewish Community of Lewiston Auburn Area," Documenting Maine Jewry, accessed March 3, 2019, https://www.mainejews.org/LocalHomePageHistory.php?city=LA; Krasne Guestbook Archive; Jensen, "Jewish Merchants of Lewiston's Lisbon Street"; Barbara Goodman Shapiro, "History of Beth Abraham Synagogue: 90th Commemorative Review," updated June 1, 2008, Documenting Maine Jewry, accessed March 6, 2019, https://mainejews.org/AuburnBethAbraham90.php; Epstein, "Fitting In and Moving Up."

10. W. Barnstone, *We Jews and Blacks*, 21–23. The *Colorado Springs City Directory* for 1946 shows that Robert Barnstone was living at the Broadmoor Hotel in room 17. He was buried in Colorado Springs.

11. Howard Barnstone received an honorary MArch degree from Yale on June 11, 1972.

12. Lily Barnstone Wells, interview by Barrie Scardino Bradley and Stephen Fox, Houston, February 22, 2018.

13. "'City Planning' Course Offered This Spring," *Cougar*, February 11, 1949, 5; see also "Houston U. Class Will Submit Ideas for Civic Beauty," *Houston Chronicle*, March 20, 1949; "Students Will Submit Civic Center Plans," *Cougar*, March 25, 1949, 6.

14. According to Lily Barnstone Wells, her grandmother Dora Barnstone and her grandmother's cousin Celia Fink were quite close and traveled together often.

15. The Barnstone Collection at the Houston Metropolitan Research Center, Houston Public Library, contains over fifty boxes of personal and general correspondence. A group of revealing letters from 1948 and 1949 were written by an architect named Peter who addressed Howard as "My Dear Barney" (Barnstone Collection, HMRC, box 29:7–8). The letters contain many endearments, suggesting the two had had an affair, perhaps when Howard was in the navy or at Yale. Peter's letters came from Paris. Both Howard and Peter eventually married women, and the correspondence ceased.

16. Kingsley and Carwile, *Modernist Architecture of Samuel and William Wiener*; Jann Patterson Mackey, "Modernism Comes to Dallas: The Architecture of Howard Meyer" (PhD diss., University of Texas at Dallas, 2010).

17. Bolton's father, Frank C. Bolton, was chairman of the electrical engineering department at Texas A&M University; he served as the university's president from 1948 to 1950. Preston Bolton was an architecture graduate of Texas A&M.

18. On Preston Bolton, see Everett Evans, "Preston Bolton, 91, Architect, Civic Leader, Pioneer in Houston's Arts," *Houston Chronicle*, November 6, 2011; see also "Bolton, Preston Morgan," in *American Architects Directory*, 3rd ed., 85.

19. C. Adams, *The Museum of Fine Arts, Houston*, 66.

20. Jonathan Marshall, "The A.F.A. Convention," *Arts* 31 (May 1957): 10–11.

21. Kevin Alter, "SOM in Houston," *Cite 40* (Winter 1997–1998): 34–37. Cowell & Neuhaus had been commissioned to design the Tenneco Building; Wilson, Morris, Crain & Anderson, the First City National Bank Building.

22. Koush, *Constructing Houston's Future*, 12–43; see also Gerald Moorhead, "Wilson, Morris, Crain & Anderson," *Texas Architect* 39 (November–December 1989): 80; Moorhead, "Hermon F. Lloyd," *Texas Architect* 39 (November–December 1989): 61; Moorhead, "Neuhaus & Taylor," *Texas Architect* 39 (November–December 1989): 65.

23. Ann Holmes, "Houston to Paris Gallery on the Way," *Houston Chronicle*, May 2, 1962; see also "Museum Is in the Spot This Week," *Houston Chronicle*, November 29, 1965; "Galvestonians and Familiar Scenes," *Houston Chronicle*, December 1, 1965.

24. Elmer Bertelsen, "School Board Election Draws 10 Candidates," *Houston Chronicle*, October 25, 1964.

25. "Party Will Honor Artist," *Houston Chronicle*, April 7, 1961; see also Betty Ewing, "Fabulous Museum Opening Ends with Splash," *Houston Chronicle*, April 5, 1965; Ewing, "The Sinister Thrush Operator Was Crying Softly," *Houston Chronicle*, November 30, 1967.

26. "Personal Listings," *Houston Chronicle*, January 21, 1962.

27. "American Institute of Architects Fellowships: Howard Barnstone, Houston, For Design, Literature, and Education," *Texas Architect* 18 (August 1968): 10.

28. "Suits Filed in District Courts and Courts of Domestic Relations," *Daily Court Review*, September 10, 1968.

29. Howard Barnstone, conversations with Barrie Scardino Bradley.

30. Howard Barnstone, "Obit: John de Menil," *Architecture Plus* 1 (August 1973): 71.

31. Karleen Koen, "Best of '77: Nine Architects and Their Projects Win Residential Honors," *Houston Home and Garden*, February 1978, 54–55, 60–61; see also Gary McKay, "Architectural Honors," *Houston Home and Garden* 11 (July 1985): 60–61.

32. Mary Jean Kempner, "Young Architects in the Spotlight," *House Beautiful* 108 (July 1966): 68; see also Moorhead, "Wilson, Morris, Crain & Anderson," 80; Aubry, *Born on the Island*, 3–4.

33. "Record Houses of 1973: 10, House, Galveston," *Architectural Record* 153 (mid-May 1973): 60–61.

34. *Howard Barnstone v. Congregation Am Echad*, 574 F.2d 286 (5th Cir. 1978), available at Court Listener, accessed March 4, 2019, https://www.courtlistener.com/opinion/355153/howard-barnstone-v-congregation-am-echad. Temple Shalom Synagogue Center, as the congregation is known today, built its synagogue and school in 1982.

35. "Architect Asks Order to Bar IRS From Seizing Property," *Houston Chronicle*, August 20, 1975.

36. "Exchange Machine Guns for Champagne," *Houston Chronicle*, January 11, 1973; see also Peter C. Papademetriou, "Report from Houston," *Progressive Architecture* 56 (May 1975): 38.

37. Ann Holmes, "TV Special to Look at City's Architecture," *Houston Chronicle*, December 31, 1976; see also "People and Programs," *Houston Chronicle*, April 26, 1977; Ann Hodges, "Galveston Highlighted Nationally," *Houston Chronicle*, June 19, 1977.

38. Gay Elliott McFarland, "Dream Houses: What Architects Would Build if They Had the Chance," *House Home and Garden* 9 (December 1982): 104, 106; see also Mark Hewitt, "Barnstone's Benchmarks," *Ultra* 4 (February 1985): 56–61.

39. Nory Miller, "Lone Stars—Howard Barnstone and Karl Kamrath," *Inland Architect* 21 (June 1977): 16; see also "Obelisk and Chapel, Houston," *Architectural Review* 164 (November 1978): 318.

40. Mary E. Osman, "Honor Awards/1978: Moved and Restored Buildings, Long Island, New York," *AIA Journal* 67 (mid-May 1978): 137; see also "Two Remodelings That Bridge 300 Years: Re-Creating the Past," *Housing* 56 (July 1979): 80–81.

41. "Schlumberger Austin Systems Center, Austin, Texas, 1987," *A + U* 206 (November 1987): 31–38; see also Joel Warren Barna, "Bridgelike Walking System Links a Set of Five Office Pavilions: Schlumberger Company, Austin, Texas, Systems Center," *Architecture* 77 (January 1988): 78–81; "Austin Systems Center: Research Center for Schlumberger Company, Joint Venture by Howard Barnstone and Robert Jackson," *Baumeister* 85 (April 1988): 50–57; Joel Warren Barna, "High Tech Office Center Fits One of a Kind Site," *Texas Architect* 38 (November–December 1988): 36; Peter Davey, "Texas Nature," *Architectural Review* 981 (September 1989): 67–70; Michael Leccese, "Hill Country Headquarters: What Happens When a Texas Corporation Meets the Endangered Species Act? Austin's Schlumberger Systems Center Finds a Perfect Solution," *Landscape Architecture* 86 (April 1996): 56, 58–63.

42. Ann Holmes, "John Staub, the Ideal Eclectic Architect," *Houston Chronicle*, January 30, 1977, 11; see also H. Barnstone, *Architecture of John F. Staub*, xi.

43. Ann Holmes, "The Architecture of John F. Staub," *Houston Chronicle*, Zest magazine, October 21, 1979; see also "John F. Staub: A New Book about Our City's Great Eclectic Architect," *Houston Home and Garden* 6 (October 1979): 53–60.

44. Wendy Haskell Meyer, "Provincial Living," *Houston Home and Garden* 5 (February 1979): 90–95; see also "Eva Rose Lempert Space," *Houston Chronicle*, June 6, 1979.

45. Jeffrey Karl Ochsner, "Bramlett House," *Texas Architect* 33 (May–June 1983): 46–47.

46. C. Smith, *Supermannerism*, 59, 75, 89–90, 103. Smith also cited Doug Michels (115–116) and John Zemanek (203–204) in his account of the postmodern turn in American architecture.

47. Joel Warren Barna, "Taft Architects," *Texas Architect* 39 (November–December 1989): 74.

48. Barnstone Collection, HMRC, box 96:9; see also "Jet Runs Off Runway," *Houston Chronicle*, April 29, 1985.

49. Barnstone Collection, box 105:13. Barnstone was baptized and confirmed in the Episcopal Church on June 17, 1985. Robert Richter was his witness, and Eugenia Preston Brooks Richardson and Stephen Fox were his sponsors. He attended the "Dean's Hour" Sunday school class often, and church services sporadically with Richter.

50. According to Margie Keeland, her husband, Barnstone's best friend, Burdette Keeland, stood in for Barnstone at the wedding ceremony, which Barnstone did not attend.

51. W. Barnstone, *We Jews and Blacks*, 216, 218–219.

52. "Krakower," *Houston Chronicle*, September 26, 1986.

53. "Architect Harwood Taylor Dies," *Houston Chronicle*, December 18, 1988.

54. W. Barnstone, *We Jews and Blacks*, 221–222.

55. Pamela Lewis, "Architect Howard Barnstone: The Legacy Lives On through His Work, Colleagues, and Students," *Houston Post*, May 2, 1987; see also "Howard Barnstone, 64, Houston Architect Dies," *Houston Post*, April 30, 1987; Michael

McCullar, "Architect Left Mark on Austin," *Austin American-Statesman*, May 5, 1987; Peter Applebone, "Howard Barnstone, 64, Dies: Texas Architect and Author," *New York Times*, May 2, 1987.

56. Peter C. Papademetriou, "Howard Barnstone, 1923–1987," *Progressive Architecture*, 68 (July 1987): 27; and Phillip Lopate, "Elegy for Houston," *Texas Observer*, May 29, 1987, 10.

57. Ann Holmes, "Tour a Tribute to the Magic of Howard Barnstone," *Houston Chronicle*, *Zest* magazine, October 23, 1988.

58. The filmmaker Jon Schwartz exposed this tension in his mesmerizing documentary about Gertrude Barnstone, shot in the Rothko Chapel in 2015 when she turned ninety. The film deals quite candidly with Howard Barnstone's disorders; see Olivia Flores Alvarez, "*Gertrude Barnstone: Home Movie*: Chronicles of a Life Well Lived," *Houston Press*, November 5, 2015, accessed March 4, 2019, https://www.houstonpress.com/arts/gertrude-barnstone-home-movie-chronicles-a-life-well-lived-7896554.

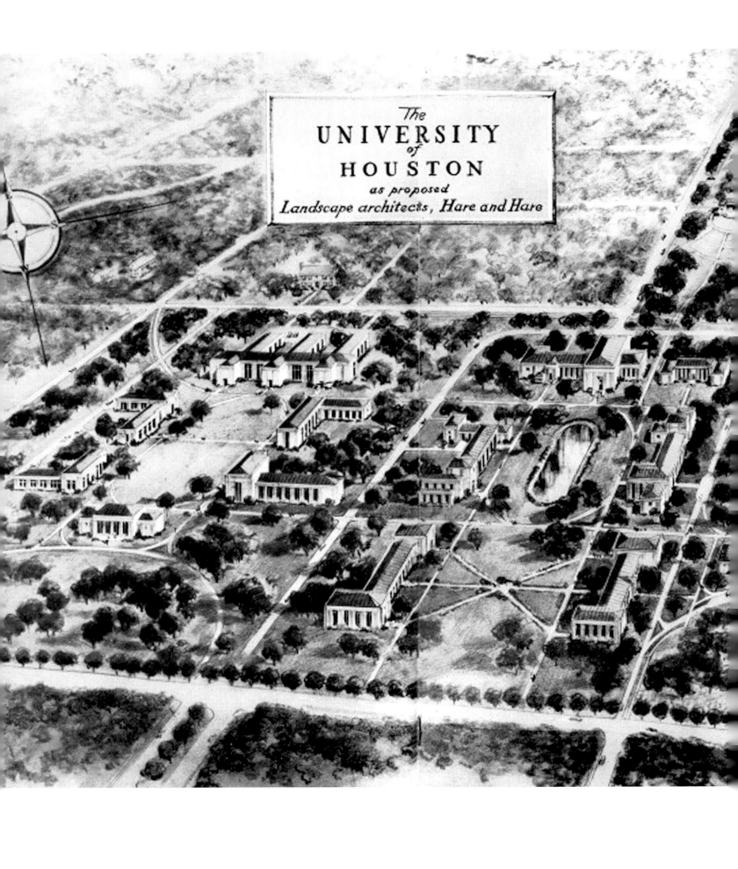

CHAPTER EIGHT

BARNSTONE AND THE UNIVERSITY OF HOUSTON

BRUCE C. WEBB

TO START A SCHOOL of architecture in a young, overextended university in mid-1940s Houston, what would it take? Whatever it might be, the University of Houston (UH) didn't have much of it. But potential students began showing up after the Second World War with GI Bill tickets in hand, asking about courses that would allow them to become architects. According to governmental information distributed to veterans, it was a field that would be much in demand because of the upsurge in building expected in the postwar, baby-booming years ahead. And Houston was one of the cities that would be leading the way. The university had nothing for them.

Just twenty years old, UH was barely settled as an offshoot of Houston Junior College, where it had existed in borrowed space in San Jacinto High School since 1927. The university had become a four-year degree-granting university in 1934, and it depended on student tuition and Houston's private wealth to sustain itself. UH moved to its present location in 1939, a 110-acre tract of isolated, forested land five miles southeast of the growing Houston downtown. The property was donated by heirs of J. J. Settegast (1875–1942) and the local philanthropist Ben Taub (1899–1982). The oilman Hugh Roy Cullen and his wife, Lillie Cranz Cullen, donated funds to erect the first buildings, the Roy Gustav Cullen Building (1939, Lamar Q. Cato), a companion to the science building (1939, Lamar Q. Cato), and, later, the Ezekiel W. Cullen Building (1950, Alfred C. Finn).[1] This ensemble of buildings was part of a quadrangle that fit into a formal campus plan prepared by the Kansas City landscape planners Hare and Hare in 1937. The legibility and commodious attributes of the original plan were abandoned as the campus grew, along with Houston, into a commuter destination. A

There is always a risk that education may put you at odds with the tasteless philistines who run the world and whose lexicon stretches only to words like oil, golf, power, and cheeseburger.

TERRY EAGLETON, *AFTER THEORY* (2003)

perimeter belt of asphalt parking lots now surrounds the inner campus, where new buildings of every architectural genus have been strung out along disjunctive grid lines. The freeway, railroad tracks, and deteriorating neighborhoods surrounding the campus did little to dispel the notion that UH was on the wrong side of town.

Always more ambitious than cautious, UH decided to establish an architecture course of study even without available space, professors, a director, or a curriculum. Like many postwar architecture programs, it would be located administratively in the School of Engineering, and studios were initially set up in the vocational education shops. The administration appointed Richard W. Lilliott Jr. (b. 1941), a peripatetic academic who had briefly studied architecture at the Rice Institute before completing undergraduate and graduate degrees in English, as interim director, to get the program started. Lilliott had taught drafting in the University of Houston's engineering school, but he was not an architect, nor did he have an architecture degree, an indication that the university may have had initially low expectations for its foray into teaching architecture. Its plan was to seek a permanent director quickly if things worked out, but plans to hire the lone candidate, Robert W. Talley, a teaching fellow at Rice, didn't materialize, and Lilliott settled in for an amazing twenty-year run as interim head, director, and, finally, dean as the architecture program moved up from department to school and finally to an independent college in 1961.[2]

Lilliott was inexperienced but willing. Entrusting him with the job of building a new school of architecture was the kind of unconventional move that the university employed to compensate for its persistent lack of resources. Lilliott was

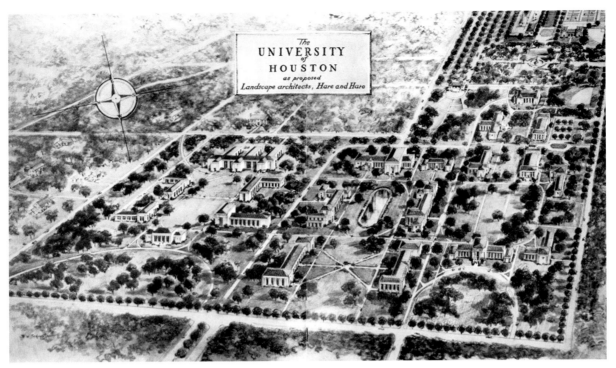

University of Houston, General Plan for Campus Development (Hare and Hare, 1937).

thoughtful, intelligent, and cultured; he had no strong agenda of his own. He was given to a brand of modernism that was not about any particular style or polemic, but embraced open-ended exploration and encouraged free-spirited design investigations. He set out a very basic curricular plan that he expected the faculty would expand and shape as the school grew. The course catalogue of 1950–1951 announced "all phases of architectural instruction are presented through four channels: design, construction, aesthetics, and graphics with emphasis on the integration of all four to remind the student of their interdependence."[3]

Lilliott's loose concept for the school allowed him to attract and be attractive to a wide variety of potential faculty members with many different points of view. At first, most of the school's embryonic design staff was local. A fortuitous first hire was the already-notable architect Donald Barthelme, a powerful personality who exercised a paternal influence over the school as it brought younger faculty members into the ranks. As a successful and busy practicing architect, Barthelme set a precedent by which instructors were tacitly expected to have private architectural offices separate from their teaching positions. Though this arrangement was not common at other schools, and the university administration was not entirely comfortable with it, it did help recruit new teachers. Barthelme set out the school's first testament: a deliberate rejection of the Beaux Arts tradition in

University of Houston College of Architecture students in studio, 1947.

favor of a strong-willed mixture of educational pragmatism and passion for discovery that he called "an integrated approach to architectural education":

The department begins a new plan in architecture training designed to attack the fundamental problem of preparing its students for practice in the profession. The University approach admits that architecture as a pattern or set of answers or formulas is inadequate in the light of current concepts. It seeks to provide each student the opportunity of developing himself to take a proper place in the architectural profession under the guidance and counsel of its staff along with the provision of a cultural background and practice in the tools of the profession.

The kernel of this plan lies in the thorough integration of all phases of architectural instruction at the exact time when they will be of most use to the student. It disallows teaching on the basis of copying either plates, drawings or construction methods. It studies history or esthetics as a useful background for current endeavor and improvement of taste. Chronology is relatively unimportant.

This program is designed to produce graduates able to dissect each problem into its essential components . . . with a thoughtful and informed understanding as well as a practiced skill . . . developed through integrated study of design, construction, graphics, free hand drawing and esthetics. It is designed to produce a person with no stock answers for any problem however common.[4]

Barthelme's polemic served the school catalogue for many years, although course listings for the most part remained unchanged: workaday descriptions of the components of a professional curriculum that didn't quite match the dynamics of Barthelme's rhetoric, and a studio sequence organized around successively more complex material design projects.

Lilliot filled out the faculty with other young architects who happened to be in the area, several of them among the first graduates of the school. He brought on William R. Jenkins, who was back from service in the US Navy and gaining recognition as a designer of modest, modern houses. Jenkins would later become a long-term dean of the college. Edmund Furley, C. R. Lively, Herbert Linnstaedter, David Red, Robert Lindsey, and, later, Burdette Keeland also joined the small faculty. John Zemanek, another veteran who was back in the United States after

Gaea I House (1968, John Zemanek), Houston.

Second World War assignments in Japan, was hired in 1962 to fill a teaching vacancy, and he too became a permanent part of the faculty. Zemanek was an arch-iconoclast whose biography began with his growing up on a Texas farm and then earning degrees from the University of Texas and Harvard. He was an "indigenous modernist" who became well known for a trio of individualistic houses that he built for himself.[5] Within the architecture school, Zemanek championed the rising interest among architects and students nationwide in addressing problems in underserved communities. With a following of students, he began to work in Houston's poorest neighborhoods, undertaking low-budget interventions that required abundant creative thinking.

BARNSTONE ARRIVES

Howard Barnstone was the most significant new faculty member. His arrival in 1948 brought social and architectural élan to the nascent school. Finding

Howard Barnstone, c. 1961.

opportunity in a city that was undergoing rapid change in an environment of economic prosperity, Barnstone started a practice and joined the UH faculty almost immediately after moving to Houston. His long association with the Menil family that began in 1952 provided continuity to his career. He was a favored member of their elite cultural circle, and his association with the family and its businesses was good for the University of Houston's architecture school. It brought the school into contact with intellectual, artistic, and architectural luminaries who otherwise would have been beyond the reach of the fledgling school. The Menils also accommodated requests for small grants for college projects and exhibitions. Barnstone made numerous visits to the job site of Philip Johnson's Menil House during construction as a teaching opportunity for his students to get an inside look at the making of a local masterwork of modern architecture.[6]

Barnstone made a vivid impression on Burdette Keeland, a UH student beginning in 1948: "He came to class wearing a cowboy hat and a white button-down Brooks Brothers' shirt with a long, stringy black knit tie. He was so short his feet dangled beneath the lectern while he lectured. But what he told us lasted: 'be daring, be creative, be great, with CLASS.'"[7] Barnstone became Keeland's mentor and lifelong friend.

Barnstone's growing reputation as a modern architect, together with the continuing presence of Barthelme, propelled the reputation of the school as a Texas outpost of vanguard design. The best students were encouraged to pursue master's degrees. William Jenkins, Burdette Keeland, and others were soon earning their share of architectural design awards and recognition, a tradition of professional excellence that has continued to enhance the college's reputation as a design school. Students, too, were frequently winners in state design competitions. Visitors often remarked on the work ethic, quality of effort, and accomplishment evident in student design work that belied the school's limited resources and shabby facilities.

As the architecture school continued to grow, even without adequate university support, there were signs of restlessness underneath the surface. In

1959, Barthelme decamped to Rice to become the director of its architecture program, an arrangement that lasted two years. Barthelme found the Rice faculty less pliable and less open to new ideas than his UH colleagues; his plans for the staid crosstown institution struck the faculty there as too radical an upheaval.

Barnstone, Keeland, and Jenkins enjoyed being the unchallenged center of power in the college during Barthelme's absence. Following his brief tenure at Rice, Barthelme returned to UH, a situation that didn't sit well with the trio. In a letter to Lilliott, Keeland and Barnstone protested and threatened to resign or take a leave of absence, "if it is preferred." The letter cited as reasons an "anti-Keeland-Barnstone-Mies climate" in the school. "A strong conviction," the letter continued, "is the only way to architectural success, and we feel that an acknowledged and overt policy against one of the most highly thought of schools of architectural thinking makes teaching a rocky and unpleasant task." In a snarly tone, they strongly criticized the "integrated program conceived by Mr. Barthelme," proclaiming that it led to "formalistic pattern [making]" and promoted "a restricted form of *Architectural Graphic Standards* architecture."[8]

Faculty members of the University of Houston, College of Architecture, c. 1950: (*left to right*) Donald Barthelme, Howard Barnstone, Edmund Furley, and Richard Lilliott.

After a semester of brooding, the secessionists returned to an atmosphere of ideological discontent and rivalry. Barthelme and Lilliott, with a few others, supported an open-ended, theoretical approach to architecture as a cultural endeavor. Barnstone's clique promoted a more disciplined, orthodox modernism. But as Zemanek noted, "Exactly what each side stood for was not clear, except to say that power threatened ideas."[9] In Zemanek's view, it was the Barnstone group that was most driven by a quest for power. Barthelme was a slightly muddleheaded thinker who couldn't resist the exciting messiness of the background issues of a problem; Barnstone was impatient with theoretical speculations. This clash of views defined the schism. The turmoil and unhappiness landed in Lilliott's lap.

Buildings X, Y, Z, University of Houston, College of Architecture (1955, Cato, Austin & Evans with Edmund R. Furley Jr., demolished).

CELEBRITY, UNREST, AND THE VANGUARD

At the time, the school was housed in an inauspicious, modestly scaled metal building. Rather than being named, the architecture studio building was simply called Building X of a three-building set: X, Y, and Z. The buildings had been assembled by assistant dean Edmund Furley with then-students C. R. Lively and Joe Skorpea from donated casement windows and an ad hoc kit-of-parts system of steel framing and panels. Drexel Turner claims that these buildings were the university's first architect-designed "modern buildings."[10] The mainly white metal boxes were symbolically and functionally augmented with two enigmatic elements (Buildings Y and Z). One was a glass box that sat under the college's second-story administration suite; it was variously used as a gallery, a studio, or faculty offices—sometimes all three simultaneously. The other was a squat cylindrical concrete-block silo that was appended to the studio building. It accommodated a succession of uses, including a shop, a studio, a student lounge, and, since there were no windows, sundry clandestine activities. A plumpish totem, it was painted over many times; among the treatments, it appeared as a Maxwell House coffee tin and an American flag. According to a student in the college in the late sixties, a female student became the first person to embellish the silo by covering her body with lavender-blue paint and stamping multiple images of herself on the curved white surface.

The architecture school's roots were pragmatic: it was founded in response to Second World War veterans looking for a degree in architecture. Barnstone talked about the working-class men who were getting their first familial chance at education: "The war wasn't won by people from Yale and Harvard and Penn; it was won by soldiers and officers from Ohio State, Michigan, University of Houston."[11] The belief that the college was educating a new wave of untapped talent and energy focused the mission of the school.

In the spring of 1960, Barnstone published his prospectus for the college, titled "Inspiration Unlimited," in *Texas Architect*. Its goals were lofty:

> A school can insure top architectural training only if the program inspires students to want to be the best architects anywhere, and that once the student is so motivated, no inconvenience, no lack of amenity or facility—be it a library too far away to be usable—becomes very important . . . To inspire such dedication, it was essential first that the permanent staff in the upper grades be accomplishing, practicing architects first and teachers second. The deep respect that the student feels for a doer cannot be simulated; no amount of book learning or erudition is a satisfactory substitute.[12]

In *Open Plan*, a history of the college, Drexel Turner fleshed out Barnstone's ideas:

> Barnstone then asserted a principle that became embedded in the modus operandi of the school: "Permanent staff in the upper levels . . . should be free [to] give any type of problem they desire . . . [especially one they might be] working on simultaneously in their office since it would permit greater realism and depth as opposed to theoretical but shallow exercises." Barnstone also railed against pedagogic tyranny and make-work.
>
> Having urged primacy for practitioners like himself and disposed of academic pompousness and drudgery, he [Barnstone] proceeded to what he called the "salt" in the recipe: a program of visiting "greats" inasmuch as the "feeling of closeness and physical contact to eminence has no substitute." The suggestion that greatness is passed from master to student is not without historical example—Frank Lloyd Wright nursing from Master Sullivan . . . Behrens to Mies, or even Bramante to Michelangelo suggests there is truth and success in the method, though he admitted that "in our time, with a hundred or more schools around, it's hard to come up with a hundred Bramantes."
>
> Barnstone then called attention to the lecture series he had championed for the college and announced his hope for enlarging the program to include extended residencies—a model adopted at Yale, Barnstone's alma mater during the 1950s where, as Robert A. M. Stern notes, the program

was staffed by a small tenured faculty in architecture with an emphasis on visiting personnel and a diversity of viewpoints.[13]

John de Menil encouraged Barnstone's academic ambitions. At a time when it was rare for architecture schools to invite well-known architects to travel cross-country to lecture on their work, Menil funded a speaker series that Barnstone organized for the University of Houston Architectural Society beginning in 1953. The series featured nationally known architects: Frank Lloyd Wright, Buckminster Fuller, Philip Johnson, Eero Saarinen, Charles Eames, and Henry-Russell Hitchcock, all of whom spoke in 1954. Richard Neutra, Craig Ellwood, Paul Rudolph, Enrico Peressutti, Bruce Goff, and Douglas Haskell spoke in 1955. Serge Chermayeff, Victor Gruen, Marcel Breuer, Finn Juhl, and Minoru Yamasaki were speakers in 1956.[14] Stephen James, writing about the lecture series, noted the striking caliber of talent that appeared in a single program of lectures: "In hindsight we recognize that many of the visitors—particularly Wright, Breuer, Neutra, and Eero Saarinen—were at peaks of legendary careers that defined modern architecture in the twentieth century. . . . And, of course, there was Philip Johnson, who became a fixture on the Houston architectural scene for the next several decades and one of the most important architects of the last fifty years."[15]

Barnstone used the series to promote the college, seeking to have the talks publicized in local magazines and newspapers as well as national professional journals. Some of his pitches to *Architectural Record* and *Architectural Forum*, for example, were strikingly audacious. They didn't result in the desired national spreads, but the lecture series and the school became known through word of mouth.[16] Barnstone polled his students to see which of the lecturers in the first year impressed them the most, and he sent the results to Douglas Haskell, editor of *Architectural Forum*. Mies was at the top, followed by Johnson, Eames, and Fuller. "Russell Hitchcock, FLW, and Eero Saarinen didn't make too much impression on our jaded boys," Barnstone wrote, commenting wryly, "There is some question whether a cobalt bomb explosion 30 miles from Houston would seriously impress our sophisticates."[17]

Dean Lilliott became an issue when the college was threatened with losing its accreditation. The National Architectural Accrediting Board (NAAB) cited Lilliott's lack of proper architectural and academic credentials as an impediment to maximizing the college's potential. And the faculty was growing restless with Lilliott's performance: each side in the schism wanted a stronger dean who would support its position. The complaints found their way to the NAAB members, as they usually do, and they became central to the visiting committee's report. Campuses at the time were hotbeds of dissension, and *Progressive Architecture* included several reports about incidents at UH in its feature on student unrest in architecture schools. In the fall of 1966, the magazine reported that UH students had been joined by some faculty members in walking out of a meeting with the university administration because the latter wouldn't turn over the results of the recent accreditation visit. Threatened with a campus-wide boycott of classes, the university capitulated and released the complete report. By April 1967, Lilliott had resigned.

But things got worse rather than better for Lilliott's replacement. W. Eugene George, former chairman of the architecture department at the University of Kansas and a Texan, took over the deanship in 1968. George quickly alienated the already revved-up students by dismissing several faculty members and pushing to impose his own brand of order. With nudges from some established instructors, students produced propaganda materials arguing the case for jettisoning George, most of the accusations to do with what students and faculty members viewed as his authoritarian attitude, his insistence on requiring the faculty and students to be on campus a certain number of hours, and the simpleminded, unimaginative program of study that he promulgated. A bomb threat phoned into George's office prompted him to move his office to a secret (and secure) location.

The university knew it had a problem on its hands. As Turner wrote, "The extent of dissatisfaction with George's agenda became apparent in 1968 when students presented the NAAB accrediting team (returning for a post-1966 follow-up visit) with a list of ten complaints taking issue with George's 'outdated' concepts as opposed to 'free school ideas.'"[18]

William Jenkins emerged as a candidate for interim dean after a 1960s-style encounter session for the faculty. Held in Galveston and managed by a team of psychologists, the meeting was intended to give a fair hearing to George's ideas. It turned out to be more like turning the beasts loose on him. John Perry, who

TOP Philip Johnson lecturing at the University of Houston College of Architecture, 1966.

BOTTOM Faculty members, University of Houston College of Architecture, c. 1968: (*left to right*) Eugene McMillin, Dean Richard W. Lilliot, Howard Barnstone, Robert F. Lindsey, William Jenkins (future dean), Myron C. Anderson, and Eugene Aubry.

had just joined the faculty as an assistant professor, found himself in the middle of the Galveston dustup before he had met his first class: "Here I was in a room full of angry men who were making the dean who just hired me into a sacrificial scapegoat."[19]

George soldiered on for several more months, enraging students further with his decision not to renew the contract of assistant professor John Zemanek; then George capitulated.[20] Jenkins was given the job of putting the school back together. The psychologist-facilitator running the show had reported to the provost that Jenkins seemed to be agreeable to almost everyone, the person most generally trusted. Burdette Keeland told me that "they" (which usually meant he and Barnstone) had made Jenkins dean because they thought they could manipulate him.

In the late 1960s, the college was enveloped in an intoxicating aura of anarchy. Barnstone had written a letter to Dean Lilliott, making his case for rejecting the model of hiring prominent architects, which was being followed by more prestigious schools. "Instead," he wrote, "UH should follow the opposite tack, that of having a group of outstanding young practitioners acting together in a vigorous way consulting with one another and with a sympathetic administration."[21]

Another equally powerful force was bubbling up in the zeitgeist of the Age of Aquarius—cultural and artistic experimentation that both entertained and outraged mainstream America. Doug Michels, guru of the San Francisco-based art and architecture collective Ant Farm, was brought onto the faculty part-time in 1969 as a "cultural catalyst." Houston wasn't nearly as wide open as California, but there were opportunities and people to support the building of inflatables, geodesics, and an amazing house. Ant Farm trafficked in the sensuous side of the zeitgeist, celebrating its liberal sexual attitudes and countercultural activities. In 1972, the group was commissioned to design a weekend house for the Houston art collector Marilyn Oshman, called the "House of the Century," which looked like a cross between a submarine and the kind of anatomical-scatological drawings that adolescent boys scrawl in bathroom stalls, although Michels described it as capturing the "NASA aesthetic."

As a faculty member, Michels was a provocateur. He once described institutions such as the University of Houston as simply information systems and resource centers. The counterculture fed off the resources of the establishment, particularly universities, with access to free libraries, free space, expertise, and Xerox machines (the proletariat's printing press). Despite or maybe because of his countercultural dash, Michels had a nomadic relationship with Philip Johnson's New York office and a more fixed involvement with Barnstone, for whom he worked for a time. Barnstone enjoyed free spirits such as Michels, who must have expressed some repressed desires of his own psyche.

Like the counterculture itself, the places changed by those times were gradually absorbed into the mainstream and became less differentiated. Today, UH tussles with goals like achieving Tier I status, and the Gerald D. Hines College of Architecture and Design is a corporate edifice that the fire marshal visits regularly to make sure no one is breaking the rules. But for a time during Barnstone's tenure, the UH architecture school was a place of bohemian counterculture on campus. It may be a testament to the resilience and openness of American universities that they became a bivouac for the counterculture in the 1960s and 1970s. It may also be the case that a revolutionary spirit and a sense of social justice and involvement, along with a hedonistic avant-garde, were shaped and softened in these proxy cities by being kept an aesthetic distance from the actual urban spaces beyond.

House of the Century (1972, Ant Farm Art Collective), Angleton, Texas, a biomorphic weekend house commissioned by the art patrons Marilyn Oshman and Alvin Lubetkin.

BARNSTONE'S VIEW

Barnstone's feelings about the disposition and atmosphere of the college were not consistent. He seemed to see the matter as a clash of attitudes that were always up for debate. He told a story in an interview with *Zero*, a short-lived college publication:

> When I graduated from Yale, even though General Eisenhower gave the commencement address (incidentally he didn't wear a uniform) Architecture marched first. The chancellor of the university came around and said, "The Governor's Connecticut Foot Guard of 1720 will play marching music. But you do not have to walk in step with the music as your ancient right to

dissent...." That's what a university is. That's what professor means: people who profess one thing or another.[22]

Barnstone was impressed by people of accomplishment and ability who distinguished themselves by both what they did and how they conducted themselves. He used an example:

> President Lyndon Johnson has said that he wants to teach political science at Texas when he retires from the presidency. You can imagine what an extraordinary experience for a student to learn political science from Lyndon Johnson. Start figuring that, and you realize what a university is. It's a series of experiences that a student goes through. Now you wouldn't expect that the administrative head of this school of political government would tell Lyndon Johnson how to teach, would you? Or if you had a college and could get Dr. Jonas Salk to teach advanced chemical drug therapy, this would be exciting and enlightening for the students. This is what a university hopefully is, this is how Harvard is, and how the great universities all are—a series of great experiences for students.[23]

Barnstone also expressed misgivings about establishing a graduate architecture program at UH, because, he charged, the faculty members often took advantage of graduate students:

> I'd like to think of ... [graduate education] ... as a series of options. We could have a Bachelor of Architecture in structural design; another in urban planning; interior architecture or the history of architecture. I think there's nothing so extraordinary about that. Consider that one can get a Doctor of Philosophy in Education or in German ... The graduate programs that I know of are largely, I feel, slave labor to the students. The student graduates from here, say, and goes to a nearby institution where he is paid a $1,000 a year in some tuition scholarship. For this he has to teach lower grades, and go through the motion of doing a thesis for a high-ranking professor. Then he's given a Master of Architecture. I think this is slave labor. And I don't respect it.[24]

Barnstone understood the importance of having allies in the college, both faculty members and students, and he often used both to stir things up. He was drawn to Keeland, a favored student in his studio in the 1940s, and helped him become a highly influential force and ally in the college. With Barnstone's encouragement, Keeland went to Yale for a master's degree in 1958, making him eligible for tenure after he returned to join the UH faculty. Barnstone and Keeland were partners in the college, supporting each other's agendas. As Barnstone became more engaged in negotiations with the administration, he copied Keeland on his correspondence. Barnstone had a patrician demeanor that was smoother, slyer, and more intellectualized than that of Keeland, but he was also more acerbic and capable of downright nastiness. In that sense, it was sometimes harder to take Keeland as seriously as Barnstone.

Jenkins was dean during these convulsive years, but he began to calm things. When I arrived in the fall of 1972, there was a lingering feeling of disorganization and palpable restlessness. First- and second-year students had hot (that is, shared) desks; third-year students were in a constant state of existential bewilderment. A paranoid mist drifted through the place; it wasn't clear what would come next. Jenkins, when he interviewed me in 1972, candidly talked about how he was trying to offset some of the influence of his old colleagues by hiring new faculty members. Jenkins's leadership style was to hire several faculty members—preferably part-time, to get more bodies for less money—let them loose in the studios, and turn on the air-conditioning. And he often brought them on part-time in his professional office as well. In three years, Jenkins hired a new generation of leaders: Art Hacker, John Perry, Robert Timme, Robert Griffen, Robert Samuelson, Shafik Rifaat, and me—a group that Barnstone referred to (using various facial expressions, depending on the occasion) as the "Young Turks." As the new hires took over coordination responsibilities for the first four years of classes, Barnstone and Keeland maintained a stronghold as coordinators of theses, controlling the final gate to a professional degree.

Barnstone had a profound effect on thesis projects. In addition to being a distinguished architect with significant critical abilities, he was the bona fide scholar and intellectual member of the faculty. He pioneered an interest in the region's historic architecture, which culminated in his two notable books. As thesis mentor, he encouraged the exploration of a wide range of topics, including planning, building design, and historical and technical research. These investigations were subjected to thorough scrutiny in formal, final reviews that frequently became well-attended occasions where families, friends, and classmates watched the student joust with the faculty jury. Food and drinks were provided by the student. Barnstone found money to allow for each thesis project to be bound and placed in the library, creating a valuable record of the passing interests and ideas of students through the years.

Both Barnstone and Keeland were sapped by medical problems that required periodic leaves of absence. Barnstone's was the more severe, since it involved bipolar disorder, which made his participation in the school uneven. Although control of the college was shifting to a younger generation, an inevitable but always bitter event in the life of an institution, Barnstone's and Keeland's influence wasn't over. Keeland was able, against considerable odds, to deliver a final coup: orchestrating the design commission for the college's new building for his friend Philip Johnson. Barnstone had introduced Johnson to Keeland, and Keeland became a huge Johnson fan. The university's announcement in 1982 that Johnson/Burgee had been commissioned to design the new architecture building came as a surprise. The workshop atmosphere of the worn-out accommodations of Building X was so much a part of the persona of the college that it took some time to imagine anything else. The faculty had proposed a competition so that diverse designs from a number of architects could be considered. The audacity of the university championing Johnson, the playful postmodern aesthete and corporate star, to be the architect of the new College of Architecture building was too much for many faculty members and students, who thought of themselves as belonging to a modernist, vanguard tradition. But their disapproval resulted in only a few short-lived protests. Keeland convinced the university's president that hiring a "starchitect" who was favored by Gerald D. Hines might be a way to induce developers to donate enough funds to build the new building. It worked, of course, and the building is officially the home of the Gerald D. Hines College of Architecture and Design. This was a Houston kind of business deal: quick, mutually beneficial, but, on the whole, not quite satisfying. Johnson had relinquished his former allegiance to Miesian abstraction (the kind of rarefied perfection he had given to the University of St. Thomas) and become something of a point man for the devilish freedoms of postmodernism. The design he delivered was a full dose of historical fiction. Going far beyond anyone's wildest dreams, he loosely modeled the college's new home on a schematic, eighteenth-century classical design for the house of education in the saltworks city of Arc-et-Senans by the French revolutionary architect Claude-Nicolas Ledoux.[25]

Keeland took unmitigated pride in his role in the debacle, and Barnstone seemed to fall in line. Johnson, who at that time referred to himself as a "functionalist-eclectic," was perhaps less impressed with his creation, calling the building "my sin" and "the building where I learned mostly what not to do." It was never easy to detect how tongue-in-cheek Johnson's commentary was meant to be; he also maintained it was the best building on the University of Houston campus. Visitors commented that it was a decent diagram for a college of architecture, wrapping everything important around an interior court and hiding everything else. But one had to strip it bare to see it. Some of the more audacious features—the reductive neoclassical decoration; the rooftop *tempietto*; the bleak, tunnel-like entrances; and even the simplistic, glib formality of the façade, which looks as thin as a drawing—were easily pointed out by visiting architects and by professors in the college, who used the building as a full-sized example of what not to do. But it caught the attention of many nonarchitects and campus officials, who admired its monumental singularity and overstated symbolism, which distinguished it from the less self-assured buildings on campus.

The architecture building's atrium quickly became a locus where the college community gathered for major lectures, exhibitions, building projects, parties (including weddings), and a gamut of creative exploits inspired by the luxury of an empty unprogrammed indoor piazza-like space partially in a state-funded building. It served, as well, as a magnet for campus and outside groups, who for the first time knew the location not only of the architecture college, but also of the campus itself when viewed from the nearby Gulf Freeway. But for a functioning, modern architecture school that had been accustomed to working in the proletarian tradition of a workshop setting, in industrial sheds, it was an awkward fit and an irritating, bourgeois symbol. Zemanek, a vociferous critic of postmodernism, and of Philip Johnson's work in particular, remarked in a public forum, to the surprise of many, that he thought the building was more important than we realized. Looking up into the volume of the atrium, he remarked that Johnson's creation was distinguished by the fact that it was such a full dose of the postmodern idea that it stood out as the best of the worst and therefore needed to be taken seriously.

John Burgee and Philip Johnson with model of their new UH College of Architecture building.

THE CHANGING OF THE GUARD

As younger faculty members took up the task of reorganizing the curriculum (a traditional ritual when there is a new dean and some new instructors), the older professors retrenched, taking positions on the margins and sniping at the way things seemed to be going. The new faculty in the 1970s spent a weekend retreat putting together a new curriculum based on objective planning concepts in educational theory, which they presented to select faculty members. Keeland (speaking for himself and Barnstone) rejected the effort: "We invite you guys down here and give you all this freedom in the world, and the first thing you do is start creating ways to tie yourselves down." To the Young Turks, it was about finding their place,

Howard Barnstone, Burdette Keeland, Jr., Philip Johnson, and John Burgee heading to the groundbreaking for the new Gerald D. Hines College of Architecture Building, c. 1985.

their own cabal, and hanging on. The college was radically entrepreneurial. Later, it became clear to me how much the campus and the college were miniature versions of Houston. At that time, both the city and the college benefited from an environment of navigable anarchy with few rules. In the case of Houston, it was the intractable no-zoning policy, which allowed more freedom for development than in zoned cities but prevented the formulating and enforcing of community standards.

The faculty talked about pedagogical order and the logic of the curriculum, but almost in defiance, the college worked best as an opportunistic incubator that kept things open and allowed people to experiment and draw others to their interests. The archive of theses shows the variety of projects that were explored: written investigations of every sort, buildings, speculative ideas, technical investigations, planning, and urban design. One of the most ambitious was a 1974 design for a moon colony by the students John Dossey and Guillermo Trotti, to be located on the St. George Crater near the landing site of Apollo 15. Barnstone served as thesis adviser for the pair, and with his help, they were able to entice the visionary designer R. Buckminster Fuller to visit Houston and discuss the project. Fuller penned a note in their thesis booklet, commending the work.

As Jenkins grew into his job as dean, he realized that things couldn't stay the same. The university was becoming more academically ambitious. He learned that university funding formulas reimbursed a college at a six-to-one rate for graduate students versus undergraduates. And only six graduate students were required to constitute a class. So he put together a graduate program in urban design with six students. He also tried to diversify the college's capstone program, organizing it into concentrations in urban design, health care, regional architecture, and space architecture—later called "experimental architecture." The initiatives were characteristically opportunistic, since there was almost no new money for such prospecting. Jenkins would get an idea, find someone who was willing to head it up, print posters (he loved puttering with graphic design), and mail them off to other schools of architecture. Then wait.

Jenkins had a talent for talking people into taking responsibility for initiating, directing, teaching, and building a research agenda in a new area for a minuscule salary, but with the promise that they could earn much more by initiating new

Lunar Colony thesis project (1974, John Dossey and Guillermo Trotti), Howard Barnstone, adviser.

activities and getting them funded. It fit the entrepreneurial spirit of Houston. A classic Jenkins pitch went something like this: "Sure, you could go up to Harvard or Princeton and be a small fish in a big pond. But here the sky's the limit. There's nothing holding you back. You can grow your own program and your salary too."

When I arrived at UH, Barnstone's participation in the college was shaky. Although usually one didn't know what mood he would be in, he continued to have a sharp mind and a razor wit that could be used insultingly. Sometimes it was difficult to know whether he was being humorous or using you as a punch line for a point he was trying to make. He could say something so caustic about you that it would never be forgotten. But Barnstone was one of the most brilliant critics I ever sat with in review: concise, witty, to the point. He never tried to talk over the student's head, but to genuinely communicate. He also had a good detector for who was serious in his or her work and who was trying to get away with something. On a bad day, he tended to err on the side of suspicion, and when he and Keeland decided to take someone apart, they could be embarrassingly cruel, picking on everything: a student's design, drawings, haircut, shoes, and speaking style. Unfortunately, it sent a lot of students running from his studio.

Cartoon of Philip Johnson and Howard Barnstone, drawn and labeled by Burdette Keeland, c. 1955. But the figure on the left could be Keeland himself instead of Johnson.

Eugene Aubry, a student in the college in the 1950s, describes his first meeting with Barnstone: "I met this guy from Maine who everyone was terrified of. He became my fourth- and fifth-year critic. He and Burdette set the ethos for design work. At UH you did Mies. Only Mies. And everything was black and white. No color. If you went into a jury with color on your boards, Howard would go crazy."[26] Aubry worked for both Keeland and Barnstone, the latter luring him away from the former. It was common for both of them to bring the best students into their offices. Jenkins did a similar thing with young faculty members whom he hired part-time at the college and then half-time in his professional office.

Barnstone's last teaching assignment was a seminar course that he put together on urbanism, in which he exercised his acerbic, sharp, stream-of-consciousness commentary on the news of the day. Little effort was required, and students either loved it or tolerated it. It seemed as if he was being pushed into the shadows, but it wasn't entirely bad for a distinguished faculty member to simply share his experience, thoughts, and ideas. Keeland created a unique course of his own, modeled on a talk show, in which he interviewed local architects. He played the moderator, sitting at the front desk, and the guest sat in a comfortable side chair; the students served as the audience, expected to clap and cheer on cue.[27]

For many of its years, the college of architecture was a wild, semistable, creative hotbed of slightly larger-than-life personalities and students working under the spell of a handful of minor philosopher-kings, like Barnstone, none of whom were deans. Seven deans have served the college up to the present time, and most of them have been enablers. Most came up through the UH teaching ranks, and they were called on to run a program they had had a hand in formulating. Having been in the dean's chair for a few years myself, I came to think of the position as being the "designated driver" for a load of academic libertarians. Some teachers thrive in such an atmosphere, especially those such as Barnstone whose eccentricities, attention deficits, and depressions are their juice. But there are risks for every player. Barnstone came to Houston for a visit, and like many others, he stayed to become a major part of a remarkable enterprise. He had a large influence on others, including students, teachers, and those who came to know the college by its work and activities. He brought the college into conjunction with a larger and more accomplished social, professional, and artistic circle, giving the faculty and students the courage to take risks, try things out, and be a little bit off center. Most of all, Howard Barnstone believed in this little proletarian school without endowed privilege where students did remarkable things. Those ideas were the genius of the college. You couldn't write it down, but you could feel it.

NOTES

1. The first UH buildings were faced with Texas fossilized limestone and designed in a modernistic style that projected a sense of academic gravitas meant to anchor the budding campus.

2. Turner, *Open Plan*.

3. University of Houston, College of Architecture Course Catalogue, 1950–1951.

4. Donald Barthelme, "A New Curriculum," *Journal of Architectural Education* (Summer 1961): 47–50; Drexel Turner, in *Open Plan*, points out that accounts of the new curriculum appeared in the *Daily Cougar*, June 16, 1950, and February 29, 1952.

5. Zemanek named the three houses Gaea I (1968), Gaea II (2000), and Gaea III (2010), after the Greek earth goddess. The houses have been extensively published. Zemanek offers his own story of their creation in his biography, *Being . . . Becoming*.

6. William F. Stern, unpublished notes, "Howard Barnstone and the de Menil family" (2012). Stern was one of the original contributors to this book before his untimely death in 2013.

7. Burdette Keeland, "The Legacy of Howard Barnstone," unpublished eulogy (1987), Burdette Keeland Architectural Papers, Special Collections, University of Houston (hereafter cited as Keeland Papers).

8. Burdette Keeland, Jr., and Howard Barnstone to Richard Lilliott, October 28, 1955, Keeland Papers.

9. Zemanek, *Being . . . Becoming*, 87.

10. Fred George, unpublished essay (1998), copy in author's possession; see also "University Building by Cato, Austin, Evans architects in association with Edward Furley," *Arts and Architecture* v. 72:7 (July 1955): 20–21, 31.

11. Author's notes from a faculty meeting of the architecture school, September 1982.

12. Howard Barnstone, "Inspiration Unlimited," *Texas Architect* (April 1960).

13. Turner, *Open Plan*, 14–15.

14. "Frank Lloyd Wright Appears as Guest Speaker for Lecture," *Daily Cougar*, January 8, 1954; see also "Noted Architect Speaks Wed.," *Daily Cougar*, February 12, 1954; "Architect Tours US Campuses," *Daily Cougar*, May 14, 1954; Mack Wilder, "Famous Men in Architecture to Appear in Lecture Week," *Daily Cougar*,

January 14, 1955; "Lecture Series Set Here Feb. 7," *Daily Cougar*, February 4, 1955; "Experts Featured in Arch. Series," *Daily Cougar*, February 18, 1955; Lynn Del Davis, "UHAS Builds for Future: Architectural Society Gains Stature By Presenting UH Lecture Series," *Daily Cougar*, November 23, 1955; "Architects Hold Lecture Series," *Daily Cougar*, February 17, 1956; "Architectural Society at U.H. Slates Talks," *Houston Chronicle*, March 11, 1956; "Several Speakers to Attend Meeting," *Daily Cougar*, March 2, 1953; "Yamasaki Talks to Arch. Group," *Daily Cougar*, April 6, 1956; "Breuer Speaks in Library," *Daily Cougar*, April 13, 1956.

15. Stephen James, "The Fond Look Back: The University of Houston Architectural Society Lecture Series of 1953–1956," unpublished manuscript (2000), copy in author's possession.

16. Ibid., 4.

17. Quoted in James, "The Fond Look Back."

18. Turner, *Open Plan*, 18.

19. John Perry, conversation with the author.

20. Zemanek offers his own account of the Eugene George affair ("Regime Change" in *Being . . . Becoming*, 88–89).

21. Howard Barnstone to Richard Lilliott, January 21, 1953, Keeland Papers.

22. Howard Barnstone, interview, *Zero* magazine, c. 1969.

23. Ibid.

24. Ibid.

25. For an extended discussion of Johnson/Burgee's design, see Welch, *Philip Johnson and Texas*, 206–215.

26. Eugene Aubry, taped interview by Catherine Essinger, October 30, 2012, Audio/Video Repository, William R. Jenkins Architecture, Design, and Art Library, University of Houston, https://av.lib.uh.edu/media_objects/3n203z130. Essinger is the architectural librarian at the Gerald D. Hines College of Architecture and Design.

27. Some episodes of the "Keeland Show" were videotaped, but they seem to have been lost.

CHAPTER NINE

THE WORST THING THAT CAN HAPPEN

Gertrude and Howard

OLIVE HERSHEY

AS HOWARD BARNSTONE landed in Texas in 1948, fresh out of Yale, it seemed as if he and Gertrude Levy were fated to meet in Houston's contemporary art scene. With a job offer to teach at the new University of Houston architecture school, Howard moved to town and settled in. That was the opening scene in the marriage play starring Gertrude Levy and Howard Barnstone. Equal parts comedy of manners and domestic melodrama, the play's action was driven by the protagonists' complex psychologies, which sometimes produced uproariously funny situations and often profoundly wrenching ones. The setting for the drama was Houston at the midpoint of the twentieth century, a city emerging simultaneously as a booming business powerhouse and a burgeoning center for modern art and culture.

Howard Barnstone and Gertrude Levy, both possessing brilliant intellects and magnetic personalities, formed a marriage that generated enormous creative energy and achievement. These two complex, talented people had professional interests and ambitions that inspired in each a powerful impulse to excel in their chosen disciplines: Howard as the Texas interpreter of Philip Johnson, and Gertrude as an actress, artist, and activist. Paradoxical characters driven by their passions and ambitions, Howard and Gertrude experienced intense emotional stress while playing their roles in a city undergoing tremendous cultural and economic change.

MIDCENTURY HOUSTON

Houston in the late 1940s and early 1950s was a youthful, boisterous city with outsized cultural ambitions. Home to the wildcatter Glenn H. McCarthy's Shamrock

Gertrude and Howard Barnstone on a bus to Mexico, 1959.

Hotel (1949), the biggest hotel built in the United States in the 1940s, and the new Texas Medical Center, the city seemed constrained only by the conventionality of its economic elite. An outpouring of cultural energy from arts pioneers challenged this complacency. In 1947, Nina Vance, an actress and public-school drama and speech teacher, founded the Alley Theatre. The Ballet Russe de Monte-Carlo considered establishing an American base in Houston during the Second World War. Although this did not happen, the Houston Foundation for Ballet was established in 1955, under the direction of Tatiana Semenova, who had performed in Houston with the Ballet Russe. The foundation's first studio was designed by Bolton & Barnstone and built in the backyard of its office at 811 Lovett Boulevard.[1] The Houston Symphony Orchestra hired Leopold Stokowski as its principal conductor in 1955. That same year, the newly founded Houston Grand Opera debuted with a controversial production of *Salome*.[2] And in November 1955, Gertrude Levy married Howard Barnstone.

THE ART SCENE

Gertrude remembers first meeting her husband-to-be at a Contemporary Arts Association (CAA) exhibition soon after he arrived in town.[3] Founded in October 1948, the CAA was housed in an unusual A-frame building designed by MacKie & Kamrath and constructed in 1949 by museum member-volunteers. Gertrude says she was immediately fascinated with Howard. The two seemed to their friends a natural match. Both were well educated, intellectually agile, extremely

Contemporary Arts Association interior with Jeannie (Mrs. Karl) Kamrath, 1949.

attractive, and Jewish. People who knew them described them as charming, witty, fun, and at ease in sophisticated circles. Their innate fearlessness struck an additional spark. Liberal, progressive, and nonconformist, Gertrude and Howard boldly expressed outrageous opinions that upended conventional notions about almost everything. In Gertrude's case, outrageousness was part of a strategically designed theatrical persona. Above all else, Gertrude Levy was a consummate actress. She was also her own favorite playwright, crafting real-life dramas in which she performed the starring role.

Gertrude and Howard were compatible not merely because they were creative, handsome, liberal, and Jewish. They were drawn to each other because both were laced with contradictions, contradictions that made sparks fly. Playful and impish, with a wicked sense of humor, Gertrude delighted in turning decorum upside down. Howard was also a provocateur, and he was excited by her high spirits, her beauty, and her refusal to behave as society expected. At the same time, Gertrude's willingness to play the rebel willing to challenge conventional elements of Houston society was risky from Howard's point of view, since an arriviste Yankee architect, no matter how charming, talented, or well educated he might be, could not afford to alienate too many potential clients. During the

LEFT Gertrude (second from left) and other cast members in *George Washington Slept Here*, Houston Little Theater, 1950.

RIGHT Gertrude and Howard stepping into Howard's convertible, c. 1955.

years of their marriage and beyond, these character traits would regularly produce conflict, stress, and drama in their relationship.

As Gertrude and Howard were shaping their careers in the 1950s and 1960s, their life as a couple seems, at least in retrospect, to have been glamorous and colorful, something like a Fellini movie being acted out on a Gulf Coast prairie. Pursuing their interest in contemporary European and American art and architecture, the two gravitated to the overlapping circles of Houston artists, architects, intellectuals, and art enthusiasts who had been part of Gertrude's life since her childhood in Houston. One circle involved theater: Gertrude was cast as the leading lady in local theater productions of *Strange Bedfellows* (1949) and *George Washington Slept Here* (1950). Another circle revolved around Dominique and John de Menil, who had wide-ranging international educations, experiences, and interests. The Menils introduced unconventional people from all over the world who embraced and espoused startlingly progressive ideas to conservative Houston society.

As a Contemporary Arts Association board member, John de Menil was a catalyst for expanding Houston's aesthetic horizons during the early 1950s. Dominique de Menil was greatly influenced by her spiritual adviser, Father Marie-Alain Couturier, who guided the couple in selecting works of art as they began to collect in the 1940s. Dominique and John de Menil would enrich Houstonians' comprehension of the connections between spirituality, art, and human rights. From Gertrude Levy's point of view as an artist, this conjunction was astounding and energizing.

Other like-minded Houstonians of the period included Marguerite Johnston, a journalist at the *Houston Post* who, beginning in 1947, covered many civic issues and launched the newspaper's first column of art reviews and criticism. She and her husband, Charles Wynn Barnes, a geologist working for the Standard Oil Company of Indiana, were newcomers themselves, having arrived in Houston in 1946. Marguerite and Charlie Barnes supported a wide range of social-justice causes.[4] Clare Fleming, the daughter of Lamar Fleming, president of Anderson, Clayton and Company, the world's largest cotton-trading company, was Gertrude's friend from painting classes at the Museum of Fine Arts' art school. She joined Gertrude and Howard, along with her fiancé, Samuel N. Sprunt, in a fast-paced whirl of art shows, art classes, and parties. Many parties and art openings were held at the Contemporary Arts Association.

The CAA's initial publication proclaimed its ambition to promote understanding of all the contemporary arts, including painting, sculpture, and graphic art. The CAA was a cultural catalyst: it focused the passions of Houstonians and newcomers eager to bring vanguard art to local audiences and to stimulate its production in Houston. This sense of purpose sparked explosions of intellectual and creative energy among Houston artists and collectors. Gertrude Barnstone remembers that the CAA was magnetic north for her and her friends. Like many of the first generation of members, she frequently volunteered at the museum, doing everything from hanging shows to sweeping the floor.

THE ROMANCE

Gertrude and Howard were instantly attracted to each other. But they took their time in getting married. For one thing, Howard had competition. The Houston architect Anderson Todd recalled: "We were both chasing her, and we both drove convertibles." Todd found Gertrude fascinating, "more interested in ideas than in fame." But he acknowledged that he never got to the point of falling in love with her.[5] It may also have been the case that Gertrude was in no great hurry to tie the knot after the breakup of an earlier marriage, an impetuous elopement to California with a naval officer when she was fresh out of the Rice Institute and still too young to marry without her parent's consent.

Soon after meeting John de Menil, Barnstone became the Menils' house architect, supervising maintenance and repairs at their house on San Felipe Road. Houstonians who had never seen modern architecture looked askance at the Menil House, which was built on the edge of River Oaks, the favorite enclave of wealthy Houstonians. The Menil House had a revolutionary impact on Houston. Bolton & Barnstone's adaptations of Philip Johnson's' designs during the 1950s drew Gertrude and Howard into the cultural orbit around John de Menil.

Clare Sprunt remembered that Gertrude's mother, Gisella Levy, did not want Gertrude to marry Howard. Gertrude said her mother didn't want her to marry anybody. As far as Gisella Levy was concerned, her daughter was going to be the artist she never had the opportunity to be. "My mother, I think, always regretted not having a career in the arts," Gertrude remembered. "Her friends in New York were artists and writers. She always said that the worst thing a woman could do was to marry and the next worst thing was to have children, because it stops her from developing herself."[6]

Tired of hearing her mother nag her not to marry or have children, Gertrude Levy vowed to do both. Gertrude's wedding story has a madcap, mischievous quality. The way she told it, she and Howard had been attending art openings and other events for two years. Howard had asked her to marry him, and she had promised to consider his proposal. "A while later," she recalled, "I remember spending the day in the Rice library reading Dylan Thomas's *A Child's Christmas in Wales*. That afternoon I drove over to Howard's office and said, 'Let's go grab a Coke.' So we got in the car, and I said, 'Let's get married.' Howard said, 'Great, I just have to cancel my dinner date.'"

The two then drove his convertible to the Levys' apartment to announce their intentions, though no version of this story ever suggests they were asking her parents' permission to marry. "We walked into the house, and I said, 'We're getting married.' My mother sat down and said, 'For God's sake, somebody get me a drink.'" Gertrude did not report what her father said.

Harris County, where Houston is located, required a waiting period between the issuance of a marriage license and the performance of a wedding ceremony. Because neighboring Fort Bend County did not have that requirement, the couple drove to Richmond, bought a license, and were directed to a justice of the peace in the adjacent town of Rosenberg. Rosenberg was a railroad depot town of about six thousand residents thirty-five miles southwest of Houston; supposedly, it was there that Bonnie and Clyde rushed through their last meal, with the car engine running outside.[7] "He [the justice of the peace] had to wake up his wife so she could act as a witness," Gertrude said. "And then the weirdest thing happened. Just as he was saying the words, 'I now pronounce you man and wife,' a little cuckoo clock he had hanging on the wall started cuckooing." Both Gertrude and Howard took delight in puncturing excessively romantic scenes with the sharp tooth of irony.

As two fearless, unconventional thinkers, two intellectual rebels, Gertrude and Howard felt a mutual attraction that created a magnetic force field with powerful positive and negative charges. Their relationship was always volatile, Gertrude reported, as her husband's need to impose order on his surroundings came into direct conflict with his wife's delight in chaos: "He could fly into a rage if he walked into the kitchen and found dishes in the sink."

Howard was often described as charming, witty, and charismatic, which is exactly the way Gertrude remembered him. "Howard was a fascinating person," she said. "He was so interesting, intelligent . . . intuitive and creative. Our sex life together was wonderful, fantastic." When asked what attracted her to Howard, she said without hesitating: "It was his mind. All the other men I knew were boring by comparison."

THE HOUSTON ART SCENE

In 1955, John de Menil brought Jermayne MacAgy from San Francisco to become the first professional director of the Contemporary Arts Association. During her four years at the CAA, Jerry MacAgy organized twenty-nine exhibitions, each with a catalogue. In 1957 she gave Mark Rothko his second single-artist museum exhibition. Many of her shows were cutting edge and unusual for this period, especially *The Disquieting Muse: Surrealism* (1958). MacAgy's installations were equally startling; they were intended to induce aesthetic and psychological reactions in their viewers. MacAgy's most popular show for the CAA, *Totems Not Taboo* (1959), was installed in Mies van der Rohe's newly completed Cullinan Hall at the Museum of Fine Arts. This was the largest, most inclusive exhibition of tribal art that had been presented in the United States up to that time. Dominique de Menil wrote of MacAgy, "Each of her installations produced an atmospheric miracle which set the work of art in such a light that that it would shine."[8]

In Houston, modern art and architecture circles overlapped. Joan Crystal and her partner, Adrian S. Rosenberg, ran the Louisiana Gallery, where Gertrude exhibited in the 1960s. Rosenberg was an architect who worked for Bolton & Barnstone in the 1950s. Kathryn Swenson, who operated the New Arts Gallery, was married to the architect Bailey Swenson. Howard Barnstone's faculty colleague Burdette Keeland designed the modern house of June Davis and Gilbert Arnold. The Arnold House was published in *Arts and Architecture*, and it featured in June Arnold's first novel, the experimental *Applesauce* (1966).[9] The Houstonian who achieved the widest recognition as a modern innovator, the

Jermayne MacAgy. Photograph by Andy Warhol, c. 1968.

writer Donald Barthelme, Jr. (1931–1989), was the son of another of Barnstone's faculty colleagues at the University of Houston, the architect Donald Barthelme. Although Houston's modern cohort was circumscribed, it generated excitement: "I remember being thrilled at one of my shows," Gertrude said. "Jim Sweeney showed up with Alexander Calder at an opening and that was great fun." James Johnson Sweeney was the Museum of Fine Arts director whom John de Menil had lured away from his directorship at the Guggenheim Museum in New York in 1961 to shake up the Houston art scene.

When the CAA board did not renew Jerry MacAgy's contract in 1959, she began lecturing at the University of St. Thomas. Along with Dominique de Menil, she created the university's art department. Jerry MacAgy was a close friend of Gertrude and Howard's. It was MacAgy's intellectual boldness and passion for art and its imaginative presentation that Gertrude remembered. Her curating was intellectually challenging to audiences, as, for example, when she juxtaposed primitive totems with medieval iconography and contemporary painting and sculpture. MacAgy's shows, like the best poetry, blew away old notions of what constitutes art. With the CAA and the University of St. Thomas exploding conventions in the world of art, and the Menil House and innovative Barnstone houses upending traditional Houstonian ideas about domestic architecture, the Menil revolution transformed Houston.

Amid this cultural ferment, Gertrude and Howard, along with their friends Clare Fleming and Sam Sprunt, were so busy that it is a wonder either couple ever slowed down long enough to consider marriage. The young men were building their careers, Howard in architecture and Sam Sprunt in navigation technology. The young women, though not salaried, worked hard at making art. The social whirl that Clare Sprunt described sounds like glamorous entertainment, and nothing like an ordinary art student's schedule: drawing and painting class in the mornings with such Museum of Fine Arts instructors as the artist and graphic designer Charles Schorre (1925–1996), followed by a hell-for-leather drive in Howard's or Sam's convertible to Clear Lake or Galveston for water skiing, and then back to town for an evening of Latin dancing at The Riviera or El Tropical. Clare Sprunt re-created the scene this way: "At the Riviera there was a one-armed trumpet player. I think that was Norma Zenteno's father, Roberto.... And so we did the merengue and the bossa nova and the cha cha cha.... In the mid-1960s we would walk into the Houston Club and the orchestra would start playing 'Laura's Theme' from *Doctor Zhivago* . . . , and so we made a great entrance."[10]

Gertrude Barnstone with Dora, Lily, and George Barnstone.

MOTHERHOOD

Gertrude and Howard Barnstone had two daughters in quick succession, Dora Lempert (1957) and Lily Elizabeth Gisella (1958), followed by a son, George Arthur (1963). Gertrude didn't let the arrival of children slow her pace. Her second daughter, Lily, tells a story about Gertrude leaving her as a premature newborn in the hospital incubator so that she and Howard could host an engagement party for Robin Hunt and Malcolm McCorquodale.[11] Gertrude always believed in letting the good times roll.

Clare Sprunt remembered that both she and Gertrude, even after marriage, had trouble with their interfering mothers. "Both our mothers wanted to control us," Clare said. "I don't think Mrs. Levy wanted Gertrude to marry Howard." This seems to be putting it mildly. Clare Sprunt elaborated: "Gertrude stayed at my parents' house on Lazy Lane right before her first child, Dora, was born. The doctor said she shouldn't stay at home." This suggests that peace of mind simply wasn't possible when Gertrude was with her mother and father. Howard, at the time, was on assignment outside the country, building company houses for Schlumberger in South America. Gertrude remembered luxuriating at the Lazy Lane home of Clare's parents, Clare and Lamar Fleming. "They waited on me hand and foot," she said. "The doctor was afraid I could lose the baby, so I was supposed to stay quiet." This was a rare, early sign of Gertrude's physical frailty. Apart from a few large-scale disasters, for most of her life Gertrude appears to have been amazingly healthy and robust.

Soon after Dora was born, the Barnstones moved into a Tudor-style house at 1720 North Boulevard near Rice University. Purchased for $30,000, the house, built in 1930, had a living room, screened porch, dining room, and kitchen downstairs, and three bedrooms, two baths, and a sitting room upstairs. Gertrude remembered that after her marriage, she still had plenty of freedom to work in her studio behind the house. "When Dora was born," Gertrude recalled, "Howard arranged for us to have a Puerto Rican housekeeper. She took care of the baby and freed me up to paint. North Boulevard was a big house. I did virtually no housework." Instead, during the 1950s and early 1960s, Gertrude concentrated on painting, drawing, and acting—as she put it, "using all my muscles" in these creative pursuits.

GERTRUDE'S ART

In 1951, Gertrude Levy was commissioned to execute her first architectural sculpture, a piece for the S&H Green Stamp Building on Holcombe Boulevard. The commission required her to work in welded aluminum, which she wasn't trained to do. She accepted the challenge with no hesitation because she wanted to try large-scale projects, even though paying to have the two pieces fabricated to her design specifications absorbed most of her fee. An article about the sculpture was published in the *Houston Chronicle*.[12] A black-and-white photo spotlights Gertrude Levy's fearless, dramatic draftsmanship, showing a curling ribbon of shiny metal twining itself like an elegant vine around the building's two columns. Her interest in and aptitude for architectural sculpture and design were apparent early in her career. Anderson Todd was surprised that she had not studied architecture at Rice, which, until the early 1960s, was the only way that Rice students could take art classes.

In addition to exhibiting her work at annual Museum of Fine Arts shows, Gertrude showed her painting and sculpture at the Louisiana Gallery at 3312 Louisiana Street; the James Bute Company Gallery at Caroline and McKinney, which became the DuBose Gallery; and Kathryn Swenson's New Arts Gallery at 3106 Brazos Street, which also featured the work of the eccentric visionary artist Forrest Bess (1911–1977), who became a good friend of Gertrude and Howard's.[13]

One motif stands out in the lifelong friendship between Gertrude Barnstone and Clare Sprunt: their drive to free themselves from their straitlaced and

S&H Green Stamp Building Sculpture (1955, Gertrude Barnstone), Holcombe Boulevard, Houston.

controlling mothers. Rebelling against anyone's attempt to impose constraints on her, Gertrude for much of her life seems to have raised a clenched fist as well as her powerful voice to assert her independence. Fiercely possessive, her mother, Gisella Levy, was quite strict. Given her daughter's independent streak, there was no way Gisella could contain her. At the same time, both of Gertrude's parents insisted that she adhere to a fixed set of principles and fight for them—evidence that her parents taught her to think independently and avoid following the herd. Throughout her years as an actress, artist, and activist, she followed these principles, taking on ambitious projects that would have frightened most women of her generation. She challenged prevailing ideas about the place of women, African Americans, and other minorities. It is ironic that Gertrude Barnstone slipped from her mother's restraining arms and fell into those of a husband who was equally controlling. People who knew the couple well say that Howard was jealous of his wife's beauty and talent and fiercely possessive of her. It was Howard

Barnstone's passionate jealousy that ultimately cut short Gertrude's blossoming theatrical career.

THE HOUSTON SCHOOL BOARD

Gertrude didn't say much about her children's childhoods, remarking only that Dora and Lily were "holy terrors" growing up; the baby, George, seems to have won her heart. Her artist's notebooks contain many pages of pen-and-ink sketches of George as a youngster. Gertrude also volunteered at the neighborhood Montessori school, on Huldy Street, where George was enrolled. Even so, he was not even two years old when Gertrude decided in 1964 to campaign for a position on the Houston Independent School District Board of Trustees. Prompted by an attack by white conservative trustees on Hattie Mae Whiting White, the lone African American liberal on the board, Barnstone felt compelled to act. As she later explained her choice, "I looked at myself in the mirror and knew I had to do something."

President John F. Kennedy had just been murdered in Dallas, and some students at Houston high schools cheered upon hearing the news. When white school board members pretended to be shocked by the students' cheers, Hattie Mae White stood up to them: "Why are you so surprised, when every week I hear you speaking against the president and our government?" When Gertrude heard the conservatives call for Mrs. White's resignation at the meeting, which was being broadcast on local television, she made up her mind to act. On the advice of her friend Woodrow Seals (later appointed to the federal bench by President Lyndon B. Johnson), she and Howard kicked off her campaign with a public tea party at the Rice Hotel in honor of Mrs. White.

The Barnstone tea party launched Gertrude's campaign in 1964 for an at-large seat on the school board. Howard threw himself wholeheartedly into Gertrude's candidacy and worked behind the scenes to help raise funds to back her. Certainly, the thousand-dollar check from John de Menil was a generous boost, and many of the couple's friends followed suit. While Gertrude enjoyed walking Houston's neighborhoods to hand out campaign literature and meet all kinds of people, the strain of the election put stress on her marriage. Many of Gertrude and Howard's friends were shocked to discover that "Mrs. Howard Barnstone" (as her campaign literature styled her) was a staunch advocate of such egalitarian, liberal, and progressive ideas as the right of all children to an equal education, which had been the law of the land since the US Supreme Court's 1954 ruling in *Brown v. Board of Education*.

THE SOCIAL SWIRL

Gertrude and Howard moved in a glamorous social circle. The fact that they were liberal and Jewish did not, apparently, diminish their popularity as hosts or guests. Gertrude was not raised in a religiously observant family. For the most part, being Jewish was not experienced by the Levy family as a social handicap. In addition, Gertrude and Howard, as artists and intellectuals, were probably viewed as elite outsiders, beyond the confines of conventional social boundaries. Gertrude reported that as a married couple, the Barnstones did not attend temple with any regularity, although they were members of Congregation Beth Israel, Houston's oldest congregation.

In addition to the Menils and Jerry MacAgy, the Barnstones' group of friends included Buckminster Fuller, whom Dominique de Menil invited to speak at the *Visionary Architects* exhibition at the University of St. Thomas in 1967. Fuller was known to deliver expansive orations over the Barnstone's dinner table. Gertrude often referred to Fuller as one of her mentors, someone who wrote positive reviews of her work. Marguerite and Charlie Barnes, Lucie Wray and Anderson Todd, Laura and Jim Sweeney, Margie Scott and Burdette Keeland, Vale Ashe and Mike Ackerman, Anne Schlumberger Melcher, and Clare and Sam Sprunt attended many of these dinner parties, where the focus was more on architecture, ideas, and drink than food. (At one dinner party, Gertrude is supposed to have tossed a tray of tuna sandwiches at her guests.)

The Barnstones valued their close friendship with Forrest Bess, who lived on a barrier island near Bay City on the Texas Gulf Coast.[14] "We would go down to Forrest's and honk," Gertrude says. "If he wanted to see us, he'd come get us in a skiff. He lived in an overturned shrimp boat. We had several of his paintings. They were damned nice. If I had one now, I'd be mighty glad." By the 2010s, Bess's small paintings were selling for $200,000 or more. In 1961, Hurricane Carla, the most intense hurricane up to that time to make landfall on the Texas coast, was approaching as the Barnstones were vacationing on the Bolivar Peninsula, along a very exposed stretch of the Texas Gulf Coast. At the time, they were tending a stray dog they had found. "I remember Hurricane Carla was blowing in," Gertrude says. "I'd been feeding a dog, and when the National Guard came by our rent house and banged on our door and told us we had to go, we took our two little babies and the dog and went to Forrest's." They needed to leave the dog with him. "Forrest decided to ride out the hurricane," she noted. "I don't know what happened to the dog. We named him Carlos, after the hurricane."

Gertrude Barnstone volunteering at River Oaks Montessori School in Houston, which her son George attended.

LEFT Gertrude Barnstone at a Houston Independent School District Board meeting, seated next to Hattie May White.

RIGHT (left to right) Burdette Keeland, Howard Barnstone, and Buckminster Fuller, at the Barnstone's house, 1720 North Boulevard, Houston, c. 1954.

Katie Robinson Edwards, in *Midcentury Modern Art in Texas*, calls Forrest Bess "one of Texas's finest modernist painters."[15] And as she points out: "Modernist painting has inverted standard tropes and expectations, tending to elevate the anti-hero and the renegade." Asked whether Howard might have been fascinated by Forrest Bess because of the artist's eccentric notion that if a man could become a hermaphrodite, he would achieve sublime happiness, Gertrude responded "Sure, because Howard was bisexual." It isn't surprising that both Gertrude and Howard were attracted to this immensely talented artist, who was determined to live his life well outside the mainstream, even though he once showed his work at the prestigious Betty Parsons Gallery in New York. Like Gertrude and Howard, Bess was a person of many, sometimes contradictory, facets. According to Stephen Fox, Howard Barnstone liked to think of himself as a revolutionary architect, and Gertrude seems to have enjoyed being outrageous in all sorts of ways. While on the Houston school board, she sometimes dressed up in costume to attend meetings, once wearing fishnet stockings and a beret and smoking a cigar. Like her husband, Gertrude championed the contrarian side of any argument, particularly if it had to do with politics.

DRAMA!

From early childhood, Gertrude Levy loved drama and the dramatic. In the first years of the Community Players, under the direction of Margo Jones, Gertrude took the stage, acting the part of Rosalind in *As You Like It* in 1941 at the age of sixteen. She appeared in Noel Coward's *Hay Fever* (1942, Rice Hotel), in *Easter* by

Gertrude Barnstone as a harem girl in *Desert Song*, Alley Theatre, c. 1954.

August Strindberg (1944–1945; Houston Little Theater on Chelsea Boulevard), in *Little Women* as Meg (1946; Little Theater), and in J. M. Synge's *Playboy of the Western World* as Pegeen Mike (1947; Little Theater). Later in her life, the actress revealed that what she most enjoyed about theater was the process of developing a character in rehearsal. The theatrical production, the finished product, was not as important to her.

As a young dancer and actress, Gertrude was a charmer, and her beauty endured for many years. Photographs of her as a dancer, actress, artist, and mother reveal that throughout her life she was a seductive enchantress, always changing costumes, metamorphosing, evolving. It wasn't until she took on the substantial role of the merchant's wife in the Alley Theatre's 1959 production of *Rashomon* that local reviewers took her seriously, as something more substantial than a great beauty.

Gertrude Barnstone as the merchant's wife in *Rashomon*, Alley Theatre, 1959, adapted by Fay Kanin and Michael Kanin from the film by Akira Kurosawa.

What Gertrude remembered most vividly about the Alley's production of *Rashomon* was how Howard's sexual jealousy nearly wrecked a dress rehearsal. The play begins as the wealthy merchant's retinue, including his gorgeous wife, is riding horseback through a forest. They are accosted by robbers, who pull them from their mounts. A bandit then rapes the wife in full view of the agonized husband, who is bound. Gertrude explained the direction for the scene: "The bandit grabs the wife, and she struggles at first, but at one point she puts her arm around his neck and gets a gleam in her eye." In telling this story, Gertrude's mischievous expression spoke volumes about how any jealous husband would have reacted while viewing that scene on stage. Something in the way Gertrude played the scene in the dress rehearsal, perhaps with too much enthusiasm and too little

THE WORST THING THAT CAN HAPPEN

resistance, triggered a furious reaction in Howard, who was watching in the audience. "He stood up and stormed out of the theater," she recalled. "I came home later and found the script nailed to my bedroom door."

Because of Howard's anger and jealousy, Gertrude abandoned live theater after *Rashomon*'s run at the Alley. "It was just too public," she said. But giving up the theater did not mean retiring from the limelight. After winning a seat on the school board, Gertrude became a passionate contender in raucous debates during weekly board meetings. Local television stations broadcast live footage of angry arguments among the trustees. The *Post* and the *Chronicle* ran articles and photos documenting these contentious gatherings, dubbed the "Friday Night Fights," with the glaring spotlight of live television broadcasts trained on Gertrude as the board's newest and most outspoken member. All this publicity must have made Howard feel insecure. In spite of his evident success—he was an influential professor at the University of Houston College of Architecture and his book *The Galveston That Was* (1966) had been widely praised—Howard seemed jealous of the constant attention his wife earned. The unremitting pressure that Gertrude faced in school board meetings every week intensified as the conservative majority blocked every progressive move she promoted. Both she and Howard were worn thin by nightly hate-filled telephone calls and angry letters. Yet in photos taken at the time, she looks serene and in command.

THE UNRAVELING

The spotlight on Gertrude grew more focused when the September 21, 1965, issue of *Look* magazine came out. In a feature on American cities, one group of articles showcased Houston, which *Look* portrayed as a boomtown swollen with oil money and filling up with newcomers from every corner of the world: "Houston booms. Skyscrapers poke above the downtown plains, traffic rarely chokes up; the Museum of Fine Arts and the Jesse H. Jones Hall for the Performing Arts throw off élan. The economy churns."[16] An article headlined "A Lady Stirs Her City's Conscience" featured Gertrude delivering a controversial message promoting racial integration to a community dragging its feet at the prospect of changing its ways. "But her insistence," the article continues, "as a member of the Houston school board, on changes in the public-school system stirs consciences and is heard as discord by many other boosters."[17] This was putting the matter politely, to say the least.

Racist attitudes were so pervasive and powerful that Gertrude's mother telephoned her one day to report that she had observed business associates of Arthur Levy's crossing a downtown street to avoid speaking to him, presumably because of Gertrude's advocacy for desegregation. At every school board meeting, Gertrude was frustrated by continuing stubborn opposition to her efforts. Gertrude, Hattie Mae White, and Asberry Butler, the three liberals (still a minority) on the board, sought, almost always unsuccessfully, to pass progressive policies affecting Houston schools. They kept trying for the duration of Gertrude's one term, which lasted from January 1965 through December 1969. The *Look* article suggests that the conservative majority, whose leader was also a member of the White Citizens' Council, blocked biracial adult education classes as well as the chance for Houston schools to receive federal funding for books and subsidized lunches.

Karl Kilian, founder of Houston's Brazos Bookstore and a protégé of Dominique and John de Menil's, described an angry, racist, anti-Semitic outburst that turned violent at a garden party hosted by the Menils for the filmmaker Michelangelo Antonioni at their home. Kilian was there with a fellow University of St. Thomas student, Helen Winkler, later a cofounder of the Dia Art Foundation. The party included Camilla Davis and John H. Blaffer, who lived next door to the Menils, and Edward J. Hudson, a Museum of Fine Arts trustee whose recent, bitterly contested divorce from John Blaffer's sister, Cecil, had been a public sensation.

Kilian recounted the episode:

> There was a party for Antonioni. He was in town to shoot a sequel to *Blowup*. Helen and I were in charge of Antonioni and his girlfriend, Claire Pepli. They were headed down to Simonton to the rodeo to replay Magritte's rodeo visit. The Menils . . . had set up tables—seven or eight round tables and chairs. Ed Hudson was sitting across the table from me. Gertrude was there. We were right up close to the house, and somewhere out in the yard was John Blaffer's table. Just the presence of Ed Hudson was offensive to him. Blaffer didn't like blacks, Jews, anybody. He hated any sort of authority. He was picking on Gertrude, calling her "Jew lady" and "nigger lover." He pushed Ed Hudson over backwards in his chair. There were [African American] people waiting on tables. John never missed an opportunity to say "nigger" in their presence. I said to him, "If you need to be offensive, talk to me." I left the table. When I came back, he grabbed me and pushed me up against a tree. John de Menil walked over and said, "John, please leave. You are not wanted here." I remember John Blaffer walking, with Camilla down on the ground holding on to one of his legs.[18]

Even among patrician guests at an exclusive party for an elite group of art collectors and patrons, blatant anti-Semitism and racial hatred were never far from the surface. In Houston during the late 1960s, a powerful wind was brewing, and Gertrude Barnstone was standing in the eye of the storm.

The *Look* article, with its flattering photographs portraying Gertrude as a beautiful wife, a busy mother, and her city's insistent conscience, was probably doubly galling to Howard, who was falling into a deep depression. Gertrude was clearly too busy with her political struggles to attend to the needs of three young children and an emotionally troubled husband. Their relationship deteriorated further as both began to seek sexual partners outside their marriage. Howard had begun having covert affairs with men, and Gertrude was involved in a passionate relationship with William P. Hobby, Jr., scion of a Houston political family, president of the *Houston Post* and KPRC Television, and later lieutenant governor of Texas. This must have been awkward: Diana and Bill Hobby were longtime friends and neighbors of Gertrude and Howard's. When asked whether she and Howard had had a so-called open marriage, Gertrude replied, "No, I wouldn't say at the beginning. I always knew he was bisexual. It was only later I knew he was having affairs with men. I didn't care, because I was doing my own thing."

Eventually, in 1968, Gertrude had reasons to fear for her physical safety.

> I remember we were in Boston or New York for the wedding of one of the Menil children. In the hotel, Howard was enraged by something. He said, "You've got a plastic shield around you but I'm going to break through it with a knife, with an axe, with a gun." He pinned my arms behind my back until they hurt, and I decided the next time this happens, I am out of here.... And when it did happen again, I left the house and walked down the street to the Hobbys' and spent the night.

The next day, she moved with her three children to her friend Ann Adams's house. Gertrude continued, "It was so sad. Poor thing. It was manic depression. . . . Howard once said that marriage is a license for cruelty."

Letters from Howard Barnstone to his lawyer, his psychiatrist, and other associates offer a window into the intense suffering he experienced after Gertrude left him and filed for divorce in September 1968. Accusing his wife of cruelty and infidelity, Howard asked his lawyer to pursue custody of the three Barnstone children, for their protection. His letters indicate Howard's jealousy and rage when confronted with clear evidence that his wife was in love with another man. On the other hand, letters to his lawyer, who assumed control of communication between the Barnstones, show that Howard was well aware that he needed to appear not crazy or hysterical when negotiating the children's visitation schedule.

After enduring Howard's unannounced visits to the North Boulevard house, Gertrude asked the family court to cite him for contempt for continuing to harass her and her friends. Her husband's efforts to win her back did not make much of an impression. One poignant note from Howard, scrawled on notepaper from the Hotel Carlyle in New York, claims, "I have every right to love you," and "Imagine the opportunities a successful and fairly good-looking man has in New York."[19] These admonitions elicited no reply from Gertrude.

Gertrude Barnstone never second-guessed her decisions. "I have no regrets," she said about her marriage and divorce. "I did what I thought was best at the time." She admitted that her children have complained about some of her choices. Once I asked her whether she felt guilty about the affair with Hobby, and she said she did. I asked her why she didn't break it off, and she said, "I tried but I couldn't. I loved him too much."

In early 1969, after Howard's release from Galveston's John Sealy Hospital, where he had been treated for depression, he moved into Dominique and John de Menil's guesthouse, which he had designed. The breakdown marked the end of the Barnstone marriage: their divorce became final that year.[20] Howard supported their three children; Gertrude had to get a job to provide for herself. For three years she worked for KPRC-TV, Houston's NBC affiliate, which was owned by the Hobby family. She started as community relations director. She soon drew on her theatrical skills and sense of play to design a weekly children's television program entitled *Sundown's Tree House*, based on the idea that an appealing educational program for children should be designed by the kids in the show. In the early 1970s, Gertrude began taking welding classes at Houston Community College and using those skills to make her living both as an artist working with steel and, on occasion, as a professional welder.

Over her lifetime, Gertrude Barnstone had many admirers, and she doubtless had love affairs with some of them. But it was her long-term friendships that helped her survive and overcome personal tribulations. Her neighbors Diana and Bill Hobby were her greatest source of emotional support and security, attempting to moderate Howard's wildly oscillating moods, and they remained friendly with both Gertrude and Howard despite Howard's jealousy and threats to expose the affair. Clare and Sam Sprunt and Dominique and John de Menil also maintained their close friendship with both Gertrude and Howard during those tumultuous years when Howard was undergoing psychiatric treatment.

After their divorce, Gertrude and Howard continued to communicate about their children, and their regard for one another never diminished. In 1986, less than six months before he killed himself, Howard telephoned Gertrude and asked whether she would remarry him so that she could receive his Social Security and University of Houston retirement benefits. Both agreed that theirs would be a secret arrangement, just a paper marriage. They were married before a justice of the peace on November 10, 1986. Howard's part was played by Burdette Keeland as proxy. At the last moment, Howard had realized that he wouldn't be able to endure the ceremony if it meant standing next to his ex-wife.

Like most children, the Barnstone siblings hold varied memories of their mother and father. For the most part, Lily Barnstone Wells asserted that Gertrude was a terrible mother, irresponsible and selfish, sometimes almost oblivious of the serious psychological problems that Lily had as a teenager. George won't say much about Gertrude as a parent: "Mother is a free spirit" was about all he would tell me. Gertrude's friends recalled that a near-fatal automobile accident involving George emotionally paralyzed his mother. This was borne out by George's account of spending many weeks recuperating at the home of his sister, who was living in Austin. "Lily was terrific," said George. "My mother came to Austin to see me, but she couldn't deal with it."

After their divorce, Gertrude lived for several years in the house at 1720 North Boulevard. Lily continued to live with her off and on, whereas Dora and George lived most of the time with their father. In 1968, during the manic phase that preceded his terrible depression, Howard purchased a house across the street at 1715 North Boulevard. Lily had a deeply sad memory of this period: "I wanted to live with my father. My brother and sister were sharing a room. My father and Bob had the other room. I begged him to let me stay, but he told me I looked too much like my mother, and he couldn't stand to live with me."[21] By this time, the house at 1720 North Boulevard had become well known around Houston as a place where artists, activists, and liberals were welcome.

The Houston animal rights activist Janice Blue described the rolling, carnival atmosphere: "We kept going to Gertrude's house. César Chávez was there, Black Panthers. Anytime there was anyone progressive in town, the reception would be at 1720 North Boulevard. And the kids were there, and the dogs were there. The house was full of cats and dogs. There was so much art. Everybody knew Gertrude. She was involved in the American Civil Liberties Union too. It was the beginning of the feminist movement. And to know Gertrude as somebody who was doing something on her own was great for me."[22]

Gertrude Barnstone in her welding gear in her garage studio, c. 1972, 1401 Harold Street, Houston.

In the mid-1970s, Gertrude moved into a modest bungalow at 1401 Harold Street. In back of the corner lot was a garage that she used as a studio. "People I bought it from were do-it-yourselfers," Gertrude said about the studio. "It had everything—all I had to do is put in more electricity for a welding machine. . . . It was wonderful. Shelves and sink and a flat cement floor. You know, it's not the biggest in the world, but it worked for thirty years, and I've done big things in it."[23] Gertrude talked about learning to weld as though it was like falling in love. When approached by friends while she was at work in her driveway with her goggles and gloves on, she would remove her protective gear to greet them, revealing a face flushed with color and enthusiasm, her silver curls dampened with perspiration. Gertrude never tired of her work; it was a joy for her, a physical and spiritual renewal.

Gertrude Barnstone's combination of curiosity, intelligence, and playfulness brought her to the high point of her creative career. Divorce from Howard Barnstone, difficult and painful as it was for both of them, enabled her to focus her energies on acquiring necessary skills and using them in her new métier, one that helped her live independently. Sculpting in steel, acrylic, and glass brought Gertrude Barnstone modest recognition in the last decades of the twentieth century. Her art injected her special joie de vivre and sense of style into Houston's landscape and architecture. She did installations for the architects Robert Morris and Cameron Armstrong, for the lawyer Eugene Harrington, and for her children at the Vassar Place Apartments, which they inherited from their father.

Gertrude and Howard each contained multiple selves, which contributed to their individual successes. Howard gave Houston remarkable buildings, and Gertrude, as an actress, political activist, television personality, and artist, pushed Houston to become a more inclusive place. The two generally encouraged each other, and when they didn't, each seemed to return to his or her preferred sphere of artistic expression to create new forms and patterns that would transcend their struggles. At their worst moments, Gertrude and Howard behaved like monsters lashing out at each other to salve their emotional wounds. At those times, I am certain that Gisella Levy's words rang loud and clear in her daughter's ears: "The worst thing a woman can do is to marry. And the next worst is having children, because then she doesn't develop herself." By insisting on having her career and a family, Gertrude disproved her mother's dire warnings. Gertrude and Howard Barnstone weathered divorce, with its emotional and professional fallout—if not with grace, with bravery.

Icons of the midcentury American scene, both Barnstones, in quite different ways, conjured in their professional work varieties of spatial, visual, and theatrical legerdemain. It may be that Howard and Gertrude were each essentially accomplished dramatic actors who adopted and played out the roles that were most appealing and useful at key moments. It isn't surprising that they both became popular models for younger activists. Gertrude's direct challenge to conservatives on the school board made her a polarizing figure, whereas Howard's sophisticated and understated style of speaking, dressing, and designing spaces was aimed at a softer sort of modern revolution. Both Barnstones aimed to overturn power structures that were overly self-important, authoritarian, and humorless. Their methods were those of the satirist, wit and irony.

NOTES

1. "1955–1967," Houston Ballet website, accessed July 25, 2018, https://www.houstonballet.org/explore/history/1955-1967.

2. "About Us," Houston Grand Opera website, accessed July 25, 2018, https://www.houstongrandopera.org/abouthgo#A_HistoryofHGO%20.

3. Gertrude Barnstone, interview by the author, April 2010, Houston.

4. Marguerite Johnston delivered the eulogy at Howard Barnstone's funeral.

5. Anderson Todd, interview by the author, July 10, 2007, Houston.

6. Gertrude Barnstone interview. All subsequent quotations from Gertrude Barnstone are taken from interviews with her by the author.

7. Joan Frances, "Bonnie and Clyde in Rosenberg: A Little Piece of History," *Absolutely Brazos*, December 30, 2015, accessed July 25, 2018, http://absolutelybrazos.com/bonnie-and-clyde-in-rosenberg.

8. Quoted in Smart, *Sacred Modern*, 61.

9. Howard Barnstone remodeled a four-story house for June Arnold on Bleecker Street in New York (Barnstone Collection, HMRC, box 18:11).

10. Clare Sprunt, interview by the author, May 14, 2014, Houston.

11. Lily Barnstone Wells, interview by the author, July 2017.

12. "Something New Under the Sun," *Houston Chronicle*, February 6, 1955, 3.

13. Patricia Covo Johnson, "Influential Houston Art Dealer Joan Crystal," *Houston Chronicle*, March 31, 2016, accessed July 25, 2018, https://www.houstonchronicle.com/lifestyle/passages/obituaries/article/Influential-Houston-art-dealer-Crystal-dies-7220075.php.

14. Michael Ennis, "In This Ramshackle Cabin on a Backwater Bay of the Gulf Lived and Worked One of the Greatest Artists Texas Has Ever Produced: His Name Was Forrest Bess," *Texas Monthly*, June 1982, 140–143.

15. Edwards, *Midcentury Modern Art in Texas*, 10.

16. George Zimmerman, "A Lady Stirs Her City's Conscience," *Look* (September 21, 1965): 66.

17. Ibid., 71.

18. Karl Kilian, interview by the author, May 2014, Houston.

19. Barnstone Collection, HMRC, box 32:1–3.

20. Barnstone Collection, HMRC, box 30:19–21 and box 31:1–4.

21. Lily Barnstone Wells interview.

22. Janice Blue, interview by the author, June 12, 2017, Houston.

23. Sarah Reynolds, interview by the author, June 2006, Houston.

CONCLUSION

Magical Modernism

BARRIE SCARDINO BRADLEY, STEPHEN FOX,
AND MICHELANGELO SABATINO

SURVEYS OF THE CAREERS of architects often make only minimal reference to their personal lives. With Howard Barnstone, this interpretive method is suitable. His body of architectural work commands respect and does not require extensive knowledge of his life to elicit appreciation. But to those acquainted with Barnstone, an impersonal interpretation would appear woefully misguided. Barnstone's forceful, charismatic personality is almost tangible in his architecture. Without some understanding of his complex and compelling personality, and what impelled him to assert cultural leadership in Houston through architecture, his buildings would likely be reduced to the well-rehearsed disciplinary discourse emphasizing the succession of formal trends in mid-twentieth-century American architecture. What insight into Barnstone's life, motivations, and contradictions yields is a much richer appreciation of what his buildings, their spaces, contents, and landscape settings, meant to their communities and to broader audiences when they were built.

Following Philip Johnson's lead, Barnstone set out in the 1950s to craft an architecture, primarily of houses, that would give form to his vision of how the modern American patrician class should live.[1] This is what separates Barnstone's translation of Miesian architecture from how it was received in Chicago (as tectonic discipline) and in the buildings associated with the Case Study Program in Los Angeles during the 1950s (as stylish, middle-class, and suburban). Dominique and John de Menil were Barnstone's ideal models of aristocrats of modern taste. His association with Johnson enabled him to translate to Houston Johnson's effort to architecturally identify a modern American aristocracy. Because Barnstone aligned himself with the architecture of Hugo Neuhaus (and ultimately

Anderson Todd, both gentleman architects as well as disciples of Mies) and then promulgated this architecture as a design critic at the University of Houston, he showed that he could, and did, function as an arbiter elegantiarum who elevated the segment of Houston society affiliated with the Menils to national recognition through publication of their houses in the architectural press.

Barnstone's compulsion to seek publicity, not only in nationally circulated architecture magazines but also through repeated publication of his buildings in the *Houston Chronicle* and *Houston Post*, represents another way that he asserted cultural leadership in Houston. Publicity enabled Barnstone to shape persuasive narratives about how spatial organization, site orientation, and construction could materialize modern realities previously unimaginable except in fairy tales, such as the hypnotic allure of gazing through transparent walls of glass at wild nature while environmentally secure in air-conditioned settings that negated threats of climatic extremes, bodily discomfort, and pernicious insects.

Making It, the autobiography that the magazine editor Norman Podhoretz published in 1967, provides a fascinating commentary on Barnstone's social transition from small-town Maine to Manhattan's Upper West Side to Yale and finally to Houston, where "making it" remains a defining local ambition. More than just the story of Podhoretz's life, *Making It* is his account of his transformation from the child of working-class Jewish immigrants into an upper-middle-class cultural authority capable of assimilating WASP manners without sacrificing "the nervous energy, the quick brilliance, and the boisterousness of spirit of the American big city," a coded characterization of an emerging postwar modern American Jewish subjectivity.[2] Podhoretz rejected the stifling restrictions of an immigrant identity (a "Jewish-Americana which was rarely free of a distressingly vulgar coziness" and "the strident note of apologetics and defensiveness ... the endless harping on the suffering of the Jews") for a newfound power to shape perceptions, ideas, and styles through the media and to use the rhetoric of class stratification to valorize the good ("a passionate interest in great matters of modernism and contempt for middlebrow philistine criticism") and exclude the undeserving: "elitism—the conviction that others were not worth taking into consideration except to attack and need not be addressed [since] integrity and standards were only possible among 'us.'"[3]

Podhoretz's unapologetic advocacy for excluding the unworthy can also be seen in Barnstone's dismissal of "middlebrow" modernisms—regionalism, the Usonian, and the contemporary—and the communities of taste they identified, in favor of Miesian elegance, the architectural counterpart to Podhoretz's "great matters of modernism." Jermayne MacAgy, James Johnson Sweeney, and eventually Dominique de Menil, through their exhibitions, shaped spaces for the exhilarating performance of modernity in Houston: in Mies's Cullinan Hall, Johnson's Gallery of Fine Arts at the University of St. Thomas, Barnstone & Aubry's Art Barn at Rice University, and Johnson, Barnstone, and Aubry's Rothko Chapel, where modernism was raised to the solemn dignity of tragedy.

The most profound way in which Barnstone and his cohorts sought to forge consensus on the superiority of their practices and legitimize their claims to cultural authority and leadership was by constructing sensations of "magic." Both MacAgy and Barnstone used the word "magic" to describe architectural settings that viscerally affected the perceptions of those who inhabited them. Barnstone used the phrase "divine float" to describe the bodily sensations of weightless euphoria and emotional elation that one experienced in Cullinan Hall, physical sensations that Sweeney intensified by suspending works of art from the ceiling rather than mounting them on walls or panels.[4] The recognition that MacAgy, Sweeney, and Dominique de Menil attracted in the 1960s in national and international art journals for their stunning exhibition installations drew on Barnstone's technique of using national publicity as a way to assert architectural superiority before a local audience and to craft narratives that represented Houston as exceptional and extraordinary rather than, as John de Menil had phrased it in 1949, "provincial."[5] Alice T. Friedman asserts in her book *American Glamour and the Evolution of Modern Architecture* that "the essence of glamour is magical storytelling."[6] The images of modern Houston that circulated in national architectural and art journals as well as local newspapers constructed mythic representations that identified the privileged settings with which Barnstone and his taste community were affiliated as sophisticated and alluring, and as Friedman observes, that "spoke directly to the aspirational fantasies of viewers."[7]

Barnstone's decision to align himself with the cosmopolitan vision of Dominique and John de Menil and what Mark Alan Hewitt described as the "progressive MoMA modern style" of Philip Johnson led him to reject, almost as a dialectical reflex, the "middlebrow" versions of modern architecture associated nationally with *House Beautiful* magazine and its editor, Elizabeth Gordon, which Monica Penick examines in her book *Tastemaker*.[8] Gordon's bizarre attack in 1953 on Mies van der Rohe's Farnsworth House, which *House Beautiful* sensationally denounced as un-American, highlighted the struggle for cultural authority occurring *within* modernist circles in the 1950s, nationally as well as in Houston.[9] Barnstone's liberal sympathies, confrontational inclination, and ambivalent sense of otherness coalesced in his effort to use architecture to materialize a particular kind of modern community and class identity in Houston.

One marker of Barnstone's otherness in mid-twentieth-century Houston was his Jewishness. A roster of Texas members of the American Institute of Architects published in 1970 reveals surprisingly few Jewish architects practicing in Texas cities.[10] Howard R. Meyer, Dallas's pioneer modern architect and a Depression-era transplant from New York who had married a Texan, was one of the few Jewish architects in practice in Texas, as were the Austrian-born Walter Wisznia in Corpus Christi, the Polish-born Ben J. Kotin in Galveston, and Kotin's partner, the Czech-born Tibor Beerman. (Morris L. Levy of Corpus Christi and Malcolm G. Simons of San Antonio belonged to the premodern generation, as had Joseph Finger of Houston, who died in 1952.) Houston, with sixteen Jewish architects, stood out among Texan cities; most of those architects headed their own practices. What distinguished Barnstone from his fellow Houston Jewish architects was that his clientele was not primarily Jewish, although he had prominent Jewish clients. Barnstone's sense of otherness extended even to communities with which he might otherwise have been automatically associated. He deliberately avoided identification with Houston's Jewish institutions. A distinction that the religious historian Matthias Henze draws between Christian and Jewish hermeneutics seems pertinent to understanding Barnstone: whereas Christian churches seek to define orthodox interpretations of biblical texts, Jewish hermeneutics promote questioning and interpretation.[11] It is in this indirect way that Barnstone's Jewishness intersected with his architecture: the confidence and enthusiasm with which he used architecture to analyze and interpret social circumstances.

Another marker of otherness was Barnstone's bisexuality. During most of his lifetime, it was not respectable, in the social circles to which he aspired to belong, to acknowledge same-sex attraction. Therefore, although some architects whom Barnstone admired were homosexual (Philip Johnson and Paul Rudolph), as were some architects he did not admire (Bruce Goff), he did not focus on sexual orientation in his architecture. In the same way that seeking Jewish cultural traces in Barnstone's architecture seems futile, so too is the effort to isolate traces of a gay identity in his buildings. More relevant is the observation of the historian of religion Jeffrey J. Kripal:

> A homoerotic orientation must put an individual in profound and irreconcilable conflict with the normative social constructions of practically any society, almost all of which are formed around some form of procreative heterosexuality . . . The homoerotic man or woman thus knows what it feels like to stand "against the law" of culture and society not abstractly, but

> physically, biologically, ontologically. He or she also possesses special gifts of transcendence, insight, and social criticism that are not easily won by those deeply embedded in the heterosexual order . . . That is why . . . the ranks of intellectuals, artists, and prophetic religious figures . . . are filled with homoerotic figures who saw through and transgressed the social and religious orders of their day . . . Quite literally, they did not "fit in."[12]

Barnstone's persistent ambivalence about fitting in—desiring to do so but retreating from commitments that might compromise his independence—imparts a melancholy resonance to Kripal's observations.

Barnstone positioned himself as a modern architect, not a Houston architect. Yet despite the wide geographic distribution of his work, Houston became an indissoluble part of his professional identity. The emergence of Dominique and John de Menil as subjects of historical scholarship and critical evaluation makes it possible to interpret Barnstone's association with Houston in terms other than "provincial" or "regional." William Middleton's biography of Dominique and John de Menil, *Double Vision*; Pamela Smart's ethnography of the Menil Collection, *Sacred Modern*; Marcia Brennan's *Curating Consciousness: Mysticism and the Modern Museum*; and Sheldon Nodelman's *The Rothko Chapel Paintings* subject Houston's Menil episode to critical investigation, leading to the potential for revising stereotypes of Houston as a crass frontier wasteland and appreciating how counternarratives, the "decent, complex alternative[s]" that Phillip Lopate recognized in Barnstone, were generated by culturally ambitious Houstonians.[13] As Houston comes to be critically reinterpreted as a distinctive American cultural landscape, the ways that Barnstone's architecture engaged the city and its particular conditions will stand out as remarkable instances of spatial invention.[14]

Phillip Lopate, who came to Houston to teach in the Creative Writing Program at the University of Houston in 1981, is one of the writers who gathered around Houston's most famous modernist, the short-story writer Donald Barthelme, eldest son of the architect Donald Barthelme. What Lopate, Barthelme, and their colleagues, the poets Cynthia McDonald and Edward M. Hirsch and the novelists Laura Furman and Rosellen Brown, brought to Houston was their ability to transform life into art: to observe the routines of their daily lives and recast them in literary form as varied reflections of the city in which they lived. Distilling lived experience into form was an art at which Barnstone excelled. His preoccupations were different from those of the writers, and the forms with which he worked were material and spatial rather than figurative and literary. The University of Houston's creative writing program nurtured a community of imaginative writers such as Joel Warren Barna, who became an architecture critic and the author of *The See-Through Years*. Barna chronicled with invention and insight the expansion and sudden contraction of Texas's building economy in the 1980s, the period corresponding to Barnstone's final phase of professional activity.[15] The junior Donald Barthelme, although he began his writing career in Houston, had to move to New York for his narrative innovations to be recognized. Barnstone, who remained in Houston, did not go unnoticed. But the lack of an interpretive apparatus for deducing the social meanings embedded in Barnstone's architecture stemmed not from neglect by New York cultural authorities but from the uneven development of a critical interpretive infrastructure in Houston.

It was while visiting a Barnstone-designed house that the architectural critic and historian Aaron Betsky noticed that Houston's most compelling domestic architecture tends to be antithetical to, rather than expressive of, the flat, hot, raucous, sprawling suburbanized metropolis in which it is built.[16] Although Barnstone's houses condense tranquility and refinement, they are enlivened by their "magical" attributes: their proportioned scale, spatial intimacy, and indoor-outdoor continuity in a climate that often discourages open doors and windows. Barnstone mobilized the technologies of his time to domesticate modern architecture in Houston and shape it to local circumstance, but with a critical twist. He formulated antitheses to prevailing conditions and made architecture out of his antithetical reactions. He sought to devise a modern power style that, through exhilarating spatial sensations, rewarded its adherents for relinquishing the architectural rhetoric of privilege that was explicitly incorporated in the eclectic country houses of Barnstone's predecessors John Staub and Birdsall Briscoe. In reacting against the excesses of mid-twentieth-century Houston, Barnstone constructed an architecture of subtle nuance that identified the modern subcultural faction whose superiority his buildings championed.

NOTES

1. Johnson's career has not been systematically analyzed from the perspective of patronage. The most thoughtful text on this facet of his career is Kazys Varnelis, "Philip Johnson's Empire: Network Power and the AT&T Building," in Petit, *Philip Johnson*, 120–135.

2. Podhoretz, *Making It*, 122. Thanks to Benjamin Moser for calling this book to our attention.

3. Ibid., 44, 115–116.

4. Howard Barnstone, "Rediscovering John Staub: The Great Eclectic of Houston's Elite," *Texas Architect* 29 (November–December 1979): 53. Barnstone coined the term "divine float" to describe the spatiality of Staub's houses.

5. Quoted in Lynn M. Herbert, "Seeing Was Believing: Installations of Jermayne MacAgy and James Johnson Sweeney," *Cite 40* (Winter 1997–1998): 30–33.

6. Friedman, *American Glamour*, 13.

7. Ibid., 93.

8. Mark A. Hewitt, "Neoclassicism and Modern Architecture: Houston Style, or The Domestication of Mies," *Cite 7* (Fall 1984): 12–15; see also Penick, *Tastemaker*.

9. Elizabeth Gordon, "The Threat to the Next America," *House Beautiful* 95 (April 1953): 126–130; Joseph A. Barry, "Report on the American Battle between Good and Bad Modern Houses," *House Beautiful* 95 (May 1953): 172–173. Earlier polemics associated with the struggle to control the direction and interpretation of postwar modern architecture in the United States include "What Is Happening to Modern Architecture?," *Bulletin of the Museum of Modern Art* 15 (Spring 1948): 4–20; and Peter Blake and Philip C. Johnson, "Architectural Freedom and Order: An Answer to Robert W. Kennedy," *Magazine of Art* 41 (October 1948): 228–231.

10. *American Architects Directory*, 3rd ed., 1098–1102.11. Matthias Henze, lecture delivered to the Rice Historical Society, September 30, 2018.

12. Kripal, *Secret Body*, 151.

13. Phillip Lopate, "Elegy for Houston," *Texas Observer*, May 29, 1987, 10.

14. Reyner Banham accomplished such a feat of critical reversal with his book *Los Angeles: The Architecture of Four Ecologies*.

15. Barna, *The See-Through Years*.

16. Aaron Betsky, conversation with Stephen Fox, October 14, 2000.

AFTERWORD

Looking toward the Future

THEODORE H. M. PRUDON

THE SECOND WORLD WAR ended in 1945, and millions of returning soldiers needed a place to live. President Franklin Delano Roosevelt's "arsenal of democracy" was being transformed into a peacetime production machine.[1] As goods unobtainable in the long period of scarcity during the Great Depression and the war became available and affordable, Americans began to foresee a time of prosperity and optimism that would radically change society. Against this background, there emerged a generation of young architects who had graduated from architectural schools during and just after the war, when architecture schools were moving from a Beaux Arts–based curriculum to one inspired by the modernism brought to the United States by Bauhaus-trained European architects who had immigrated just before the war. These events played themselves out in Houston and across the country in new residential subdivisions.

When Howard Barnstone entered practice and joined the faculty of the University of Houston architecture school in 1948, it was the beginning of a decades-long professional and academic career. His portfolio consists of a substantial number of single-family houses that reflect not only a modernist rigor but also a personal stylistic diversity and originality in plan and volume. Barnstone's work, while nationally and locally recognized at the time, is emblematic of an entire generation of American architects who were working throughout the country during the 1950s and 1960s. This important nationwide legacy represents a challenge to preservation architects and historians.

In Houston, as elsewhere, it is precisely these single-family residences that have become the subject of pitched preservation battles. Located near urban centers and on prime lots in mature and desirable neighborhoods, these once au courant modern houses are now considered inadequate in size and amenities. Because they no longer satisfy contemporary requirements such as gigantic bathrooms and open-plan public areas, real estate pressures to resell them are severe. Disturbingly, these original, modern, modestly sized houses are being demolished and replaced by much larger ones, nicknamed McMansions. These new houses, vaguely classical or Victorian, are reminiscent of a past that never existed. In a few instances, the consternation around the sudden demolition of a significant modern house has had a positive outcome: greater community awareness, leading to greater vigilance and, more importantly, the implementation of appropriate legislation aimed at safeguarding this mid-twentieth-century heritage.

Although most cities have no formal or strong legal frameworks to assist in preservation efforts, national organizations such as Docomomo US, with chapters across the country, and local groups such as Houston Mod are taking the lead in advocating for preservation of modern buildings and sites. In some cities, this increased attention has led to the passage of preservation ordinances. Where this modernist residential heritage has become a source of pride and celebration, new economic opportunities are developing. Palm Springs with its Modernism Week and Sarasota with a similar event are prime examples, along with the frequent tours and publications of Houston Mod.

In other cases, demolition has been avoided through the use of renovations and additions to an existing house that provide the spatial requirements of today while respecting the character of the original architecture. In fewer instances, the original house is treated with respect and restored and adapted thoughtfully. Here the challenge is a different one: to not make the original more perfect than it ever was. In Houston, one good example of the right approach is the restoration and conservation of the Menil House, designed by Philip Johnson in 1951. After the deaths of Dominique and John de Menil, their house was carefully restored by the Houston architectural firm Stern and Bucek for the Menil Foundation, which maintains the house for special events. This is an ideal but rare circumstance. But to preserve the many excellent examples of modern residences in the Houston suburbs, people must want to live in them. With the cyclical and fickle nature of architectural types and styles, appreciation of the beauty of modernism will return, as will the desire of some to downsize their living arrangements to be more economical and environmentally responsible.

By raising awareness and appreciation of one exceptional modern architect, this monograph on Howard Barnstone should contribute significantly to the advocacy efforts for the preservation of modern architecture. It adds to the meaningful education and discussion nationally about what can and should be saved and treasured. Such efforts must involve the general public as well as professional architects and educators. Barnstone's work is a fine example of architecture produced by the first postwar generation of architects. Today, schools and advocates for preservation of modern buildings must train and educate the next generation of architects, designers, and preservationists to take care of that legacy.

Preservation of modern architecture in general, and modern residential architecture in particular, has come to the foreground in the last decade. More and more communities are becoming attuned to the losses and potential losses of this domestic heritage. *Making Houston Modern* adds to the literature on one city's modern architecture and explains the many reasons the architecture of this defining American generation deserves to be preserved. It also shows, in its illustrations, both historic and current, the beauty and future possibilities of preserving these buildings.

NOTE

1. The term "arsenal of democracy" was first used by President Roosevelt in a radio broadcast on December 29, 1940.

APPENDIX 1

Interview with Eugene Aubry

CONDUCTED BY STEPHEN FOX AND
MICHELANGELO SABATINO
MAY 5, 2010, GALVESTON, TEXAS

Q: *When did you first encounter Howard Barnstone? What was your reaction?*
A: I first encountered Howard when I was a student at the University of Houston. He was always around, but I didn't get to know him until I got to fourth year and had him for studio. I was intrigued because I wanted to find out who he was. I wasn't afraid of him, but many of the guys were. He was known for being ruthless in juries and made some guys cry. A lot of people who started out with me quit long before graduation.

Q: *What was Howard Barnstone like as a teacher?*
A: In fourth year, you were assigned a project and had a certain amount of time in which you were expected to at least put something on paper. With Howard, you didn't have to put much down on paper, because it was always easy to talk to him about the project. I also had Burdette Keeland, and he was very predictable; you pretty much knew what he was looking for. But with Howard, I didn't try to second-guess him by drawing something that I thought he would like. I could do something that was in my head, so I was not designing for Howard, but creating a solution that I thought was right. This rather fascinated Howard, so our friendship started because our minds worked alike. At that time, Don Palmer was working for Howard (and had for many years). So I was familiar with the houses, such as the Owsley House and the Winterbotham House, that his office was producing.

Q: *What project did you first work on with Barnstone?*
A: When I was still a student, he asked me to build a model of the Owsley House. He found out I could make models and that I loved doing that. I remember going out to the construction site with him. The steel frame and wood joists were up. I

was standing up in the house, and I asked, "Where is the lateral bracing?" I wasn't an experienced architect, but I knew something was wrong. At the time, I was in fourth year and working part-time for Burdette, and out of nowhere, Howard asked me if I would like to come to work in his office because Don was leaving. I was a little worried because I knew Burdette and Howard were great friends, but Burdette thought it was a great idea. I worked in Howard's office at 811 Lovett, and Preston Bolton was there. Preston had a very formal office. Howard's office was at the very end, upstairs in the attic, and he had a secretary, Virginia Hess. Don left the first day I was there; he just walked out and said, "Good Luck!" Adrian Rosenberg from Rice also worked there. Preston and Howard didn't get along. Preston has nothing to do with Howard; he just ran the financial side of the office. They really didn't work as a partnership.

Q: *What aspects most intrigued you about Barnstone?*
A: What intrigued me about him was his mystery. You couldn't figure him out. I was very young, and about this time, between my fourth and fifth year, I fell in love with Elizabeth Hunter, the daughter of a wealthy Galveston man, so I'm in society. Howard thought that was great. I took his social climbing as a sign of insecurity; part of Howard was very insecure. His brother, Willis, was the ultimate intellectual. He was a poet and translator who had an MA from Columbia and a PhD from Yale. Willis was rather ethereal and could go off on some pretty interesting tangents, but he was very impatient with Howard. Beatrice, his sister, was wonderful, and I used to go visit her in Sarasota, and we would talk about Howard.

Q: *What aspects most troubled you?*
A: Talking to Howard was like talking to Frederick Kiesler or Bucky [Buckminster Fuller]. You couldn't follow the bouncing ball because oftentimes there was no ball. Howard only cared about how the building came together, if he thought he was doing something nobody else had ever done before. The reality is that there isn't anything that hasn't been done. He wanted to do things that were all-new, totally fresh. Otherwise he just wasn't interested. I was always intrigued by Howard's tastes. Here was a guy that could look at something and understand if it was good or bad aesthetically. He had no idea if it was bad structurally, only if it was good aesthetically, like the Maher House. We worked with Philip Johnson, and in a way, Howard patterned himself after Johnson. He loved Philip and loved to have him over to his house. Philip would sit on the floor and talk to the kids—not preaching or anything like that. Howard always wanted that to happen with him, but it didn't. Howard did pattern himself a lot.

Q: *Did you work with Preston Bolton or only with Barnstone? Did Bolton have his set of draftsmen? Did Bolton and Barnstone consult or collaborate on each other's designs?*

A: I only worked with Howard. I said, "Good Morning" and "How are you?" every day with Preston, but that was it. Adrian Rosenberg did drawings for both Preston and Howard. Adrian was very proficient in detailing; he really knew the Johnson details. If you look at the houses he worked on for Bolton & Barnstone, they were all Johnson's details. All the details in the Menil House were used in the Cook House in Friendswood and in the Gordon House—they were all Philip's details. John Manley was Johnson's guy. The Seagram Building wouldn't be what it is without the Johnson office—that is, Manley—as associate architects for Mies.

When Howard did the house for Ruth Ann and Charlie Smithers, which was very Miesian—a very simple house in New Canaan, Connecticut—Don Palmer did all the drawings, the details. Howard was very captivated by the social milieu. Smithers was a Wall Street guy and very wealthy. The addition he did later was a box with rounded corners and oval windows. They didn't know how to build it, and Howard didn't know what to tell them. That was finished in 1961, then we added yet another addition in 1968, which bore no relationship to the first one. This is the history of modern architecture—the Miesian period, then the brutalist period, then postmodernism—I was rather ignorant, but I did it.

Q: *How did you come to advance from new employee to partnership? What were your areas of responsibility?*

A: In the office, I worked on jobs where I knew the client. Howard had other clients that he would sneak around and do himself. For example, I knew Marti, his stepmother in Laredo. Howard really didn't design anything for her. One day when Howard came up to talk to me, I just said, "I think we should be partners." I was terrified because I understood what liability meant, and I knew, signing up to dance and sleep with Howard, that I'd better cover my ass. We needed a partnership agreement, so we went to Adrian Levy, a onetime Galveston mayor and society man whose office was in the US National Bank Building. Levy happened to be one of Mr. Hunter's very good friends. Elisabeth and I were married, and Howard was working this scene. So we got a partnership agreement in 1965. We spent months designing a brochure, deciding on the type style. We didn't argue about it; that was fun.

Q: *What led to the dissolution of the Barnstone & Aubry partnership?*

A: There weren't any disagreements. We completely agreed about what we each did, we just decided that it wasn't in our best interests to be partners anymore.

We did not part on angry terms. Unfortunately, as in all divorces, the anger comes out after the divorce. All of a sudden, the emotions spill over. I totally understood Howard, but he didn't understand himself. The reason I had to leave was because Howard and I were very close friends. We worked with Mr. de Menil, and I became very close to the Menils. After our split, I did quite a number of jobs that Howard never knew about. The Menils protected him and took care of him.

After my discussion with Howard, I went to Mr. de Menil and talked to him about going to New York to work with Philip Johnson. I was also offered the opportunity to work with S. I. Morris. I asked Mr. de Menil what he thought I should do. I really had no interest in running a firm, at least not the business of a firm. I didn't want to be an accountant or office manager and didn't like the idea of having architects work for me. Even though I was hired by Howard, our agreement was that I worked with him, not for him. I wasn't the employee, and he never made me feel like that, which I thought was a pretty unique relationship. You didn't become a member of the Count Basie band because you did what he said. If you weren't good, you just weren't there anymore. Howard had special relationships with people in the office, and if you got out of that circle, he could be difficult. With Howard, it wasn't if you were a good architect; it was more about what kind of person you were that was more important to him. In the office, we had Newman Sherman, the first black architect from the University of Texas, and we had this guy Alex Wong, whom Howard drove crazy. Don Emerson was a really good technical guy whose father was a vet in the Barnum & Bailey Circus. Bill Anderson was also a very good technical architect; he just didn't talk to Howard. Social image was everything for Howard, so we moved downtown to the Niels Esperson Building. There you had lunch at the counter with the boys in the famous drugstore in the Esperson Building—and that was a big deal!

Q: *What were Barnstone's contributions to the office designs that aren't necessarily obvious?*

A: Howard was very judgmental about other people. I was like a conduit. We could work, and I could get done what needed to be done the way he wanted it. He wouldn't go too far, because he got out of bounds quickly. I could develop his ideas. In the Puerto Vallarta job, for example, we had a conversation, and from there it got done. He never went down to see it, but it got done. What Howard gave me was emotional, a spiritual thing. He created drive in me, and he gave me a desire to excel, because I knew what his expectations were.

Q: *Which architects did Barnstone most admire? Could any be considered his mentor?*

A: He was a very good friend of Philip Johnson. How much he admired him, I don't know, but Howard always paid attention to him. Philip was the Andy Warhol of architecture—you never knew which door he was going to come out of, and when he did, you paid attention. I'm not sure what he felt about Mies. There wasn't anything romantic about Mies. Johnson warmed up modernism. Howard was intrigued by Paul Rudolph. Howard got a number of guys from UH into Yale, such as Burdette. Years later, I went up to New Haven because Burdette was having a birthday, and I wanted to interview Rudolph and Johnson. Rudolph ran us out of the office.

Q: *Did Barnstone think of himself as an "insider" or an "outsider" with respect to his clients?*
A: Oftentimes he thought no one understood him—what he wanted and what he was doing and why he was trying to push them. Budgets were non-discussion points. Like Philip Johnson, he had no interest in budgets. Which is what happened for the Center for the Retarded. In the beginning, with a new client, he was good at dating and seducing them, but then, when you pass to the day-to-day marriage part, it often fell apart.

Q: *Did Barnstone seek out jobs? Or did clients come to him?*
A: He literally got the majority of his work through the Menils, one way or the other.

Q: *What was most significant about* The Galveston That Was?
A: People have different abilities or ways to address their thoughts. Howard had ways of expressing himself which made sense to me. Other times, he greatly angered people. He could lay a big dead fish on the table, for which I have always applauded him. This was the basic story of Galveston, and everyone knew part of the story, but they didn't know the punch line. During the last quarter of the nineteenth century, Galveston was jumping, with a deepwater port, railroads, Henry Rosenberg. Then the 1900 storm hit, and people had to start over. One group of guys went to High Island and hit oil. If you look at the family trees of these guys, they all came from Galveston. Some of the powers that be in Galveston basically said, "We are not going to do that." So these wildcatters went up to Houston and built the Houston Ship Channel and shut Galveston down. The real tragedy to me and to Howard—we talked about this a lot—was that I couldn't go back to Galveston where I grew up. You cannot accomplish anything in a brain drain.

Social climbing is public relations. The Galveston book was like one great, gigantic date. It was great PR. Howard and I were both very concerned about all the old architecture being torn down. The extraordinary thing about the book was that it created an awareness of what was going on. One of Howard Barnstone's greatest contributions in his life was to write that book. And it wasn't just the architecture; he did it because of his intellect.

Q: *What buildings from the Barnstone & Aubry partnership do you value most highly?*
A: The Harris County Center for the Retarded, which was completely private. The name is misleading. New question: why didn't Howard do more public buildings? Because they were a bureaucratic nightmare. Piney Point Elementary School was a nightmare—going to meetings with Howard to deal with officials. We did design the recreation center for Tuffly Park in northeast Houston.

Q: *Do you see any special architectural qualities, traits, or details that you would identify as distinctively "Howard Barnstone"?*
A: The one job that was typically Howard that he had a lot to do with was the house for Anne Schlumberger and Leroy Melcher on Tiel Way. The doorbell was a gong. Howard managed all the spatial-relationship sequences. He insisted on the bedroom arrangement, and they just built it. All the switch plates were lowered to wrist level and always placed horizontally, which was difficult in frame houses. Plugs were as low as you could get them and sideways, which is more logical. Howard thought one should never see light directly. Indirect light avoided glare, and he insisted on high-quality lighting. The handles on the doors and the cabinets in the kitchen had to be horizontal. Howard loved to go into the philosophy and psychology of your eyes or whatever.

Q: *What did you learn from Howard Barnstone?*
A: Howard did not like to be questioned. When he decided that he was being questioned by a client, he withdrew from the project and turned everything over to his staff. When he realized he'd "lost" a client, he disappeared, because he knew he could rely on the staff. It caused a lot of disorientation, because I liked Howard and knew what the issues were. I still wanted to carry the job through with the original intent. I'm very much a realist; however, I learned how to go off on tangents from one of best—he taught me that. He taught me to be a freethinker.

Q: *Why did the office's design change from the Miesian architecture of the Bolton & Barnstone period?*
A: It changed because the staff changed. And Howard changed the way he did things. One thing he did not like about Miesian buildings was that they all looked alike. Howard never wanted two things to look alike. Pelli, SOM, HOK—if that

is really what you like, then go to them. Now, if you want a building that is your building, specifically designed for you, then you needed to hire us. So Barnstone's modernism was tailored. We didn't have a cookie cutter. No two clients are alike, so why should two buildings be alike? Every day is a new day. Don left, and I was there. It was like being back in school. I just did what I wanted to—the Mermel House, for example. Howard would get into fights with clients and lose the commission.

Q: *Was Barnstone's practice profitable?*
A: It was fairly consistent, but not highly profitable. He relied on the school for his income. He owned 811 Lovett and got rent money from that. I will say, Howard was a completely fair employer. He never cheated you out of your salary. We always got paid, and we had a lot of fun.

Q: *Anything else?*
A: Howard was pedigreed, and he was the first to bring a cosmopolitan vision to the college of architecture. Others were very practical and grounded; he was an inspiration—ethereal, charismatic, imaginative. He made you think. Howard never drew anything, and when he did, it was like a third grader. Philip couldn't draw either, but he could talk and inspire you. He talked like he drew, vague and mystical. With Howard, you didn't talk about patio doors and windowsills, and you never talked about the theory of architecture; you talked about other subjects. He was very smart and was good at improvisation. He was also the ultimate social climber.

APPENDIX 2

Interview with Anne Schlumberger Brown

CONDUCTED BY BARRIE SCARDINO BRADLEY AND STEPHEN FOX, SEPTEMBER 28, 2018, HOUSTON, TEXAS

Q: *Do you remember when you first met Howard?*
A: Not exactly, but it was when he worked on our house on Tiel Way in 1962. My parents had given me some money, and I decided to buy a house with it. We found the house on Tiel Way, designed by Ham Brown, and bought it because of its location and beautiful site, but it needed a lot of work and an addition to have enough room for our three boys. My father either brought Howard over or suggested that we get in touch with him to help us with the house.

Q: *Did you know he had worked on your aunt's house on San Felipe and the Schlumberger offices?*
A: I had heard of him, of course, but as a busy young mother, I didn't really pay attention. I had probably met him and Gertrude at parties, but I honestly don't remember.

Q: *What did he do with your house on Tiel Way?*
A: He made the house wonderful. He took out a couple of walls and opened it up. There was a strange door from the den that went directly outside. Howard explained that the door was not unusual. It was for the man of the house to use when he came home tired from work; he could slip into his den and knock back a few drinks before having to face his wife and children! We left it there. The main thing Howard did that improved the house was to add on a glass-walled extension to the living room on the back of the house, overlooking the yard and a woodsy ravine. Above it we had a wide porch off of the bedrooms. The only problem was that it always leaked! Every time it rained hard, I called Howard to complain. We had it repaired several times—but it still leaked. Howard would say something

like how lucky we were to live in such a marvelous house, and that a little leak shouldn't spoil it for us. We lived there fifteen years and did love it, leak and all. It was a great place for the boys to grow up, riding their bicycles everywhere, playing in the ravine.

Q: *When you were an architecture student at UH, did you have Howard for a studio?*
A: You know, it was Howard's idea for me to go to architecture school. We were good friends by that time, and I guess I complained about being bored with the children all in school. He said he thought I would make a terrific architect and, with all of my experience as a client, I should just start in second year. Well, I was admitted, and in my first class the professor told us he had to be gone for six weeks, or something like that, and gave us a design problem and told us to work it up with drawings, a model, and working drawings, and he'd review them when he got back. I had no idea how to do any of that, so I dropped back to first year and did the whole five years! And no, I didn't have Howard in studio, but he did sit on juries for my studios.

Q: *What was that like?*
A: Oh, it was horrible. Howard and Burdette were known, of anyone on the faculty, to be the toughest on students. They could be ruthless. We'd all have our models, for example, and Howard would pick out one and say it was the worst one and then tear it, and the poor student, apart. Sometimes he'd pick out the best one and talk about it, but he would find fault with it too. We'd all be scared to death, but we'd remember what not to do.

Q: *Didn't you have him for a city-planning course?*
A: Yes, I did, and it was my favorite class. It was mostly a gossip session. Howard loved gossip, and we'd talk about who was having an affair with whom, or some party that he'd been to or was in the newspaper. He'd sometimes bring in gossip-column clippings. But I actually remember more from that class than any other one I took in architecture school. In order not to have to write up a final exam, Howard gave us a final assignment. Each person in the class was to make up a question, and each person had to answer one of the questions. You got two grades, one for how good your question was, and the other for how well you answered another person's question.

Q: *Tell us about your relationship with your father's cousin, Dominique de Menil, and her husband, John.*
A: Dominique admitted she was a terrible mother, but she was such an interesting person and did so much for everyone else—she and John. My mother died just

before I was to get married, and John in particular was so sweet and helpful to me. But they and my father took advantage of Howard. My father called Howard in the middle of the night one time because he was trying to sleep in a new bed—that Howard had probably ordered for him—and he couldn't go to sleep because something was wrong with the mattress. He asked Howard to come over and take a look at it. Howard did, and found that whoever had made up the bed put no mattress pad on it, and the little buttons on the top of the mattress were uncomfortably sticking up.

Q: *That sounds like Simone Swan's story of John calling Howard to fly up to New York because the house smelled bad. When Howard got there the next morning, he found a dead rat in the air-conditioning system. Did Howard think they were taking advantage of him?*
A: Oh yes. He complained to me all the time about how he felt used by the Menils. I'd go over to his house in the evening and have a few drinks; he felt like he could talk to me. He was a very open person. You know he used to wrap all their Christmas presents—my father's, too. It was those kinds of things.

Q: *Do you think he felt that was the price he had to pay to remain in the exciting Schlumberger-Menil orbit?*
A: I guess so, but it was sad. One thing that I think is funny is that when my father was courting my stepmother, he had Howard write his love letters to her because my father was afraid his English wasn't good enough to impress her.

Q: *What do you remember about Howard during his last depression? Do you think there was something specific that pushed him over the edge and caused him to commit suicide?*
A: You know, his father committed suicide, and so did his half brother. Depression can be a familial trait. I don't think there was one specific thing. He was very upset about losing jobs he wanted and thought he should have gotten. His life just seemed to come unraveled. He didn't believe he ever got the recognition he deserved. I believe he was thinking about committing suicide for a long time before he actually did it. Everyone wished he could have known what a huge void he would leave.

APPENDIX 3

Architectural Awards

AMERICAN INSTITUTE OF ARCHITECTS ARCHITECTURE AWARDS

1959, AIA Homes for Better Living Awards
Aaron J. Farfel House, Houston

1978 Honor Award for Extended Use: Menil-Carpenter Houses, East Hampton, Long Island, New York (with Daniel M. C. Hopping, consulting architect; William Chaffee and Morey & Hollenbeck, prior architects)

TEXAS SOCIETY OF ARCHITECTS HONOR AWARDS

1952 Award of Merit: Herbert Blum House, Beaumont

1953 Award of Merit: Morris G. Rosenthal House, Houston

1954 Award of Merit: Lawrence Blum House, Beaumont
Commendation: Schlumberger office renovation (with Knoll Design Associates), Houston

1955 Award of Excellence: Richard Hardison House, Houston

1956 Award of Honor: Gerald S. Gordon House, Houston

1957 First Honor Award: Aaron J. Farfel House, Houston

1958 Award of Merit: Dr. Harris Hosen House, Port Arthur

1959 First Honor: M. L. Cook House, Friendswood

1960 Architecture of Merit in the Past Ten Years
Gerald S. Gordon House, Houston
Marc Demoustier House, Houston
Mrs. David Lindsay House, Houston
Aaron J. Farfel House, Houston
M. L. Cook House, Friendswood
Dr. Harris Hosen House, Port Arthur

1961 Award of Merit: Alvin M. Owsley, Jr., House, Houston

1962 Award of Merit: John M. Winterbotham House, Houston (Bolton & Barnstone)

1972 First Honor Award: P. G. Bell House, Houston (Barnstone & Aubry)

1974 Rothko Chapel, Houston (Barnstone & Aubry)
Frank Herzog House, Houston (with Anthony E. Frederick)

1976 Honorable Mention: Jean Riboud House, Scottsdale (with Anthony E. Frederick)

1977 First Honor: Menil-Carpenter Houses, East Hampton, Long Island, New York (with Daniel M. C. Hopping, consulting architect; William Chaffee and Morey & Hollenbeck, prior architects)

1980 Honor Award: Encinal Condominiums, Austin (with Alan Nutt, associate architect)
Honor Award: Schlumberger-Doll Research Center, Ridgefield, Connecticut

1988 Honor Award: Schlumberger Austin Systems Center (with Robert T. Jackson, joint venture architect)

AMERICAN INSTITUTE OF ARCHITECTS, HOUSTON CHAPTER

Biennial Design Awards
1956 Gerald S. Gordon House, Houston
1958 Aaron J. Farfel House, Houston

1962 Commendation: Irving Mermel House, Houston

1972 Award of Merit: Rothko Chapel (Barnstone & Aubry)

Award of Merit: Guinan Hall, University of St. Thomas, Houston (Barnstone & Aubry)

1974 Honor Award: Crispin Company rehabilitation, Houston

Honor Award: Dr. William J. Levin House, Galveston (Barnstone & Aubry)

Honorable Mention: Frank Herzog House (with Anthony E. Frederick)

HOUSTON HOME DESIGN AWARDS

Sponsored by *Houston Home and Garden* magazine and AIA, Houston

1977 Graustark Family Townhouses, Houston

AMERICAN INSTITUTE OF STEEL CONSTRUCTION ARCHITECTURAL AWARD OF EXCELLENCE

1961 John M. Winterbotham House, Houston (Bolton & Barnstone)

Gerald S. Gordon House, Houston (Bolton & Barnstone)

HOWARD BARNSTONE'S ARCHITECTURAL OFFICES

1949–1951	3106 Brazos Street	1971–1973	1224 Barkdull Street
1952–1961	811 Lovett Boulevard	1974–1979	1303 Vassar Place
1962	630 Niels Esperson Building, 808 Travis Street	1980–1986	5200 Bayard Lane
1963	14th floor, Niels Esperson Building	1986	17 Shadowlawn (May to August)
1963–1969	1914 West Capitol Avenue	1986–1887	1200-C Bissonnet

CATALOGUE RAISONNÉ

NOTES

1. Several projects inexplicably have the same job number.
2. The first two digits of a job number indicate the date when the project was initiated, which was not necessarily the date of completion.
3. Some jobs that were begun in the Barnstone office—and thus were given a job number and are represented in the Howard Barnstone Collection (MSS 178) of the Houston Metropolitan Research Center, Houston Public Library—were completed by another architect, which is noted in the catalogue entry.
4. If an entry lists no location for a project, it is unknown.

HOWARD BARNSTONE, ARCHITECT 1949–1952

[no job number]
HOUSE FOR DR. AND MRS. LEE E. HARTMAN

525 Yount Street, Beaumont, Texas

1949 "House Without a Living Room: Residence for Dr. and Mrs. Lee E. Hartman, Beaumont, Texas, Howard Barnstone, Architect," *Architectural Record* 112 (November 1952): 188–189.

503
HOUSE FOR MR. AND MRS. HERBERT M. BLUM

780 East Drive, Beaumont, Texas (demolished)

1950–1952

"More Space for Less Money," *House and Home* 2 (November 1952): 136–139.

[no job number]
ROSENSTOCK MOTORS BUILDING

2101 San Jacinto Street, Houston, Texas (altered)

1951, Richard S. Colley, architect; Howard Barnstone, associate architect

"Rosenstock Motors New Home Opens," *Houston Chronicle*, April 20, 1951, 6A.

[no job number]
COLT STADIUM WATER MAIN

Houston, Texas

1951

[no job number]
COUNCIL FOR RETARDED CHILDREN

1951

5012

H. M. COHEN HOUSE

Houston, Texas

1950–1951

5101

SHOPPING CENTER

1951

5155

ELEVATOR

1411 West Gray, Houston, Texas

1951

[no job number]

HOUSE FOR DR. AND MRS. GERHARD HERZOG

2523 Maroneal Boulevard, Houston, Texas (altered)

1952, Paul László, architect; Howard Barnstone, associate architect

Mary Ellen Preusser, "West Coast Architect Designs Special Home for Houstonians," *Houston Post*, March 15, 1953, Section 6, 1; "Modern Homes Are Open Saturday and Sunday," *Houston Chronicle*, April 9, 1954, Section D, 1.

(See also job number **6603**.)

BOLTON & BARNSTONE 1952–1961

Note: When the Bolton & Barnstone partnership was dissolved, the two partners divided the drawings, based on which partner was the primary architect for each project. The name in boldface indicates who received the materials from that project.

[no job number]

HOUSE FOR MR. AND MRS. DAN BLOXSOM

22 E. Shady Lane, Houston, Texas (demolished)

1952, Bolton & **Barnstone**

521

HOUSE FOR MR. AND MRS. SEYMOUR G. ROSENTHAL

615 Yount Street, Beaumont, Texas

1952, Bolton & **Barnstone**

522

HOUSE FOR MR. AND MRS. R. E. MING

11617 Monica Lane, Piney Point Village, Texas (demolished)

1955, Bolton & **Barnstone**

"Ming Residence Bids Due December 9," *AGC News Service*, November 30, 1954, 8.

523

RANCH ESTATE FOR JOHN BENNICK

Old Richmond Road (Bissonnet Avenue and Wilcrest Drive), Houston, Texas

1952, Bolton & **Barnstone**

524

HOUSE FOR MR. AND MRS. EDWIN C. ROTTERSMANN

4611 Parkwood Drive, Houston, Texas (extensively altered)

1952–1953, Bolton & **Barnstone**

5201

TAYLOR & RUSSELL OPERATING ROOM

1857 Richmond Avenue, Houston, Texas

1952, Bolton & **Barnstone**

5299

ALTERATIONS TO COTTON BUILDING

3106 Brazos Street, Houston, Texas (demolished)

1952, Bolton & **Barnstone**

531

ALTERATIONS AND ADDITIONS TO HOUSE OF CHARLES SHUMAKE

422 Doucette Street, Beaumont, Texas

1953, **Bolton** & Barnstone

5312: kitchen renovation

532

HARTMAN CLINIC

1953, Bolton & **Barnstone**

533

ALTERATIONS TO HOUSE OF MR. AND MRS. JOHN DE MENIL

3363 San Felipe Road, Houston, Texas

1953, Bolton & **Barnstone**

    5412: alterations to service wing
    5914: painting storage
    6004: servants' house (subsequently guesthouse)
    6027: renovations
    6147: courtyard canopy
    6153: Christmas decorations
    6510: addition of collection room (not built)
    6822: renovation, storage additions
    7517: windows
    7531: kitchen, oven

534

HOUSE FOR MR. AND MRS. LAWRENCE H. BLUM

1030 23rd Street, Beaumont, Texas

1954, Bolton & **Barnstone**

    5504: cabinet buffet details

"Texas Architecture—1954: Awards of Merit—Residence," *Texas Architect* 5 (December 1954): 12.

"Small House Designed for the Gulf Coast Region of Texas," *Arts & Architecture* 72 (March 1955): 28–29.

"South Central: Lawrence H. Blum House, Beaumont, Texas, Bolton and Barnstone, Architects," *Architectural Record* 117 (May 1955): 182–183.

535

HAROLD FREEMAN APARTMENTS

Houston, Texas

1953, Bolton & **Barnstone**

536

HOUSE FOR MR. AND MRS. GERALD S. GORDON

2307 Blue Bonnet Boulevard, Houston, Texas

1955, Bolton & **Barnstone**; Thomas D. Church, landscape architect; Knoll Planning Unit, interiors

    6106: addition, new fence
    7110: furnishings
    7608: dining room expansion
    8035: swimming pool and deck

"Residence Job in Plan Stage," *AGC News Service*, March 23, 1954, p. 5.

"Steel and Glass: Contract Let for Unusual House," *Houston Chronicle*, August 15, 1954, B9.

"Gordon Residence to Van Cleve," "Residence Job Is Planned," *AGC News Service*, August 20, 1954, 1.

"House by Bolton & Barnstone, Architects," *Arts & Architecture* 72 (December 1955): 22–23.

Anna Beth Morris, "Walled-In Sunshine," *Houston Post*, March 4, 1956, NOW section, 7.

"Modern House Tour Set for April 14–15," *Houston Chronicle*, April 1, 1956, section I, 7.

"Record Houses of 1956: Disciplined Elegance Marks Home Design," *Architectural Record* 119 (mid-May 1956): front cover and 134–138.

"Value of Fitting Home to Climate and Site Spotlighted by 2 Awards," *Houston Chronicle*, July 1, 1956, section C, 9.

"Winner: 'Texas Architecture—1956,'" *Texas Architect* 7 (November 1956): 15.

"Description of Winner in 'Texas Architecture—'56,'" *Texas Architect* 8 (January 1957): 4.

"New Scale for Living: This House Sets Trends with 2-Story Rooms, 2-Part Plan," *House and Garden* 113 (January 1958): front cover and 32–35.

Ten Years of Houston Architecture (Houston: Contemporary Arts Museum, 1959). Exhibition catalogue.

"New Talent USA: Architecture," *Art in America* 48, no. 1 (1960): 156–157.

"Architecture of Merit in the Past Ten Years: Gordon Residence, Houston," *Texas Architect* 12 (June 1961): 9.

Thomas W. Ennis, "Architects Find New Steel Uses: Nine Buildings Cited for Outstanding New Designs," *New York Times*, July 2, 1961, section R, 1.

Charlotte Tapley, "Use of Steel In 2 Houston Homes Wins Recognition," *Houston Post*, July 2, 1961, section 9, 1.

Ben Koush, "Houston Lives the Life: Modern Houses in the Suburbs, 1952–1962," MArch thesis, Rice University, 2002, 157–161.

537

SOUTHERN ABSTRACT & TITLE CO. OFFICE INTERIOR FOR MORRIS G. ROSENTHAL

Giesecke Building, 1106 Rusk Avenue, Houston, Texas (demolished)

1953, Bolton & **Barnstone**

539

APARTMENT FOR DR. GERHARD HERZOG

1953, **Bolton** & Barnstone

[no job number]

FIRST STATE BANK OF GREENS BAYOU BUILDING FOR S. MILES STRICKLAND, JR.

1420 Federal Road, Houston, Texas (extensively altered)

1955, Bolton & **Barnstone**

    589: alterations
    7113: alterations

"Green's Bayou 'Treasure Hunt,' Ground-Breaking Set," *Houston Post*, April 17, 1955, section 3, 3.

"Green's Bayou Bank Will Move into Its New Quarters Monday," *Houston Post*, September 11, 1955, section 3, 1.

"Open New Bank Home Saturday," *Houston Chronicle*, September 11, 1955, section F, 2.

"Bank Which Once Used Red Ink Now Shows Profit," *Houston Post*, November 6, 1955, section 3, 1–2.

"First State Bank Building," *Houston Chronicle*, January 5, 1975, section 3, 18.

"Building for Sale," *Houston Chronicle*, October 12, 1975, 46.

5301

MUSEUM OF FINE ARTS, HOUSTON

1001 Bissonnet, Houston, Texas

1953–54, Bolton & **Barnstone**

    5417: Blaffer addition

5307

SOUTHERN ABSTRACT & TITLE CO.

1953, Bolton & **Barnstone**

5308

PAUL LOWRY HOUSE

1953, Bolton & **Barnstone**

5310

ALTERATIONS AND ADDITIONS TO HOUSE OF MR. AND MRS. CHARLES W. BARNES

5319 Cherokee Street, Houston, Texas (demolished)

1953, **Bolton** & Barnstone

562	1956: kitchen alterations
5907	1959: garage apartment
6218	1962: garage

7006   1970: porch

5311

SCHLUMBERGER-SURENCO OFFICE INTERIOR FOR JOHN DE MENIL

Schlumberger Building, 2720 Leeland Avenue, Houston, Texas (dismantled)

1954, Bolton & **Barnstone**

"Texas Architecture—1954 Winner," *Texas Architect* 6 (January 1955): 9.

5313

ALTERATIONS TO SPIEGEL, INC.

Houston, Texas

1952 **Bolton** & Barnstone

5315

HOUSE FOR MR. AND MRS. RICHARD M. HARDISON

233 Merrie Way Lane, Piney Point Village, Texas (demolished)

1954, **Bolton** & Barnstone

    5512: alterations
    5920: alterations

"Will Open Five Homes on Modern House Tour," *Houston Chronicle*, March 20, 1955, section I, 1.

Marjorie Paxson, "New Houses Feature Good Plans, Look and Construction," *Houston Chronicle*, March 27, 1955, section I, 1, 10.

"Three Awards of Excellence for Residence: Richard M. Hardison Residence, Houston," *Texas Architect* 6 (November 1955): 12.

"Houston: Bolton & Barnstone: Goodbye, Miesian Asymmetry," *House and Home* 12 (September 1957): 155.

Ben Koush, "Houston Lives the Life: Modern Houses in the Suburbs, 1952–1962," MArch thesis, Rice University, 2002, 149–150.

5316

HOUSE FOR ROBERT M. BRUCE

1953, **Bolton** & Barnstone

5317

PELICAN ISLAND DEVELOPMENT

Galveston, Texas

1953, Bolton & **Barnstone**

5318
HOUSE FOR DR. AND MRS. FRANZ V. GRÜNBAUM

8939 Newcastle Street, Bellaire, Texas (demolished)

1953, Bolton & **Barnstone**

6101: alterations
7132: studio addition

5319
HOUSE FOR MR. AND MRS. MORRIS G. ROSENTHAL

4506 North Roseneath Drive, Houston, Texas

1953, Bolton & **Barnstone**

"Galbreath Gets Residence Job," *AGC Newsletter*, July 6, 1951, 5.

"Houston Architectural Firms Take Awards in TSA Contest," *Houston Post*, October 11, 1953, Section 3, 2.

"Residence of Mr. and Mrs. M. G. Rosenthal," *Texas Architect* 5 (August 1954): 7.

"Houses on Difficult Sites: An Almost-Triangular Lot, Wide End to Street," *Architectural Record* 116 (October 1954): 170–171.

5320
CONSULATE OF FRANCE

1953, Bolton & **Barnstone**

5325
HOUSE FOR MR. AND MRS. MARC DEMOUSTIER

608 Little John Lane, Houston, Texas (demolished 1995)

1955, Bolton & **Barnstone**

5801 1958: remodeling for Henry David
1965: renovations for Lawrence Marcus

"Residence Job Is Planned," *AGC News Service*, March 23, 1954, 5.

"Demoustier Residence Due September 3," *AGC News Service*, August 24, 1954, 2.

"Dent Awarded Residence Job," *AGC News Service*, September 28, 1954, 1.

"Steel and Glass: Contract Let for Unusual House," *Houston Chronicle*, August 15, 1954, section B, 9.

Anna Beth Morris, "Bayou House," *Houston Post*, October 14, 1956, section 5, 1, 14.

"Modern House Tour Homes Are Listed," *Houston Chronicle*, March 6, 1957, section C, 4.

"Houston: Bolton & Barnstone: Goodbye, Miesian Asymmetry," *House + Home* 12 (September 1957): 155.

"House in the Southwest: Gulf Coast Region of Texas," *Arts & Architecture* 74 (December 1957): 22–23.

"Sherwood Forest Distinctive Home Being Sold for Close to $100,000," *Houston Chronicle*, February 2, 1958, section F, 5.

"Strong Emphasis on Privacy," *Architectural Record* 123 (April 1958): 199–202.

Colin Rowe, "Neo-'Classicism' and Modern Architecture I," in *The Mathematics of the Ideal Villa, and Other Essays* (Cambridge: MIT Press, 1977), 120, 137.

Ben Koush, "Houston Lives the Life: Modern Houses in the Suburbs, 1952–1962," MArch thesis, Rice University, 2002, 154–156.

5326
ACME WAREHOUSE COMPANY BUILDING

Roanoke Street and Jensen Drive, Houston, Texas (demolished)

1954, Bolton & **Barnstone**

5701: alterations

"Warehouse Planned on Jensen," *Houston Chronicle*, January 10, 1954, B5.

"$300,000 Warehouse Planned on Jensen," *Houston Post*, January 10, 1954, section 3, 3.

5327
HOUSE FOR M. B. BETHEA

Houston, Texas

1953, **Bolton** & Barnstone

5328
APARTMENT REMODELING FOR J. W. LINK, JR.

Chilton Court Apartments, Houston, Texas

1953, Bolton & **Barnstone**

5621: alterations

5328
HOUSE FOR DR. AND MRS. HARRIS HOSEN

3708 Lakeshore Drive, Port Arthur, Texas

1953, Bolton & **Barnstone**

(See also job number **5519**.)

541

E. P. CONGDON, JR., BUILDERS

1954, **Bolton** & Barnstone

542

H. V. SLOCUM BUILDERS

1954, **Bolton** & Barnstone

543

ROTTERMAN BUILDERS, INC.

1954, **Bolton** & Barnstone

544

RENOVATION OF HOUSE OF JOHN P. KLEP

1954, **Bolton** & Barnstone

5604 1956: remodeling

545

BEN KAUFMAN APARTMENTS

1954, Bolton & **Barnstone**

546

HOUSE FOR MR. AND MRS. HENRY D. GREENBERG

2230 Sheridan Road, Houston, Texas

1955, Bolton & **Barnstone**

"Greenberg Residence Plans Are Released," *AGC News Service*, October 19, 1954, 7.

"Residence Let to Copeland," *AGC News Service*, November 9, 1954, 1.

547

REMODELING OF HOUSE OF W. S. HAWES

1954, **Bolton** & Barnstone

549

CARIBBEAN AND SOUTH AMERICAN PROJECTS FOR SCHLUMBERGER-SURENCO

1954–1957, Bolton & **Barnstone**

A. St. Joseph Village, County of Victoria, San Fernando, Trinidad and Tobago

Three houses, 1954 and 1957, Colin Laird, supervising architect

"Company House in Trinidad, B.W.I." *Arts & Architecture* 74 (April 1957): 28–29.

"Houston Designed Home Picked by Britannica, *Houston Post*, March 20, 1960, section 4, 2.

"A Company's Castle: A Houston Architectural Firm Has Given Trinidad Something Besides Oil and Asphalt to Brag About," *Texas Architect* 10 (April 1960): 8–9.

B. Anaco, Anazoátegui, Venezuela

C. Comodoro Rivadavia, Chubut, Argentina

Manager's house

D. Las Morochas 1 and 2, Ciudad Ojeda, Zulia, Venezuela

Office building, 1957

E. El Tigre, Anazoátegui, Venezuela

Community House no. 2, 1955

School and dormitory, 1957

"House in Venezuela by Bolton and Barnstone," *Arts & Architecture* 73 (November 1956): 28–29.

F. Caracas office

6304: Majani furniture

G. Bachaquero, Zulia, Venezuela

Houses

H. Talara, Talara, Peru

I. Maracaibo, Zulia, Venezuela

Manager's house, scheme 2, 1952

Country club, 1957

J. Zapatos, Venezuela

K. Punta de Mata, Monagas, Venezuela

5410

HOUSE FOR PAUL LUCAS

1954, Bolton & **Barnstone**

5411

REMODELING OF HOUSE OF LEON L. LESHIKAR

1954, **Bolton** & Barnstone

5412

ALTERATIONS TO APARTMENT OF MR. AND MRS. JOHN DE MENIL

120 East 80th Street, New York, New York (dismantled)

1955, Bolton & **Barnstone**

5414

INTERIOR ALTERATIONS OF BOLTON & BARNSTONE OFFICE

811 Lovett Boulevard, Houston, Texas (demolished)

1954, **Bolton** & Barnstone

5514 garage apartment renovation

5415
ALTERATIONS TO FIRST LIBERTY NATIONAL BANK BUILDING

Liberty, Texas

1954, **Bolton** & Barnstone

5416
ADDITION TO HOUSE OF DR. AND MRS. FRANK BROUSSARD

5131 Doliver Drive, Houston, Texas (demolished)

1955, **Bolton** & Barnstone

5606 1956: remodeling

"Galbreath Is Awarded Broussard Residence," *AGC News Service*, November 9, 1954, 9.

5418
ALTERATIONS AND ADDITIONS TO HOUSE OF DR. AND MRS. WARREN M. JACOBS

3202 South MacGregor Way, Houston, Texas

1954, Bolton & **Barnstone**

5510: alterations

5420
HOUSE FOR MR. AND MRS. PAUL D. MCNAUGHTON

234 Bylane Drive, Piney Point Village, Texas (not built)

"McNaughton Residence Due September 15," *AGC News Service*, September 2, 1955, 7.

"McNaughton Residence Bids Are Rejected," *AGC News Service*, October 18, 1955, 7.

5421
BOLTON & BARNSTONE HOUSE NO. 1

1954, Bolton & **Barnstone**

5422
HOUSE FOR MR. AND MRS. M. L. COOK

150 Providence Drive, Friendswood, Texas (extensively altered)

1959, **Bolton** & Barnstone; Knoll Planning Unit, interiors

"Build Fine Home in Quaker Region," *Houston Chronicle*, March 23, 1958, section E, 22.

"Architecture, 1959—First Honor Awards: Residence of Mr. and Mrs. M. L. Cook, Friendswood," *Texas Architect* 10 (November 1959): 30.

"Variation on the Court House Theme," *Architectural Record* 127 (May 1960): 190–192.

"Architecture of Merit in the Past Ten Years: Cook Residence, Friendswood," *Texas Architect* 12 (July 1961): 9.

5423
APARTMENTS

1954, Bolton & **Barnstone** (not built)

5423
HOUSE FOR MR. AND MRS. GREGG C. WADDILL

5528 Holly Springs Drive, Houston, Texas (demolished)

1956, **Bolton** & Barnstone

"Waddill Residence Due December 9," *AGC News Service*, November 29, 1955, 5.

"Tanglewood Residence Awarded to Boessling," *AGC News Service*, April 3, 1956, 8.

May Del Flagg, "House and Garden Are United Area," *Houston Post*, October 19, 1958, section 6, 1.

Ben Koush, "Houston Lives the Life: Modern Houses in the Suburbs, 1952–1962," MArch thesis, Rice University, 2002, 172–173.

5424
SUPERVISION OF THE HOUSE OF FRANK S. HAINES, JR.

1954, **Bolton** & Barnstone

5425
REMODELING OF HOUSE OF MR. AND MRS. JULES H. TALLICHET, JR.

1954, Bolton & **Barnstone**

5426
COMPETITION ENTRY FOR ALL FAITHS CHAPEL

Texas A&M University, College Station, Texas

1954, **Bolton** & Barnstone

"Religious Buildings: Building Types Study No. 223: Interfaith Chapel for Texas A&M College," *Architectural Record* 117 (June 1955): 194–196.

5427

WEEKEND HOUSE FOR DAVID FARNSWORTH

1954, **Bolton** & Barnstone

551

HOUSE FOR MR. AND MRS. AARON J. FARFEL

18 Westlane Place, Houston, Texas

1956, Bolton & **Barnstone**

7207: alterations

"One of Best 25 Home Designs," *Houston Chronicle*, March 17, 1957, section D, 3.

"Record Houses of 1957: Design Expressing Dignity," *Architectural Record* 121 (mid-May 1957): 164–167.

Charlotte Millis, "Home Here Wins Design Laurels," *Houston Chronicle*, October 24, 1957, section C, 1.

"Forecast '58: Your Intimate Outdoors" and "Trend 25: Texture Is the New Dimension," *House and Garden* 113 (January 1958): 37, 38–40.

"Description of Winners in 'Texas Architecture, '57,'" *Texas Architect* 8 (April 1958): 8–9.

"Custom-House Winners of the 1959 Homes for Better Living Awards Sponsored by the AIA: Honorable Mention: Architects: Bolton & Barnstone," *House and Home*, 15 (June 1959): 128.

"A Complex Family Problem Is Solved; The Results Win Merit Award for Houston Architects," *Texas Architect* 10 (August 1959): 8–9.

"Architecture of Merit in the Past Ten Years: Farfel Residence, Houston," *Texas Architect*, 12 (September 1961): 11.

556

SUPERVISION OF THE HOUSE OF R. B. LIVINGSTON

1955, **Bolton** & Barnstone

558

LAW OFFICE INTERIOR FOR GERALD S. GORDON

1955, Bolton & **Barnstone**

559

HOUSE FOR MR. AND MRS. CONSTANTINOS A. PAPAVASSILIOU

1955, Bolton & **Barnstone**

5510

HOUSE FOR WARREN M. JACOBS

Houston, Texas

1955, Bolton & **Barnstone**

5511

HOUSE FOR FRANK M. ALLEN

1955, **Bolton** & Barnstone

5513

REMODELING OF RENTAL HOUSE FOR MRS. ABRAHAM I. FINK

2206 Sampson Street, Houston, Texas (demolished)

1956, Bolton & **Barnstone**

5515

MEDICAL OFFICE INTERIORS FOR DOCTORS WARREN S. JACOBS AND STANLEY ROGERS

Medical Towers Building, 1709 Dryden Road, Houston, Texas (dismantled)

1956, Bolton & **Barnstone**

"The Medical Towers," *Progressive Architecture* 38 (June 1957): 195.

5516

HOUSE

1955, Bolton & **Barnstone**

5517

OFFICE INTERIOR FOR AARON J. FARFEL

1955, Bolton & **Barnstone**

5518

APARTMENT FOR MR. AND MRS. MARC DEMOUSTIER

New York, New York

1957, Bolton & **Barnstone**

5519
HOUSE FOR DR. AND MRS. HARRIS HOSEN

3708 Lakeshore Drive, Port Arthur, Texas (extensively altered)

1957, Bolton & **Barnstone**

"Rectangular Houses: 6, Port Arthur, Texas: Dr. and Mrs. Harris Hosen, Owners; Bolton & Barnstone, Architects." *Architectural Record* 122 (November 1957): 162–163.

"Houston Architects Score New First on Port Arthur Home," *Houston Chronicle*, October 12, 1958, section C, 8.

"Texas Architecture '58." *Houston Post*, October 12, 1958, NOW section, 4.

"Winners: 'Texas Architecture—1958:' Residence of Dr. and Mrs. Harris Hosen, Port Arthur, Texas," *Texas Architect* 9 (November 1958): 26.

"Architecture of Merit in the Past Ten Years: Hosen Residence, Port Arthur," *Texas Architect* 12 (September 1961): 10.

(See also job number **5328**.)

5520
HOUSE FOR MR. AND MRS. JOHN DE MENIL

Connecticut

1955, Bolton & **Barnstone**

5521
HOUSE FOR MR. AND MRS. EARL LEWIS SUNESON

Paseo Colón and Calle Reynosa, Colonia Madero, Nuevo Laredo, Tamaulipas, Mexico (demolished)

1958, Bolton & **Barnstone**

  5810: revisions
  6105: remodeling

"Modern Home, Yet Mexican in Styling," *Houston Chronicle,* February 19, 1956, section D, 6.

"Architects Here Design Mexico Home," *Houston Post*, February 19, 1956, section 3, 3.

5522
GARDEN OF THE GOOD SHEPHERD

1955, Bolton & **Barnstone**

5523
803 LOVETT PROPERTY

Houston, TX

1955, **Bolton** & Barnstone

563
CARRIER CORPORATION BUILDING AND THE BLACK ANGUS

2925–2929 Weslayan Street, Houston, Texas (demolished)

1958, 1959, **Bolton** & Barnstone

"Carrier Erects Office Building on Weslayan," *Houston Chronicle*, August 11, 1957, section D, 4.

"Work Begun on Restaurant," *Houston Chronicle*, December 14, 1958, section G, 4.

"Steak House Sets Opening," *Houston Post*, December 14, 1958.

565
SWIMMING POOL FOR HOUSE OF MR. AND MRS. S. MILES STRICKLAND, JR.

Houston, Texas

1956, Bolton & **Barnstone**

  575: addition

567
HOUSE FOR MR. AND MRS. EARL LEWIS SUNESON NO. 2

Laredo, TX

1956, Bolton & **Barnstone**

568
SKYSCRAPER OFFICE BUILDING FOR A. J. FARFEL

Houston, Texas (not built)

1956, Bolton & **Barnstone**

569
HOUSE FOR MR. AND MRS. CHARLES SMITHERS, JR.

Cross Ridge Road, New Canaan, Connecticut

1956, Bolton & **Barnstone**

  6011: second phase, Bolton & Barnstone
  6713: third phase, Barnstone & Aubry

"One House—Past, Present and Future," *Houston Post*, May 1, 1960, section 5, 3.

5610
REMODELING OF HOUSE OF MR. AND MRS. J. LEWIS THOMPSON, JR.

1715 North Boulevard, Houston, Texas

1956, **Bolton** & Barnstone

5611

UNIVERSITY OF ST. THOMAS

3800–3900 blocks of Yoakum Boulevard, Houston, Texas

1958, 1959, Philip C. Johnson Associates, architect; Bolton & **Barnstone**, associate architects

> **5727:** stage two
> **6006:** alterations to Jones Hall

(See also job numbers **6402, 6619,** and **6817**.)

"The University of St. Thomas," *Architectural Record* 122 (August 1957): 138, 142–143.

"First Units in the Fabric of a Closed Campus," *Architectural Record* 126 (September 1959): 180–182.

William H. Jordy, "The Mies-less Johnson," *Architectural Forum* 111 (September 1959): 120.

"The University of St. Thomas," *Liturgical Arts* 28 (November 1959): 15.

Henry-Russell Hitchcock, "The Current Work of Philip Johnson," *Zodiac* 8 (1961): 64–81.

John M. Jacobus, Jr., *Philip Johnson* (New York: Braziller, 1962), 35–36, plates 68–71.

"Université St.-Thomas, Houston: Auditorium et Salles de Cours," *L'Architecture d'Aujourd'hui* 107 (April–May 1963): 97–99.

"Processional Elements in Houston," *Architectural Record* 137 (June 1965): 159.

5612

HOUSE FOR W. W. GREENE

1956, **Bolton** & Barnstone

5613

HOUSE FOR R. B. LITTLE

1956, **Bolton** & Barnstone

5614

HOUSE FOR JACK R. CARROLL

Houston, Texas (not built)

1956, Bolton & **Barnstone**

5616

HOUSE FOR MR. AND MRS. I. FALLIS

Briar Drive, Houston, Texas (not built)

1956, Bolton & **Barnstone**

5617

CO-OP APARTMENT

1956, Bolton & **Barnstone**

5618

ADDITIONS TO THE HOUSE OF JAMES S. HUGHES

1956, **Bolton** & Barnstone

5619

REMODELING OF HOUSE OF J. W. LINK, JR.

Lovett Boulevard, Houston, Texas

1956, **Bolton** & Barnstone

5622

REHEARSAL HALL FOR HOUSTON GRAND OPERA ASSOCIATION

1956, **Bolton** & Barnstone

572

PLEASANTVILLE FURNITURE COMPANY

8438 Market Street Road, Houston, Texas

1957, **Bolton** & Barnstone

573

HOUSE FOR R. W. MAYE

1957, **Bolton** & Barnstone

574

HOUSE FOR H. W. BLACKSTOCK

1957, **Bolton** & Barnstone

577

HOUSE FOR MR. AND MRS. LE MAY E. SHANE

1957, Bolton & **Barnstone**

(See also job number **6419**.)

578

HOUSE FOR MRS. DAVID LINDSAY

7623 River Pointe Drive, Houston, Texas

1959, **Bolton** & Barnstone

"Lindsay Residence Bids Due November 20," *AGC News Service*, November 8, 1957, 4.

"Lindsay Residence Contract Awarded," *AGC News Service*, December 27, 1957, 2.

Arnold Rosenfeld, "Houston Has Home 'One of 20,'" *Houston Post*, February 22, 1959, section 6, 1.

"Record Houses of 1959: Garden Affords Private Views," *Architectural Record* 125 (mid-May 1959): 80–83.

"Architecture and The Outdoors," *Houston Post*, April 30, 1961, NOW section, 34.

"Architecture of Merit in the Past Ten Years: Lindsay Residence, Houston," *Texas Architect* 12 (August 1961): 11.

[no job number]
APARTMENT BUILDING FOR HENRY D. GREENBERG AND BEN L. APPELBAUM

2207 Sheridan Road, Houston, Texas (not built)

"Sheridan Street Apartment Job Plans Released," *AGC News Service*, August 19, 1958, 4.

5710
OFFICE INTERIOR FOR JOHN DE MENIL

Bank of the Southwest Building, 910 Travis Street, Houston, Texas (dismantled)

1957, Bolton & **Barnstone**

5711
OFFICE INTERIORS FOR SCHLUMBERGER LTD.

Bank of the Southwest Building, 910 Travis Street, Houston, Texas (dismantled)

1957, **Bolton** & Barnstone

5712
ALTERATIONS AND ADDITIONS TO HOUSE OF MR. AND MRS. MERRICK W. PHELPS

Boulder, Colorado

1957, Bolton & **Barnstone**

  5936: addition
  6109: addition
  6404: addition
  7011: greenhouse
  7509: window treatment

5713
HOUSE FOR MRS. RICHARD W. NEFF, JR.

Houston, Texas

1957, **Bolton** & Barnstone

5714
SWIMMING POOL FOR MR. AND MRS. ARON S. GORDON

2339 Underwood Boulevard, Houston, Texas

1958, Bolton & **Barnstone**

  6033: dressing rooms

5716
FRANK TAMBURINE MOTEL

1957, **Bolton** & Barnstone

5717
ARTIST STUDIO

1957, **Bolton** & Barnstone

5718
HOUSE FOR DRS. LENORA AND JOHN ANDREW

Houston, Texas

1957, Bolton & **Barnstone**

5719
MOTEL FOR GORDON AND MORRISON

Greens Bayou, Houston, Texas

1957, Bolton & **Barnstone**

5720
ECHOLS DEVELOPEMENT PROJECT

1957, **Bolton** & Barnstone

  5726: remodeling

5721
ALTERATIONS TO HOUSE OF MR. AND MRS. SAMUEL N. SPRUNT

2517 Stanmore Drive, Houston, Texas (demolished)

1958, Bolton & **Barnstone**

  5911: remodeling

5722
HOUSE FOR MR. AND MRS. ALVIN M. OWSLEY, JR.

Leeland, Michigan

1957, Bolton & **Barnstone**

5723

HOTEL FOR W. E. COX

Venezuela

1957, **Bolton** & Barnstone

5725

JOHN'S RESTAURANT

Houston, Texas

1957, **Bolton** & Barnstone

5728

HOUSE FOR MR. AND MRS. ALVIN M. OWSLEY, JR.

65 Briar Hollow Lane, Houston, Texas

1960, Bolton & **Barnstone**

- **6012:** fire damage repairs
- **6151:** alterations and additions
- **6523:** alterations and additions

"Home to Have Frame Design beyond Walls," *Houston Post*, February 22, 1959, section 2, 3.

"Personal Listings," *Houston Chronicle*, February 11, 1962, section 2, 1.

Ann Minick Criswell, "If You Need Design Ideas, Plan to Take C.A.A. Tour," *Houston Chronicle*, April 27, 1962, section 6, 2.

Esther McCoy, "Young Architects in the United States: 1963," *Zodiac* 13:186–187.

"Steel and Glass House on Buffalo Bayou," *Interiors* 123 (November 1963): 72–79.

5729

HOUSE FOR HOWARD BARNSTONE

Houston, Texas

1957, Bolton & **Barnstone**

5730

ALTERATIONS AND ADDITIONS TO HOUSE OF DR. AND MRS. IRVIN A. KRAFT

2423 Gramercy Boulevard, Houston, Texas

1960, Bolton & **Barnstone**

- **6005:** alterations
- **8305:** alterations

5799

MENIL BUNGALOW PROJECTS

1957, Bolton & **Barnstone**

582

OFFICE INTERIORS FOR SCHLUMBERGER-SURENCO

1602–1612 Commerce Building, 914 Main Street, Houston, Texas (dismantled)

1958, Bolton & **Barnstone**

583

HOUSE FOR ELSIE TURNER

3013 Barbee, Houston, Texas

1958, Bolton & **Barnstone**

- **5899:** alterations

584

HOUSE FOR MR. AND MRS. MARVIN WALDMAN

Hollywood Drive and Oak Avenue, Liberty, Texas (not built)

1958, Bolton & **Barnstone**

586

TEXACO SERVICE STATION FOR MARVIN WALDMAN

Liberty, Texas

1958, Bolton & **Barnstone**

588

SERVICE STATION & RESTAURANT FOR R. W. WELLS

1958, **Bolton** & Barnstone

5813

HOUSE FOR ROBERT PRESSLER

1958, Bolton & **Barnstone**

5814

RENOVATION OF HOUSE OF MR. AND MRS. FRANK FREED

1958, Bolton & **Barnstone**

5815

MCCRACKEN PROJECT

1958, **Bolton** & Barnstone

5817

DOWNTOWN VICTORIA PROJECT

Victoria, Texas

1958, Bolton & **Barnstone**

"Model City," *Victoria Advocate*, October 8, 1958, 5.

5818

HOUSE FOR MR. AND MRS. JOHN M. WINTERBOTHAM, JR.

54 Briar Hollow Lane, Houston, Texas (demolished)

1960, **Bolton** & Barnstone

6402: alterations and additions

"Plans Released for Residence on Briar Hollow," *AGC News Service*, January 30, 1959, 6.

"Residence Job Low Bid Is Given," *AGC News Service*, February 13, 1959, 2.

"Contract Awarded on Residence Job," *AGC News Service*, April 14, 1959, 2.

Thomas W. Ennis, "Architects Find New Steel Uses: Nine Buildings Cited for Outstanding New Designs," *New York Times*, July 2, 1961, section R, 1, 4.

Charlotte Tapley, "Use of Steel in 2 Houston Homes Wins Recognition," *Houston Post*, July 2, 1961, section 9, 1.

"Ordered Calm: House Planned with Formal Beauty," *House and Garden* 123 (January 1963): 104–109.

"A Formal House That Exploits a Sloping Site," *Architectural Record* 134 (September 1963): 169–172.

5819

HOUSE FOR MR. AND MRS. JAMES O. LEWIS, JR.

10919 Wickwild Drive, Piney Point Village, Houston, Texas (demolished)

1960, Bolton & **Barnstone**

"Lewis Residence Is Planned for 2-Stage Construction," *Houston Post*, April 5, 1959, section 3, 3.

"Unusual Two-Stage Home Planned for Willowick," *Houston Chronicle*, April 8, 1959, section 4, 8.

"House in the South West," *Arts & Architecture* 76 (July 1959): 22–23.

5820

KTRK-TV

Houston, Texas

1958, Bolton & **Barnstone**

5821

APARTMENT FOR JIM A. WHITLAW

1958, Bolton & **Barnstone**

5822

T. L. LEONARD COMPANY WAREHOUSE

Meadow Avenue, Laredo, Texas

1958, Bolton & **Barnstone**

[no job number]

ALTERATIONS AND ADDITIONS TO HOUSE OF HOWARD BARNSTONE

2050 Banks Street, Houston, Texas

1958, Bolton & **Barnstone**

[no job number]

TOWNHOUSE PROJECT

1958, Bolton & **Barnstone**

5901

SHOP FOR MR. AND MRS. EARL LEWIS SUNESON

Nuevo Laredo, Tamaulipas, Mexico

1959, Bolton & **Barnstone**

5902

HOUSE FOR MR. AND MRS. W. GORDON WING

33 East Rivercrest Drive, Houston, Texas

1961, Bolton & **Barnstone**

"Residence Job Plans Under Way," *AGC News Service*, August 25, 1959, 4.

Esther McCoy, "Young Architects in the United States: 1963," *Zodiac* 13:188–189.

5903

LAW OFFICE INTERIOR FOR GERALD S. GORDON

Houston, Texas

1959, Bolton & **Barnstone**

5904

HOUSE FOR MR. AND MRS. MAURICIO FRANK

Laredo, Texas (not built)

1959, Bolton & **Barnstone**

5908
REMODELING OF HOUSE OF JOHN MARSHALL
Houston, Texas
1959, **Bolton** & Barnstone

5909
HOUSE FOR MR. AND MRS. JACK FINKELSTEIN
307 W. Friar Tuck Lane, Houston, Texas
1961, P. M. Bolton Associates

"Interior of House Yet to Be Built," *Houston Post*, July 26, 1959, section 4, 3.

"Four Level Home Started in Memorial," *Houston Chronicle*, October 30, 1960, section 4, 4.

5910
HOUSE FOR DR. AND MRS. FLETCHER HESTER
1208 Carey Drive, Sweeny, Texas
1961, **Bolton** & Barnstone

5912
BEACH HOUSE FOR MR. AND MRS. J. J. ELLIOTT
1959, **Bolton** & Barnstone

5913
HOUSE FOR MR. AND MRS. SEARCY BRACEWELL
1959, **Bolton** & Barnstone

5914
MENIL PAINTING STORAGE
Houston, Texas
1959–1960, Bolton & **Barnstone**

5915
HOUSE FOR MR. AND MRS. STEPHEN P. FARISH, JR.
1959, **Bolton** & Barnstone

5916
HOUSE FOR MR. AND MRS. IRVING MERMEL
5043 Glenmeadow Drive, Houston, Texas (extensively altered)
1961, Howard Barnstone & Partners

"Sketch of Houston Home of Tomorrow" and Mary Rice Brogan, "Home Designing in for Revolution: 'Togetherness' on Wane, New Separate Living Areas Seen," *Houston Chronicle*, January 31, 1960, section 13, 10.

"'House of Light' Attracts Visitors," *Houston Chronicle*, June 18, 1961, section 11, 2.

"House by Howard Barnstone and Partners, Architects," *Arts & Architecture* 79 (February 1962): 26–27.

"Houston Chapter Awards for Design Excellence: Commendation: Mermel Residence, Houston," *Texas Architect* 12 (September 1962): 14.

Esther McCoy, "Young Architects in the United States: 1963," *Zodiac* 13:190.

Ben Koush, "Houston Lives the Life: Modern Houses in the Suburbs, 1952–1962," MArch thesis, Rice University, 2002, 197–199.

5917
5000 LONGMONT FOR PRESTON M. BOLTON
5000 Longmont Lane, Houston, Texas
1961, P. M. Bolton Associates

6018: Townhouse for W. H. Griffin
6019: Townhouse for Preston M. Bolton
6020: Townhouse for Dr. and Mrs. Arthur L. Glassman
6021: Townhouse for Richard E. Rolle
6022: Townhouse for Fred R. Williams
6023: Townhouse for Robert U. Parish
6024: Townhouse for Mrs. R. W. Neff, Sr.
6025: Townhouse for Mrs. H. G. Safford

"Cooperative Housing Settlement Planned," *Houston Chronicle*, April 10, 1960, section 4, 6.

"8 Fine Homes in Town Houses Will Be Built," *Houston Chronicle*, October 9, 1960, section 4, 4.

Charlotte Tapley, "The Town House Idea Rising in Houston," *Houston Post*, July 23, 1961, section 7, 1.

"Safford Residence, Houston," *Texas Architect* 13 (August 1963): 8–11.

G. O'Brien, "Past and Present House: Houston, Texas, Home Designed by P. M. Bolton Associates," *New York Times Magazine*, October 6, 1963, 126–127.

"Record Houses: Residence for Mr. and Mrs. Preston M. Bolton, Houston, Texas," *Architectural Record* 133 (mid-May 1963): 62–65.

Paul B. Farrell, Jr., "Architect Develops His Own Environment," *Progressive Architecture* 51 (May 1970), 90–91.

Ben Koush, "Houston Lives the Life: Modern Houses in the Suburbs, 1952–1962," MArch thesis, Rice University, 2002, 200–202.

5918
HOUSE FOR MR. AND MRS. HAROLD FREEMAN

Houston, Texas

1959, **Bolton** & Barnstone

> **7106:** alterations

"Architects Design Eight-Sided Home," *Houston Chronicle*, December 6, 1959, section 17, 4.

"New Dwelling Will Be Octagonal in Design," *Houston Post*, December 9, 1959, section 4, 3.

5919
HOUSE FOR MR. AND MRS. DAVID CHALLINOR, JR.

121 Deepwood Drive, Hamden, Connecticut

1960, Bolton & **Barnstone**

> **6238:** alterations

"Here Are Two New Experiments in Geometric Form," *House and Home* 17 (January 1960): 136–137.

R. E. Connor, "Wide Interest Shown in Houstonians' Plan," *Houston Chronicle*, February 7, 1960, section 3, 5.

Elizabeth Mills Brown, *New Haven: A Guide to Architecture and Urban Design* (New Haven: Yale University Press, 1976), 38.

5921
REMODELING OF HOUSE OF MR. AND MRS. R. B. SMITH

Houston, Texas

1959, Bolton & **Barnstone**

5922
REMODELING OF HOUSE OF PROFESSOR AND MRS. ANDREW N. JITKOFF

Houston, Texas

1959, **Bolton** & Barnstone

5923
ADDITION TO HOUSE OF MR. AND MRS. RICHARD W. NEFF, JR.

Houston, Texas

1959, **Bolton** & Barnstone

5925
HOUSE FOR MR. AND MRS. ARNOLD SUSSMAN

884 Little John Lane, Houston, Texas

1959, **Bolton** & Barnstone

> **5929:** changes
> **7225:** pool deck

5926
ALTERATIONS TO HOUSE OF DR. AND MRS. JACK J. BLANKFIELD

1959–1960, **Bolton** & Barnstone

5928
HOGG BUILDING, CHILD GUIDANCE CENTER

3214 Austin Street, Houston, Texas (demolished)

1961, Howard Barnstone & Partners

"Mansion Rebuilt for Child Guidance," *Architectural Forum* 117 (November 1962): 137.

5929
PROJECT FOR BUCK KING, BUILDER

1959, **Bolton** & Barnstone

5930
REMODELING OF ALLEY THEATRE

Houston, Texas (demolished)

1959, **Bolton** & Barnstone

5931
HOUSE FOR SAM J. SHAPIRO

Houston, Texas

1959, **Bolton** & Barnstone

5932
SHELVING FOR TEXAS DAILY NEWS

1959, **Bolton** & Barnstone

5935

SOUTHSIDE STATE BANK

Houston, Texas

1959, **Bolton** & Barnstone

5938

PREFABRICATED HOUSE

1959, Bolton & **Barnstone**

Arnold Rosenfeld, "Plan Room with Cut-Outs," *Houston Post*, January 3, 1960, section 5, 2.

6001

ALTERATIONS TO HOUSE OF PROFESSOR AND MRS. EDMUND L. PINCOFFS

32 Crestwood Drive, Houston, Texas (demolished)

1961, Bolton & **Barnstone**

   6138: library
   6416: addition

6002

CABINETS FOR DR. ELLIOTT

1960, **Bolton** & Barnstone

6003

MODULAR SERVICE STATION

1960, Bolton & **Barnstone**

6007

DUPLEX RENOVATION

1568 Castle Court, Houston, Texas

1961, Bolton & **Barnstone**

6008

ALTERATIONS TO TOWNHOUSE OF MR. AND MRS. JOHN DE MENIL

111 East 73rd Street, New York, New York

1961, Bolton & **Barnstone**

6009

APARTMENT FOR DR. GERHARD HERZOG

1960, Bolton & **Barnstone**

6010

APARTMENT COMPLEX FOR JENARD GROSS

Houston, Texas

1960, Bolton & **Barnstone**

6015

REMODELING OF HOUSE OF MRS. MARTIN WARREN

1960, Bolton & **Barnstone**

6016

MOTEL FOR WARREN PINNEY, JR.

Nuevo Laredo, Tamaulipas, Mexico (not built)

1960, Bolton & **Barnstone**

6017

ALTERATIONS TO HOUSE OF F. W. CONRAD

1960, Bolton & **Barnstone**

6026

HOUSE FOR W. E. ECKLES

1960, **Bolton** & Barnstone

6027

CLUBHOUSE FOR DALLAS POLO CLUB

Dallas, Texas

1960, Bolton & **Barnstone**

6028

REMODELING OF HOUSE OF I. E. CLARK

1960, **Bolton** & Barnstone

6029

ALTERATIONS TO HOUSE OF SARITA KENEDY EAST

La Parra Ranch, Kenedy County, Texas

1961, P. M. Bolton Associates

6031

STEWART & STEWART

1960, **Bolton** & Barnstone

6034

PINEY POINT ELEMENTARY SCHOOL

8921 Pagewood Lane, Houston, Texas (demolished)

1962, Howard Barnstone & Partners, architects; Harvin C. Moore, consulting architect

"New Piney Point Elementary Will Feature Precast Concrete Design," *Houston Post*, October 22, 1961, section 7, 11.

"Houston School," *Architectural Forum* 116 (June 1962): 52.

Emily Grotta, "Whatever Happened to . . . Unique HISD School?" *Houston Post*, February 22, 1982, section C, 4.

6035
RENOVATION OF HOUSE OF GERTRUDE AND HOWARD BARNSTONE
1720 North Boulevard, Houston, Texas
1960, Bolton & **Barnstone**
  6103: addition
  6136: alterations
(See also job number **7819**.)

6036
OFFICE INTERIORS FOR ISTEL, LEPERCQ & COMPANY
63 Wall Street, New York, New York (dismantled)
1961, Bolton & **Barnstone**

6037
OFFICE BUILDING FOR LORRAINE GEORGE INTERESTS
Bagby Street and McIlhenny Avenue, Houston, Texas (not built)
1960, Bolton & **Barnstone**

6102
HOUSE FOR K. L. LAIRD
1961, **Bolton** & Barnstone

6103
RENOVATION OF FERNDALE TOWNHOUSES
2912 Ferndale Street, Houston, Texas (not built)
1961, Bolton & **Barnstone**

6104
PERLMAN TOWNHOUSES
Houston, Texas
1961, Bolton & **Barnstone**

6108
HOUSE FOR PROFESSOR AND MRS. WILLIS BARNSTONE
Florida (not built)
1961, Bolton & **Barnstone**

6110
OFFICE INTERIOR FOR HENRI DOLL, SCHLUMBERGER LTD.
Getty Building, 900 Madison Avenue, New York, New York (dismantled)
1963, Howard Barnstone & Partners
"Contemporary at Its Best," *Interiors* 122 (April 1963): 98–101.

6111
ADDITION TO HOUSE OF J. J. PAUL
1518 Ronson Road, Houston, Texas (not built)
1961, Bolton & **Barnstone**

6112
HEADQUARTERS BUILDING FOR PAN AMERICAN HEALTH ORGANIZATION
1961, Bolton & **Barnstone**

6113 and 6114
HOUSE FOR WILLIAM J. SALMAN
Houston, Texas (not built)
1961, Bolton & **Barnstone**

6116
HOUSE FOR MR. AND MRS. JOHN F. MAHER
2930 Lazy Lane, Houston, Texas (altered)
1964, Howard Barnstone & Partners
"Record Houses of 1965: 'Treetop' Living Pavilion of Steel and Glass," *Architectural Record*, 137 (mid-May 1965): 66–69.
Mary Jane Kempner, "Young Architects in the Spotlight," *House Beautiful* 108 (July 1966): 67.
Gary McKay, "Architectural Honors," *House Home and Garden*, 11 (July 1985): 60.
  6142: revisions
  6230: landscaping

6117
VILLA FOR H. PESLE
St. Maxime Commune, Lotissement, Les Alques, France
1961, Bolton & **Barnstone**

6118
CHURCH
Chile
1961, Bolton & **Barnstone**

6119
ADDITIONS TO HOUSE OF ALEXANDRE IOLAS

Athens, Greece

1961, Bolton & **Barnstone**

6121
OFFICE INTERIOR FOR HOWARD BARNSTONE & PARTNERS

Niels Esperson Building, 808 Travis Street, Houston, Texas (dismantled)

1962, Howard Barnstone & Partners

6124
APARTMENT INTERIOR FOR MR. AND MRS. JAMES JOHNSON SWEENEY

Apartment 15G, 1400 Hermann Drive, Houston, Texas (dismantled)

1962, Howard Barnstone & Partners

6126
HOUSE REMODELING FOR JANE HEYER TALLICHET

Houston, Texas

1961, Howard Barnstone & Partners

    6204: alterations

6127
SCHLUMBERGER AIRPLANE INTERIORS

1961, Howard Barnstone & Partners

    8021: Falcon Jet

6129
LAW OFFICE INTERIOR FOR GERALD S. GORDON

Tennessee Life Insurance Co. Building, Houston, Texas (dismantled)

1961, Bolton & **Barnstone**

6130
HOUSE FOR MR. AND MRS. ST. JOHN GARWOOD, JR.

Houston, Texas (not built)

1961, Bolton & **Barnstone**

    6424: alterations

6134
APARTMENT REMODELING FOR MR. AND MRS. HENRI DOLL

31B and 31C, Ritz Tower, 50 Central Park South, New York, New York (dismantled)

1963, Howard Barnstone & Partners

6135
EMBLEM FOR SCHLUMBERGER LTD.

1961, Howard Barnstone & Partners

6137
SCHLUMBERGER LTD. AIRPLANE HANGAR

Hobby Airport, Houston, Texas

1961, Bolton & **Barnstone**

6137
ATLANTIC REFINING CO. BUILDING

Houston, Texas

1961, Bolton & **Barnstone**

6139
SCHLUMBERGER LTD. GARAGE

1961, Bolton & **Barnstone**

6140
HOUSE FOR MR. AND MRS. JEAN RIBOUD

38850 North Spanish Boot Road, Scottsdale, Arizona

1961–1965, Howard Barnstone & Partners

    7355: furniture
    7524: furniture

(See also job number **7355**.)

6145 and 6146
ALTERATIONS TO HOUSE OF MR. AND MRS. PIERRE M. SCHLUMBERGER

2970 Lazy Lane, Houston, Texas

1963, Howard Barnstone & Partners

    6210: dressing room and bathroom
    6227: alterations

[no job number]
BOUTIQUE AND APARTMENT FOR KATRINA SNELL

1961, Bolton & **Barnstone**

HOWARD BARNSTONE & PARTNERS 1962–1965

6203
MUSEUM OF PRIMITIVE ART
15 West 54th Street, New York, New York
Design of advertisements for the *New Yorker*

6206
HOUSE REMODELING FOR JUNE DAVIS ARNOLD
5006 San Felipe Road, Houston, Texas (demolished)
1962, Howard Barnstone & Partners
Ben Koush, "Houston Lives the Life: Modern Houses in the Suburbs, 1952–1962," MArch thesis, Rice University, 2002, 147–148, 179–180.
"Small House in Texas by Burdette Keeland," *Arts & Architecture* 76 (October 1959): 18–19.

6208
HOUSTON TEACHERS CREDIT UNION BUILDING
2102 Austin Street, Houston, Texas (altered)
1963, Howard Barnstone & Partners
"Teachers Credit Union Buys Tract for Office," *Houston Chronicle*, October 21, 1962, section 4, 4.
"Two-Story Building Planned by Teachers," *Houston Chronicle*, December 8, 1962, section 2, 3.

6209
ALTERATIONS AND ADDITIONS TO HOUSE OF MR. AND MRS. FRANK FREED
11310 Smithdale Road, Piney Point Village, Houston, Texas
1963, Howard Barnstone & Partners
  7604: alterations
  7913: alterations

6211
ALTERATIONS AND ADDITIONS TO HOUSE OF MR. AND MRS. LEROY MELCHER, JR.
13 Tiel Way, Houston, Texas (extensively altered)
1964, Howard Barnstone & Partners
  6605: alterations
  7008: alterations
(See also job number **7339**.)

"Award Winners," *Houston Post*, September 18, 1949, section 2, 6.

6213
APARTMENTS FOR JIM A. WHITLAW
Houston, Texas
1962, Howard Barnstone & Partners

6215
HOUSE REMODELING FOR MR. AND MRS. CONSTANTINOS A. PAPAVASSILIOU
4610 Bryn Mawr Lane, Houston, Texas
1964, Howard Barnstone & Partners
  8407: alterations
(See also job number **559**.)

6219
MOTEL FOR WARREN PINNEY, JR.
Houston, Texas
1962, Howard Barnstone & Partners

6222
HOUSE FOR DEAN L. EBELS
Houston, Texas
1962, Howard Barnstone & Partners

6223
REMODELING OF HOUSE OF MR. AND MRS. CLIVE RUNNELLS
Houston, Texas
1962, Howard Barnstone & Partners

6226
HOUSE FOR MR. AND MRS. HAROLD V. GOODMAN
Houston, Texas
1962, Howard Barnstone & Partners

6228
ALTERATIONS AND ADDITIONS TO HOUSE OF DR. AND MRS. WILLIAM K. WRIGHT
3671 Del Monte Drive, Houston, Texas
1964, Howard Barnstone & Partners

6325: driveway
8123: renovations
8202: renovations

6229
HOUSTON INDEPENDENT SCHOOL DISTRICT ELEMENTARY SCHOOL COMPETITION

1962, Howard Barnstone & Partners

6231
HOUSE REMODELING FOR MR. AND MRS. THEODORE P. ELLSWORTH

250 Chimney Rock Road, Houston, Texas

1962, Howard Barnstone & Partners

7375: alterations

6232
ALTERATIONS TO HOUSE OF MR. AND MRS. WILLIAM P. HOBBY, JR.

1506 South Boulevard, Houston, Texas (altered)

1964, Howard Barnstone & Partners

6307: kitchen
6516: air conditioning
7009: alterations
7368: roof
7529: porch

6233
MOTEL FOR OCTAVIANO LONGORIA THERIOT AND EDUARDO LONGORIA THERIOT

Nuevo Laredo, Tamaulipas, Mexico (not built)

1962, Howard Barnstone & Partners

6235
APARTMENT REMODELING FOR CHRISTOPHE DE MENIL THURMAN

New York, New York

1962, Howard Barnstone & Partners

6239
BARNSTONE-KEELAND OFFICES

630 Niels Esperson Building, 808 Travis Street, Houston, Texas

1962, Howard Barnstone & Partners and Burdette Keeland, Jr.

6239
OFFICE BUILDING FOR HOWARD BARNSTONE & PARTNERS AND BURDETTE KEELAND, JR.

1914 West Capitol Avenue, Houston, Texas (not built)

1962, Howard Barnstone & Partners and Burdette Keeland, Jr.

"Construction to Start on Odd Building," February 24, 1963, *Houston Chronicle*, section 7, 2.

"Houston Offices," *Architectural Forum* 118 (May 1963): 59.

8502 (job number out of sequence)
OFFICE INTERIOR FOR RELIANCE TITLE CO.

Fannin Bank Building, Houston, Texas (demolished)

1962, Howard Barnstone & Partners

6306
BARNSTONE & PARTNERS OFFICE

14th floor, Niels Esperson Building, 808 Travis, Houston, Texas

1963, Howard Barnstone & Partners

6308
DANBURY INDEPENDENT SCHOOL DISTRICT SCHOOL

Danbury, Connecticut

1963, Howard Barnstone & Partners

6311
BUILDING FOR THE LIGHTHOUSE FOR THE BLIND

Houston, Texas (not built)

1963, Howard Barnstone & Partners

6312
GALVESTON COUNTY PUBLISHING COMPANY BUILDING

8522 Teichman Road, Galveston, Texas

1965, Howard Barnstone & Partners; William Ginsberg & Associates, consulting architects

8327: remodeling

"Industrial Buildings: Building Types Study No. 366: Publishing Company Building, Galveston, Texas," *Architectural Record* 141 (January 1967): 158–159.

6313
AMERICAN BANK BUILDING
Galveston, Texas (not built)
1963, Howard Barnstone & Partners

6314
ALTERATIONS AND ADDITIONS TO HOUSE OF MR. AND MRS. SAMUEL N. SPRUNT
3702 Knollwood Drive, Houston, Texas (altered)
1964, Howard Barnstone & Partners
    6401: alterations
    7114: alterations

6315
IOLAS GALLERY INTERIOR FOR ALEXANDRE IOLAS
15 East 55th Street, New York, New York (demolished)
1963, Howard Barnstone & Partners
"Iolas Gallery New Address: 15 E. 55th Street, New York," *Art in America* 51 no. 6 (1963): 130.

6318
OFFICE BUILDING FOR HOWARD BARNSTONE & PARTNERS AND BURDETTE KEELAND
1914 West Capitol Avenue, Houston, Texas (altered)
1965, Howard Barnstone & Partners and Burdette Keeland
"The Architect's Own Office: Showplace and Workspace," *Progressive Architecture* 47 (September 1966): 129.

6319
INTERIOR ALTERATIONS TO BROWN BOOKSTORE
Houston, Texas
1963, Howard Barnstone & Partners

6321
APARTMENT INTERIOR FOR MR. AND MRS. LEOPOLD MEYER
2016 Main Street, Houston, Texas (dismantled)
1964, Howard Barnstone & Partners

6322
ADDITIONS TO HOUSE OF MR. AND MRS. JOHN STETSON
1314 South Boulevard, Houston, Texas (demolished)
1963, Howard Barnstone & Partners

6324
HARRIS COUNTY SOCIETY FOR CRIPPLED CHILDREN
Houston, Texas
1963, Howard Barnstone & Partners

6326
ADDITION TO HOUSE OF LENORA DETERING
10002 Memorial Drive, Houston, Texas
1964, Howard Barnstone & Partners
    6401: studio addition

6403
ALTERATIONS TO HOUSE OF MR. AND MRS. CHARLES DILLINGHAM
4 Waverly Court, Houston, Texas
1965, Howard Barnstone & Partners
    6514: renovations
    6909: garage

6402
M. D. ANDERSON BIOLOGY BUILDING
University of St. Thomas, Houston, Texas
1966, Barnstone & Aubry

6403
MONTESSORI SCHOOL OF HOUSTON
1800 Huldy Street, Houston, Texas (not built)
1964, Howard Barnstone & Partners

6405
ALTERATIONS AND ADDITIONS TO HOUSE OF MR. AND MRS. BERNARD WOLF
1749 Milford Street, Houston, Texas
1964, Howard Barnstone & Partners
    6706: alterations, Barnstone & Aubry
    7512: alterations, Howard Barnstone, FAIA

6407
REMODELING OF FORMER CENTRAL PRESBYTERIAN CHURCH FOR ANTA THEATER

Houston, Texas (not built)

1964, Howard Barnstone & Partners

Ann Holmes, "A New Theater Is Born; What of the Others?," *Houston Chronicle*, *Zest* magazine, May 17, 1964, 6.

Ann Holmes, "Cronyn, Miss Tandy Likely ANTA Stars," *Houston Chronicle*, May 28, 1964, section 6, 8.

Ann Holmes, "Steepled Theater? It's a Possibility," *Houston Chronicle*, June 5, 1964, section 2, 2.

Ann Holmes, "Ambitious First Year Plan Announced by ANTA Theater," *Houston Chronicle*, July 7, 1964, section 1, 22.

6409
ALTERATIONS TO HOUSE OF DR. AND MRS. GEORGE JORDAN, JR.

2336 Robinhood Road, Houston, Texas

1964, Howard Barnstone & Partners

6411
OFFICE BUILDING FOR CLEAR LAKE REALTY

Seabrook, Texas

1964, Howard Barnstone & Partners

6412
HOUSE FOR DR. AND MRS. FRANK HILL

Houston, Texas

1964, Howard Barnstone & Partners

6419
HOUSE FOR MR. AND MRS. LE MAY E. SHANE

119 Tuscany, Sugar Land, Texas

1965, Howard Barnstone & Partners

(See also job number **577**.)

6421
TUFFLY PARK RECREATION CENTER, CITY OF HOUSTON, DEPARTMENT OF PARKS AND RECREATION

3200 Russell Street, Houston, Texas

1966, Barnstone & Aubry

6422
HOUSE FOR DR. AND MRS. WILLIAM C. LEVIN

1301 Harbor View Drive, Galveston, Texas (demolished)

1970, Barnstone & Aubry

7906: alterations

"Record Houses of 1973: 10, House, Galveston," *Architectural Record* 153 (mid-May 1973): 60–61.

Madeleine McDermott Hamm, "Open, Cheerful House Captures Galveston's Sea and Sun," *Houston Chronicle*, June 12, 1975, section 5, 1, 5.

Nory Miller, "Lone Stars—Howard Barnstone and Karl Kamrath," *Inland Architect* 21 (July 1977): 16–17.

[no job number]
VASSAR PLACE APARTMENTS FOR HOWARD BARNSTONE

1303 Vassar Place, Houston, Texas (altered)

1965, Howard Barnstone & Partners

6727: alterations, Barnstone & Aubry
7209: H. Barnstone apartment, Howard Barnstone, FAIA
7519: H. Barnstone office
8006: courtyard plan, floor plan
8012: pool
8111: condo conversion
8208: renovations
8310: swimming pool

"Thirteen Award-Winning Apartments and Townhouses," *House and Home* 29 (August 1966): 73.

"Village-Like Garden Apartment Addition Coordinates Parking, Outdoor Living, and Privacy on a Limited Half-Round Site," *Architectural Record* 143 (January 1968): 152–153.

[no job number]
CENTER FOR THE RETARDED

3500 West Dallas Avenue, Houston, Texas (demolished)

1966, Barnstone & Aubry

"Council for Retarded Children Ready to Begin Work on Center," *Houston Chronicle*, March 11, 1965, section 4, 4.

"'Waffles' for a Houston Walkway," *Houston Chronicle*, November 6, 1966, section 3, 12.

"Center for the Retarded Dedication Is Today," *Houston Chronicle*, December 4, 1966, section 3, 1.

"Advanced Center for the Retarded," *Architectural Forum* 127 (December 1967): 48–53.

6501
COMMERCIAL AND HOTEL BUILDING
Houston, Texas (not built)
1965, Howard Barnstone & Partners

6502
JOHN A. BERNATH CONDOMINIUM APARTMENTS
Galveston, Texas
1965, Howard Barnstone & Partners

6503
COMMERCIAL BUILDING AND HOTEL
Preston at Travis Streets, Houston, Texas
1965, Howard Barnstone & Partners

6504
CASA DE PIEDRAS FOR MR. AND MRS. EARL LEWIS SUNESON
Calle Santa Bárbara 454, Puerto Vallarta, Jalisco, Mexico
1967, Barnstone & Aubry
Betty Ewing, "Long Live Liz in Vallarta," *Houston Chronicle*, June 19, 1968, section 2, 2.

6505
INSTITUTE OF INTERNATIONAL EDUCATION
Houston, Texas
1965, Howard Barnstone & Partners

6505
HOUSE FOR MR. AND MRS. MAURICIO FRANK
Laredo, Texas
1965, Howard Barnstone & Partners

6507
HOUSE FOR JAMES O. LEWIS, JR.
Houston, Texas
1965, Howard Barnstone & Partners

6509
ALTERATIONS TO HOUSE OF JUDGE AND MRS. WILMER B. HUNT
526 West Friar Tuck Lane, Houston, Texas (demolished)
1967, Barnstone & Aubry

6511
ALTERATIONS TO HOUSE OF DR. AND MRS. GENE E. BURKE
515 Little John Lane, Houston, Texas
1967, Barnstone & Aubry

6512
EDUCATIONAL BUILDING FOR WHEELER AVENUE BAPTIST CHURCH
3826 Wheeler Avenue, Houston, Texas (demolished)
1966, Barnstone & Aubry; John S. Chase, associate architect
   6915: alterations

6513
HOUSE FOR PROFESSOR AND MRS. WILLIS BARNSTONE
4930 East Heritage Woods Road, Bloomington, Indiana
1967, Barnstone & Aubry

6518
OFFICE INTERIORS FOR SCHLUMBERGER LTD.
277 Park Avenue, New York, New York
1966, Barnstone & Aubry
   6711: furniture
   7204: 4th-floor offices, Howard Barnstone, FAIA
   7802: office for Jean Riboud
   8040: alterations
   8402: office for Michel Gouilloud

"New Angles on the Executive Floor," *Fortune* 73 (June 1966): 169.
"Wiggle Walls," *Progressive Architecture* 47 (August 1966): 160–163.
"Angling the Rectangle . . . The Park Avenue Offices of Schlumberger, Ltd.," *Interiors* 126 (September 1966): 132–133.
C. Ray Smith, *Supermannerism: New Attitudes in Post-Modern Architecture* (New York: Dutton, 1977), 103.

6519
COTLAR HIGHRISE APARTMENT BUILDING
Rosewood at Scott, College Oaks, Houston, Texas (not built)
1965, Howard Barnstone & Partners

6520

ALTERATIONS AND ADDITIONS TO HOUSE OF MR. AND MRS. THOMAS STEPH

28 South Shore Drive, Galveston, Texas (extensively altered)

1965, Howard Barnstone & Partners

6522

MOSIER RESEARCH LABORATORIES

1965, Barnstone & Aubry

[no job number]

ALUMINUM COMPANY OF AMERICA

1965, Barnstone & Aubry

BARNSTONE & AUBRY 1966–1969

6601

BENJAMIN FELD WAREHOUSE

Houston, Texas

1966, Barnstone & Aubry

6602

HOUSE FOR MR. AND MRS. OSCAR KAMMERMAN

(Beatrice Barnstone Kammerman)

1966, Barnstone & Aubry

6602

ADDITIONS TO HOUSE OF CHARLES MCRAE

Houston, Texas

1966, Barnstone & Aubry

6603

ALTERATIONS TO HOUSE OF DR. AND MRS. LOUIS DAILEY

2523 Maroneal Boulevard, Houston, Texas

1967, Barnstone & Aubry

  7010: roof
  7216: remodeling

6604

COMMERCIAL DEVELOPMENT

Clear Lake City, Texas

1966, Barnstone & Aubry

6604

PRINTING BUILDING FOR JACK CAMPBELL

Galveston, Texas

1966, Barnstone & Aubry

6606

BEACH HOUSE FOR JACK CAMPBELL

Clear Lake City, Texas

1966, Barnstone & Aubry

6608

OFFICE BUILDING FOR DR. JOSEPH BARNHART

Houston, Texas

1966, Barnstone & Aubry

6608 and **6610**

REMODELING OF HOUSE OF MR. AND MRS. BERNARD SAMPSON

526 Ripple Creek Drive, Hunters Creek Village, Texas

1966, Barnstone & Aubry

6609

HOUSE FOR MR. AND MRS. STANLEY RINZLER

Atlanta, Georgia

1966, Barnstone & Aubry

6613

HOUSE REMODELING FOR MENIL FOUNDATION HEADQUARTERS

1506 Branard Avenue (moved to 1427 Branard Avenue), Houston, Texas (altered)

1967, Barnstone & Aubry

  7365: garage renovations, air-conditioning, heat

6614
HIGHWAY MOTEL FOR EARL LEWIS SUNESON
Puerto Vallarta, Jalisco, Mexico (not built)
1966, Barnstone & Aubry

6616
REHABILITATION OF WASHINGTON HOUSE FOR APARTMENTS AND OFFICES
Galveston, Texas (not built)
1966, Barnstone & Aubry

6618
HOUSE FOR DR. RICHARD BENUA
126 San Moreck Drive, Galveston, Texas
1966, Barnstone & Aubry

6619
DOHERTY LIBRARY
University of St. Thomas, Houston, Texas
1970, Eugene Aubry and Wilson, Morris, Crain & Anderson

6620
TOWNHOUSE AND GALLERY FOR RICHARD FEIGAN
New York, New York
1966, Barnstone & Aubry

6621
ALTERATIONS TO HOUSE FOR ALLIANCE FRANÇAISE
4006 Mount Vernon Street, Houston, Texas
1966, Barnstone & Aubry

6622
HACIENDA MOTOR HOTEL
Puerto Vallarta, Jalisco, Mexico (not built)
1966, Barnstone & Aubry

6623
HOUSE FOR MR. AND MRS. FRANCIS BUTLER
109 Hillcrest Drive, Richmond, Texas (altered)
1968, Barnstone & Aubry

7349: alterations for Maydee Butler

6625
BAY HOUSE FOR AGNES ARNOLD AND DR. JOSEPH BARNHART
Texas Corinthian Yacht Club, Kemah, Texas
1967, Barnstone & Aubry

6626
REGATTA INN CABAÑAS AND CLUB FOR ALBERT B. FAY
Seabrook, Texas
1966, Barnstone & Aubry

6627
INTERIOR ALTERATIONS, MASON BUILDING
711 Main Street, Houston, Texas
1966, Barnstone & Aubry

6654
RENOVATION OF THE HOUSTON POST BUILDING
2410 Polk Avenue, Houston, Texas
1966, Barnstone & Aubry

6703: alterations

[no job number]
BUTLER BINION LAW FIRM
Houston, Texas
1966, Barnstone & Aubry

[no job number]
HOUSE FOR JOSÉ RAMÓN ASTEINZA
1966, Barnstone & Aubry

[no job number]
INSTITUTE FOR STORM RESEARCH
4104 Mount Vernon Street, Houston, Texas (demolished)
1967, Barnstone & Aubry

6702
CARVER BAKERY
1967, Barnstone & Aubry

6704
TIDELAND SIGNAL CORPORATION FOR SAMUEL N. SPRUNT

Houston, Texas
1967, Barnstone & Aubry

6705
WILLIAMS HOUSE

Houston, Texas
1967, Barnstone & Aubry

  7612: greenhouse

6707
REMODELING OF BRICK ROW BOOK SHOP

3600 Mount Vernon Street, Houston, Texas
1967, Barnstone & Aubry

6708
ALTERATIONS TO HOUSE OF MR. AND MRS. MARION S. ACKERMAN III

3396 Del Monte Drive, Houston, Texas
1967, Barnstone & Aubry

6709
SKI CHALET FOR DR. AND MRS. FRANK HILL

Crested Butte, Colorado
1967, Barnstone & Aubry

  7012: alterations

6710
ADDITION TO HOUSE OF LEROY MELCHER, JR.

4527 West Alabama Avenue, Houston, Texas (demolished)
1967, Barnstone & Aubry

6714
PAVILION FOR HEMISFAIR '68

San Antonio, Texas (not built)
1967, Barnstone & Aubry

6717
TOWNHOUSE COMPLEX FOR PAUL AND SIDNEY CROFT

61 units, Houston, Texas (not built)
1967, Barnstone & Aubry

6718
POOL PAVILION FOR MR. AND MRS. PIERRE M. SCHLUMBERGER, JR.

528 West Friar Tuck Drive, Houston, Texas (demolished)
1968, Barnstone & Aubry

6722
APARTMENT INTERIOR FOR MR. AND MRS. JEAN RIBOUD

3rd floor, 211 East 49th Street, Amster Yard, New York, New York (dismantled)
1968, Barnstone & Aubry

6723
BOATHOUSE AND PAVILION FOR LEROY MELCHER, JR.

816 Shorewood Drive, Timber Grove, Seabrook, Texas
1969, Barnstone & Aubry

Madeleine McDermott Hamm, "The Grahams' Life by the Lake Includes Early A.M. Water Skiing, Lincoln's Desk," *Houston Chronicle*, July 27, 1980, section 5, 6.

6725
HOUSE FOR MR. AND MRS. PAUL GERVAIS BELL, JR.

5135 Bayou Timber Lane, Houston, Texas
1970, Barnstone & Aubry

  7226: library and staircase remodeling

"New England Comes to Houston," *Texas Architect* 23 (November–December 1973): 22–24.

6726
ALTERATIONS TO HOUSE OF JUDGE AND MRS. WILMER B. HUNT

Houston, Texas
1967, Barnstone & Aubry

6729
TOWNHOUSE DEVELOPMENT FOR PALMER WIGBY

Houston, Texas
1967, Barnstone & Aubry

6732

LAW OFFICE INTERIORS FOR PAUL, WEISS, GOLDBERG, RIFKIND, WHARTON & GARRISON

345 Park Avenue, New York, New York

1968, Barnstone & Aubry with Sally Walsh, interior designer

7007: alterations

Maxine Mesinger, "Big City Beat," *Houston Chronicle*, October 4, 1967, section 1, 1.

Maxine Mesinger, "Big City Beat," *Houston Chronicle*, November 10, 1967, section 2, 1.

"S. I. Morris Associates," *Interiors* 134 (June 1975): 79.

6733

BARCELONA POINT DEVELOPMENT

Sag Harbor, Suffolk County, Long Island, New York

1967, Barnstone & Aubry

Maxine Mesinger, "Big City Beat," *Houston Chronicle*, November 10, 1967, section 2, 1.

6734

LAW OFFICE INTERIORS FOR STRICKLAND, GORDON & SHEINFELD

Houston, Texas

1967, Barnstone & Aubry

6736

BOAT HOUSE FOR SCOTT ROYCE

Timber Grove, Houston, Texas

1967, Barnstone & Aubry

6737

ALTERATIONS TO UNIVERSAL SECURITY LIFE BUILDING

Pease Avenue and Main Street, Houston, Texas (demolished)

1967, Barnstone & Aubry

6799

INTERIOR ALTERATIONS TO PLAZA HOTEL

5020 Montrose Boulevard, Houston, Texas

1967, Barnstone & Aubry

6801

HOUSE

Lazy Bend, Kemah, Texas

1968, Barnstone & Aubry

6802

SUNESON SHOPS

Puerto Vallarta, Jalisco, Mexico

1968, Barnstone & Aubry

6804

FIRST STATE BANK OF GREENS BAYOU BUILDING

12605 East Freeway (I-10), Houston, Texas (not built)

1968, Barnstone & Aubry

7113: alterations

6805

ART MUSEUM OF SOUTH TEXAS

1902 North Shoreline Boulevard, Corpus Christi, Texas (altered)

1972, Johnson/Burgee, architects; Barnstone & Aubry, associate architects

7130: alterations

6809

HOUSE FOR MR. AND MRS. I. H. KEMPNER III

3811 Del Monte Drive, Houston, Texas

1969, Barnstone & Aubry

6810

OFFICE INTERIORS FOR LEPERQ, DE NEUFLIZE & COMPANY

23rd floor, 345 Park Avenue, New York, New York

1969, Barnstone & Aubry

8121: office extension

Beverly Maurice, "Only the Very Rich Need Apply to This Financier Who Advises Millionaires," *Houston Chronicle*, August 19, 1974, section 6, 5.

6811

ROTHKO CHAPEL

1409 Sul Ross Avenue, Houston, Texas

1971, Barnstone & Aubry

Ann Holmes, "Important Changes as New Year Looms," *Houston Chronicle Sunday Magazine*, December 27, 1970, 23.

Eleanor Freed, "A Triumph of Austerity: The Rothko Chapel—An Essence and a Crescendo, a Conception of Vast Beauty to Stir Men's Souls," *Houston Post*, February 28, 1971, 6.

"Art and Faith in Houston," *Newsweek*, March 15, 1971, 63.

"Shades of Red and Black," *Architectural Forum* 134 (April 1971): 5.

Katherine Kuh, "A Maximum of Poignancy," *Saturday Review*, April 17, 1971, 52.

D. Frédéric Debuyst, "La chapelle Rothko à Houston," *Art d'Eglise* 155 (April–June 1971): 161–165.

Dominique de Menil, "Rothko Chapel," *Art Journal* 30 (Spring 1971): front cover and 249–251.

"Reflections on the Rothko Chapel," *AIA Journal* 57 (April 1972): 52.

Jean-Patrice Marandel, "Une Chapelle Oecuménique au Texas," *L'Oeil* 197 (May 1971): 16–18.

Pierre Restany, "Notes de Voyage Houston–New York," *Domus* 498 (May 1971): 45–46.

Dore Ashton, "The Rothko Chapel in Houston," *Studio International* 181 (June 1971): 273–275.

Brian O'Doherty, "The Rothko Chapel," *Art in America* 61 (January–February 1973): 14–20.

"Texas Architecture 1974: Rothko Chapel, Houston," *Texas Architect* 24 (November–December 1974): 34.

"Obelisk and Chapel; Houston; Architects: Howard Barnstone and Eugene Aubry," *Architectural Review* 981 (November 1979): 318.

Susan J. Barnes, *The Rothko Chapel: An Act of Faith* (Houston: Rothko Chapel, 1989).

Sheldon Nodelman, *The Rothko Chapel Paintings: Origins, Structure, Meaning* (Austin: University of Texas Press, 1997).

6812
RENOVATION OF HOUSE FOR MR. AND MRS. FAYEZ SAROFIM

Houston, Texas (not built)
1968, Barnstone & Aubry

6814
W. A. TAYLOR WAREHOUSE

Houston, Texas
1968, Barnstone & Aubry

6816
ALTERATIONS TO HOUSE FOR W. A. HORNE CO. REALTOR OFFICES

1401 Sul Ross Avenue, Houston, Texas
1968, Barnstone & Aubry

6817
GUINAN HALL, UNIVERSITY OF ST. THOMAS

1300 Branard Avenue, Houston, Texas (demolished)
1971, Barnstone & Aubry

"Advertisement for Bids," *Houston Chronicle*, April 22, 1968, section 3, 23.

"New St. Thomas Dormitory," *Houston Chronicle*, September 2, 1969, section 1, 13.

6819
ALTERATIONS TO HOUSE OF HOWARD BARNSTONE

1715 North Boulevard, Houston, Texas (not built)
1968, Barnstone & Aubry

6820
B. WALSH PROPERTY PLAN

Houston, Texas
1968, Barnstone & Aubry

6823
APARTMENT FOR SAM KATZ

Houston, Texas
1968, Barnstone & Aubry

6824
HOUSE FOR WILLIAM E. LADIN, JR.

Houston, Texas
1968, Barnstone & Aubry

[no job number]
ST. THOMAS HIGH SCHOOL

Houston, Texas
1968, Barnstone & Aubry

6901
OFFICE INTERIORS FOR ART AND ART HISTORY DEPARTMENT
Allen Center Building, Rice University, Houston, Texas (dismantled)
1969, Barnstone & Aubry

6901
FOURTH WARD PARK
Houston, Texas
(See also job number **6917**.)

6901 A
ADDITIONS TO HOUSE OF MRS. MORRIS G. ROSENTHAL
4 West 11th Place, Houston, Texas (altered)
1970, Howard Barnstone, FAIA
- **7001:** alterations
- **7532:** draperies
- **8210:** alterations

6902
OFFICE INTERIORS FOR INSTITUTE OF RELIGION
Texas Medical Center, Houston, Texas
1970, Howard Barnstone, FAIA

6902
RICE MUSEUM (ART BARN) FOR THE INSTITUTE FOR THE ARTS
Rice University, Houston, Texas (demolished)
1969, Barnstone & Aubry
Helaine Wayne, "Rice Gets an 'A' for Its Art Home," *Houston Post*, March 27, 1969, section 5, 2.
Elinor Freed, "Machine Show in Machine Shop," *Houston Post, Spotlight* magazine, December 29, 1968, 8.
"Machine Shop for Art," *Architectural Forum* 131 (July–August 1969): 95.

6902
MEDIA CENTER BUILDING FOR INSTITUTE FOR THE ARTS
Rice University, Houston, Texas
1970, Eugene Aubry

6903
OFFICE BUILDING FOR THE HONORABLE ALBERT B. FAY
515 Houston Avenue, Houston, Texas
1971, Howard Barnstone, FAIA
- **8320:** monument for Ambassador Fay
- **8373:** garden addition
- **8406:** addition

6905
PHOTOGRAPHY STUDIO FOR L. BLAINE HICKEY AND OGDEN ROBERTSON
Houston, Texas
1969, Barnstone & Aubry

6907
CINEMA CORPORATION OF AMERICA
1969, Barnstone & Aubry

6908
DEPARTMENT STORE FOR MARTI FRANCO DE SUNESON
Laredo, Texas (not built)
1969, Howard Barnstone, FAIA

6916
OFFICE INTERIOR FOR RONALD HOBBS
New York, New York
1969, Barnstone & Aubry

6917
MENIL PARK
Houston, Texas
1969, Howard Barnstone, FAIA

HOWARD BARNSTONE, FAIA, ARCHITECT
1970–1987

7002
POCKET PARK PROJECT
Houston, Texas
1970, Howard Barnstone, FAIA

7003
MARTI'S SPECIALTY STORE FOR MARTI FRANCO DE SUNESON
Calle Victoria 2923, Nuevo Laredo, Tamaulipas, Mexico
1971, Howard Barnstone, FAIA

- **7221:** plaza display
- **7343:** display front
- **7821:** courtyard expansion
- **8011:** display windows
- **8301:** fire repair and new roof

7005
ALTERATIONS TO TOWNHOUSE OF ADELAIDE DE MENIL AND EDMUND S. CARPENTER
163 East 69th Street, New York, New York (not built)
1970, Howard Barnstone, FAIA

7008
PROJECT FOR LEROY MELCHER, JR.
1970, Howard Barnstone, FAIA

7101
GRAUSTARK FAMILY TOWNHOUSES FOR HOWARD BARNSTONE
4923, 4925, and 4927 Graustark Street, Houston, Texas
1970–1972, Howard Barnstone, FAIA

- **7230:** alterations
- **7516:** improvements

4923 Graustark
- **7516:** improvements

4925 Graustark
- **7002:** alterations
- **7823:** residence for Dr. Sam Ross

4927 Graustark
- **7101:** alterations
- **7107:** alterations

- **7201:** skylight, closets

Ann Holmes, "Refreshing Designs for Small Buildings," *Houston Chronicle Sunday Magazine*, August 13, 1972, 33.

Madeleine McDermott Hamm, "Top Designs Good to Look At, Live In," *Houston Chronicle*, January 18, 1978, section 8, 7.

Karleen Koen, "Best of '77: Nine Architects and Their Projects Win Residential Honors," *Houston Home and Garden* 4 (February 1978): 54–55, 60–61.

7102
REHABILITATION OF THE FEDERAL RESERVE BRANCH BANK OF DALLAS FOR THE CRISPIN COMPANY
1301 Texas Avenue, Houston, Texas
1973, Howard Barnstone, FAIA

- **7108:** phase 2
- **7205:** renovations
- **7227:** furnishings
- **7229:** tenant
- **7338:** office for Patricia Teed
- **7340:** fire marshal
- **7533:** alterations

"Exchange Machine Guns for Champagne," *Houston Chronicle*, January 11, 1973, section 5, 2.

Peter C. Papademetriou, "Report from Houston," *Progressive Architecture* 56 (May 1975): 38.

7103
ALTERATIONS TO HOUSE OF THE RIGHT REVEREND AND MRS. J. MILTON RICHARDSON
14 Shadowlawn Circle, Houston, Texas (altered)
1972, Howard Barnstone, FAIA

- **7232:** guesthouse
- **7235:** elevator
- **7505:** remodeling

7104
ALTERATIONS TO HOUSE OF MR. AND MRS. WILLIAM L. WAYNE
2232 Stanmore Drive, Houston, Texas
1971, Howard Barnstone, FAIA

CATALOGUE RAISONNÉ

7105
INSTITUTE OF RESEARCH
1714 Rice Boulevard, Houston, Texas
1971, Howard Barnstone, FAIA

7106
OFFICE INTERIOR FOR COMMUNICATIONS GROUP
Houston, Texas
1971, Howard Barnstone, FAIA

7109
ALTERATIONS TO HOUSE OF MR. AND MRS. JERRY E. BATTLESTEIN
9201 Memorial Drive, Houston, Texas (demolished)
1972, Howard Barnstone, FAIA

7111
OFFICE INTERIOR FOR JERRY E. BATTLESTEIN
Houston, Texas
1971, Howard Barnstone, FAIA

7112
MILFORD TOWNHOUSES FOR HOWARD BARNSTONE
1213, 1215, and 1217 Milford Street, Houston, Texas (altered)
1973, Howard Barnstone, FAIA
   7316: swimming pool
"New Building Permits for Houston," *Daily Court Review*, September 1, 1972, 8.

7116
ADDITION TO HOUSE OF BARBARA KIBLER DILLINGHAM
Round Top, Texas
1971, Howard Barnstone, FAIA

7117
ALTERATIONS TO HOUSE OF CHARLES DILLINGHAM
Round Top, Texas
1971, Howard Barnstone, FAIA

7122
PROJECT FOR DR. IRVIN M. COHEN
1971, Howard Barnstone, FAIA

7126
ALTERATIONS TO HOUSE OF MR. AND MRS. ROBERT COZENS
6619 Belmont Street, West University Place, Houston, Texas (demolished)
1971, Howard Barnstone, FAIA

7129
HOUSE FOR MR. AND MRS. JERRY E. BATTELSTEIN
9201 Memorial Drive, Houston, Texas (not built)
1971, Howard Barnstone, FAIA

7131
LAW OFFICE INTERIOR FOR STRICKLAND & GORDON
2505 Houston Natural Gas Building, 1200 Milam Street, Houston, Texas (dismantled)
1971, Howard Barnstone, FAIA

7133
ALTERATIONS TO HOUSE OF MR. AND MRS. WILLIAM PERLMAN
250 Pine Hollow Lane, Houston, Texas
1971, Howard Barnstone, FAIA
   7504: remodeling

7201
CONFERENCE ROOM INTERIOR FOR MCA FINANCIAL GROUP
One Shell Plaza, 910 Louisiana Street, Houston, Texas (dismantled)
1972, Howard Barnstone, FAIA

7201
ALTERATIONS AND ADDITIONS TO HOUSE OF DR. AND MRS. JULES H. BOHNN
1411 North Boulevard, Houston, Texas
1973, Howard Barnstone, FAIA
   7232: table
   7342: garage office

7202
TOWNHOUSE AND DUPLEX
Houston, Texas
1972, Howard Barnstone, FAIA

7202
ADDITION TO COUNTRY HOUSE OF MR. AND MRS. JERALD D. MIZE
Brenham, Texas
1972, Howard Barnstone, FAIA

7203
HOUSE
1972, Howard Barnstone, FAIA

7206
PEDEN SQUARE FOR JERRY E. BATTELSTEIN
Houston, Texas (not built)
1972, Howard Barnstone, FAIA

7208
ALTERATIONS TO CAMPBELL SEWALL HOUSE FOR CHILDREN'S MENTAL HEALTH SERVICES, INC.
1304 Elgin Avenue, Houston, Texas
1972, Howard Barnstone, FAIA
   7212: master plan
   7213: offices for Dr. Donald Young and psychological group

7210
HOUSE FOR MARILYN ELLIOTT SEE
914 Shorewood Drive, Seabrook, Texas (not built)
1972, Howard Barnstone, FAIA

7214
ALTERATIONS AND ADDITIONS TO HOUSE OF MR. AND MRS. FRANK HERZOG
21 Robin Lake Lane, Houston, TX
1973, Howard Barnstone, FAIA
(See also job number **8330**.)
"Texas Architecture 1974: The Herzog Residence, Houston," *Texas Architect* 24 (November–December 1974): 35.
"Glass and Crossbeams," *Texas Architect* 25 (July–August 1975): 16–17.

Frances Stamper, "Houston: Artistic Renovations," *Texas Homes* 1 (March–April 1978): 40–43.

7215
LAW OFFICE INTERIOR FOR FRANK HERZOG
2424 Two Shell Plaza, 777 Walker Avenue, Houston, Texas (dismantled)
1973, Howard Barnstone, FAIA

7217
SUMMER HOUSE FOR SIMONE SWAN
Peconic, Long Island, New York (not built)
1972, Howard Barnstone, FAIA

7220
KIPLING-YUPON TOWNHOUSES
Houston, Texas
1972, Howard Barnstone, FAIA

7222
HOUSE FOR THE HONORABLE AND MRS. FRED HOFHEINZ
111 North Post Oak Lane, Houston, Texas
1972, Howard Barnstone, FAIA, with Neuhaus & Wingfield, architects

7223 and 7228
ALTERATIONS TO BARKDULL APARTMENTS FOR ANTHONY WILSON
1214 Barkdull Street, Houston, Texas
1972, Howard Barnstone, FAIA
   7714: lot division

7224
MENIL TOWNHOUSE DEVELOPMENT
Rothko Chapel area, Houston, Texas (not built)
1972, Howard Barnstone, FAIA

7231
OFFICE INTERIOR FOR DOW CHEMICAL CO. LEGAL DEPARTMENT
6th floor, 3636 Richmond Avenue, Houston, Texas
1972, Howard Barnstone, FAIA

7233

TOWNHOUSES FOR WILLIAM C. COOLEY, JR.

Fairview Street and Persa Street, Houston, Texas

1972, Howard Barnstone, FAIA

7299

APARTMENTS FOR HOWARD BARNSTONE

1972, Howard Barnstone, FAIA

7344

LANDSCAPE IMPROVEMENTS FOR MR. AND MRS. WILLIAM L. WAYNE

1419 Kirby Drive, Houston, Texas

1973, Howard Barnstone, FAIA

7336

ALTERATIONS TO HOUSE OF CARTER B. CHRISTIE

2247 Troon Road, Houston, Texas

1973, Howard Barnstone, FAIA

7337

ALTERATIONS TO HOUSE OF DR. AND MRS. BERNARD FRIEDMAN

11145 South Country Squire Lane, Piney Point Village, Texas

1973, Howard Barnstone, FAIA

7339

CONSULTATION ON ALTERATIONS TO HOUSE OF DR. AND MRS. JOHN BARKSDALE

13 Tiel Way, Houston, Texas

1973, Howard Barnstone, FAIA

(See also job number **6211**.)

7345

ADDITION TO BAY HOUSE OF THE HONORABLE AND MRS. ALBERT B. FAY

1215 Kipp Avenue, Kemah, Texas

1973, Howard Barnstone, FAIA

7346

OFFICE INTERIOR FOR WILLIAM PERLMAN AND WINDSOR GAS CORPORATION

Niels Esperson Building, 606 Travis Street, Houston, Texas (dismantled)

1973, Howard Barnstone, FAIA

7348

ALTERATIONS TO HOUSE OF THE RIGHT REVEREND AND MRS. SCOTT FIELD BAILEY

5309 Mandell Street, Houston, Texas

1973, Howard Barnstone, FAIA

7350

GALVESTON HISTORICAL FOUNDATION

Galveston, Texas

1973, Howard Barnstone, FAIA

7351

TOWNHOUSES FOR KALDIS REAL ESTATE

San Felipe Road, Houston, Texas (not built)

1973, Howard Barnstone, FAIA

7352

INTERIOR OF SPEEDBY'S OLD PRINT GALLERY FOR ELSA ROSS

5017 Montrose Boulevard, Houston, Texas (demolished)

1974, Howard Barnstone, FAIA

7919: renovation

7353

CONSULTATION WITH MR. AND MRS. RAY PRICE ABOUT TOWNHOUSE

Indian Hills, Houston, Texas

1973, Howard Barnstone, FAIA

7354

ALTERATIONS AND ADDITIONS TO AUTRY HOUSE

6221 Main Street, Houston, Texas

1975, Bailey & Belanger

"Autry House," *Texas Architect* 27 (July–August 1977): 42–43.

7355
HOUSE FOR MR. AND MRS. JEAN RIBOUD

38850 North Spanish Boot Road, Scottsdale, Arizona

1974, Howard Barnstone, FAIA

7524: alterations
7808: additions

Nory Miller, "Lone Stars—Howard Barnstone and Karl Kamrath," *Inland Architect* 21 (July 1977): 16–17.

(See also job number **6140**.)

7358
PROJECTS FOR THE MENIL FOUNDATION

Mulberry Street and Branard Avenue, Houston, Texas

1973, Howard Barnstone, FAIA

7401: position and install Tony Smith sculptures *The Snake Is Out* (1962), *Elevens Are Up* (1963), *Marriage* (1965), *New Piece* (1966), and *Spitball* (1966) (sculptures subsequently moved to different sites)
7506: Menil Conference Center (not built)
7510: Art Storage Building, Branard at Mulberry (not built)
7918: Menil area street lighting

(See also job numbers **7503, 7908,** and **8022**.)

Douglas Milburn, with photographs by Tom Richmond, *The Last American City* (Houston: Texas Chapbook Press, 1979), 46, 49.

7359
TOWNHOUSES FOR JAY STERLING

2655 South Braeswood Boulevard, Houston, Texas (not built)

1973, Howard Barnstone, FAIA

7607: revised plan

7360
EMANUEL MORGAN PROJECT

Ecuador (not built)

1973, Howard Barnstone, FAIA

7362
HOUSE FOR MARTI FRANCO

Laredo, Texas (not built)

1973, Howard Barnstone, FAIA

7363
HOUSE FOR MARILYN OSHMAN LUBETKIN

Houston, Texas (not built)

1973, Howard Barnstone, FAIA

7364
ALTERATIONS, ADDITIONS, AND RESTORATION OF HOUSES FOR ADELAIDE DE MENIL AND EDMUND S. CARPENTER

Farther Lane, East Hampton, Long Island, New York (disassembled and moved to new sites, 2008)

1977, Howard Barnstone, FAIA, with William Chaffee, Morey & Hollenbeck, and Daniel M. C. Hopping, architects; Zion & Breen, landscape architects

Peach House converted to a guesthouse

Baker Barn remodeled for the gatehouse

Erwitt (Phoebe House) converted to the caretaker's house

Hand House converted to a guesthouse

Cutchogue converted to a guesthouse

Garden shed restored

7601: Purple House and Bridgehampton Barn connected by a new greenhouse
8103: alterations

Ann Holmes, "New Environment for Old Houses," *Houston Chronicle*, *Zest* magazine, October 23, 1977, 12, 32.

"First Honor Awards: The De Menil–Carpenter Project—East Hampton, Long Island," *Texas Architect* 27 (November–December 1977): 48.

"Farm House Sanctuary," *Texas Architect* 28 (March–April 1978): 36–37.

"National Awards for Two Houston Architects," *Houston Chronicle*, April 5, 1978, section 1, 21.

Mary E. Osman, "Honor Awards / 1978: Moved and Restored Buildings, Long Island, New York," *AIA Journal* 67 (mid-May 1978): 137.

"Two Remodelings That Bridge 300 Years: Re-Creating the Past," *Housing* 56 (July 1979): 80–81.

7366
HOUSTON COTTON EXCHANGE

Houston, Texas

1973, Howard Barnstone, FAIA

7367
CONSULTATION WITH JUDITH AND BARRY KAPLAN
1973, Howard Barnstone, FAIA

7369
ALTERATIONS TO APARTMENT OF ADELAIDE DE MENIL AND EDMUND S. CARPENTER
222 Central Park South, New York, New York
1977, Howard Barnstone, FAIA
7513: alterations

7371
ALTERATIONS TO HOUSE OF MR. AND MRS. MALCOLM S. McCORQUODALE
3470 Locke Lane, Houston, Texas
1975, Howard Barnstone, FAIA
8114: renovations

[no project number]
CONSULTATION WITH HARRY LICATA
1974, Howard Barnstone, FAIA

7501
RENOVATION OF ASHTON VILLA
2328 Broadway, Galveston, Texas (not built)
1975, Howard Barnstone, FAIA

7501
APARTMENT COMPLEX
22–24 units, garage, Houston, Texas
1975, Howard Barnstone, FAIA

7502
ALTERATIONS TO HOUSE OF SHIRLEY SCHLEIN
11114 Wickdale Drive, Piney Point Village, Texas
1975, Howard Barnstone, FAIA

7503
ALTERATIONS TO BUNGALOW FOR MENIL FOUNDATION
1412 Sul Ross Avenue, Houston, Texas
1973, Howard Barnstone, FAIA

7505
ALTERATIONS TO DUPLEX APARTMENT BUILDING FOR ROBERT BARNSTONE
202 West 31st Street, Austin, Texas
1975, Howard Barnstone, FAIA
7605: alterations

7506
ARCHITECTURE OFFICE INTERIOR FOR HOWARD BARNSTONE
1303 Vassar Place, apartment 5, Houston, Texas (altered)
1975, Howard Barnstone, FAIA
7806: renovations

7507
ALTERATIONS AND ADDITIONS TO HOUSE OF MR. AND MRS. ROBERT BARNSTONE
114 West Eleventh Street, Austin, Texas
1977, Howard Barnstone, FAIA
7508: lamps
7607: alterations
7917: furniture

7511
ALTERATIONS TO HOUSE OF DR. AND MRS. CHARLES DOUGLASS
1007 Spanish Moss Lane, Piney Woods, Houston, Texas
1975, Howard Barnstone, FAIA

7514
SYNAGOGUE CENTER FOR CONGREGATION AM ECHAD
74 Bradman Street, Auburn, Maine (not built)
1976, Howard Barnstone, FAIA
7810: alternative plans

7515
ALTERATIONS TO HOUSE OF JERRY E. BATTELSTEIN
1640 Banks Street, Houston, Texas (demolished)
1975, Howard Barnstone, FAIA

7518
ALTERATIONS TO HOUSE AND OFFICE OF CHARLES THOBAE
1420 Sul Ross Avenue, Houston, Texas
1975, Howard Barnstone, FAIA

7520
COUNTRY HOUSE FOR MR. AND MRS. P. G. BELL, JR.
Chappell Hill, Texas
1975, Howard Barnstone, FAIA

7521
OFFICE BUILDING FOR KAHN & MAIERSON
Houston, Texas
1975, Howard Barnstone, FAIA

7522
ALTERATIONS TO TOWNHOUSE OF PHILIP S. GREENE
1630 Cherryhurst Street, Houston, Texas
1975, Howard Barnstone, FAIA

7523
RENOVATION OF FIRE HOUSE FOR CONVERSION TO MASJID AL-FARA FOR DIA ART FOUNDATION
155 Mercer Street, New York, New York
1975, Howard Barnstone, FAIA

7525
ADDITION TO RUGGLES RESTAURANT
903 Westheimer Road, Houston, Texas (not built)
1975, Howard Barnstone, FAIA

7526
ADDITION TO HOUSE OF J. P. POMEROY, JR.
3832 Chevy Chase Drive, Houston, Texas
1975, Howard Barnstone, FAIA

7527
ALTERATIONS TO HOUSE OF MR. AND MRS. JOE B. KNAUTH
2409 Ella Lee Lane, Houston, Texas
1975, Howard Barnstone, FAIA

7528
ALTERATIONS TO HOUSE OF DR. JOSEPH BARNHART
3507 Inwood Drive, Houston, Texas (demolished)
1975, Howard Barnstone, FAIA

7601
BARNSTONE MINI-STORAGE WAREHOUSE
Houston, Texas
1976, Howard Barnstone, FAIA

7603
MATCH FACTORY
Belize
1976, Howard Barnstone, FAIA

7609
LAKE HOUSE FOR ROBERT BARSTOW
Comanche Point, Lake Travis, Austin, Texas
1976, Howard Barnstone, FAIA

7610
RICHTER-BARNSTONE PROPERTY
4912 Mount Vernon Street, Houston, Texas
7812: alterations

7611
ALTERATIONS TO HOUSE OF MR. AND MRS. ANDRÉ CRISPIN
Houston, Texas
1976, Howard Barnstone, FAIA

7612
ALTERATIONS TO HOUSE OF MR. AND MRS. WILLIAM GUEST
2243 Stanmore Drive, Houston, Texas
1976, Howard Barnstone, FAIA

7613
SCHLUMBERGER-DOLL RESEARCH CENTER
Old Quarry Road, Ridgefield, Connecticut (demolished)
1980, Howard Barnstone FAIA; Zion & Breen, landscape architects
7825: phase 2
8018: library
8019: library storage shed

CATALOGUE RAISONNÉ

8020: Linac (linear particle accelerator) Building
8119: Linac research wing
8120: research lab and offices
8207: alterations
8212: basement library
8318: technical library

"Design Awards: 18 Projects Cited in TSA's 1980 Design Awards Program," *Texas Architect* 30 (November–December 1980): 85.

"Schlumberger-Doll Research Center, Ridgefield, Conn.," *Texas Architect* 31 (March–April 1981): 40.

7614
GREENHOUSE FOR MR. AND MRS. J. J. FARBSTEIN
1976, Howard Barnstone, FAIA

7615
HOUSE FOR MR. AND MRS. WILLIAM E. LADIN
1976, Howard Barnstone, FAIA

7616
ALTERATIONS TO HOUSE OF RICHARD MILLER
Houston, Texas
1976, Howard Barnstone, FAIA
8002: remodeling
8098: alterations

7701
ALTERATIONS TO APARTMENT OF MR. AND MRS. MICHEL GOUILLOUD
34 East 30th Street, Murray Hill, New York, New York
1979, Howard Barnstone, FAIA

7701
ALTERATIONS TO HOUSE OF HOWARD BARNSTONE
17 Shadowlawn Circle, Houston, Texas (altered)
1977, Howard Barnstone, FAIA
7910: garage apartment
8550: floor plans for alterations

Gay E. McFarland, "Architectural Delights Can Be Noted on Tour," *Houston Chronicle*, April 7, 1978, section 6, 1.

Wendy Haskell Meyer, "Provincial Living," *Houston Home and Garden* 5 (February 1979): 90–95.

7702
LAW OFFICE INTERIOR FOR FRANK HERZOG
Pennzoil Place, 711 Louisiana Street, Houston, Texas
1977, Howard Barnstone, FAIA

77003
ADDITION TO HOUSE OF MR. AND MRS. RISHER RANDALL
3249 Chevy Chase Drive, Houston, Texas
1977, Howard Barnstone, FAIA

77004
ELEVATOR FOR CHANCERY OF THE EPISCOPAL DIOCESE OF TEXAS
520 San Jacinto Street, Houston, Texas
1977, Howard Barnstone, FAIA

7705
HOUSE FOR HOWARD BARNSTONE
16 Shadowlawn Circle, Houston, Texas
1977, Howard Barnstone, FAIA
(See also job number **7927**.)

7706
ENCINAL CONDOMINIUMS FOR ROBERT BARNSTONE
1106 West Sixth Street, Austin Texas
1978, Howard Barnstone, architect; Allan Nutt, associate architect
7924: alterations

"Design Awards: 18 Projects Cited in TSA's 1980 Design Awards Program," *Texas Architect* 30 (November–December 1980): 85.

"Encinal Condominiums," *Texas Architect* 31 (March–April 1981): 39.

Katherine Liapi and Charles W. Moore, "Court Living," in "Ah Mediterranean! Twentieth-Century Classicism in America," special issue, *Center: A Journal for Architecture in America* 2 (1985): 86.

7707
ALTERATIONS TO HOUSE OF MR. AND MRS. BENJAMIN KITCHEN
3614 Piping Rock Lane, Houston, Texas (demolished)
1977, Howard Barnstone, FAIA
7811: addition

7708

CULLEN PARK, CITY OF HOUSTON, PARKS AND RECREATION DEPARTMENT

19008 Saums, Houston, Texas

1977, Howard Barnstone, FAIA

8302: promotional materials

7709

OFFICE INTERIOR FOR LEPERCQ, DE NEUFLIZE & CO.

641 Lexington Avenue, New York, New York (not built)

1977, Howard Barnstone, FAIA

7710

ALTERATIONS TO DUPLEX OF ROBERT C. RICHTER, JR.

1222 Barkdull Street, Houston, Texas

1977, Howard Barnstone, FAIA

7711

ALTERATIONS TO HOUSE OF DR. AND MRS. S. J. KURZBARD

4130 North Round Hill Road, Arlington, Virginia

1977, Howard Barnstone, FAIA

7803: furnishings

7712

ALTERATIONS TO HOUSTON NATIONAL BANK BUILDING FOR JERRY E. BATTELSTEIN

202 Main Street at Franklin, Houston, Texas (not built)

1977, Howard Barnstone, FAIA

7712

SITE PLAN FOR INSTITUTE TOWNHOUSES FOR JOHN KNAPP AND AKCO BUILDERS

5328–5336 Institute Lane, Houston, Texas

1977, Howard Barnstone, FAIA

1978, Ziegler Cooper, architects for the three houses built on the site

(See also job number **7913**.)

7713

BUILDING

Teetshorn Street and Taylor Street, Houston, Texas

1977, Howard Barnstone, FAIA

7715

ALTERATIONS TO HOUSE OF MRS. GLADYS SIMMONS

125 Hubbard Avenue, Stamford, Connecticut

1977, Howard Barnstone, FAIA

7716

SHADYSIDE PLACE TOWNHOUSE COMPLEX

1500 Bissonnet Avenue, Houston, Texas (not built)

1977, Howard Barnstone, FAIA

7907: alternate plan

7801

ALTERATIONS TO HOUSE OF MR. AND MRS. HOWARD MARCUS

26 North Wynden Drive, Houston, Texas

1978, Howard Barnstone, FAIA

7804

ALTERATIONS TO HOUSE OF A. T. ERWIN

21 Hedwig Circle, Hedwig Village, Texas

1978, Howard Barnstone, FAIA

7805

ALTERATIONS FOR MR. AND MRS. MELVIN A. SONDOCK

Seawall Boulevard, Galveston, Texas

1978, Howard Barnstone, FAIA

7807

ADDITION TO HOUSE OF DR. JOSÉ D. MDALEL

Sugar Land, Texas

1978, Howard Barnstone, FAIA

7807
FURNITURE FOR APARTMENT OF MR. AND MRS. JEAN RIBOUD
No. 912, Carlton House, 608 Madison Avenue, New York, New York
1978, Howard Barnstone, FAIA

7809
PROPOSAL FOR MARTI'S STORE FOR MARTI FRANCO
San Francisco, California (not built)
1978, Howard Barnstone, FAIA

7813
LAW OFFICE INTERIOR FOR GERALD S. GORDON
6th floor, Siteman Building, 6900 Fannin Street, Houston, Texas (dismantled)
1978, Howard Barnstone, FAIA

7814
INTERNATIONAL BONDED WAREHOUSE FOR HIGHLAND MALL PROPERTIES
Austin, Texas
1978, Howard Barnstone, FAIA
 8118: alterations

7815
DRYDEN SHOPPING MALL
Laredo, Texas
1978, Howard Barnstone, FAIA

7816
ALTERATIONS TO HOTEL GÁLVEZ
Galveston, Texas (not built)
1978, Howard Barnstone, FAIA

7817
SUGARCREEK TOWNHOUSES FOR GREENMARK, INC.
Country Club Boulevard, Sugar Land, Texas (not built)
1978, Howard Barnstone, FAIA

7818
POSADA DEL REY CONDOMINIUMS FOR ROBERT BARNSTONE
505 West 7th Street, Austin, Texas (not built)
1978, Howard Barnstone, FAIA

7819
ALTERATIONS TO HOUSE OF SUE LAWSON
1720 North Boulevard, Houston, Texas
1978, Howard Barnstone, FAIA
(See also job number **6035**.)

7820
LAW OFFICE INTERIOR FOR ROBERT C. RICHTER, JR.
7718 West Bellfort Boulevard, Houston, Texas
1978, Howard Barnstone, FAIA

7822
ELMCOURT CONDOMINIUMS FOR ROBERT BARNSTONE
1103 Elm Street, Austin, Texas
1978, Howard Barnstone, FAIA
 8044: condo for Jackson Giles

7823
OFFICE AND APARTMENT FOR DR. SAM ROSS
5001 Milam Street, Houston, Texas
1979, Howard Barnstone, FAIA

7824
ALTERATIONS TO MOSCHINI HOUSE
2104 Pelham Drive, Houston, Texas
1978, Howard Barnstone, FAIA

7826
OFFICE BUILDING FOR ROBERT BARNSTONE
West Fifth Street and Baylor Street, Austin, Texas (not built)
1978, Howard Barnstone, FAIA

7901
ALTERATIONS TO JETT GROCERY CO. BUILDING FOR OFFICES

5021 Montrose, Houston, Texas (not built)
1979, Howard Barnstone, FAIA

7902
ALTERATIONS TO HOUSE OF HERMAN E. DETERING III

2134 Tangley Road, Houston, Texas
1979, Howard Barnstone, FAIA

- **8081:** additions
- **8205:** rear addition

7903
ALTERATIONS TO TOWNHOUSE OF ROBERT CHAFFIN

1010 Potomac Drive, Houston, Texas
1979, Howard Barnstone, FAIA

7905
HOUSE FOR MR. AND MRS. ERNEST B. FAY

3910 Willowick Road, Houston, Texas (not built)
1979, Howard Barnstone, FAIA

- **8506:** new proposals

7908
ART MUSEUM FOR THE MENIL FOUNDATION

3900 block of Mulberry Street, Houston, Texas (not built)
1979, Howard Barnstone, FAIA

7909
ADDITION TO HOUSE OF MR. AND MRS. LOUIS ADLER

3680 Inwood Drive, Houston, Texas (not built)
1979, Howard Barnstone, FAIA

7911
GORDON CHAPEL, CONGREGATION BETH ISRAEL

8600 North Braeswood Boulevard, Houston, Texas (not built)
1979, Howard Barnstone, FAIA

7912
HOUSE FOR CAROL EADS

107 Sage Road, Houston, Texas (not built)
1979, Howard Barnstone, FAIA

7913
ALTERATIONS TO HOUSE OF ELEANOR K. FREED

5328 Institute Lane, Houston, Texas
1979, Howard Barnstone, FAIA

7914
ADDITION TO TOWNHOUSE OF ROBERT FRIEDMAN

1012 Potomac Drive, Houston, Texas
1979, Howard Barnstone, FAIA

7916
APARTMENT BUILDING FOR ROBERT BARNSTONE

McAllen, Texas (not built)
1979, Howard Barnstone, FAIA

7920
ALTERATIONS TO RESURRECTION AVENUE BAR AND GRILL

East 11th Avenue and Studewood Street, Houston, Texas
1979, Howard Barnstone, FAIA

7921
ALTERATIONS TO HOUSE OF MR. AND MRS. ANDREW E. SPECTOR

8832 Chatsworth Drive, Houston, Texas

- **8311:** renovation

7922
TOWNHOUSES

Bissonnet Avenue and Dora Lane, Houston, Texas (not built)
1979, Howard Barnstone, FAIA

7923
ALTERATIONS TO HOUSE OF MR. AND MRS. OLIVER WILLIAMS

11558 Memorial Drive, Houston, Texas
1979, Howard Barnstone, FAIA

7925
HOUSE FOR DR. AND MRS. BRENT MASEL
Beluche Drive, Galveston, Texas (not built)
1979, Howard Barnstone, FAIA

7927
HOUSE FOR MR. AND MRS. ROBERT BRAMLETT
16 Shadowlawn Circle, Houston, Texas
1982, Howard Barnstone, FAIA
(See also job number **7705**.)
Jeffrey Karl Ochsner, "Bramlett House," *Texas Architect* 33 (May–June 1983): 46–47.

7928
DE SALIGNY CONDOMINIUMS FOR ROBERT BARNSTONE
1111 West 12th Street, Austin, Texas
1982, Howard Barnstone, FAIA, and Robert T. Jackson

7929
FRENCH LEGATION PARK
Austin, Texas
1979, Howard Barnstone, FAIA

[no job number]
PROPOSAL FOR BUTERA'S GROCERY STORE BUILDING
Houston, Texas
1979, Howard Barnstone, FAIA

8001
TOWNHOUSES
The Woodlands, Texas
1979, Howard Barnstone, FAIA

8003
COUNTRY HOUSE FOR MARC FLATOW
Bluebonnet Hills, Washington County, Texas (not built)
1980, Howard Barnstone, FAIA

8004
ALTERATIONS TO BANK BUILDING FOR MIKE PERRIN
1980, Howard Barnstone, FAIA

8005
ALTERATIONS TO HOUSE FOR BARNSTONE ARCHITECTURAL OFFICE
5200 Bayard Lane, Houston, Texas (altered)
1980, Howard Barnstone, FAIA
   8300: renovations
   8403: proposal for Museum Townhouses on site

8007
ALTERATIONS TO OFFICE OF ROBERT BRAMLETT
429 Woodland Street, Houston, Texas
1980, Howard Barnstone, FAIA

8008
GREENWAY PLAZA
Austin, Texas
1980, Howard Barnstone, FAIA

8009
HOUSE FOR MR. AND MRS. GEORGE PETERKIN, JR.
5787 Indian Circle, Houston, Texas
1983, Howard Barnstone, FAIA
Katherine Liapi and Charles W. Moore, "Court Living," in "Ah Mediterranean! Twentieth-Century Classicism in America," special issue, *Center: A Journal for Architecture in America* 2 (1985): 88.

8013
LANSDALE PARK RECREATION CENTER, CITY OF HOUSTON, PARKS AND RECREATION DEPARTMENT
8201 Roos Road, Houston, Texas
1980, Howard Barnstone, FAIA

8014
ALTERATIONS TO HOUSE FOR SALE
3826 Olympia Drive, Houston, Texas (not built)
1980, Howard Barnstone, FAIA

8022
PHOTO ARCHIVE BUILDING FOR MENIL FOUNDATION
1414 Sul Ross Avenue, Houston, Texas (not built)
1980, Howard Barnstone, FAIA

8026
WEBB COUNTY ADMINISTRATION BUILDING AND RESTORATION OF WEBB COUNTY COURTHOUSE

Laredo, Texas (not built)

1980, Howard Barnstone, FAIA

8032
HOUSE FOR MR. AND MRS. CHARLES R. HOUSSIERE III

2003 Arrowwood Circle North, Piney Point Village, Texas

1983, Howard Barnstone, FAIA

8033
ALTERATIONS TO HOUSE FOR PHOTO ARCHIVE BUILDING FOR MENIL FOUNDATION

1503–1507 Branard, Houston, Texas

1983, Howard Barnstone, FAIA

8034
ALTERATIONS AND ADDITIONS TO HOUSE OF THE HONORABLE AND MRS. ROBERT J. O'CONOR, JR.

3831 Del Monte Drive, Houston, Texas

1981, Howard Barnstone, FAIA

8036
ALTERATIONS TO APARTMENT OF MR. AND MRS. CLAUD B. HAMILL

Apt. 2D, Inwood Manor, 3711 San Felipe Road, Houston, Texas (dismantled)

1982, Howard Barnstone, FAIA

8037
LAREDO COUNTRY CLUB

Laredo, Texas

1980, Howard Barnstone, FAIA

8038
HOUSE FOR MR. AND MRS. HAROLD BLUDWORTH

Green Tee Drive, Green Tee Terrace, Baytown, Texas

1980, Howard Barnstone, FAIA

8204: alterations

8039
YOAKUM CONDOMINIUMS

4901 Yoakum Boulevard, Houston, Texas (not built)

1980, Howard Barnstone, FAIA

8101
ALTERATIONS TO HOUSE OF DIANA MARSHALL

322 Isolde Drive, Houston, Texas

1981, Howard Barnstone, FAIA

8102
ALTERATIONS TO DRUCKER HOUSE

Stratford Lane, Laredo, Texas

1981, Howard Barnstone, FAIA

8104
ALTERATIONS TO HOUSE OF PAM AND TOM RICKS

2421 Southgate Boulevard, Houston, Texas (demolished)

1981, Howard Barnstone, FAIA

8105
MASTER PLAN PROPOSAL FOR SCHLUMBERGER AUSTIN

Interstate Highway 35 and Yager Lane, Austin, Texas

1981, Howard Barnstone, FAIA

(See also job number **8413**.)

8106
ADDITIONS TO HOUSE OF DRS. ALICE HENIKER AND TIMOTHY SHARMA

1311 South Boulevard, Houston, Texas

1980, Howard Barnstone, FAIA

8107
ALTERATIONS TO HOUSE

1803 Banks Street, Houston, Texas

1981, Howard Barnstone, FAIA

8108
MERCADO

1981, Howard Barnstone, FAIA

8109
ADDITIONS TO RANCH HOUSE OF HERMAN E. DETERING III
Detering Ranch, Rio Frio, Texas
1981, Howard Barnstone, FAIA

8110
GARDEN LIGHTING FOR JANE BLAFFER OWEN
300 Pinewold Drive, Houston, Texas
1981, Howard Barnstone, FAIA

8112
ALTERATIONS AND ADDITIONS TO HOUSE OF DR. AND MRS. BRENT MASEL
2908 Dominique Drive, Galveston, Texas (not built)
1981, Howard Barnstone, FAIA

8113
KALDIS BATH HOUSE
1981, Howard Barnstone, FAIA

8115
ALTERATIONS TO THE MUSEUM OF THE SOUTHWEST
1705 West Missouri Avenue, Midland, Texas
1981, Howard Barnstone, FAIA

8116
ALTERATIONS TO SANTA ANITA RESTAURANT FOR GEORGE O. JACKSON, JR.
1919 Louisiana Street, Houston, Texas (not built)
1981, Howard Barnstone, FAIA

8117
HOUSE FOR MR. AND MRS. WILLIAM PERLMAN
Lakewood Yacht Club, Seabrook, Texas (not built)
1981, Howard Barnstone, FAIA

8201
INN OF THE REPUBLIC OF TEXAS
Willow Street, Austin, Texas
1982, Howard Barnstone, FAIA

8203
ALTERATIONS TO HOUSE OF MR. AND MRS. JOE B. DURRET
5508 Sturbridge Drive, Houston, Texas (demolished)
1982, Howard Barnstone, FAIA

8209
ALTERATIONS TO HOUSE OF DR. CAL COHN
Bayard Lane, Houston, Texas
1982, Howard Barnstone, FAIA

8211
RENOVATION OF HOUSE OF MR. AND MRS. RICHARD P. KEETON
410 Spiller Lane, Austin, Texas
1982, Howard Barnstone, FAIA with Robert T. Jackson

8213
CONSULTATION WITH JUDY AND ROBERT ALLEN
1982, Howard Barnstone, FAIA

8213
ALTERATIONS TO DETERING BOOK GALLERY FOR HERMAN E. DETERING III
2311 Bissonnet Avenue, Houston, Texas (dismantled)
1982, Howard Barnstone, FAIA
  8507: extension
  8603: addition

8214
CALHOUN PARK
Houston, Texas
1982, Howard Barnstone, FAIA

8215
TOWNHOUSES FOR CAMARERO-BARNSTONE-LUNDELL PARTNERSHIP
1110 Barkdull Street, Houston, Texas (not built)
1982, Howard Barnstone, FAIA

8216
PROJECT FOR A NEW LAGUNA GLORIA ART MUSEUM

Downtown Austin, Texas (not built)
1982, Howard Barnstone, FAIA

8216
DESIGN ENTRY FOR *DREAMS AND SCHEMES* EXHIBITION

Contemporary Arts Museum Houston, Houston, Texas
1982, Howard Barnstone, FAIA
Ann Holmes, "CAM Makeover," *Houston Chronicle*, Zest magazine, October 17, 1982, 13.

8217
CONDOMINIUM COMPLEX FOR HARVEY CONWELL

Mustang Island, Texas
1982, Howard Barnstone, FAIA

8218
REHABILITATION OF JEFFERSON DAVIS HOSPITAL

1101 Elder Street, Houston, Texas (not built)
1982, Howard Barnstone, FAIA

8301
CONSULTATION WITH MARY KATHERINE ALONSO

1983, Howard Barnstone, FAIA

8302
CONSULTATION WITH DR. AND MRS. LARRY LIPSCHULTZ RE: HERZOG HOUSE

1983, Howard Barnstone, FAIA
(See also job number **7214**.)

8303
ALTERATIONS AND ADDITIONS TO HOUSE OF MR. AND MRS. WILLIAM PERLMAN

4846 Post Oak Timber, Houston, Texas (altered)
1983, Howard Barnstone, FAIA

8304
HOUSE FOR HELEN GORDON AND ROBERT DE YOUNG

1983, Howard Barnstone, FAIA

8304
GILBANE HOUSE

1983, Howard Barnstone, FAIA

8306
HOLMES HOUSE

130 Summerwood Drive, Beaumont, Texas
1985, Howard Barnstone, FAIA

8307
MOUNT VERNON MANOR HOUSE

1202 Milford Street, Houston, Texas (not built)
1983, Howard Barnstone, FAIA

8307
TEXAS COMMERCE BANK

1983, Howard Barnstone, FAIA

8308
ALTERATIONS TO 1215 BANKS APARTMENTS

1215 Banks Street, Houston, Texas (altered)
1983, Howard Barnstone, FAIA

8308
ALTERATIONS TO ST. JOSEPH HOSPITAL

Houston, Texas (not built)
1983, Howard Barnstone, FAIA

8309
MONTESSORI SCHOOL

Arnold Street, Houston, Texas (not built)
1983, Howard Barnstone, FAIA

8310
ALTERATIONS TO PAUL CRAVEY HOUSE

East Texas (not built)
1983, Howard Barnstone, FAIA

8312
LEE HOUSE
1983, Howard Barnstone, FAIA

8312
ALTERATIONS TO DAVID E. KAZDAN HOUSE
327 Tealwood Drive, Houston, Texas
1983, Howard Barnstone, FAIA

8313
ADDITION TO GROSSBERG HOUSE
8939 Briar Forest Drive, Piney Point Village, Texas
1983, Howard Barnstone, FAIA

8313
HOUSE FOR ROGER SURI
1983, Howard Barnstone, FAIA (not built)

8314
TOWNHOUSES FOR MICHAEL ROBINSON
Colquitt Avenue, Houston, Texas
1983, Howard Barnstone, FAIA

8314
RENOVATION OF HOUSE OF WILLIAM PERLMAN
1814 Larchmont Road, Houston, Texas
1983, Howard Barnstone, FAIA

8315
NEW BEACH HOTEL
8811 Seawall Boulevard, Galveston, Texas (not built)
1983, Howard Barnstone, FAIA

8316
BRENHAM GUESTHOUSE
Brenham, Texas
1983, Howard Barnstone, FAIA

8317
CHEESE FACTORY
Fredericksburg, Texas (not built)
1983, Howard Barnstone, FAIA

8319
ALTERATIONS TO PASTERNAK HOUSE
1819 Lauderdale, Houston, Texas
1983, Howard Barnstone, FAIA

8319
ALTERATIONS TO HOUSE OF VIRGINIA AND ROBERT J. HOELSCHER
2116 Chilton Road, Houston, Texas
1983, Howard Barnstone, FAIA

8320
YANG HOUSE
2320 Chimney Rock Road, Houston, Texas
1983, Howard Barnstone, FAIA

8321
ALTERATIONS TO HOUSE OF FRANK HERZOG
165 Sage Road, Houston, Texas
1983, Howard Barnstone, FAIA

8324
AUDUBON STREET ARTS CENTER
New Haven, Connecticut
1983, Howard Barnstone, FAIA

8328
AUSTIN CITY HALL
Austin, Texas (not built)
1983, Howard Barnstone, FAIA

8330
ALTERATIONS TO HOUSE OF MR. AND MRS. A. BRUCE LAWRENCE
21 Robin Lake Lane, Houston, Texas
1983, Howard Barnstone, FAIA
(See also job number **7214**.)

8331
TEO CORPORATION FOR JAMES STIRLING
1983, Howard Barnstone, FAIA

8332

BARNSTONE-RICHTER PROPERTY

1136 Berthea Street, Houston, Texas

1983, Howard Barnstone, FAIA

8401

ALTERATIONS TO HOUSE OF MR. AND MRS. JAMES R. DOTY

2333 Claremont Lane, Houston, Texas

1984, Howard Barnstone, FAIA

8404

LAW OFFICE INTERIORS FOR GERALD S. GORDON

16th floor, Two Post Oak Central, 1980 Post Oak Boulevard, Houston, Texas

1984, Howard Barnstone, FAIA

8407

KOSTOS PAPAVASSILIOU HOUSE

4610 Bryn Mawr Lane, Houston, TX

1984, Howard Barnstone, FAIA

8408

ALTERATIONS TO HOUSE OF MR. AND MRS. MICHAEL R. JODEIT

5551 Tupper Lake Lane, Houston, Texas (demolished)

1984, Howard Barnstone, FAIA

8409

ALTERATIONS TO HOUSE OF SARA E. WHITE

3345 Del Monte Drive, Houston, Texas

1984, Howard Barnstone, FAIA

8410

HOUSE FOR MR. AND MRS. PABLO JÁCOBO SUNESON

La Brisas del Mar subdivision, Laredo, Texas

1984, Howard Barnstone, FAIA

8411

ADDITION TO HOUSE OF LARRY GOODMAN

15707 Craighurst Drive, Clear Lake City, Texas

1984, Howard Barnstone, FAIA

8412

INTERIOR OF DAVIS-MCLAIN GALLERY

2615 Colquitt Street, Houston, Texas (dismantled)

1984, Howard Barnstone, FAIA

Patricia C. Johnson, "Moving Experiences for Houston Galleries," *Houston Chronicle*, *Zest* magazine, March 17, 1985, 17.

8413

SCHLUMBERGER AUSTIN SYSTEMS CENTER

11400 Concordia University Drive, Austin, Texas (altered)

1988, Howard Barnstone, FAIA, and Robert T. Jackson; J. Robert Anderson, landscape architect

8604: recreation center

(See also job number **8105**.)

"Schlumberger Austin Systems Center, Austin, Texas, 1987," *A + U: Architecture & Urbanism* 11 (November 1987): 31–38.

"Austin Systems Center: Research Center for Schlumberger Company, Joint Venture by Howard Barnstone and Robert Jackson," *Baumeister* 85 (April 1988): 50–57.

Joel Warren Barna, "High Tech Office Center Fits One of a Kind Site," *Texas Architect* 38 (November–December 1988): 36.

Peter Davey, "Texas Nature," *Architectural Review* 111 (September 1989): 67–70.

Michael Leccese, "Hill Country Headquarters: What Happens When a Texas Corporation Meets the Endangered Species Act? Austin's Schlumberger Systems Center Finds a Perfect Solution," *Landscape Architecture* 86 (April 1996): 56, 58–63.

[no job number]

AUSTIN CIVIC CENTER

Austin, Texas (not built)

1984, Howard Barnstone, FAIA

8501

ALTERATIONS AND ADDITION TO HOUSE OF DR. AND MRS. GEORGE EHNI

16 Sunset Boulevard, Houston, Texas

1986, Howard Barnstone, FAIA

8502
OFFICE INTERIOR OF RELIANCE TITLE CO.
Fannin Bank Building, Fannin Street at Holcombe Boulevard, Houston, Texas (demolished)
1985, Howard Barnstone, FAIA

8504
ALTERATIONS TO GEORGE HOUSE
River Oaks, Houston, Texas
1985, Howard Barnstone, FAIA

8505
DRAWINGS FOR COMPETITION TO EXTEND THE NATIONAL GALLERY
Pall Mall, London, England (not submitted)
1985, Howard Barnstone, FAIA

8509
MONTESSORI SCHOOL
West Bell Street, Houston, Texas
1985, Howard Barnstone, FAIA

8599
ARIZONA HISTORICAL SOCIETY MUSEUM
1300 North College Avenue, Tempe, Arizona
1985, Howard Barnstone, FAIA

8602
HOUSE FOR JAMES DUNAWAY
Fort Worth, Texas
1986, Howard Barnstone, FAIA

8605
HOUSE FOR OLIVE LIU
1986–1987, Howard Barnstone, FAIA

8799
LAW OFFICE INTERIOR FOR ROBERT C. RICHTER, JR.
12727 Featherwood Drive, Houston, Texas
1987, Howard Barnstone, FAIA

[no job number]
JEDAH HOUSE
1987, Howard Barnstone, FAIA

[no dates or job numbers]
ADDITION TO HERMAN BROWN LAKE HOUSE, LAKE AUSTIN, TEXAS

ALTERATIONS TO GEORGE CONSTRUCTION CO. OFFICE, HOUSTON, TEXAS

APARTMENTS FOR MARTI FRANCO, PUERTO VALLARTA, MEXICO

CARTER CHRISTIE HOUSE, AUSTIN, TEXAS

COOPERATIVE APARTMENTS, HOUSTON, TEXAS

HOUSE FOR MARTI FRANCO, PUERTA VALLARTA, JALISCO, MEXICO

LAREDO AUTOS S.A. DEALERSHIP, LAREDO, TEXAS

MARTI'S SAN ANTONIO

SEVEN-STORY OFFICE BUILDING

TOWNHOUSE

TOWNHOUSE FOR HOWARD BARNSTONE, HOUSTON, TEXAS

TWO-STORY OFFICE BUILDING

SELECTED BIBLIOGRAPHY

Adams, Celeste Marie, ed. *The Museum of Fine Arts, Houston: An Architectural History, 1924–1986*. Houston: Museum of Fine Arts, 1992.

Adams, Nicholas. *Skidmore, Owings & Merrill: SOM since 1936*. Milan: Electa Architecture, 2007.

Akcan, Esra. *Architecture in Translation: Germany, Turkey, and the Modern House*. Durham, NC: Duke University Press, 2012.

Allaud, Louis A., and Maurice H. Martin. *Schlumberger: The History of a Technique*. New York: Wiley, 1977.

Alofsin, Anthony. *The Struggle for Modernism: Architecture, Landscape Architecture, and City Planning at Harvard*. New York: Norton, 2002.

American Architects Directory. 3rd ed. New York: American institute of Architects and Bowker, 1970.

American Institute of Architects, Dallas Chapter. *The Prairie's Yield: Forces Shaping Dallas Architecture from 1840 to 1962*. New York: Reinhold, 1962.

Apple, Max. *Three Stories*. Dallas: Pressworks, 1983.

Aubry, Eugene. *Born on the Island: The Galveston We Remember*. College Station: Texas A&M University Press, 2012.

Auletta, Ken. *The Art of Corporate Success: The Story of Schlumberger*. New York: Putnam's Sons, 1984.

Banham, Reyner. *A Critic Writes: Essays by Reyner Banham*. Edited by Mary Banham, Paul Barker, Sutherland Lyall, and Cedric Price. Berkeley: University of California Press, 1996.

———. *Los Angeles: The Architecture of Four Ecologies*. Baltimore: Penguin, 1973.

Barna, Joel Warren. *The See-Through Years: Creation and Destruction in Texas Architecture and Real estate, 1981–1991*. Houston: Rice University Press, 1992.

Barnes, Susan J. *The Rothko Chapel: An Act of Faith*. Houston: Rothko Chapel, 1989.

Barnstone, Howard. *The Architecture of John F. Staub: Houston and the South*. Austin: University of Texas Press, 1979.

———. *The Galveston That Was*. New York and Houston: Macmillan and the Museum of Fine Arts, Houston, 1966.

Barnstone, Willis. *We Jews and Blacks: Memoir with Poems*. Bloomington: Indiana University Press, 2004.

Beasley, Ellen. *The Alleys and Back Buildings of Galveston: An Architectural and Social History*. College Station: Texas A&M University Press, 2007.

Beeth, Howard, and Cary D. Wintz, eds. *Black Dixie: Afro-Texan History and Culture in Houston*. College Station: Texas A&M University Press, 1992.

Benjamin, Susan, and Michelangelo Sabatino. *Modern in the Middle: Chicago Houses, 1929–1975*. New York: Monacelli, 2020.

Bernard, Richard M., and Bradley R. Rice, eds. *Sunbelt Cities: Politics and Growth Since World War II*. Austin: University of Texas Press, 1983.

Bernhard, Virginia. *Ima Hogg: The Governor's Daughter*. Austin: Texas Monthly Press, 1984.

Birmingham, Stephen. *Our Crowd: The Great Jewish Families of New York*. New York: Harper and Row, 1967.

Bjone, Christian. *Philip Johnson and His Mischief: Appropriation in Art and Architecture*. Victoria, Australia: Images, 2014.

Blaser, Werner. *Atrium: Five Thousand Years of Open Courtyards*. Basel: Wepf, 1985.

———. *Gene Summers: Art/Architecture*. Basel: Birkäuser, 2003.

———. *Mies van der Rohe: Continuing the Chicago School of Architecture*. Boston: Birkäuser Verlag, 1981.

———. *Myron Goldsmith: Buildings and Concepts*. New York: Rizzoli, 1987.

Boyce, Robert. *Keck & Keck: The Poetics of Comfort*. New York: Princeton Architectural Press, 1993.

Bradley, Barrie Scardino. *Improbable Metropolis: Houston's Architectural and Urban History*. Austin: University of Texas Press, 2020.

Brennan, Marcia. *Curating Consciousness: Mysticism and the Modern Museum*. Cambridge, MA: MIT Press, 2010.

Brutvan, Cheryl A. *In Our Time: Houston's Contemporary Arts Museum, 1948–1982*. With Marti Mayo and Linda L. Cathcart. Houston: Contemporary Arts Museum, 1982.

Canizaro, Vincent B. *Architecture Regionalism: Collected Writings on Place, Identity, Modernity, and Tradition*. New York: Princeton Architectural Press, 2007.

Cannady, William T. *Four Houses: Designs for Change*. Houston: Rice University School of Architecture, 2017.

Caragonne, Alexander. *The Texas Rangers: Notes from the Architectural Underground*. Cambridge, MA: MIT Press, 1995.

Carleton, Don E. *Red Scare! Right Wing Hysteria, Fifties Fanaticism, and Their Legacy in Texas*. Austin: Texas Monthly Press, 1985.

Caudill, William W. *Architecture by Team: A New Concept for the Practice of Architecture*. New York: Van Nostrand Reinhold, 1971.

Cole, Thomas R. *No Color Is My Kind: The Life of Eldrewey Stearns and the Integration of Houston*. Austin: University of Texas Press, 1997.

Coleman, Elizabeth Ann. *The Genius of Charles James*. New York: Brooklyn Museum and Holt, Rinehart and Winston, 1982.

Comazzi, John. *The Miller House and Gardens: A Biography of Modern Living*. New York: Princeton Architectural Press, 2018.

Cook, John W., and Heinrich Klotz. *Conversations with Architects*. New York: Praeger, 1973.

Cooke, Catherine. *The Russian Avant-Garde: Art and Architecture*. New York: St. Martins, 1984.

Danz, Ernst. *Architecture of Skidmore, Owings & Merrill, 1950–1962*. New York: Praeger, 1963.

Davis, Susan O'Connor. *Chicago's Historic Hyde Park*. Chicago: University of Chicago Press, 2013.

Dillon, David. *The Architecture of O'Neil Ford: Celebrating Place*. Austin: University of Texas Press, 1999.

Dobie, J. Frank. *The Mustangs*. New York: Little, Brown, 1952.

Duany, Andres, Elizabeth Plater-Zyberk, and Jeff Speck. *Suburban Nation: The Rise of Sprawl and the Decline of the American Dream*. New York: North Point, 2010.

Dulaney, H. G., and Edward Hake Phillips, eds. *Speak, Mister Speaker*. Bonham, TX: Sam Rayburn Foundation, 1978.

Eagleton, Terry. *After Theory*. London: Penguin, 2004.

Edwards, Katie Robinson. *Midcentury Modern Art in Texas*. Austin: University of Texas Press, 2014.

Fairbanks, Robert B., and Kathleen Underwood. *Essays on Sunbelt Cities and Recent Urban America*. College Station: Texas A&M University Press, 1989.

Fenberg, Steven. *Unprecedented Power: Jesse Jones, Capitalism, and the Common Good*. College Station: Texas A&M University Press, 2011.

Ferber, Edna. *A Kind of Magic*. Garden City, NY: Doubleday, 1963.

Ferguson, Cheryl Caldwell. *Highland Park and River Oaks: The Origins of Garden Suburban Community Planning in Texas*. Austin: University of Texas Press, 2014.

Ford, O'Neil. *O'Neil Ford on Architecture*. Edited by Katherine E. O'Rourke. Austin: University of Texas Press, 2019.

Fox, Stephen. *AIA Houston Architectural Guide*. Houston: AIA Houston, 2012.

———. *Braeswood: An Architectural History*. Houston: Old Braeswood Civic Club, 1988.

———. *The Country Houses of John F. Staub*. College Station: Texas A&M University Press, 2007.

Friedman, Alice T. *American Glamour and the Evolution of Modern Architecture*. New Haven, CT: Yale University Press, 2010.

Fuermann, George. *Houston: Land of the Big Rich*. Garden City, NY: Doubleday, 1951.

George, Mary Carolyn Holler. *O'Neil Ford: Architect*. College Station: Texas A&M University Press, 1992.

Germany, Lisa. *Harwell Hamilton Harris*. Austin: University of Texas Press, 1991.

Graham, Don. *Cowboys and Cadillacs: How Hollywood Looks at Texas*. Austin: Texas Monthly Press, 1983.

Graves, John. *Goodbye to a River*. New York: Knopf, 1960.

Gray Is the Color: An Exhibition of Grisaille Painting, XIIIth–XXth Centuries. Houston: Institute for the Arts, Rice University, 1974.

Hardwick, Susan Wiley. *Mythic Galveston: Reinventing America's Third Coast*. Baltimore, MD: Johns Hopkins University Press, 2002.

Helfenstein, Josef, and Laureen Schipsi. *Art and Activism: Projects of John and Dominique de Menil*. Houston: Menil Collection, 2010.

Hitchcock, Henry-Russell. *Philip Johnson Architecture, 1949–1965*. New York: Holt, Rinehart and Winston, 1966.

Holmes, Ann Hitchcock. *The Alley Theatre: Four Decades in Three Acts*. Houston: Alley Theatre, 1986.

Houston: Text by Houstonians. Marrero, LA: Hope Haven, 1949.

Howey, John. *The Sarasota School of Architecture: 1941–1966*. Cambridge, MA: MIT Press, 1995.

Hoyt, Vernita Bridges, ed. *Flashbacks: Images from the First Fifty Years of the College of Architecture, University of Houston, 1945–1995*. Houston: Atrium Press, 1995.

Hunting, Mary Anne. *Edward Durell Stone: Modernism's Populist Architect*. New York: Norton, 2013.

Isenstadt, Sandy. *The Modern American House: Spaciousness and the Middle-Class Identity*. Cambridge: Cambridge University Press, 2006.

Jackson, Kenneth T. *Crabgrass Frontier: The Suburbanization of the United States*. Oxford: Oxford University Press, 1985.

Jackson, Neil. *California Modern: The Architecture of Craig Ellwood*. New York: Princeton Architectural Press, 2002.

Jencks, Charles. *The Language of Post-Modern Architecture*. New York: Rizzoli, 1991.

Johnson, Philip. *Mies van der Rohe*. New York: Museum of Modern Art, 1947.

———. *Writings*. New York: Oxford University Press, 1979.

Jordy, William H. *American Buildings and Their Architects*, vol. 5: *The Impact of European Modernism in the Mid-Twentieth Century*. Oxford: Oxford University Press, 1972.

Kacmar, Donna. *Victor Lundy: Artist, Architect*. New York: Princeton Architectural Press, 2018.

Kamps, Toby, and Meredith Goldsmith, eds. *No Zoning: Artists Engage Houston*. Houston: Contemporary Arts Museum, 2009.

Kiesler, Frederick. *Inside the Endless House: Art, People, and Architecture; A Journal*. New York: Simon and Schuster, 1966.

———. *Selected Writings*. Edited by Siegfried Gohr and Gunda Luyken. Ostfildern, Germany: Verlag Gerd Hatje, 1996.

King, Jonathan, and Philip Langdon, eds. *The CRS Team and the Business of Architecture*. College Station: Texas A&M University Press, 2002.

Kingsley, Karen, and Guy W. Carwile. *The Modernist Architecture of Samuel G. and William B. Wiener: Shreveport, Louisiana, 1920–1960*. Baton Rouge: Louisiana State University Press, 2016.

Kirkland, Kate Sayen. *The Hogg Family and Houston: Philanthropy and the Civic Ideal*. Austin: University of Texas Press, 2009.

Koush, Ben. *Booming Houston and the Modern House: Residential Architecture of Neuhaus & Taylor*. Houston: Houston Mod, 2006.

———. *Constructing Houston's Future: The Architecture of Arthur Evans Jones and Lloyd Morgan Jones*. Houston: Houston Mod, 2017.

———. *Donald Barthelme: A Modernism Suitable for Everyday Use, 1939–1945*. Houston: Houston Mod, 2005.

———. *Hugo V. Neuhaus, Jr.: Residential Architecture, 1948–1966*. Houston: Houston Mod, 2007.

Kripal, Jeffrey J. *Secret Body: Erotic and Esoteric Currents in the History of Religions*. Chicago: University of Chicago Press, 2017.

Lambert, Phyllis, ed. *Mies in America*. New York: Abrams, 2001.

Lange, Christiane. *Ludwig Mies van der Rohe: Architecture for the Silk Industry*. Berlin: Nicolai, 2011.

Lerup, Lars. *One Million Acres and No Zoning*. London: Architectural Association, 2011.

Maas, Elaine. *The Jews of Houston: An Ethnographic Study*. New York: AMS, 1989.

Martin, Guy. *Lake|Flato Houses: Embracing the Landscape*. Austin: University of Texas Press, 2014.

McCarthy, Muriel Quest. *David R. Williams: Pioneer Architect*. Dallas: Southern Methodist University Press, 1984.

McComb, David G. *Houston: The Bayou City*. Austin: University of Texas Press, 1969.

McCoy, Esther. *Modern California Houses: Case Study Houses, 1945–1962*. New York: Reinhold, 1962.

McMurtry, Larry. *Horseman, Pass By*. New York: Harper, 1961.

Melosi, Martin V., and Joseph A. Pratt, eds. *Energy Metropolis: An Environmental History of Houston and the Gulf Coast*. Pittsburgh: University of Pittsburgh Press, 2007.

Middleton, William. *Double Vision: The Unerring Eye of Art World Avatars Dominique and John de Menil*. New York: Knopf, 2018.

Miller, Char, ed. *Cities and Nature in the American West*. Reno: University of Nevada Press, 2010.

Moser, Benjamin. *Why This World: A Biography of Clarice Lispector*. New York: Oxford University Press, 2009.

Mumford, Lewis. *The South in Architecture: The Dancy Lectures, Alabama College*. New York: Harcourt, Brace, 1941.

Neumeyer, Fritz. *The Artless Word: Mies van der Rohe on the Building Art*. Cambridge, MA: MIT Press, 1991.

Nodelman, Sheldon. *The Rothko Chapel Paintings: Origins, Structure, Meanings*. Austin: University of Texas Press, 1997.

Payne, Richard. *The Architecture of Philip Johnson*. Boston: Bulfinch, 2002.

Penick, Monica. *Tastemaker: Elizabeth Gordon, "House Beautiful," and the Postwar American Home*. New Haven, CT: Yale University Press, 2017.

Perloff, Nancy Lynn, and Brian Reed, eds. *Situating El Lissitzky: Vitebsk, Berlin, Moscow*. Los Angeles: Getty Research Institute, 2003.

Petit, Emmanuel, ed. *Philip Johnson: The Constancy of Change*. New Haven, CT: Yale University Press, 2009.

Podhoretz, Norman. *Making It*. New York: Random House, 1967.

Polyzoides, Stefanos, Roger Sherwood, and James Tice. *Courtyard Housing in Los Angeles: A Typological Analysis*. New York: Princeton Architectural Press, 1992.

Pratt, Joseph A. *Growth of a Refining Region*. Greenwich, CT: JAI Press, 1980.

Reed, Christopher, ed. *Not at Home: The Suppression of Domesticity in Modern Art and Architecture*. New York: Thames and Hudson, 1996.

Richards, J. M. *New Buildings in the Commonwealth*. New York: Praeger, 1962.

Riley, Terence, and Barry Bergdoll, eds. *Mies in Berlin*. New York: Museum of Modern Art, 2001.

Rosales, Francisco A., and Barry J. Kaplan, eds. *Houston: A Twentieth-Century Urban Frontier*. Port Washington, NY: Associated Faculty Press, 1983.

Rothman, Hal. *LBJ's Texas White House: "Our Heart's Home."* College Station: Texas A&M University Press, 2001.

Rowe, Colin. *The Mathematics of the Ideal Villa, and Other Essays*. Cambridge, MA: MIT Press, 1977.

Rudofsky, Bernard. *Architecture without Architects*. New York: Museum of Modern Art, 1964.

Rudolph, Paul. *Writings on Architecture*. New Haven, CT: Yale School of Architecture, 2008.

Scardino, Barrie, William F. Stern, and Bruce Webb, eds. *Ephemeral City: Cite Looks at Houston*. Austin: University of Texas Press, 2003.

Scardino, Barrie, and Drexel Turner. *Clayton's Galveston: The Architecture of Nicholas J. Clayton and His Contemporaries*. College Station: Texas A&M University Press, 2000.

Seal, Mark, William Middleton, Lisa Gray, and Hilary Lewis, eds. *Hines: A Legacy of Quality in the Built Environment*. Bainbridge Island, WA: Fenwick, 2007.

Slotboom, Erik. *Houston Freeways: A History and Visual Journey*. Houston: Slotboom, 2003.

Smart, Pamela. *Sacred Modern: Faith, Activism, and Aesthetics in the Menil Collection*. Austin: University of Texas Press, 2010.

Smith, C. Ray. *Supermannerism: New Attitudes in Post-Modern Architecture*. New York: Dutton, 1977.

Smith, Elizabeth A. T., ed. *Blueprints for Modern Living: History and Legacy of the Case Study Houses*. Cambridge, MA: MIT Press, 1989.

Smith, Jason A. *High Style in the Suburbs: The Early Modern Houses of William R. Jenkins, 1951–1958*. Houston: Houston Mod, 2009.

Sonzogni, Valentina, and Heinz Krjci, eds. *Friedrich Kiesler: Endless House*. Ostfildern-Ruit, Germany: Verlag Gerd Hatje, 2003.

Speyer, A. James. *Mies van der Rohe*. Chicago: Art Institute of Chicago, 1968.

Stern, Robert A. M., Peggy Deamer, and Alan Plattus, eds. *Re-reading "Perspecta": The First Fifty Years of the Yale Architectural Journal*. Cambridge, MA: MIT Press, 2004.

Stern, Robert A. M., Gregory Gilmartin, and John Massengale. *New York 1900: Metropolitan Architecture and Urbanism, 1890–1915*. New York: Rizzoli, 1983.

Stern, Robert A. M., Thomas Mellins, and David Fishman. *New York 1960: Architecture and Urbanism between the Second World War and the Bicentennial*. New York: Monacelli, 1995.

Stern, Robert A. M., and Jimmy Stamp. *Pedagogy and Place: 100 Years of Architecture Education at Yale*. New Haven, CT: Yale University Press, 2016.

Stone, Bryan Edward. *The Chosen Folks: Jews on the Frontiers of Texas*. Austin: University of Texas Press, 2010.

Summerson, John. *The Classical Language of Architecture*. Cambridge, MA: MIT Press, 1963.

Tegethoff, Wolf. *Mies van der Rohe: The Villas and Country Houses*. New York: Museum of Modern Art, 1985.

Ten Years of Houston Architecture. Houston: Contemporary Arts Museum, 1959. Exhibition catalogue.

Tupitsyn, Margarita. *El Lissitzky: Beyond the Abstract Cabinet; Photography, Design, Collaboration*. New Haven, CT: Yale, 1999.

Turner, Drexel. *Open Plan: The History of the College of Architecture, University of Houston, 1945–1995*. Houston: Atrium Press, 1995.

Vinci, John, ed. *A. James Speyer: Architect, Curator, Exhibition Designer*. Chicago: University of Chicago Press, 1997. Exhibition catalogue.

Welch, Frank D. *On Becoming an Architect*. Fort Worth: Texas Christian University Press, 2015.

———. *Philip Johnson and Texas*. Austin: University of Texas Press, 2000.

Wells, Christopher. *Car Country: An Environmental History*. Seattle: University of Washington Press, 2014.

Whitney, David, and Jeffrey Kipnis, eds. *Philip Johnson: The Glass House*. New York: Pantheon, 1993.

Wiegman, John. *His Story: A Personal History of Morris Architects*. Houston: privately printed, 2001.

Witte, Ron, ed. *Counting: In Honor of Anderson Todd's 90th Birthday*. Houston: School of Architecture, Rice University, 2011.

Zemanek, John. *Being . . . Becoming: An Acorn Becomes an Oak*. Privately printed, 2016.

CONTRIBUTORS

DEBORAH ASCHER BARNSTONE, the niece-in-law of Howard Barnstone, is professor of architecture at the University of Technology Sydney. Barnstone's primary research interests are in exploring the origins of classical modernism and the relationships between art, architecture, and, more broadly, culture. Recent publications include the books *The Break with the Past: German Avant-garde Architecture, 1910–1925* (Routledge, 2018) and *Beyond the Bauhaus: Cultural Modernity in Weimar Breslau, 1918–1933* (University of Michigan Press, 2016), and articles in the *Journal of Architecture*, the *Journal of Design History*, and *New German Critique*. She coauthored, with Elizabeth Otto, *Art and Resistance in Germany* (Bloomsbury, 2018), which looks at how artists resisted political oppression in Germany during the last one hundred years.

ROBERT V. BARNSTONE, the nephew of Howard Barnstone, is an award-winning architect and sculptor. He graduated from Bennington College with a BA in architecture and sculpture (1984) and received his MArch from the Graduate School of Design, Harvard University (1991). He has published articles on architecture in the *Journal of Architectural Education*, *Wood Design Focus*, *OnSite*, and *A.D.: Architectural Design*. Barnstone, who has taught architecture at universities around the world, is currently at the University of New South Wales, Sydney. Barnstone's scholarly research looks at architectural applications of wood and plastic extrusions, cardboard for emergency housing, phosphate and pozzolanic cements, and thermal chromic coatings.

BARRIE SCARDINO BRADLEY has written and lectured about Houston history and Texas architecture for more than thirty-five years. She is a graduate of Duke University (BA, English) and the University of Southern California (MS, library science), and she attended the Graduate School of Architecture and Urban Planning at UCLA. Her most recent publications are *Improbable Metropolis: Houston's Architectural and Urban History* (University of Texas Press, 2020), *Fair Winds: The History of Kirby Corporation* (Herring Press, 2017), and *Houston's Hermann Park: A Century of Community* (Texas A&M University Press, 2014). She is a past editor of *Cite: The Architecture and Design Review of Houston*. In addition, she worked as a research associate in the Rice University School of Architecture, as the executive director of the Houston Chapter of the American Institute of Architects, and as the architectural archivist of the Houston Metropolitan Research Center of the Houston Public Library.

STEPHEN FOX is an architectural historian and a fellow of the Anchorage Foundation of Texas.

JOSHUA J. FURMAN is the inaugural director of the Houston Jewish History Archive at Rice University. He received his PhD in modern Jewish history from the University of Maryland in 2015. His published works include "Across the Ocean and across Town: Migration and Mobility in American Jewish History," a chapter in the edited volume *Interpreting American Jewish History at Museums and Historic Sites* (Rowman and Littlefield, 2016). Currently, Furman is at work on a book about the history of Houston's Jewish community.

OLIVE HERSHEY, a native Houstonian, is a Texas writer, poet, and novelist. She attended Connecticut College and received a BA (1968), an MA (1970), and a PhD (1978) from the University of Texas at Austin. Hershey also earned an MA (1987) from the University of Houston's Creative Writing Program, where she studied under the American postmodern novelist Donald Barthelme Jr. She has published *Floating Face Up* (1984), a book of poetry, and *Truck Dance: A Novel* (HarperCollins, 1989). Hershey is currently working on a biography of the actress and artist Gertrude Barnstone, who was married to Howard Barnstone from 1955 to 1969.

KATHRYN E. HOLLIDAY is an architectural historian whose research and teaching focuses on the built environment in American cities. Her background is in architecture, art history, and environmental studies. She is the author of *Leopold Eidlitz: Architecture and Idealism in the Gilded Age* (Norton, 2008) and *Ralph Walker:*

Architecture of the Century (Rizzoli, 2012); both explore changing conceptions of modern architecture in the American city. As founding director of the David Dillon Center for Texas Architecture, she has helped create new venues for public discussion of design and urbanism in Dallas–Fort Worth, and she recently edited the collection *The Open-Ended City: David Dillon on Texas Architecture* (University of Texas Press, 2019). She is currently at work on a book investigating the often-mysterious telephone buildings built by the thousands by the Bell Telephone monopoly during the twentieth century.

CARLOS JIMÉNEZ teaches undergraduate and graduate studios and a seminar on architecture, film, literature, and music case studies. He began his teaching career at Rice as a visiting critic in 1987 and has been a full-time faculty member since 1997. Jiménez graduated with honors from the University of Houston College of Architecture (1981). He established his architectural practice, Carlos Jiménez Studio, in Houston in 1983. Its work has been exhibited nationally and internationally. He frequently lectures, serves as a juror, and teaches as a visiting critic at universities and cultural institutions in the United States and internationally. He served as a jury member of the Pritzker Architecture Prize, 2001–2011.

THEODORE H. M. PRUDON, a native of the Netherlands, is a practicing architect and preservationist. He received his education in the United States (MS Arch and PhD, Columbia University) and the Netherlands (MS ArchEng, University of Delft). He is a Fellow of the American Institute of Architects and the Association of Preservation Technology International. He has been on the faculty of the Graduate Programs in Historic Preservation at Columbia University and the Pratt Institute for over thirty years. He is the author of *Preservation of Modern Architecture* (Wiley, 2008), which received the Lee Nelson Book Award from the Association for Preservation Technology. He is currently the president of Docomomo US and serves on the Advisory Board of Docomomo International, based in Lisbon, Portugal. In 2016 he was awarded the architecture prize by the American Academy of Arts and Letters.

MICHELANGELO SABATINO trained as an architect, preservationist, and historian whose research broadly addresses intersections between culture, technology, and design in the built and natural environments. From 2017 to 2019 he served as dean of the College of Architecture of the Illinois Institute of Technology, where he held the Rowe Family College of Architecture Endowed Dean Chair and was the inaugural John Vinci Distinguished Research Fellow. His monograph *Pride* *in Modesty: Modernist Architecture and the Vernacular Tradition in Italy* (University of Toronto Press, 2011) received multiple awards, including the Society of Architectural Historians' Alice Davis Hitchcock Award. He recently coauthored, with Rhodri Windsor Liscombe, *Canada: Modern Architectures in History* (Reaktion, 2016) and coedited, with Ben Nicholson, *Avant-Garde in the Cornfields: Architecture, Landscape, and Preservation in New Harmony* (University of Minnesota Press, 2019).

BRUCE C. WEBB is an emeritus professor in the Gerald D. Hines College of Architecture and Design at the University of Houston, where he formerly served as dean. He has written and lectured extensively on Houston and its unique culture and urban form. He received degrees from Montana State University (BArch, 1970) and Virginia Polytechnic and State University (MArch, 1972). He served on the editorial board of *Cite: The Architecture and Design Review of Houston*, and as a board member and design editor of the *Journal of Architectural Education*. He cofounded the Center for the Advancement of Studies in Architecture (CASA), a joint venture between Texas A&M University and the University of Houston, and coedited titles in the CASA publication series, including *The Culture of Silence: Architecture's Fifth Dimension* (1997), *Urban Form, Suburban Dreams* (1993), and *Constancy and Change in Architecture* (1991). He also coedited, with Barrie Scardino Bradley and William F. Stern, *Ephemeral City: Cite Looks at Houston* (University of Texas Press, 2003).

IMAGE CREDITS

p. 5 Photograph by Henri Cartier-Bresson. Courtesy Magnum Photos.

p. 7 Photograph by Paul Hester. Courtesy Hester + Hardaway.

p. 9 Photograph by Jack F. Laws. From *Cite* 7 (Fall 1984). Courtesy private collection.

p. 10 (*left*) Photograph by R. M. Luster. From *River Oaks: A Pictorial Presentation of Houston's Residential Park* (1929). Courtesy Houston Metropolitan Research Center, Houston Public Library.

p. 10 (*right*) Courtesy Houston Metropolitan Research Center, Houston Public Library.

p. 11 Photograph by Tom Colburn. Courtesy Houston Metropolitan Research Center, Houston Public Library 178–202.

p. 12 From Insulux advertisement, *Architectural Record* (April 1938): 149.

p. 13 Courtesy Ben Koush.

p. 14 Photograph by Ulrich Meisel, 1948. Courtesy University of Houston Libraries, Special Collections, Donald Barthelme, Sr., Architectural Drawings and Photographs.

p. 15 Photograph by Paul Hester. Courtesy Hester + Hardaway.

p. 17 Courtesy MacKie & Kamrath Collection, Houston Metropolitan Research Center, Houston Public Library (MSS 422-J1115K2133).

p. 18 Photograph by Eve Arnold. Courtesy Magnum Photos.

p. 19 Photograph by Eve Arnold. Courtesy Magnum Photos.

p. 23 Photograph by Ezra Stoller. Courtesy Texas A&M University Press and the Museum of Fine Arts, Houston.

p. 25 Photograph by Rob Muir. Courtesy University of Texas Press and the Museum of Fine Arts, Houston.

p. 26 Photograph by Paul Hester. Courtesy Hester + Hardaway.

p. 27 Courtesy Rafael Longoria, photographer.

p. 28 Courtesy Benjamin Hill, photographer.

p. 41 From *Texas Architect* (April 1960). Courtesy Texas Society of Architects.

p. 42 Photograph by Myron Wood, 1960. From Jonathan King and Philip Langdon, eds., *The CRS Team and the Business of Architecture*, 49.

p. 43 Photograph by Fred Winchell. From the cover of *Architectural Record* (mid-May 1956).

p. 44 Courtesy Howard Barnstone Collection, Houston Metropolitan Research Center, Houston Public Library (MSS 178-5593-PRE-001).

p. 45 Photograph by Paul Hester. Courtesy Hester + Hardaway.

p. 46 (*top*) Photograph by Fred Winchell. Courtesy private collection.

p. 46 (*bottom*) Courtesy Eames Foundation.

p. 47 From *Zodiac: The International Magazine of Contemporary Architecture* 13 (1964).

p. 48 Photograph by Richard Payne. Courtesy Payne & Ladner.

p. 49   Courtesy George Barnstone.

p. 50 (*left*)   Photograph by Anderson Todd. Courtesy Woodson Research Center, Fondren Library, Rice University.

p. 50 (*right*)   From *Arts and Architecture* (December 1957): 23. Courtesy © Travers Family Trust. Used with permission.

p. 51   Photograph by Fred Winchell. From *Arts and Architecture* 72 (March 1955): 28–29. Courtesy © Travers Family Trust. Used with permission.

p. 52   From Bethlehem Steel advertisement; publication unknown.

p. 54   Courtesy Howard Barnstone Collection, Houston Metropolitan Research Center, Houston Public Library (MSS 178-1499-A4).

p. 55 (*top*)   Photograph by Paul Hester. Courtesy Hester + Hardaway.

p. 55 (*bottom*)   Photograph by Frank Lotz Miller. From *Architectural Record* (mid-May 1965): 68.

p. 57   Photograph by Frank Lotz Miller. Courtesy Howard Barnstone Collection, Houston Metropolitan Research Center, Houston Public Library (MSS 178-203).

p. 68   Photograph by Ezra Stoller. Courtesy Esto.

p. 68   Photograph by Ezra Stoller. Courtesy Esto.

p. 69   Photograph by Hedrich-Blessing Architectural Photography. Courtesy Chicago History Museum.

p. 70   Photograph by Hedrich-Blessing Architectural Photography. Courtesy Chicago History Museum.

p. 73   Courtesy private collection.

p. 74   Courtesy private collection.

p. 74   Courtesy private collection.

p. 75   Photograph by Paul Hester. Courtesy Hester + Hardaway.

p. 76   From *Zodiac: International Magazine of Contemporary Architecture* 13 (1964): 187.

p. 77   Photograph by Maurice Miller. From *Arts and Architecture* (October 1965): 12. Courtesy © Travers Family Trust. Used with permission.

p. 78   Courtesy private collection.

p. 79   Photograph by Ronny Jaques. From *Town & Country Magazine*, September 1957, 94.

p. 81 (*top*)   Photograph by Paul Hester. Courtesy Hester + Hardaway.

p. 81 (*bottom*)   Photograph by Douglas Jones. From *Look* (September 21, 1965): 68–71. From Library of Congress, *Look* Magazine Photograph Collection.

p. 83   Courtesy Museum of Modern Art.

p. 84   Photograph by William Leftwich. Courtesy Museum of Modern Art.

p. 86   Courtesy Benjamin Hill, photographer.

p. 87   Courtesy Benjamin Hill, photographer.

p. 89 (*top*)   Photograph by Maurice Miller. Courtesy private collection.

p. 89 (*bottom*)   Photograph by Frank Lotz Miller. Courtesy private collection.

p. 90   Photograph by Alexandre Georges. Courtesy private collection.

p. 100   Courtesy Warner Bros. Pictures.

p. 101   From Texas Instruments advertisement. *Fortune* magazine, 1957. Courtesy Texas Instruments.

pp. 102–103   From American Institute of Architects, Dallas Chapter, *The Prairie's Yield: Forces Shaping Dallas Architecture from 1840–1962*, 6–7. Courtesy AIA Dallas.

p. 104   Courtesy Texas Society of Architects.

p. 105   From James Pratt Papers, Dallas Public Library.

p. 106   From Howard Barnstone, *The Galveston That Was*. Photograph by Ezra Stoller. Courtesy Esto.

p. 107   From Howard Barnstone, *The Galveston That Was*. Photograph by Henri Cartier-Bresson, 1962. Courtesy Magnum Photos.

p. 108   From Howard Barnstone, *The Galveston That Was*. Photograph by Ezra Stoller, 1965. Courtesy Esto.

p. 109 (*top*)   Courtesy Ben Koush, photographer.

p. 109 (*bottom*)   Photograph by Paul Hester. Courtesy Hester + Hardaway.

p. 110   Photograph by M. P. N. Texan. Creative Commons.

p. 112   © San Antonio Express-News/ZUMA Press. Courtesy Special Collections, University of Texas, Arlington.

p. 112   © San Antonio Express-News/ZUMA Press. Courtesy Special Collections, University of Texas, Arlington.

p. 114   From the Bell System Promotion Kit: HemisFair '68, San Antonio, Texas, April 6 to October 6, 1968. Courtesy AT&T Archives and History Center, San Antonio.

p. 115   From *Progressive Architecture* (February 1953). Courtesy Progressive Architecture.

p. 123   Courtesy Menil Archives, Menil Collection.

p. 126   Courtesy Benjamin Hill, photographer.

p. 127   Photograph by Paul Hester. Courtesy Hester + Hardaway.

p. 128   Courtesy Howard Barnstone Collection, Houston Metropolitan Research Center, Houston Public Library (MSS 178-draw).

p. 130   Courtesy Howard Barnstone Collection, Houston Metropolitan Research Center, Houston Public Library (MSS 178-3306).

p. 131   From *Arts & Architecture* (April 1957). Courtesy © Travers Family Trust. Used with permission.

p. 134   Courtesy Howard Barnstone Collection, Houston Metropolitan Research Center, Houston Public Library (MSS 178-3006-draw01).

p. 135   Courtesy Howard Barnstone Collection, Houston Metropolitan Research Center, Houston Public Library (MSS 178, box 23-5).

p. 136   From *Progressive Architecture* (August 1966): 162.

p. 137   From *Progressive Architecture* (August 1966): 162.

p. 139   Courtesy Howard Barnstone Collection Houston Metropolitan Research Center, Houston Public Library (MSS 178-3018-A1).

p. 140   Courtesy Howard Barnstone Collection, Houston Metropolitan Research Center, Houston Public Library (MSS 178-804r).

p. 141   Courtesy Benjamin Hill, photographer.

p. 145 (*top*)   Courtesy Howard Barnstone Collection Houston Metropolitan Research Center, Houston Public Library (MSS 178-0870r).

p. 145 (*bottom*)   Courtesy Howard Barnstone Collection, Houston Metropolitan Research Center, Houston Public Library (MSS 178-29333-draw01).

p. 147   Photographs by Bill Marks. From Mark Hewitt, "Barnstone's Benchmarks," *Ultra* (February 1965). Courtesy Howard Barnstone Collection, Houston Metropolitan Research Center, Houston Public Library.

p. 148   Courtesy David Crossley, photographer.

p. 151   Photograph by Paul Hester. Courtesy Hester + Hardaway.

p. 153   Photograph by Hickey-Robertson. Courtesy Menil Archives, Menil Collection.

p. 154 (*top*)   Courtesy Menil Archives, Menil Collection.

p. 154 (*bottom*)   Courtesy Benjamin Hill, photographer.

p. 155   Courtesy Howard Barnstone Collection, Houston Metropolitan Research Center, Houston Public Library (MSS 178-b42f03).

p. 156   Courtesy Howard Barnstone Collection, Houston Metropolitan Research Center, Houston Public Library (MSS 178-5869-SKE-001).

p. 157   Courtesy Howard Barnstone Collection, Houston Metropolitan Research Center, Houston Public Library (MSS 178-2949-draw01).

p. 159   From Docomomo-USA website. Courtesy Michael Biondo, photographer.

p. 160 (*top*)   Courtesy Thomas Quick Kimball.

p. 160 (*middle*)   Courtesy Howard Barnstone Collection, Houston Metropolitan Research Center, Houston Public Library (MSS 178, box 62-5).

p. 160 (*bottom*)   Courtesy Thomas Quick Kimball.

p. 162   From J. Robert Anderson, FASLA, website.

p. 163   Courtesy Howard Barnstone Collection, Houston Metropolitan Research Center, Houston Public Library (MSS 178-5620-draw01).

p. 178   Courtesy Benjamin Hill, photographer.

p. 179   Courtesy Aliki Barnstone.

p. 181   Courtesy Robert Barnstone.

pp. 182–183   Courtesy Howard Barnstone Collection, Houston Metropolitan Research Center, Houston Public Library (MSS 178-3086-REN-001).

p. 184   Courtesy Robert Barnstone.

p. 185 (*top*)   Courtesy Howard Barnstone Collection, Houston Metropolitan Research Center, Houston Public Library (MSS 178-5622-3).

p. 185 (*bottom*)   Courtesy Howard Barnstone Collection, Houston Metropolitan Research Center, Houston Public Library (MSS 178-5622-8).

p. 187   Courtesy Howard Barnstone Collection, Houston Metropolitan Research Center, Houston Public Library (MSS 178-5683-SKE-006).

p. 189 (*top*)   Courtesy Howard Barnstone Collection, Houston Metropolitan Research Center, Houston Public Library (MSS 178-2973-PRE-003).

p. 189 (*bottom*)   Courtesy Howard Barnstone Collection, Houston Metropolitan Research Center, Houston Public Library (MSS 178-2973-PRE-001).

p. 191 (*top*)   Courtesy Howard Barnstone Collection, Houston Metropolitan Research Center, Houston Public Library (SS 178-2973-REN-003).

p. 191 (*bottom*)   Courtesy Howard Barnstone Collection, Houston Metropolitan Research Center, Houston Public Library (MSS 178-2973-REN-001).

p. 192   Courtesy Robert Barnstone.

p. 193 (*left*)   Courtesy Howard Barnstone Collection, Houston Metropolitan Research Center, Houston Public Library (MSS 178-396).

p. 193 (*right*)   Courtesy Robert Barnstone.

p. 194   Courtesy Howard Barnstone Collection, Houston Metropolitan Research Center, Houston Public Library (MSS 178-3146-REN-01).

p. 195 (*top*)   Courtesy Howard Barnstone Collection, Houston Metropolitan Research Center, Houston Public Library (MSS 178-5842-2a).

p. 195 (*bottom*)   Courtesy Benjamin Hill, photographer.

p. 196   Photograph by Paul Hester. Courtesy Hester + Hardaway.

p. 197   Photograph by Paul Hester. Courtesy Hester + Hardaway.

p. 201   Created by Minor Design Group. Courtesy Craig Minor.

p. 203   From *Architectural Record* 116 (October 1954): 170.

p. 204   Photograph by Paul Hester. Courtesy Hester + Hardaway.

pp. 206-207   Courtesy Benjamin Hill, photographer.

p. 207 (*right*)   From the cover of *House & Garden* 113 (January 1958). Photograph by Ulric Meisel.

p. 209 (*left*)   From "Design Expressing Dignity," *Architectural Record* 121 (May 1957): 166. Photograph by Maurice Miller. Courtesy Lois Farfel Stark and Gail Farfel Adler.

p. 209 (*right*)   From Charlotte Millis, "Home Here Wins Design Laurel," *Houston Chronicle*, October 24, 1957. Courtesy Lois Farfel Stark and Gail Farfel Adler.

p. 210 (*top*)   Photography by Paul Hester. Courtesy Hester + Hardaway.

p. 210 (*bottom*)   From "Design Expressing Dignity," *Architectural Record* 121 (May 1957): 166.

p. 211 (*top left*)   From *House & Home* (September 1955): 142. Burdette Keeland Architectural Papers, Special Collections, University of Houston Libraries. Courtesy Keeland family.

p. 211 (*top right*)   From *House & Home* (September 1955): 143. Burdette Keeland Architectural Papers, Special Collections, University of Houston Libraries. Courtesy Keeland family.

p. 211 (*bottom*)   Photograph by Ewing Galloway. From Alamy.

p. 213   From *Zodiac: The International Magazine of Contemporary Architecture* 13 (1964): 190.

p. 213   From *Zodiac: The International Magazine of Contemporary Architecture* 13 (1964): 190.

p. 214 (*left*)   From *Zodiac: The International Magazine of Contemporary Architecture* 13 (1964): 190.

p. 214 (*right*)   Photograph by Paul Hester. Courtesy Hester + Hardaway.

p. 215   Photographs by Paul Hester. Courtesy Hester – Hardaway.

p. 223 (*left*)   Courtesy Aliki Barnstone.

p. 223 (*middle*)   Photograph by Brian Bartlett. From Google Earth.

p. 223 (*right*)   Courtesy Lily Barnstone Wells.

p. 224 (*left*)   Courtesy Howard Barnstone Collection, Houston Metropolitan Research Center, Houston Public Library (MSS 178, box 98:27).

p. 224 (*right*)   Courtesy Lily Barnstone Wells.

p. 225 (*top*)   From "Yale Students Have Plans for Westport, Conn.," *New York Herald Tribune*, May 8, 1947. Reprinted in Robert A. M. Stern and Jimmy Stamp, *Pedagogy and Place: 100 Years of Architecture Education at Yale*, 152. Photograph by Ted Kell.

p. 225 (*bottom*)   Courtesy Lily Barnstone Wells.

p. 227   Photograph by Inge Morath. Courtesy Lily Barnstone Wells.

p. 231   From Wendy Haskell Meyer, "Provincial Living," *Houston Home and Garden*, 5 (February 1979): 90–95. Courtesy Rob Muir, photographer.

p. 231   From Wendy Haskell Meyer, "Provincial Living," *Houston Home and Garden*, 5 (February 1979): 90–95. Courtesy Rob Muir, photographer.

p. 233   Courtesy Howard Barnstone Collection, Houston Metropolitan Research Center, Houston Public Library (MSS 178-48).

p. 244   Courtesy University of Houston.

p. 245   From Vernita Bridges Hoyt, ed., *Flashbacks: Images from the First Fifty Years of The College of Architecture, University of Houston, 1945–1995*. Courtesy Atrium Press, Gerald D. Hines College of Architecture and Design, University of Houston.

p. 246   Photograph by Paul Hester. Courtesy Hester + Hardaway.

p. 247   Courtesy Howard Barnstone Collection, Houston Metropolitan Research Center, Houston Public Library (MSS 178-47).

p. 248   From Vernita Bridges Hoyt, ed., *Flashbacks: Images from the First Fifty Years of The College of Architecture, University of Houston, 1945–1995*. Courtesy Atrium Press, Gerald D. Hines College of Architecture and Design, University of Houston.

p. 249   From Vernita Bridges Hoyt, ed., *Flashbacks: Images from the First Fifty Years of The College of Architecture, University of Houston, 1945–1995*. Courtesy Atrium Press, Gerald D. Hines College of Architecture and Design, University of Houston.

p. 252 From Vernita Bridges Hoyt, ed., *Flashbacks: Images from the First Fifty Years of The College of Architecture, University of Houston, 1945–1995*. Courtesy Atrium Press, Gerald D. Hines College of Architecture and Design, University of Houston.

p. 252 From Vernita Bridges Hoyt, ed., *Flashbacks: Images from the First Fifty Years of The College of Architecture, University of Houston, 1945–1995*. Courtesy Atrium Press, Gerald D. Hines College of Architecture and Design, University of Houston.

p. 254 Courtesy Chip Lord.

p. 258 From "Pedagogy and Place" research files. Courtesy Atrium Press, Gerald D. Hines College of Architecture and Design, University of Houston.

p. 259 Courtesy Howard Barnstone Collection, Houston Metropolitan Research Center, Houston Public Library (MSS 178-75).

p. 260 From "Pedagogy and Place" research files. Courtesy Atrium Press, Gerald D. Hines College of Architecture and Design, University of Houston.

p. 261 From Burdette Keeland Architectural Papers, Special Collections, University of Houston Library (33:1). Courtesy Keeland family.

p. 267 Photograph by Myron Anderson. Courtesy Dean Patricia Oliver, Gerald D. Hines College of Architecture and Design, University of Houston.

p. 268 Photograph by F. Wilbur Seiders. Courtesy private collection.

p. 269 (*left*) Courtesy Gertrude Barnstone.

p. 269 (*right*) Courtesy Houston Metropolitan Research Center, Houston Public Library (RGD6N-5981).

p. 273 Photograph by Andy Warhol. Courtesy Menil Archives, Menil Collection.

p. 274 Courtesy Gertrude Barnstone.

p. 276 Courtesy Gertrude Barnstone.

p. 278 Photograph by Douglas Jones. From *Look* (September 21, 1965): 71. Library of Congress, *Look* Magazine Collection.

p. 279 (*left*) Photograph by Douglas Jones. From *Look* (September 21, 1965): 71. Library of Congress, *Look* Magazine Collection.

p. 279 (*right*) Courtesy George Barnstone.

p. 280 Courtesy Gertrude Barnstone.

p. 281 Courtesy Gertrude Barnstone.

p. 287 Courtesy Gertrude Barnstone.

INDEX

NOTE: Page numbers in italics indicate illustrations. For buildings, no location indicates that the site of the structure is either Houston, Texas, or unknown.

3D/International, 41
811 Lovett Boulevard, 45, 49, *49*, 267, 301, 306, 311, 317
1215 Banks Apartments, 355
5000 Longmont Townhouses, 325–326

Aalto, Alvar, 176
Ackermann, Vale Ashe and Mike, 278
Ackerman House (Marion S. III), alterations, 337
Acme Warehouse Company Building, 316
Adams, Ann, 284
Adler House (Louis), addition, 351
African American settlement in Houston, 5, 202
Afton Oaks subdivision, 141
AIA Houston, 165n1, 226; design awards, 205, 215, 310–311
AIA Journal, 230
Akco Builders Townhouses, site plan, 349
Alexandre Iolas Sculpture Gallery, New York, 135
Alfred's Delicatessen, 201, 212
Allen, Judy and Robert, consultation, 354

Allen, Richard, 110
Allen, Robert E., 4, 30n2
Allen House (Frank M.), 319
Allen House (L. D.), 10, *12*
Alley Theatre, 16, 226, 267, 280, 326
All Faiths Chapel, Texas A&M University, competition entry, 318
Alliance Française, alterations, 336
Alofsin, Anthony, x, 40
Aluminum Company of America, 335
Ambasz, Emilio, 161
Ambrose, Serge, x, 171n90
American Bank Building, Galveston, Texas, 332
American Civil Liberties Union, 286
American Federation of Arts, 124, 226
American Institute of Architects (AIA): design awards, 12, 146, 159, 230, 310; fellowship, 231
American Institute of Architects, Houston Chapter. *See* AIA Houston
American Institute of Steel Constructions Award, 311
Amherst College, 224
Amster Yard, New York, 133, 168n40
Anderson, Clayton and Company, 270

Anderson, J. Robert, 58, 162
Anderson, Myron C., *252*
Anderson, Ralph A. Jr., 226
Anderson, William J. "Bill," Jr., 42, 303
André Istel & Co., 137
Andrew House (Leonora and John), 322
Andrews, Lavone Dickensheets, 42, 231
ANTA Theater, remodeling, 333
Ant Farm Art Collective, 57, 91, 253, 254
Antioch Missionary Baptist Church, 109–110, *110*
Antonioni, Michelangelo, 283
Apollo 15, moon landing site, 259
Arab oil embargo (1983), 232
Architectural Forum, 43, 229, 251
Architectural Record, 43, *43*, 48, 203–204, 205, 208, 229, 230, 251
Architectural Review, 229
Architecture of John F. Staub, The, vi, 25, 82, 98, 230
Architecture Plus, 228, 229
Arizona Historical Society Museum, Tempe, Arizona, 358
Armour Institute of Technology (now IIT), Chicago, Illinois, 66

373

Arnold, Eve, 19
Arnold House (June Davis and Gilbert), 272, 330
Art Barn, Rice University, *15*, 152, 163–164, 340
Art Museum of South Texas, Corpus Christi, Texas, 338
Arts and Architecture, 43, 48, 272
Ashton Villa (J. M. Brown House), Galveston, Texas, 108, *108*, 346
Asplund, Gunnar, 196
Assembly of God church, 203
Asteinza House (José Ramón), 336
Astrodome, 84
Atlantic Refining Co. Building, 329
Aubry, Eugene, ix–x, 7, 40, 43, 45, 47, 49, 54, 59, 87, 133, 143, 228, 234, *252*, 261, 300–306
Auburn/Lewiston, Maine, 56, 222, 223, 279, 346; Jewish community, 235n1
Audubon Street Arts Center, New Haven, Connecticut, 356
Auletta, Ken, 138
Austin City Hall, Austin, Texas, 356
Austin Civic Center, Austin, Texas, 357
Autry House, alterations and additions, 344
Aydelotte, Alfred L., 30n2

Bailey House (Scott Field), alterations, 344
Baker, Andrew C., 8
Baker, Jim, 161
Baldwin, Billy, 133
Ballet Russe de Monte Carlo, 267
Bang, Lars, 14
Banham, Reyner, 66–67
Bank Building, alterations for Mike Perrin, 352
Bank of Houston, 72, *73*
Bank of the Southwest Building, 128
Banque Schlumberger, France, 169n58
Barber, Gary, 234
Barcelona Point Development, Sag Harbor, Long Island, New York, 338
Barkdull Apartments, alterations for Anthony Wilson, 343

Barksdale House (John), consultation, 344
Barna, Joel Warren, x, 162, 295
Barnes, Charles Wynn, 270, 278
Barnes, Marguerite Johnston, 233, 270, 278
Barnes House (Marguerite J. and Charles W.), 315
Barnhart, Joseph, Office Building, 335
Barnhart Bay House (Agnes Arnold and Joseph), Kemah, Texas, 53, 336
Barnhart House (Joseph), alterations, Inwood Drive, 347
Barnstone, Aliki (niece), x
Barnstone, Beatrice (sister), 178, 222, *223*, 301, 335
Barnstone, Deborah Ascher, ix, 234, 364
Barnstone, Dora (daughter), 227, *227*, 230, 234
Barnstone, Doris Ida Lempert "Dora" (mother), 222, *223*, 224, 225, 274, *274*
Barnstone, George Arthur (son), x, 227, *227*, 271, 274, *274*, 278, 286
Barnstone, Gertrude Levy, x, 6–7, 19, *81*, 226, 227, *227*, 232; art of, 275; and entertaining, 286; as HISD trustee, 18–19, 227, *279*; as mother, 274, *274*, 277, 286; personality of, 268; political activities of, 110; and *Rashomon* (1959, Alley Theatre), 281–282, *281*; television program of, 285; theatrical career of, 16, *269*, 276–277, 279–280, *280*, *281*; studio of, 286; welding and sculpting of, 285, 287–288, *287*
Barnstone, Gertrude Levy and Howard, 19, *81*, 266, *267*, *269*; divorce of, 54, 228, 284–285; marriage of, 226, 267, 272, 281–282; remarriage of, 286; social life of, 307; wedding of, 271
Barnstone, Howard, 5, 11, *11*, *41*, *123*, *225*, 227, *227*, 233, *259*; and academia, 254–255; and AIA fellowship, 228; and airplane crash, 232; and architectural details, 50–51, 305; as author,

viii, 22, *23*, *25*, 82, 91, 98, 102, 105–106; and automobiles, 20, 29, 177, 178, 188, 192, 196, 227, 273; bipolar disorder of, 6, 23–24, 54, 91, 143–144, 150, 152, 228, 232–233, 239n58, 256–257; and Bolton, 301; and budgets, 135, 304; cartoon of, *261*; childhood of, 222–224, *223*, *224*, 235n8; and class identity, 292; clientele of, 83, 91, 293; as design critic, 291; and Do-ville, 172n111; education of, 8, 69, 224, 236n11; and entertaining, 25, 227, 278, *279*; and Marti Franco, 223; funeral of, 233; graphic skills of, 306; influence of, on UH College of Architecture, 250–251, 261–262; Jewish clients of, 202, 225; Jewish identity of, 5–6, 72, 93; and Philip Johnson, 266, 290, 301, 302, 304; and litigation, 229, 231; and mass transit, 34n50; and Melcher House, 140–141; and Menil House, 125–127, 270; and Miesian modernism, 225; offices of, vii, 45, *49*, 53, *57*, 193, *194*, 311; personality of, 6–7, 21, 25, 57, 272, 290; and postmodernism, 27, 57–58, 231–232, 257, 258, 302; and publicity, 19, 229, 291, 304; and religion, 232–233, 238n49; and Rice Museum (Art Barn), 340; and Rothko Chapel, vi, 148, 149, *149*, 150, 152; sexuality of, 24, 80, 234, 236n15, 279, 284, 293–294; social image of, 59, 303; suicide of, 29, 233, 234; and teaching, 24, 49, 91, 224, 246–247, 248, 250–251, 253, 256, 260, 300, 307–308; and travel, 227, 232, 235; and UH faculty, 115, *252*; and UH lecture series, 250–251; and University of St. Thomas Library, 148; and US Navy, 224, *224*; at Yale, 7, 8, 69, 78, 224, *225*, 236, 250, 254
Barnstone, Lily Elizabeth Gisella (daughter), 227, *227*, 234, 274, *274*, 266, 291
Barnstone, Morris, formerly Bornstein (grandfather), 223

Barnstone, Robert (half-brother), 57–58, 178, 190, 350–351
Barnstone, Robert Carl (father), 222–223, *223*, 228, 232
Barnstone, Robert V. (nephew), ix, 176, 178, 190, 364
Barnstone, Ronald A. (half-brother), 178, 223–224
Barnstone, Willis (brother), x, 6, 178–179, 222, *223*, 233, 301
Barnstone & Aubry, vi, 20, 88, 134, 136, 137, 139, 152–153, 228, 229, 303; Art Barn, 292; dissolution of, 228, 302–303
Barnstone & Co., jewelry, 223
Barnstone & Partners/Burdette Keeland office building, 1914 W. Capitol, 332
Barnstone & Partners office, Niels Esperson Building, 303, 331
Barnstone apartments (Carl and Dora), New York, 223, 235n8
Barnstone Duplex (Robert), alterations, Austin, Texas, 346
Barnstone House (Ann Bauer and Robert), Austin, Texas, 232
Barnstone House (Elli Tzalopoulou and Willis), Bloomington, Indiana, 179–184, *179*, *181*, 227, 334
Barnstone House (George and Francine), 234
Barnstone House (Gertrude and Howard), 1720 North Boulevard, 275, 328
Barnstone House (Gertrude and Howard), alterations and additions, 2050 Banks Street, 324
Barnstone House (Howard), 17 Shadowlawn Circle, 230, *231*, 232, 348
Barnstone House (Howard), alterations, 1715 North Boulevard, 339
Barnstone House (Robert), alterations, Austin, Texas, 346
Barnstone House (Robert), project, Austin, Texas, 57
Barnstone House (Willis), Florida, 328

Barnstone-Keeland faction, UH College of Architecture, 248, 253, 255, 256, 257
Barnstone-Keeland offices, Niels Esperson Building, 331
Barnstone office building (Robert), Austin, Texas, 350
Barnstone-Richter Property, 1136 Berthea, 357
Barragán, Luis, 187
Barstow Lake House (Robert), Austin, Texas, 347
Barthelme, Donald (architect), 10, 11, 14, 20, 30n3, 42, 49, 58, 244, 247–248
Barthelme, Donald, Jr., (writer), 272–273, 294
Basilica of Santa Maria Assunta, Torcello, Italy, 149
Batey & Mack, 58
Battelstein family, 205
Battelstein House (Jerry E.), 342, 346. *See also* Peden Square for Jerry E. Battelstein
Bayou Bend (Ima Hogg and William C. Hogg House), River Oaks, 8–9, *11*
Beaux Arts tradition, 243, 297
Beerman, Tibor, 293
Behrens, Peter, 250
Bell, P. Gervais, x, 152
Bell Country House (Sue Ledbetter and Paul Gervais, Jr.), Chappell Hill, Texas, 347
Bell House (Sue Ledbetter and Paul Gervais, Jr.), 7, 27, 54, 310, 337
Bennick Ranch (John), 313
Bennington College, 176
Bentsen, Kenneth E., 14, 20, 30n2, 42, 76, 231
Bentsen, Mary Bates and Kenneth, 226
Benua House (Richard), Galveston, Texas, 336
Bernath Condominium Apartments (John A.), Galveston, Texas, 334
Bertoia, Harry, furniture, 128
Bess, Forrest, 7, 275, 278–279
Best Products showroom, 91
Beth Abraham Synagogue, Auburn, Maine, 222

Bethea House (M. B.), 316
Betsky, Aaron, 295
Betty Parsons Gallery, New York, 279
Birkerts, Gunnar, 4, 30n2
Black Angus restaurant, 320
Blackstock House (H. W.), 321
Blaffer, Camilla Davis, 283
Blaffer, John H., 283
Blake, Peter, 7, 27, 228, 229
Blankfield House (Jack J.), alterations, 326
Block-Oppenheimer Building, 105, 106, *107*
Bloxsom House (Dan), 43, 44, *44*, *45*, 313
Bludworth House (Harold), Baytown, Texas, 353
Blue, Janice, 286
Blum House (Faye Byer and Lawrence H.), Beaumont, Texas, 48, *51*, 225, 310, 314
Blum House (Herbert), Beaumont, Texas, 225, 310, 312
Bohnn House (Anne Schlumberger and Jules), 141, 342
Boissonnas, Eric H., 124
Boissonnas House (Sylvie Schlumberger and Eric H.), New Canaan, Connecticut, 44, 48
Bolivar Hall, San Antonio, Texas, 111
Bolton, Frank C., 236n17
Bolton, Preston M., 14, 20, 40, *41*, 225–226, 300, 302
Bolton & Barnstone, ix, 15, 17, 22, 25, 26, 28, 43–45, 47, 48, 49, 50, 51, 53, 67, 70–73, 76, 85, 108, 109, 128, 130, 131, 137, 138, 142, 178, 183, 225, 272; ballet studio 267; dissolution of, 226–227; and office alterations, 811 Lovett Boulevard, 317–318; and publicity, 43; University of St. Thomas, 148, 271
Bornstein, Morris and Bessie, 222
Bouguereau, William-Adolphe, 53
Box, John Harold "Hal," 30n2, 101–103, 106
Bradley, Barrie Scardino, viii, ix, 365
Braeswood subdivision, 10, 16, 201, 204, 205
Bramante, Donato, 250

INDEX 375

Bramlett House (Beth Carson and Robert S.), 58, 231, 348, 352
Bramlett Office (Robert S.), alterations, 352
Brays Bayou, 15, 17, 204
Brazos Bookstore, 283
Brennan, Marcia (*Curating Consciousness*), 23, 294
Breuer, Marcel, 251
Briar Hollow subdivision, 15
Brink, Peter, 143
Briscoe, Birdsall P., 8, 141, 295
Brochstein family, 205
Brogniez, Raymond H., 42
Broken Obelisk, 150, *151*, 171–172n99
Brooks & Brooks, 14
Broussard House (Frank), addition, 318
Brown, Anne Schlumberger, x, 24, 141, 278, 305, 307–308, 342
Brown, Hamilton, 140, 307
Brown, Rosellen, 294
Brown Bookstore, alterations, 332
Brown v. Education (1954), 277
Bruce House (Robert M.), 315
Brutalist architecture, 86, 87, 302
Buckham, Charles W., 134
Buenos Aires, Argentina, 130
Buffalo Bayou, 15, 53, 54, 61n24, 74
Buildings X, Y, Z, UH College of Architecture, 249, *249*, 257
Bunker Hill Village, 11
Buñuel, Luis, 7
Burgee, John, *258*, *259*
Burke House (Gene E.), alterations, 334
Bush, President George H. W., 225
Butera's Grocery Store proposal, 352
Butler, Asberry, Jr., 18–19, 283
Butler Binion law offices, 336
Butler House (Francis), 336

Caesar, Jack, 17
Cage, John, vii
Calder, Alexander, 273
Calhoun Park, 354
Callery, Caroline Staub and Charles, 226, 230
Camarero-Barnstone-Lundell Partnership Townhouses, 354

Campbell, Jack, printing building, Galveston, Texas, 335
Campbell Beach House (Jack), Clear Lake City, Texas, 335
Cannady, William T., 42, 228
Caracas, Venezuela, 72, 128–129, 130, 166n24, 169, 317
Carleton, Don E., 18
Carlos Jimenez Studio, vi
Carlton House, New York, 133
Carpenter, Adelaide de Menil, 133–134, 135
Carpenter, Edmund Snow "Ted," 133, 135
Carpenter, J. E. R., 223
Carpenter Apartment (Adelaide and Edmund S.), New York, 134–135, 146
Carpenter East Hampton complex (Adelaide and Edmund S.), New York, 146–147, *147*, 163
Carpenter Townhouse (Adelaide and Edmund S.), New York, 133–134, 341
Carrier Corporation Building, 320
Carroll House (Jack R.), 321
Cartier-Bresson, Henri, 23, 106, 142–143, 227
Carver Bakery, 336
Casa de Piedras (Marti Franco and Mel Suneson, House), Puerto Vallarta, Mexico, 184–186, *184*, *185*, 334
Casbarian, John J., 231
Case Study House No. 8 (Eames House), Los Angeles, California, 44, *46*, 77–78
Case Study program, Los Angeles, California, 16, 290
Castle Court Duplex renovation, 327
Cato, Austin & Evans, 249
Cato, Lamar Q., 242
Caudill, Rowlett, Scott (CRS), 40–41, *42*, 43
Caudill, William W., 30n3, 41, *42*, 42
Central Presbyterian Church, remodeling, 333
Century Properties, 41
Chafee, William P., 146

Challinor House (Joan Ridder and David, Jr.), Hamden, Connecticut, 50, 227, 326
Chapel of the Rosary, Vence, France, 148
Chase, John Saunders, 5, 12, 30n2
Chávez, César, 286
Cheese Factory, Fredericksburg, Texas, 356
Chermayeff, Serge, 251
Child Guidance Center, alterations and additions, 326
Childress House (Virgil), 10
Choucroun, Norbert, 230
Christ Church Cathedral, 232, 233
Christie House (Carter B.), alterations, 344
Church, Chile, 328
Church, Thomas D., 46, 48
Cinema Corporation of America, 340
Cite: The Architecture and Design Review of Houston, x
Clark House (I. E.), remodeling, 327
Clayton, Nicholas J., 105, 106
Clear Lake Realty office building, 333
climate and architecture, 69, 70, 73, 82, 84, 92, 98–99, 106, 178, 291, 295
Cohen, Irvin M., project, 342
Cohen House (H. M.), 313
Colbert, Charles R., 4, 30n2
Colby, Rudolph "Rudy," vi, 7, 57, 234
College of Architecture, UH. *See* University of Houston
Colley, Richard S., 30n3, 101, 113–114, 115
Colorado College, Olin Hall of Science, Colorado Springs, Colorado, 41
Colorado Sterling Silver Company, 223
Columbia University, New York, 301
Commerce Building, 128, 166, 323
Communications Group offices, 342
Community Players, 279
Condominium Complex for Harvey Conwell, Mustang Island, Texas, 355
Congdon Builders, 317
Congregation Am Echad Synagogue, Auburn, Maine, 56, 229, 346

Congregation Beth Abraham Synagogue, 222, 255n2
Congregation Beth Israel, 212, 278
Congregation Beth Israel Temple (1925), 200, 201; (1967), 201, 205; Gordon Chapel, 351
Congregation Beth Yeshurun Temple, 201, 212
Congregation Emanu El Temple, *15*, 201, 203
Conrad House (F. W.), alterations, 327
Contemporary Arts Association (CAA), 16, *17*, 272, 267, 270
Contemporary Arts Association building (1949), 267, *268*
Contemporary Arts Museum (CAM), 16, *17*, 22, 71, 226, 232, 355
Contemporary Music Society, 226
Conwell, Harvey, Condominium Complex, Mustang Island, Texas, 355
Cook House (M. L.), Friendswood, Texas, 48, 302, 310, 318
Cooley Townhouses (William C., Jr.), 344
Coonley House (Avery), Riverside, Illinois, 71
Copley House (George N.), 17 Shadowlawn; 231. *See also* Barnstone House (Howard)
Corpus Christi City Hall, 113–114, *115*
Cotlar Highrise Apartment Building, 334
Cougar, University of Houston campus newspaper, 225
Courtwright, David T., *11*, 230
courtyards, 71, 72, 76, *78*, 139, *159*, *183*, 184, *203*, 204, 333, 341
Couturier Father Marie-Alain, 269
Cowell, C. Herbert, 14
Cowell & Neuhaus, 47, 71, 226
Cox Hotel (W. E.), Venezuela, 323
Cozens, Elsian Rooney Davidson and Robert S., 229
Cozens, Robert S., 229
Cozens House (Elsian and Robert), alterations, 342
Cravey House (Paul), East Texas, 355
Crispin, André, 229

Crispin Company Building, rehabilitation, 311, 341
Crispin House (André), alterations, 347
Croft Townhouse Development (Paul and Sidney), 337
Crystal, Joan, 227, 272
Cullen, Lillie Cranz and Hugh Roy, 242
Cullen Park, 349
Cullinan, Alison Prescott (Mrs. Craig F., Jr.), 79
Cullinan, Nina, 19
Cullinan Hall, Museum of Fine Arts, Houston, 11, 18, *18*, 19, *19*, 22, 23, 39, 67, *69*, 72, 272, 292
Cullinan House (Nina), 76, 77, 78, *79*

Dailey House (Louis), alterations, 335
Dallas Polo Club Clubhouse, Dallas, Texas, 327
Dallas Tower proposal, Dallas, Texas, 104, *104*, 105
Danbury Independent School District School, Danbury, Connecticut, 331
Daniel Construction Co., 161
David, Grace McMillan, 169–170n68
David House (Grace McMillan and Henry), 139–140, 169–170n68
Dean, James, as Jett Rink in *Giant*, 99, *100*
deed restrictions in Houston, 17, 72, 83, 204, 231
Delano & Aldrich, 135
Demoustier Apartment (Germaine and Marc), New York, 132, 319
Demoustier House (Germaine and Marc), 48, *50*, 70–71, 72, 132, 139, 169–170n68, 310, 316
De Saligny Condominiums, Austin, Texas, 57–58, *174–175*, 190, *192*, 232, 352
Desforges, Bruno, 138
Detering Book Gallery, alterations, 354
Detering House (Herman E. III), alterations, 351
Detering House (Lenora), addition, 332
Detering Ranch House (Herman III), Rio Frio, Texas, 354

Dewey, John, 144
De Young House (Helen Gordon and Robert), 355
Dia Art Foundation, 138, 283, 347
Dickey, George E., 105
Dillingham House (Barbara K. and Charles), alterations, 332
Dillingham House (Barbara Kibler) addition, Round Top, Texas, 342
Dillingham House (Charles), alterations, Round Top, Texas, 342
Di Sunno, Anthony, 56
Dobbins, Roger, 57, 234
Dobie, J. Frank, 99
Docomomo US, 298
Doll, Henri-Georges, 124, 133
Doll, Henri-Georges, Office, Schlumberger Ltd., Getty Building, New York, 328
Doll Apartment (Annette Schlumberger and Henri-George), Ritz Tower, New York, 132–133, 167n37, 329
Donald Barthelme & Associates, 14
Dossey, John, 259
Dossey-Trotti Lunar Colony thesis project, 260, *260*
Doty House (Joan Richardson and James R.), alterations, 357
Douglass House (Charles), alterations, 346
"Do-ville," Menil Montrose holdings, 148, 155, *155*, 156, 164, 172n111
Dow Chemical Co., legal department offices, 343
Dreams and Schemes, Contemporary Arts Museum exhibition, design entry, 355
Drucker House alterations, Laredo, Texas, 353
Dryden Shopping Mall, Laredo, Texas, 350
DuBose Gallery, 275
Dudok, Willem, 196
Dunaway House (James), Fort Worth, Texas, 358
Durret House (Joe B.), alterations, 354

Eads House (Carol), 351
Eagleton, Terry, 243

Eames, Charles, 251
Eames House (Ray and Charles), 44, 46, 77–78
Ebels House (Dean L.), 330
Echols Development Project, 322
Eckles House (W. E.), 327
École des Mines, Paris, France, 124
economic depression in Houston, 41, 42, 232–233
economic prosperity in Houston, 8, 41, 42, 202, 232, 247, 266, 298
Edwards, Katie Robinson, 279
Ehni House (George), alterations and addition, 357
Einstein, Albert, 144
Eisenhower, Dwight David, 254
Elliott Beach House (J. J.), 325
Ellsworth House (Theodore P.), remodeling, 331
Ellwood, Craig, 4, 30n2, 77, 251
Elmcourt Condominiums for Robert Barnstone, Austin, Texas, 350
El Tropical, night club, 273
Emerson, Don, 303
Emery Roth & Sons, 135
Encinal Condominiums, Austin, Texas, 190, 192, *193*, 196, 232, 310, 348
Entenza, John, 77
Erdman, R. H. Donnelley, 42
Erickson, Arthur, 30n2
Erwin House (A. T.), alterations, 349
Evenflo Company, Inc., 208
Expo 67, Montreal, Canada, 123, *123*

Fair Park, Dallas, Texas, 105
Falla, Manuel del, vii
Farbstein Greenhouse (J. J.), 348
Farenthold, Sissy, 25
Farfel, Aaron J., offices, 319
Farfel, Esther Susholtz and Aaron Joseph, 208, *209*, 229
Farfel, Gail, *209*
Farfel House (Esther Susholtz and Aaron J.), 48, 25, *26*, 201, 205–206, 208, *209*, *210*, 310, 319
Farfel Office Building, 320
Farish House (Stephen P., Jr.), 325
Farnsworth House (David), 319
Farnsworth House (Edith), Plano, Illinois, 67, 72, 194

Fay, Albert Bel, office building, 228, 340
Fay Bay House (Albert Bel), addition, Kemah, Texas, 344
Fay House (Carolyn Grant and Ernest Bel), project, 57
Fay House (Ernest Bel), 351
Federal Reserve Branch Bank of Dallas, remodeling for the Crispin Company, 229, 341
Fehr, Arthur, 30n3
Feigan, Richard, Townhouse and Gallery, New York, 336
Feld, Benjamin, Warehouse, 335
Fellini, Federico, 269
Ferber, Edna, 22
Ferndale Townhouses, renovation, 328
Finger, Joseph, 205, 293
Fink, Celia Cohen, 224, *225*
Finkelstein House (Jack), 325
Fink Rental House (Mrs. Abraham I.), remodeling, 319
Finn, Alfred C., 242
First City National Bank Building, 67, *68*
First Colony, 20
First Liberty National Bank, alterations, Liberty, Texas, 318
First State Bank of Greens Bayou Building, 315, 338
Fishman, David, 137
Fitzgerald, Richard, 66
Flatow Country House (Marc), Bluebonnet Hills, Washington County, Texas, 352
Flavin, Dan, light installation, 138
Fleming, Clare, 226, 270, 273
Fleming, Lamar, 270, 274
Floyd, William N., 14
Foley's department store, 12
Fondren, W. W., Jr., 205
Ford, O'Neil, 20, 21, 30n3, 59, 99, 101, 110–111, 113, 114
Ford, Powell, & Carson, 111, 114
Forest Park East Cemetery, 233
Fourth Ward Park, 340
Fox, Stephen, viii, ix, xi, 162–163, 230, 365
Franco, Marti, 25, 54, 56, 178, *183*, 184, 223, 227

Franco, Marti, store, Laredo, Texas, 340
Franco-Béjar, Matilde, 223
Franco House (Marti), Laredo, Texas, 345
Frank, Adela Franco-Bejar, 223, 234
Frank, Viviana, 234
Frankenstein, Alfred, 142
Frank House (Mauricio), Laredo, Texas, 324, 334
Franzen, Ulrich, 4, 30n2
Franzheim, Kenneth, 12
Frederick, Anthony E. "Tony," 54, 56, 144, 234
Fred Winchell Photography Studio and Apartment, 77
Freed House (Eleanor and Frank), alterations and additions, Piney Point Village, 323, 330
Freed House (Eleanor K.), alterations, Institute Lane, 351
Freeman, John H., Jr., 42
Freeman House (Harold), 50, 326
French Legation Park, Austin, Texas, 352
Friedman, Alice T., 292
Friedman House (Bernard), alterations, 344
Friedman Townhouse (Robert), 351
Friedrich, Heiner, 138
Frost, Charles Sumner, 222, 223
Fuller, R. Buckminster, 123, 251, 259, 278, *279*, 301
Furley, Edmund R., Jr., 245, 249
Furman, Joshua J., ix, 365
Furman, Laura, 294

Gabert, Lenard, 12, 15, 205
Gaea I House (Zemanek House), *246*
Gainsborough Studios, New York, 134–135, 146, 168n45
Galveston County Publishing Company Building, Galveston, Texas, 53, 88, *89*, 331
Galveston Historical Foundation, Galveston, Texas, 344
Galveston That Was, The, 22–23, *23*, 82, 98, 105, 142–143, 147, 164, 227, 229, 282, 304–305
Garden of the Good Shepherd, 320
Gardner, Rick, 230

Garland, Robert D., Jr., 30n2
Gartner House (Elizabeth Reynolds and Herman), Fort Worth, Texas, 106, 109, *109*
Garwood House (St. John, Jr.), 329
Gehry, Frank, 138
General Dynamics, Fort Worth, Texas, 100
George, Mary Carolyn Hollers, 114
George, W. Eugene, 252
George House, alterations, 358
George Pierce-Abel B. Pierce, 14
George Washington Slept Here (1950), 269
Gerald D. Hines College of Architecture and Design, UH. *See* University of Houston
Gerald D. Hines Interests, 20
Giant (1956), 99, *100*
Giedion, Sigfried, and Carola Giedion-Welcker, 102
Gilbane House, 355
Gillette, Sharon, *114*
Giurgola, Romaldo, 4, 30n2
Glass House (Philip Johnson), New Canaan, Connecticut, 73–74, 76, 194
Glenbrook Valley subdivision, 15
Goff, Bruce, 251, 293
Golemon & Rolfe, 11, 12
Goodman House (Harold V.), 330
Goodman House (Larry), Clear Lake City, Texas, 357
Gordon, Elizabeth, 292
Gordon and Morrison Motel, 322
Gordon House (Lillian Guberman and Gerald), *2–3*, 28, *43*, *44*, *46*, 71, 72, 201, 204–205, *206*, *207*, *302*, 310, 311, 314
Gordon House (Aaron S.) swimming pool, 322
Gordon (Gerald S.) law offices, 319, 324, 357; Siteman Building, 350; Tennessee Life Insurance Co. Building 357; Two Post Oak Central, 329
Gornick, Vivian, 6
Gouilloud Apartment (Michel-Marie), New York, 135, 348
Granger, Charles, 30n3

Graustark Family Townhouses, 25–26, 56, 91, 228, 311, 341
Graves, John, 99
Gray Is the Color exhibition (1973–1974); 154, *154*, 156
Greacen, Thomas E., II, 42
Greacen & Brogniez, 14
Great Depression, 31n12, 232, 297
Greenberg and Appelbaum apartment building, 322
Greenberg House (Henry D.), 317
Greene, Herb, 12, 30n2
Greene House (W. W.), 321
Greene Townhouse (Philip S.), alterations, 347
GreenMark, Inc., Gerald D. Hines Interests, 20; Sugarcreek Townhouses, 350
Greenwald House (Rose and Morris), Weston, Connecticut, 67
Greenway Plaza, Austin, Texas, 352
Gropius, Walter, 30n2, 40, 78, 98
Gross, Jenard, apartment complex, 327
Grossberg House, addition, 356
Gruen, Victor, 251
Grünbaum House (Franz V.), 316
Guest House (William), alterations, 347
Guggenheim Foundation, 142
Guggenheim Museum, New York, 142, 273
Guizot, François, 165n7
Gupton, Ted B., 56–57, 234
Gwathmey, Charles, 138

Hacienda Motor Hotel, Puerto Vallarta, Mexico, 336
Haid, David, 74, 77
Haines House (Frank S., Jr.), supervision, 318
Halprin, Sarah (Mrs. Hyman Lempert), 222
Hamill Apartment (Claud B.), alterations, 353
Hanover Building, New York, 135
Hardison House (Richard M.), 310, 315
Hare and Hare, 204, 242, 244
Hamilton, E. G., 30n2
Hampton, Mark, 30n2

Harris, Harwell Hamilton, 30n3, 98
Harris County Center for the Retarded, 54, 88, *90*, 305, 333
Hartman Clinic, 314
Hartman House (Nona Cook and Lee E.), Beaumont, Texas, 225, 312
Harvard University, Graduate School of Design (GSD), Cambridge, Massachusetts, 21, 45, 78, 98, 102
Haskell, Doug, 251
Hawes House (W. S.), remodeling, 317
Heim, Glenn, 135
Heimsath, Clovis, 228
Hellmuth, Obata & Kassabaum (HOK), 41, 305
Helmich, D. A., *106*
Hemisfair '68, San Antonio, Texas, 111, 113, 114, *114*, 337
Henderson, Philip, 101, 103
Henze, Matthias, 293
Hermann Park, 204
Hershey, Olive, ix, x, 365
Herzog Apartment (Gerhard), 327
Herzog House (Doreen Wolfson and Frank C.), 54, 56, 201, 214–215, *215*, 310, 311, 343, 355, 356
Herzog House (Gerhard), 313
Herzog (Frank) law offices, Two Shell Plaza, 343; Pennzoil Place, 348
Hess, Virginia, 45, 301
Hester House (Fletcher), 325
Hewitt, Mark Alan, 292
Hickey and Robertson, photography studio, 340
Highland Mall Properties International Bonded Warehouse, 350
Highway Motel, Nuevo Laredo, Mexico, 188–190, *189*, *191*
Hilles, David E., 30n2
Hill Ski Chalet (Frank), Crested Butte, Colorado, 337
Hines, Gerald D., 77, 227
Hines College of Architecture. *See* University of Houston, Gerald D. Hines College of Architecture
Hirsch, Edward, 294
historic preservation, 82, 111, 113, 114, 143, 164, 229, 297–298
Hitchcock, Henry-Russell, 7, 48, 71, 251

Hobbs Office (Ronald), New York, 340
Hobby, Diana Stallings, and William P., Jr., 226, 284, 285
Hobby, Oveta Culp, 53–54
Hobby, William P., 205
Hobby Airport, 15
Hobby House (Dianna and William P., Jr.), alterations, 331
Hoelscher House (Virginia and Robert J.), alterations, 356
Hofheinz House (Fred), 230, 343
Hogg, Ima, 8–9, 19, 25
Hogg, William C., 8–9
Hogg Foundation for Mental Health, 9
Holliday, Kathryn, ix, 365–366
Holmes, Ann, 146
Holmes House, 355
Holt House, Corpus Christi, Texas, 58
Hood, Lucian T., Jr., 12, 14
Hosen House (Dorothy Brookner and Harris), Port Arthur, Texas, 20, 44, 68, 83, 108, 225, 310, 316, 320
Hotel Carlyle, New York, 285
House, Kemah, Texas, 338
House and Garden, 43, 205
House and Home, 43, 229, 230
House Beautiful, 292
House of the Century (1972, Ant Farm), 253, *254*
Houssiere House (Charles R. III), 353
Houston, Texas, 19; aerial view of (1952), 9; deed restrictions in, 17, 72, 83, 204, 231; economy of, 8, 41, 42, 202, 232–233, 247, 266, 298; Main Street, 204; oil and gas industry in, 8, 100, 102, 122, 129, 232, 282, 304; racism in, 5, 8, 15–19, 124, 202, 277, 283–284; society in, 19, 226–227, 247, 269, 270, 278; South End, 204; suburban sprawl in, 101; tin house movement in, 28; urban planning in, 8, 24, 103, 108, 109, 110; zoning of, 20, 68, 83, 108–109, 259
Houston Area Teachers Credit Union Building, 53, 330
Houston Arts Council, 226
Houston Ballet Foundation, 226, 267
Houston Chronicle, 19, 146, 208, 212, 225, 227, 275, 291

Houston Club, 273
Houston College for Negroes (now Texas Southern University), 16
Houston Community College, 285
Houston Cotton Exchange, 345
Houston Country Club, 15
Houston Grand Opera, 267; rehearsal hall, 321
Houston Home and Garden, 229
Houston Home design awards, 311
Houston Independent School District, 9, 18–19; elementary school competition, 331
Houston Junior College, 242
Houston Little Theater, 269, 280
Houston Metropolitan Research Center, Houston Public Library, x, xi, 234
Houston Mod, 298
Houston National Bank Building, alterations, 349
Houston Post, 19, 227, 233, 270, 284, 291
Houston Post Building, renovation, 336
Houston Ship Channel, 8, 304
Houston Symphony Orchestra, 9, 267
Houston Teachers Credit Union Building, 330
Howard, George F., 204
Hudson, Edward J., 283
Hughes, Fred, *123*
Hughes House (James S.), additions, 321
Hunter, Elizabeth, 301
Hunt House (Wilmer B.), alterations, 334, 337
Hurricane Carla (1961), 278

Illinois Institute of Technology (IIT), Chicago, Illinois, iv, 66, 366
I. M. Pei & Partners, 20
Inland Architect, 229
Inn of the Republic of Texas, Austin, Texas, 354
Institute for Storm Research, 53, 336
Institute of International Education, 334
Institute of Religion Offices, Texas Medical Center, 340
Institute of Research, 342

International Bonded Warehouse for Highland Mall Properties, 350
Inwood Manor, 25
Iolas Gallery, New York, 332
Iolas House (Alexandre) additions, Athens, Greece, 143, 329
Iowa, Jerome, 230
Isabella Court, 21
ISD, Inc., 162
Istel, Lepercq & Co. offices (Wall Street), New York, 135, 137–138, 328

Jackson, Robert T., 56, 58, 161, 192, 230, 234
Jacobs and Rogers medical office, Medical Towers Building, 319
Jacobsen, Hugh Newell, 4, 30n2
Jacobs House (Warren M.), alterations and addition, 319
James, Charles, 125, 166n14
James, Stephen, 153, 251
James Bute Company Gallery (later Dubose Gallery), 275
Japanese architectural influences, 51, 62n30
Jedah House, 358
Jefferson, Thomas, University of Virginia, 73
Jefferson Davis Hospital, rehabilitation, 355
Jenkins, William R., 7, 14, 30n2, 42, 76, 245, 248, 252, *252*, 256, 259–260, 261
Jesse H. Jones Hall for the Performing Arts, 282
Jett Grocery Co. offices, alterations, 351
Jewish Community Center, 201, 212
Jewish community in Houston, 200
Jewish Home for the Aged, 212
Jewish settlement patterns in Houston, 200–201, 215
Jiménez, Carlos, ix, 366
Jitkoff House (Andrew N.), remodeling, 326
Jodeit House (Michael R.), alterations, 357
Johansen, John M., 4, 30n2
Johansen House (John M.), Fairfield, Connecticut, 71

John Sealy Hospital, Galveston, Texas, 228, 285
Johnson, Lyndon B., 100, 255, 277
Johnson, Philip, 5, 7, 11, 14, 27, *84*, *261*, 290, 293, 301, 302, 303–304; and Gerald Hines, 20; Harvard GSD, 21, 45, 49; Hodgson House, 72; and Mies van der Rohe, 22; Menil House, 67, 122–123, 125, 247, 298; Oneto House, 71, 72; personality of, 21–22; and postmodernism, 231; Schlumberger-Doll Research Center, administration building, 159, *159*; Seagram Building, 138; UH Hines College of Architecture Building, 257, *258*, *259*; as UH visiting lecturer, 251, *251*; University of St. Thomas, 148, 292
Johnson/Burgee, 20, 93, 135, 257, *258*, 263, 338
Johnson House (Imogene and Sam), Racine, Wisconsin, 71
John's Restaurant, 323
Jones, Jesse H., and Reconstruction Finance Corporation, 31n12
Jones, Margo, 279
Jones, Robert, 109
Jordan House (Francis M.), Auburn, Maine, 222, *223*
Jordan House (George, Jr.), alterations, 333
J. Paul Getty Building, New York, 135
Juhl, Finn, 251
J. Weingarten supermarket sit-in, 17–18

Kahn, Louis I., 58, 78, 88, 153
Kaldis Bath House, 354
Kaldis Real Estate Townhouses, 344
Kammerman, Mrs. Oscar. *See* Barnstone, Beatrice
Kammerman House (Beatrice Barnstone and Oscar), 335
Kamrath, Jeannie (Mrs. Karl), *268*
Kamrath, Karl, 10
Kaplan, Barry J., 17
Kaplan, Judith and Barry, consultation, 346
Katz Apartment (Sam), 339
Kaufman Apartments, 317
Kaufman family, 205

Kazdan House (David E.), alterations, 356
Keeland, Burdette, 7, 14, 30n2, 42, 49, 76, 77, 234, 245, 247, 248, 253, 255–256, *259*, 260, 261, *279*, 286, 301, 308
Keeland, Margie Scott and Burdette, 278
Kellogg House (Lois and Spencer, Jr.), Scottsdale, Arizona, 144
Kempner House (Helen Hill and I. H. III), 53, 86, *86*, 87, *87*, 338
Kennedy, John F., 277
Kiesler, Frederick, 7, 80, 301
Kilian, Karl, 156, 283
Kimball Museum, Fort Worth, Texas, 58
Kipling-Yupon Townhouses, 343
Kitchen House (Benjamin), alterations, 348
Klein, Irving, 205
Klep House (John P.), renovation, 317
Knapp, John, Townhouses, site plan, 349
Knauth House (Joe B.), alterations, 347
Knoll Planning Unit, furniture, New York, 48, 50, 127–128, 132
Knoll, Florence Schust, 128
Knowles, James P., 143–144
Koenig, Pierre, 4, 30n2, 77
Kotin, Ben J., 293
Koush, Ben, x, 16, 41, 47
KPRC television, 284, 285
Kraft House (Irvin A.), alterations and additions, 323
Krakower, Joseph, 12, 233
Kripal, Jeffrey J., 293
KTRK-TV, 208, 324
Kurzbard House (S. J.), alterations, 349

Lackland Air Force Base, San Antonio, Texas, 100
Ladin House (William E., Jr.), 339, 348
La Fin du Monde (1963, Magritte), *209*
Laguna Gloria Art Museum project, Austin, Texas, 355
Laird, Colin, 130
Laird House (K. L.), 328

Lake/Flato, 99
Lambert, Phyllis, 30n2
Landes House (Henry), Galveston, 105–106, *106*
Lansdale Park Recreation Center, 352
La Parra Ranch House for Sarita Kenedy East, Kenedy County, Texas, 327
Laredo Country Club, Laredo, Texas, 353
La Villita, San Antonio, Texas, 111, *112*, 117n27
Lawrence House (A. Bruce), alterations, 356
Lawson House (Sue), alterations, 350. *See also* Barnstone House, 1720 North Boulevard
Le Corbusier (Charles-Édouard Jeanneret), 77, 176, 188
Ledoux, Claude-Nicolas, 257
Lee House, 356
Lempert, Hyman Michael "Mike," 222–223
Lempert House (Sarah and Mike), 222–223
Lent, Robert F., 42
Leonard Company Warehouse, Laredo, Texas, 324
Lepercq, de Neuflize & Co., 137–138, 169n58; offices, Lexington Avenue, New York, 349; offices, Park Avenue, New York, 139, *139*, 338; offices, Wall Street, New York, 137–138
Lepercq, Paul A., 138
Leshika House (Leon L.), remodeling, 317
Letzerich Ranch House (Louis), Friendswood, Texas, 74, 77
Levin House (Edna Seinsheimer and William C.), Galveston, Texas, 53, 311, 333
Levittown, New York, *211*, 212
Levy, Arthur, 283
Levy, Gisella, 271, 274, 276, 288
Levy, Morris L., 293
Lewis House (James O., Jr.), 324, 334
Lewiston, Maine, 222, 223. *See also* Auburn/Lewiston, Maine
Lewiston Evening Journal, 222

Licata, Harry, consultation, 346
Lichter, Jennie Lempert, 229
Lilliott, Richard W., Jr., 224, 243–244, 248, 251, *252*
Lindsay House (Alice Boyd), 28, 310, 321–322
Lindsey, Robert F., 245, *252*
Link Apartment (James Wiley, Jr.), Chilton Courts, 316
Link House (James Wiley, Jr.), Montrose Boulevard, 148
Link House (James Wiley, Jr.), remodeling, Lovett Boulevard, 321
Linnstaedter, Herbert, 245
Lipchitz, Jacques, 7
Lipschultz, Barbara and Larry, consultation, 355
Lissitzky, El (*Cloud Irons*, 1924), 194
Little House (R. B.), 321
Little Theater of Houston, 16
Liu House (Olive), 358
Lively, C. R., 245, 249
Livingston House (R. B.), supervision, 319
Lloyd, Hermon, 10
Lloyd, Morgan & Jones, 14, 41, 152, 226–227
Longoria Motel, Nuevo Laredo, Mexico, 188–190, *189*, *191*, 331
Longoria-Therot, Octaviano L. and Eduardo, 188
Look magazine on Houston (1965), 282–283
Lopate, Philip, 6, 29, 233–234, 294
Louisiana Gallery, 227, 272, 275
Lowe, Mary Ralph, 53
Lowery House (Paul), 315
Lubetkin, Alvin, 254
Lubetkin House (Marilyn Oshman), 345
Lucas House (Paul), 317
Lundy, Victor, 4, 24, 30n2
Lyndon B. Johnson Presidential Library, Austin, Texas, 88

Maas, Elaine, 214
MacAgy, Jermayne, 12, 19, 22, 25, 26, 226, *273*, 278, 291, 292; exhibitions, 272
MacGregor Park, 203
MacKenzie, James C., 141

MacKie & Kamrath, 10, 11, 12, 15, 16, 17, 58, 166n20, 226, 267
MacKie, Fred, 10
magical architecture, 7, 22, 25, 49, 80, 82–83, 85, 86, 91, 163, 177, 292, 295
Magritte, René, 209
Maher, John, 208
Maher House (Lois Lasater and John F.), 38–39, 53, *54*, *55*, *81*, 85, 301, 328
Mahler, Gustav, vii
Maiden Lane, New York jewelry district, 223, 235n7
Making It (1967, Norman Podhoretz), 291
Manley, John, 43, 302
Maple Terrace, Dallas, Texas, 113
Maracaibo, Zuila, Venezuela, 129, 130, *130*, 167n25, 317
Marcus, Stanley, 226
Marcus House (Howard), alterations, 349
Marcus House (Lawrence), 140. *See also* Demoustier House, Houston
Marshall House (Diana), alterations, 353
Marshall House (John), remodeling, 325
Martin, Milton Foy, 14
Marti's specialty store, Nuevo Laredo, Mexico, 25, *27*, 54, 56, 187–188, *187*, 196, 341
Marti's specialty store proposal, San Francisco, California, 350
Masel House (Brent), alterations and additions, Dominique Drive, Galveston, Texas, 354
Masel House (Brent) project, Beluche Drive, Galveston, Texas, 352
Masjid Al-Fara for Dia Art Foundation, 138, 347
Mason Building, alterations, 336
Match Factory, Belize, 347
Matisse, Henri, 148
Maverick, Mayor Maury, 111
Maye House (R. W.), 321
MCA Financial Group Conference Room, One Shell Plaza, 342
McCarthy, Glenn H., 266

McCormick House (Isabella Gardner and Robert Hall III), Elmhurst, Illinois, 67
McCorquodale, Robin Hunt and Malcolm, 274
McCoy, Esther, 7, 20, 71, 80
McDanald, Eugene, M.D., 228, 169–170n68
McDonald, Cynthia, 294
McFarland, Shawn, 56
McGehee, J. Pittman, 233
McKim, Mead & White, 142
McMillin, Eugene, *252*
McMurtry, Larry, 99
McNaughton House (Paul D.), 318
McRae House (Charles), additions, 335
Mdalel House (José D.), Sugar Land, Texas, 349
Medical Towers Building, 11, *13*
Melcher, C. Leroy, Jr., 141
Melcher, C. Leroy, Jr., project, 341
Melcher Boathouse and Pavilion (C. Leroy, Jr.), 337
Melcher House (Anne Schlumberger and C. Leroy, Jr.), 140, *140*, 141, *141*, 305, 307–308, 330
Melcher House (C. Leroy, Jr.), addition, West Alabama, 337
Mellins, Thomas, 137
Memorial Bend, 15
Memorial Coliseum, Corpus Christi, Texas, 113
Memorial Park, 214
Memorial villages, 11, 15, 33n35, 140, 202, 214
Menil, Dominique Schlumberger de, 11, *19*, 72, 122, *123*, 124, 153, 165n1, 229, 269, 291; and art exhibitions, 165n10; education of, 124–125; and family, 124, 308; and Menil Collection, 158; and Rothko Chapel, 149; and University of St. Thomas, 125, 135; Val-Richer, 124, 165n7, 165n8
Menil, Dominique S., and John de, 21–23, 59, 208, 225, 226, 247, 285, 290, 294, 303; art collection of, 125; and entertaining, 283; and Rice University, 152; and University of St. Thomas, 150–151

Menil, John de, 5, 6, 11, 19, 122, *123*, 136, 226, 251, 269, 270, 272; and G. Barnstone, 277; and H. Barnstone, 304, 309; death of, 228; education of, 123; and family, 123, 308–309; and *The Galveston That Was*, 142–143; name change of, 124; office of, in Bank of the Southwest Building, 322; and UH visiting lectureship program, 250–251; US citizenship of, 124; and World War II, 123

Menil, Francois de, 138

Menil, Georges de, 139

Menil, Philippa de (Fariha Fatima al-Jerrahi), 138

Menil Apartment (Dominique and John de), New York, 131–132, 317

Menil bungalow projects, 323, 346

Menil-Carpenter Apartment, Gainsborough Studios, New York, 56, 346

Menil-Carpenter Complex, East Hampton, Long Island, New York, 56, 146–147, *147*, 163, 230, 310, 345

Menil Collection, 66, 72, 85, 153, 172n112

Menil Foundation, 125, 298; art museum, 351; art storage building proposals, 57; gray bungalows in Montrose area, *154*; headquarters remodeling, 352; holdings in Montrose, 155, *155*, 158; photo archive building, 352; photo archives building project, 58; projects, 345

Menil Guesthouse (Dominique and John de), 126, 228, 285

Menil House (Dominique and John de), Caracas, Venezuela, *128*

Menil House (Dominique and John de), Connecticut, 320

Menil House (Dominique and John de), San Felipe Road, 14, *74*, 122–123, 125–127, *126*, *127*, 247, 270–271, 302, 314; preservation, 298

Menil museum proposals, *156*, *157*, 158

Menil Park, 340

Menil Townhouse (Dominique & John de), alterations and additions, New York, 132, 167n33, 327

Menil Townhouse development, 343

Menil trust funds, 139

Menu de Menil family, 123

Mermel House (Ann and Irving), 51, *198–199*, 201, 209–210, 212, *213*, *214*, 306, 311, 325

Meyer, George, 209

Meyer, Howard R., 30n3, 293

Meyer, Joseph F., 209

Meyer Apartment (Leopold), 332

Meyerland, 15, 17, 51, 201, 209, *211*, 212, 214, 215; Parade of Homes, 209, *211*, 212

Michels, Doug, 57, 156, 158, 238n, 253–254

Middleton, William (*Double Vision*), 294

Miesian architecture, 290, 302

Mies van der Rohe, Ludwig, 11, 14, *19*, 58, 66, 69, 70, 80, *84*, 98, 193–194, 205, 250–251; and H. Barnstone, 304; Cullinan Hall, Museum of Fine Arts, Houston, 11–12, *19*, *64–65*, 67, *69*, 72, 226, 272, 292; MOMA exhibition (1947), 80, *83*; Resor House, 71; Seagram Building, 138, 302; UH College of Architecture, 261

Milford Townhouses, 342

Miller, Nory, 59

Ming House (R. E.), 313

Mize Country House (Jerald D.), addition, Brenham, Texas, 343

modular construction, 14, 327

Moody Foundation, 142

Montessori School, Arnold Street, 355

Montessori School, West Bell Street, 358

Montessori School of Houston, 332

Moore, Charles W., 4, 30n2, 83, 143, 170n80, 228

Moore, Harvin, 10

Morey & Hollenbeck, 146

Morris, Robert, 56

Morris, S. I., 41, 54

Morris Architects, 41

Morgan, Emanuel, project, 345

Moschini House, alterations, 350

Moser, Benjamin, 29, 296n2

Mosier Research Laboratories, 335

Moss, Arthur, 12

Mount Vernon Manor House, 355

Muir, Rob, 230

Mumford, Lewis, 82

Museum District, Houston, 56

Museum of Fine Arts, Houston, 9, 16, 22, 142, 226, 275, 315; Brown Pavilion, 67, *70*, 72; Cullinan Hall, 11–12, *19*, *64–65*, 67, *69*, 72, 226, 272, 292; school, 270, 273

Museum of Modern Art, New York, 21, 78, 83, *84*, 85, 224

Museum of Primitive Art, advertisements, New York, 330

Museum of the Southwest, alterations, Midland, Texas, 354

MVRDV (Maas, Van Rijs, De Vries), 194

Napoleon I, 123

NASA, Manned Spacecraft Center, 84, 100

National Architectural Accrediting Board (NAAB), 252

National Gallery, Berlin, Germany, 72

National Gallery, London, England, competition entry for extension, 358

National Youth Administration, 111

Neff House (Richard W., Jr.), 322, 326

Neuhaus, Hugo V., Jr., 14, 20, 21, 42, 74, 78, 122, 125, 226, 231, 290

Neuhaus, J. Victor III, 14, 30n2, 41

Neuhaus, Mary Wood, 122

Neuhaus & Taylor, 41, 226–227

Neuhaus House (Hugo V., Jr.), 71

Neutra, Richard, 80, 251

New Arts Gallery, 272, 275

New Beach Hotel, Galveston, Texas, 356

Newman, Barnett, 150

New York, jewelry district, 223, 235n7

New York Times, 24, 133, 138, 233

New York University, New York, 208

Nixon, Richard M., 209

Nodelman, Sheldon (1997, *The Rothko Chapel Paintings*), 294

Noguchi, Isamu, 133

INDEX 383

Nueces County Courthouse, Corpus Christi, Texas, 114
Nuevo Laredo, Tamaulipas, Mexico, 54, 56, 227

Obata, Gyo, 4, 30n2
O'Conor House (Robert J., Jr.), 353
Oglesby, Enslie O., 20, 30n2
Oliver, Charles W., 141
OMA, 194
Oneto House (George J.), Irvington, New York, 71, 72
Open Gates, The (George Sealy House), Galveston, Texas, 142
Oshman, Marilyn, 253, 254
Oskouie, Hossein, 234
Owen, Jane Blaffer, 7
Owen House (Jane Blaffer), garden lighting, 354
Owsley House (Barbara Robinson and Alvin M., Jr.), 28, 48, 49, *52*, 67, 73–74, *76*, 300–301, 310, 323
Owsley House (Barbara Robinson and Alvin M., Jr.), Leeland, Michigan, 322
Ozad, Sheikh Muzaffer, 138

Palmer, Donald M., 43, 300–301, 302, 306
Pan American Health Organization Headquarters, 328
Papademetriou, Peter C., 71–72, 233
Papavassiliou House (Constantinos A.), remodeling, 319, 330
Papavassiliou House (Kostos), 357
Parker, Alfred Browning, 30n2
Pasternak House, alterations, 356
Paul, Weiss, Goldberg, Rifkind, Wharton & Garrison law offices, New York, 338
Paul House (J. J.), addition, 328
Peabody and Stearns, 222
Peden Square for Jerry E. Battelstein, 343
Pei, I. M., 4, 20, 30n2
Pelican Island Development, Galveston, Texas, 315
Pelli, Cesar, 30n2, 305
Penick, Monica, 292
Pepli, Claire, 283
Peressutti, Enrico, 251

Perlman, William, office, 344
Perlman House (William), alterations and additions, Pine Hollow Lane, 342
Perlman House (William), alterations and additions, Post Oak Timber, 355
Perlman House (William), renovation, Larchmont Road, 356
Perlman House (William), Seabrook, Texas, 354
Perlman Townhouses, 328
Perrin, Mike, Bank Building, alterations, 352
Perry, John, 252–253
Perspecta: The Yale Architectural Journal, 78
Pesle Villa, Les Alques, France, 328
Peterkin House (Nancy Girling and George), 58, 352
Peterson, Robert E., 228
Pevsner, Nikolaus, 102
P. G. Bell Construction Company, 152
Phelps House (Merrick W.), alterations and additions, 322
Phillips, W. Irving, Jr., 228
Piano, Renzo, 66, 72, 158
Pierce, Abel B. and George, 14
Pincoffs House (Edmund L.), alterations, 327
Piney Point Elementary School, 53, 87, *89*, 305, 327–328
Pinney Motel (Warren, Jr.), Nuevo Laredo, Mexico, 327
Pinney Motel (Warren, Jr.), Houston, 330
Plaza Hotel, alterations, 338
Pleasantville Furniture Company, 321
Pocket Park project, 341
Podhoretz, Norman, 291
Pomeroy House (J. P., Jr.), alterations, 347
Portman, John C., Jr., 30n2
Posada del Rey Condominiums for Robert Barnstone, Austin, Texas, 350
postmodernism, 27, 57, 231–232, 257, 258, 302
postwar urbanization, 101–103
Powers, Jim, 56

Prairie's Yield, The, 101–103, *102*, 105
Pratt, Box, & Henderson, 104, 105, 113
Pratt, James Reece, 30n2, 101–103, 106
preservation. *See* historic preservation
Pressler House (Robert), 323
Price Townhouse (Ray), consultation, 344
Progressive Architecture, 229, 230, 233, 252
Proler House (Ben), 10
Prudon, Theodore H. M., ix, 366

racism in Houston, 5, 8, 15–19, 124, 202, 277, 283–284
ranch house type, 12, 14, 15, 77, 94
Randall House (Katherine Risher and Edward), Galveston, Texas, 142
Randall House (Risher), addition, Chevy Chase Drive, 348
Rauch family, 205
Rayburn, Sam, 100
Red, David, 245
Regatta Inn Cabañas and Club for Albert Bel Fay, Seabrook, Texas, 336
regionalism, 5, 21, 27–28, 30n3, 83, 84, 99, 291
Reich, Steve, vii
Reliance Title Company Offices, 331, 358
Resor House project, Jackson Hole, Wyoming, 71
Resurrection Avenue Bar and Grill, alterations, 351
Riboud, Jean, 133, 135, 136, 137, 138, 142, 158
Riboud, Krishna Roy, 54, 144
Riboud Apartment (Krishna Roy and Jean), Amster Yard, New York, 337
Riboud Apartment (Krishna Roy and Jean), Carlton House, New York, 350
Riboud Apartment (Krishna Roy and Jean), East 49th Street, New York, 133, *134*, 135

Riboud House (Krishna Roy and Jean), Scottsdale, Arizona, 45, 54, 56, 144, *145*, 164, 310, 329
Rice Design Alliance, xi, 21, 234
Rice Hotel, 277
Rice University (formerly Rice Institute), 148, 150, 152, 203, 204, 224, 243, 270, 271, 275; Allen Center, 152, 340; Institute for the Arts, 152–153, 154, 156; Media Center, 54, 152, 340; Museum (Art Barn), 28, 53, *120–121*, 152, *153*, 163–164, 292, 340; Performing and Visual Arts Center project, 153; School of Architecture, ix, 248
Richardson, Eugenia Preston Brooks and Bishop J. Milton, 25
Richardson House (Eugenia and J. Milton), alterations, 341
Richter, Robert C. "Bob," Jr., 232, 286
Richter, Robert C., Jr., law office, 12727 Featherwood Drive, 358
Richter, Robert C., Jr., law office, West Bellfort Boulevard, 350
Richter-Barnstone Property, alterations, 347
Ricks House (Pam and Tom), alterations, 353
Rinzler House (Stanley), 335
Ritz Tower, New York, 133
River Oaks, 8, 10, *10*, 16, 53, 85, 86, 141, 200, 201, 205, 214, 270–271
River Oaks Corporation, 8
River Oaks Country Club, 205
River Oaks Montessori School, 278
Riverside Park, New York, 223
Riverside Terrace, 10, 14, 16, 17, 85, 200, 201, 202, 203, 204
Riverview High School, Sarasota, Florida, 82
Riviera night club, 273
Robinson, Michael, Townhouses, 356
Rogers, Edward, 57, 234
Roosevelt, Franklin Delano, 297, 299
Rosenberg, Adrian S., 43, 272, 300, 302
Rosenberg, Henry, 304
Rosen House (Arlene and Gerald), Brentwood, California, 77
Rosenstock Motors Building, 312
Rosenthal, Evelyn Fink, 203, 224

Rosenthal, Morris G., 203
Rosenthal House (Evelyn Fink and Morris G.), alterations, West 11th Place, 340
Rosenthal House (Evelyn Fink and Morris G.), North Roseneath Drive, 178, 184, 201, 203, *203*, *204*, 316
Rosenthal House (Seymour G.), Beaumont, Texas, 225, 313
Ross, Elsa, Speedby's Old Print Gallery, 344
Ross, Sam, Office and Apartment, 350
Roth, Emery, 133
Rothko, Mark, 23, 91, 148–150
Rothko Chapel, vi, 91, 148–149, *149*, *151*, 292, 310, 338–339
Rotnofsky, Frank, 234
Rotterman Builders, 317
Rottersmann House (Edwin C.), 43, 313
Rowe, Colin, 7, 47–48, 51, 70–71
Royal Dutch Shell Pension Fund development, 20
Royce Boat House (Scott), 338
Rudofsky, Bernard, 176
Rudolph, Paul, 4, 30n2, 78, 80, 82, 251, 293, 304
Ruggles Restaurant, addition, 347
Rummel Creek, 15
Runnells House (Clive), remodeling, 330
Russell Brown Company, 127
Ryan, Milton A., 30n3

Saarinen, Eero, 128, 184, 251
Sabatino, Michelangelo, viii, ix, xi, 148, 366–367
Sakowitz family, 200
Salman House (William J.), 328
Sampson House (Bernard), remodeling, 335
Samuels, Danny Marc, 21, 231
SANAA architects, 188
S&H Green Stamp sculpture (1955, Gertrude Barnstone), 275, *276*
San Fernando, Trinidad, 130
Sanguinet, Staats & Barnes, 148
San Jacinto High School, 200, 201
San Jacinto Trust Company, 204

Santa Anita Restaurant for George O. Jackson, Jr., alterations, 354
Sarasota (Florida), school of architecture, 78
Sarofim House (Fayez), renovation, 339
Saturday Review, 19
Schinkel, Karl Friedrich, 98
Schlumberger, Anne. *See* Brown, Anne Schlumberger
Schlumberger, Conrad, 124
Schlumberger, Louise Delpech, 124
Schlumberger, Marcel, 123
Schlumberger, Maria da Diniz Conceição, 141–142
Schlumberger, Pierre M., 124, 136
Schlumberger Apartments, New York, 132
Schlumberger Austin Systems Center, vii, 58, 161–163, *162*, *163*, 164, 173n125, 230, 310, 357; master plan, 353
Schlumberger Building, Leeland Avenue, 127–128, 166n20, 170n75, 315
Schlumberger-Doll Research Center (SDRC), Ridgefield, Connecticut, vii, 56, 158–161, *159*, *160*, 164, 310, 347–348
Schlumberger European division, 124
Schlumberger family, 123–124, 165n8
Schlumberger House (Claire Simone Schwob d'Héricourt and Pierre M.), 141
Schlumberger House (Lesley and Pierre M., Jr., "Pete"), 140, 337
Schlumberger House (Pierre M.), alterations, 329
Schlumberger Ltd., 20, 122, 123, 232; airplane hangar, Hobby Airport, 329; airplane interiors, 329; emblem, 329; executive offices, Houston, 128; garage, 329; motto, 128; offices, Madison Avenue, New York, 135; offices, Park Avenue, New York, 53, 135, 136, *136*, 137, *137*, 163, 334; during World War II, 131
Schlumberger-Surenco, Latin American division, 124, 127–129; camps, 129–131, 166n24;

Maracaibo House, *130*; offices, Leeland Avenue, 310, 315; offices, Commerce Building, 323; projects, 317; Trinidad Company House, 130–131, *131*
Schlumberger Well Surveying Corporation, North American division; 123–124; Houston building, 166n20
Schnitzer, Kenneth, 227
Schoenberg, Kerry, 161
Schorre, Charles, 273
Seagram Building, New York, 138, 302
Seals, Woodrow, 277
Sealy, Bob, 142
See House (Marilyn Elliott), Seabrook, Texas, 343
Semenova, Tatiana, 267
Settegast, J. J., 242
Sewall House (Campbell), alterations for Children's Mental Health Services, 343
Shadowlawn Circle, 24, 76, 81, 95n53, 230–231, 232, 311, 341, 348, 352
Shadyside, 85, 205
Shadyside Place Townhouses, 349
Shamrock Hotel, 124, 266–267
Shane House (Le May E.), 321
Shane House (Le May E.), Sugar Land, Texas, 333
Shapiro House (Sam J.), 326
Sharma House (Alice Heniker and Timothy), additions, 353
Shelley v. Kramer (1948), 17
Sheraton Marina Inn, Corpus Christi, 113
Sherman, Newman, 303
Sherwood Forest subdivision, 139
Simmons House (Gladys), alterations, 349
Simons, Malcolm G., 293
S. I. Morris Associates, 228
Sims Bayou, 15
SITE, 91
Six Flags Over Texas, 105
Skidmore, Owings & Merrill (SOM), 11, 12, 20, 67, 68, 88, 226
Skorpea, Joe, 249
Slocum Builders, 317
Smart, Pamela, G., 23, 294

Smith, C. Ray, 231
Smithers House (Ruth Ann and Charles, Jr.), New Canaan, Connecticut, 227, 302, 320
Smith House (R. B.), remodeling, 326
Smith v. Allwright (1944), 16
Snell, Katrina, Boutique and Apartment, 329
Société de Prospection Électrique, Paris, France, 123
Solar Hemicycle House, 44
Soleri, Paolo Soleri, 30n2
Sondock, Melvin, Building, alterations, Galveston, Texas, 349
Sorchan, Charlotte, 133
Soriano, Raphael, 77
Southern Title Company, 203
Southern Title Guaranty Company, 203
Southside State Bank, 327
Space, Eva Lempert, 230
Spaulding sports products, 208
Speck, Lawrence W., 21
Spector House (Andrew E.), alterations, 351
Speedby's Old Print Gallery, 344
Sprunt, Clare Fleming, 270, 274, 275–276
Sprunt, Clare Fleming and Samuel N., 226, 278, 285
Sprunt, Samuel N., 270
Sprunt House (Clare and Samuel N.), alterations and additions, 322, 332
Stark, Lois Farfel, 208, 229
Staub, John Fanz, vi, 8, *11*, 24–25, 109, 230, 231, 295
Staub, Rather & Howze, 69
Steph House (Thomas), alterations and additions, Galveston, Texas, 335
Sterling, Jay, Townhouse, 345
Stern, Robert A. M., 137, 250–251
Stern, William F., x, 262n6
Stern & Bucek, 298
Stetson House (John), additions, 332
Stirling, James, TEO Corporation, 356
St. Joseph Hospital, alterations, 355
St. Moritz Hotel, New York, 133
Stokowski, Leopold, 267
Stoller, Ezra, 106, 142–143

Stone, Edward Durrell, 78, 224
Stoneleigh Hotel, Dallas, Texas, 113
Straus House (Robert D.), 10
Strecker, Ian, 161
Strickland, Gordon & Sheinfeld law offices, 338
Strickland, S. Miles, Jr., 315
Strickland & Gordon law offices, Houston Natural Gas Building, 342
Strickland House (S. Miles, Jr.), swimming pool, 320
St. Rose of Lima Catholic Church, 12, *14*
St. Thomas High School, 339
Sufi mosque, New York, 138
Sugarcreek Townhouses for GreenMark, Inc., Sugar Land, Texas, 350
Sullivan, Louis, 250
sunbelt, 31n10, 100, 116n8,
Suneson, Earl L., 54, 56
Suneson, Earl Lewis, Highway Motel, Puerto Vallarta, Mexico, 336
Suneson-Franco House (Marti Franco and Earl Lewis "Mel"), Laredo, Texas, 227, 320
Suneson-Franco House (Marti Franco and Earl Lewis "Mel"), Nuevo Laredo, Mexico, 183, *183*, 184–186, *185*, 320
Suneson-Franco House (Marti Franco and Earl Lewis "Mel"), Puerto Vallarta, Mexico, 227
Suneson House (Pablo Jácobo), Laredo, Texas, 357
Suneson Shop, Nuevo Laredo, Mexico, 324
Suneson Shops, Puerto Vallarta, Mexico, 338
Susholtz, Ben and Ida, 208
Sussman House (Arnold), 326
Swan, Simone, 25, *123*, 125, 132, 143, 309
Swan Summer House (Simone), Peconic, Long Island, New York, 343
Sweatt v. Painter (1950), 16
Sweeney, James Johnson, 22, 26, 273, 291

Sweeney Apartment (Laura Harden and James Johnson), 142, 329
Swenson, Bailey A., 10, 12, 14, 225, 272
Swenson, Kathryn (Mrs. Bailey), 272, 275

Taft Architects, 21, 231
Talley, Robert W., 243
Tallichet House (Jane Heyer), remodeling, 329
Tallichet House (Jules H., Jr.), 318
Tamburine Motel (Frank), 322
Tanglewood subdivision, 15
Taniguchi, Alan Y., 30n2
Tapley, Charles, 59, 169–170n68, 228
Taub, Ben, 242
Taut, Bruno, 196
Taylor, Harwood, 14, 30n2, 41, 76, 77, 87, 233
Taylor, W. A. Warehouse, 339
Tenneco Building, 67, *68*
TEO Corporation for James Stirling, 356
Texaco Service Station, 323
Texas Architect, 19, 43, 103, *104*, 250
Texas Commerce Bank, 355
Texas Corinthian Yacht Club, 53
Texas Hill Country, 99, 111
Texas Homes, 229
Texas Instruments, Dallas, Texas, 100, *101*
Texas Medical Center, 11, 267
Texas Monthly, 229
Texas Observer, 233–234
Texas prairie, *102*
Texas Rangers, University of Texas architecture school, 98
Texas regionalism, 5, 21, 27–28, 83, 84, 99, 27–28, 30n3
Texas Society of Architects, 19; design awards, 204, 205, 208, 214–215, 310
Texas Southern University (TSU), 16, 17–18, 202
Texas State University for Negroes (now TSU), 202
Thaxton House (William L., Jr.), 11
Third Ward, Houston, 16, 202
Thobae House and Office (Charles), alterations, 347

Thomas, Dylan, 271
Thompson House (J. Lewis, Jr.), remodeling, 320
Thurman Apartment (Christophe de Menil), remodeling, 331
Tideland Signal Corporation, 337
Tigerman, Stanley, 7
Tillich, Paul, 7
Timbercrest, 234
Timme, Robert H., 231
tin house movement, 28
Todd, Anderson, 4, 14, 19, 28, 30n2, 42, 47, 58, 76, 78, 226, 231, 270, 275, 290–291
Todd House (Lucie Wray and Anderson), 76, *81*
Tombesi, Paolo, 41
Totems Not Taboo exhibition (1959, Cullinan Hall, MFAH), *18*, 19, 272, 273
Tower of the Americas, San Antonio, Texas, 111, 113
Towler, Martin L., M.D., 228
Tracy, Michael, 7, 24
Trinidad, British West Indies, 128, 129, 130, 131
Trinity University, San Antonio, Texas, 111
Trotti, Guillermo, 259
Tuffly Park Recreation Center, 305, 333
Tunnard, Christopher, *225*
Turner, Drexel, 249–251, *252*
Turner House (Elsie), 323

Ultra, 229
Universal Security Life Building, alterations, 338
University of Dallas, bell tower, 111
University of Houston (UH), vi, viii, 91, 208, 300; campus, 242–243, *244*; Ezekiel W. Cullen Building, 242; Roy Gustav Cullen Building, 242; School of Engineering, 243
University of Houston, Gerald D. Hines College of Architecture, 242, *245*; Architectural Society, 251; architecture program at, 225; and Barnstone-Keeland agenda, 248, 253; buildings X, Y, Z (1955), 249, *249*, 257; counterculture

atmosphere of, 253–254, 261; curriculum of, 244–245, 248; faculty factions at, 247–248; Johnson/Burgee building (1986), 257–258, *258*; Southcoast Team Number 1, 91; students at, 249–250, *252*, 256; urban design program at, 259
University of Kansas, 252
University of Massachusetts, Dartmouth Campus, 78
University of Paris, France, 123
University of St. Thomas, 11, 22, 67, *75*, 135, 147–148, 188, 227, 257, 273, 278, 292, 321; Cullen Hall, 148; Doherty Library, 54, 336; Guinan Hall, 53, 148, 311, 339; Institute for Storm Research, 53; Jones Hall, 22, 148; 321; Malloy Hall, 148; master plan for, 72–73, *74*; M. D. Anderson Biology Building, 148, 149, 332; and Menils, 66, 148, 150, 152, 155, 165, 172n102, 273, 278; Robertson Hall, 148; Strake Hall, 148; Welder Hall, *75*
University of Texas School of Architecture (Austin), 102, 230; (Arlington), 110; School of Law, 16
University of Virginia, 73
urban design in Texas, 102–103
Usonian modernism, 10, 11, 44, 84, 291
US Reconstruction Finance Corporation, 8

Vale, Wylie W., 12
Val-Richer, France, 124, 165n7, 165n8
Vance, Nina, 267
Vassar Place apartments, 25–26, 51, 195–196, *195*, *196*, *197*, 228, 232, 234, 333; apartment No. 5, alterations for Howard Barnstone, 346
Venturi, Robert, 4, 30n2
Victoria, Texas, Project, 324
Vierendeel trusses, 53

Waddill House (Greg C.), 318
W. A. Horne Company, realtor offices, 339
Waldman House (Marvin), 323

Walker Guest House (Walt), Sanibel Island, Florida, 78
Walsh, Sally Sherwin, 25–26, 48, 136
Walsh Property plan, 339
Wareing, William A. III, 230
Warhol, Andy, *123*, 304
Warren House (Martin), remodeling, 327
Warwick Hotel (now Hotel Zaza), 230
Washington House hotel rehabilitation, Galveston, Texas, 336
Washington Terrace, 16, 17, 200, 201, 202
Watkin, William Ward, 232
Wayne House (William L.), alterations, Stanmore Drive, 341
Wayne House (William L.), landscaping, Kirby Drive, 344
Webb, Bruce C., ix, 59, 367
Webb County Administration Building, project, Laredo, Texas, 58, 353
Webb County Courthouse, restoration, 353
Weingarten family, 200
Welch, Frank D., 4, 20, 30n2, 99, 214
Wellesley College, Wellesley, Massachusetts, 144
Wells, Clinton, 234
Wells, Lily Barnstone, x, 234, 286
Wells Service Station and Restaurant, 323
Westwood Country Club, 205, 214
Wheeler Avenue Baptist Church, Educational Building, 334

White, Hattie Mae Whiting, 18–19, 277, *279*, 283
White, Stanford, 117n17
White Citizens Council, 283
White House (Sarah E.), alterations, 357
Whitlaw, Jim A., Apartments, 324, 330
Wiegman, John, 41
Wier House (Robert), 141
Wigby, Palmer, Townhouse Development, 337
Wiley House (Robert C.), New Canaan, Connecticut, 44
Willard, Philip G., 12, 14
William P. Hobby Airport, 15
Williams, David R., 99
Williams House, 337
Williams House (Oliver), alterations, 351
Wilson, Anthony, Barkdull Apartments, alterations, 343
Wilson, Morris, Crain & Anderson, 14, 41, 54, 72, 73, 226–227, 228
Windsor Gas Corporation office, Niels Esperson Building, 344
Wingfield, Jr., B. Magruder, 42
Wing House (Louise Harbour and W. Gordon), 44, *47*, 324
Winkler, Helen, 283
Winterbotham House (Wandy Renfert and John M., Jr.), 108, 109, *109*, 300, 310, 311, 324
Wirtz & Calhoun, 10, 12
Wisdom, W. Jackson, 12
Wisznia, Walter, 293

Wolfe, Elsie de, 142
Wolf House (Bernard), alterations and additions, 332
Wong, Alex, 303
Woollen, Evans, 4, 30n2
Wright, Frank Lloyd, 10, 11, 44, 58, 71, 250, 251
Wright House (William K.), alterations and additions, 330–331
Wynne, Angus, 105

Yale University, New Haven, Connecticut, 7, 8, 78, 82, 184, 224, 225, 228, 250, 254, 255, 236, 291, 301, 304; Ezra Stiles College, 184; Forestry Building, 88; School of Architecture, 228
Yamasaki, Minoru, 251
Yang House, 356
Yoakum Condominiums, 353
York, John G., 30n3

Zemanek, John, 4, 24, 30n2, 58, 245–246, 248, 253, 258
Zenteno, Norma and Roberto, 273
Zion & Breen, landscape architects, 161, 345, 347
Zionism, 203
Zodiac, 20, 71, 88, 177
zoning in Houston, 20, 68, 83, 108–109 20, 259